MADONNA

ALSO BY J. RANDY TARABORRELLI

Jackie, Janet & Lee: The Secret Lives of Janet Auchincloss and Her Daughters

Jacqueline Kennedy Onassis and Lee Radziwill

After Camelot: A Personal History of the Kennedy Family – 1968 to the Present

Jackie, Ethel, Joan: Women of Camelot

Once Upon a Time: Behind the Fairy Tale of Princess Grace and Prince Rainier

Elizabeth

The Secret Life of Marilyn Monroe

Michael Jackson: The Magic, the Madness, the Whole Story (1958–2009)

The Hiltons: The True Story of an American Dynasty

Sinatra: Behind the Legend

MADONNA

An Intimate Biography of an Icon at Sixty

J. RANDY TARABORRELLI

SIDGWICK & JACKSON

First published 2001 by Sidgwick & Jackson

First published in paperback 2002 by Pan Books

This updated edition first published 2018 by Sidgwick & Jackson
an imprint of Pan Macmillan
20 New Wharf Road, London N1 9RR
Associated companies throughout the world
www.panmacmillan.com

ISBN 978-1-5098-4277-3 HB
ISBN 978-1-5098-4278-0 TPB

1 3 5 7 9 8 6 4 2

A CIP catalogue record for this book is available from the British Library.

Typeset by Palimpsest Book Production Ltd, Falkirk, Stirlingshire
Printed and bound by CPI Group (UK) Ltd, Croydon, CR0 4YY

Contents

Author's Note

When I first met her at a press conference in the spring of 1983, Madonna Louise Ciccone – twenty-four at the time – struck me as brash, cocky, petulant and self-indulgent. Never one to put on an act for a journalist, she was just what she was – and without hesitation. 'Look, I never had money,' she told me of her early, struggling days in New York. 'Each month it was a scramble to pay the rent and get some food in the apartment. I literally had to eat out of garbage cans in those days. Now that I have a record out and it looks like it'll be a success, hell yeah, I feel like I deserve it,' she concluded. She fixed her hazel eyes on me. 'People don't know how good I am yet,' she said, holding me with her gaze. 'But they will soon. In a couple of years everyone will know. Actually,' she concluded, 'I plan on being one of this century's biggest stars.'

'And with no last name?' I asked, uncertain that 'Madonna' was even her real name. (Surely, it couldn't have been.)

'It's Madonna,' she snapped. 'Just like Cher. Remember it.'

It was difficult to argue with her, mostly because she wouldn't hear of it. Poor thing, I thought. Let her have her illusions. No reigning beauty she, and – judging from her first record – equipped with only a fair voice, yet she thinks she's going to become a dominant influence in pop music, a big star. Well, we'll see . . .

Of course, it didn't take long for Madonna's prediction to come true.

Everything she is today has been hard earned. With nothing ever handed to her on the proverbial silver platter, her life and career have been built on single-mindedness of intention, the most exhausting work (in recording studios, on movie and video sound stages, and on concert tours), dogged determination and, often, unmerciful and extreme sacrifice. In the years since that first interview, Madonna went on to become one of the most memorable, celebrated and highest-paid women in show business . . . and to think that I doubted her resolve.

I first began the challenge of writing this book in 1990, but decided to put it away for a few years. I thought then that Madonna should have an opportunity to do more living before I, as her biographer, would be able to do her story justice. Though she was already one of the most famous people on the planet, it takes more than just the accurate documentation of a person's celebrity to make for a good character study. Most subjects need time for evolution and personal growth before their stories are ripe enough to commit to paper. At the time, Madonna was in an ambitious, self-involved phase during which nothing mattered more to her than her career.

When I picked up work on this book again in 1994, I felt the same way about her. She had prioritized her life – career first, above all else – and would still do almost anything to get to a certain point of creative freedom and financial security. I anticipated that when she was finally satisfied with her career, she would begin to work on her *life*. Happily, just such a personal evolution began to occur in 1996 when she had Lourdes, her first child.

In 2001, I went back to this book and ultimately finished it and had it published. At that time, I saw that Madonna had greater concerns than just the next big public relations spectacle in her career – especially since giving birth to another child, a brother for Lourdes, named Rocco. She had grown, changed and transformed herself (again) and, this time, in a way that had not only inspired me to want to write about her, but admire her as well. Yes, she was still driven, still ambitious and still self-involved – that hadn't changed. She was still Madonna, after all, an artist of calculation known for inventing and reinventing her image, usually for the purpose of publicity. However, as I saw it back in 2001, she was also shedding certain layers, slowly revealing who she really is as a person, as a woman.

Here's what I wrote in the original edition of this book:

> *Affluent, powerful and famous people like Madonna are, generally, different from most other people – at once more and less human, they're walking paradoxes, thoughtful and inconsiderate, generous and parsimonious, disciplined and uncontrolled, self-denigrating and self-important. While it may not always be easy to find the real Madonna amidst the hocus-pocus of public relations she manufactures to hide her true self, she's there just the same. In pursuit of her, one only has to be perceptive enough to look beyond the thick smoke, away from the confusing mirrors. There hides the real woman. As I found in the years of researching and then finally writing* Madonna: An Intimate Biography, *finding her is worth the effort.*

I still feel that way, all these years later. Since 2001, I have written a number of addendums to this book as Madonna's life story has evolved, the last edition being back in 2008 when she turned fifty and was still married to Guy Ritchie. Now, ten years later, here we are in 2018 and Madonna is about to turn sixty. Yes, you read that right: *Madonna is about to turn sixty.* That seems hard to believe, doesn't it? I think this milestone represents great success for her, though, because with the passing of the years she has only changed for the better. I would also argue that if we are at sixty what we were at twenty, something in our lives has gone seriously off the rails. Just like, hopefully, all of us, Madonna continues to evolve, be creative and be philanthropic, while at the same time working toward what sometimes seems like an elusive goal of simple happiness.

While she's still the ballsy person she's always been, she's obviously smarter than she was in her rabble-rousing youth. She now at least knows how to pick and choose her battles. She doesn't waste time on pettiness and, like most of us, realizes the clock is ticking and that there's no time like the present to not only be happy but maybe even find a way to be of service to others.

Of course, she's still Madonna, and some of her decisions tend to baffle her critics, such as the penchant she has for young men – *very* young men. We're talking men young enough to be her children and – dare I say it? – maybe even her grandchildren. Her boyfriends since her divorce from Guy have been in their early to mid-twenties. She knows what she likes, she has a 'type', in other words, and why shouldn't she? After all, she's been used to having pretty much everything else her way for a very long time. Such entitlement comes with being a star, and if anyone doesn't think she's given her all to that endeavour since she was just a kid, that would be a person who hasn't been paying much attention. Can we really begrudge her a sexy, young partner? (Would we be as critical of an older man with a much younger woman?) Even if just for the sheer entertainment value of it all, I say more power to her. As long as she can rope them in, good for her. She's earned it.

I have never stopped writing about Madonna since that day I first met her thirty-five years ago. Countless magazine and newspaper articles about her have carried my byline, not to mention new editions of this book all over the world. She remains one of the most fascinating women on the planet. I'm proud to be one of her biographers.

You should know that this isn't just an update of my original book; it's also a reconstructing of it. As you read it, you'll find that I have a few different thoughts and opinions to some of those I had almost twenty years ago. Therefore, stories on these pages may vary a little in viewpoint from what I wrote back in the day. I have also added a number of tales I think are now relevant to her history.

In the end, one thing remains constant, and that's the fierce, defiant and unapologetic character at the centre of all of it . . . and long may she live.

J. RANDY TARABORRELLI

Los Angeles, May 2018

List of Illustrations

18. On stage during the 'Blond Ambition' tour, 1990. *(Top: Retro; bottom: Photofest)*
19. Madonna aged thirty-three. *(Lorraine Day/Photofest)*
20. As sultry torch singer Breathless Mahoney in *Dick Tracy*, opposite Warren Beatty. *(Retro Photo)*
21. Madonna and Warren Beatty made a striking couple, but there were major differences that kept them apart. *(Vinnie Zuffante/Star File)*
22. In February 1991, during a contemplative moment with Tony Ward, Madonna's rebound relationship after Warren. *(Bob Scott/Neal Peters)*
23. On 25 March 1991 Madonna performed 'Sooner or Later' from *Dick Tracy* during the Academy Awards presentation. *(Paragon Photo Vault)*
24. From her critically panned film *Body of Evidence* in 1992. *(Photofest)*
25. At the New York party to celebrate her *Sex* book in October 1992. *(Louie De Filippis)*
26. Gender-breaking, as always. *(Photofest)*
27. In 1994, with basketball star Dennis Rodman. *(Paragon Photo Vault)*
28. Madonna at a party with Tupac Shakur. (© *Patrick McMullan/Patrick McMullan via Getty Images)*
29. As Evita in 1996, Madonna shone like never before. Some felt it was the performance of a lifetime for her. *(Photofest)*
30. The first photo of Madonna taken with Carlos Leon. He was understanding and patient. *(Louie De Filippis)*
31. Lourdes, photographed in 1999. *(Louie De Filippis)*
32. Madonna, Guy and Rocco outside Dornoch cathedral after the christening, December 2000. *(Rex Features)*
33. Madonna with her boyfriend, Jesus Lux, and her children David and Mercy, in 2009. *(© MCP/REX/Shutterstock)*
34. Madonna performs during the charity concert Hope for Haiti Now 2010. *(© Philip Ramey/Corbis via Getty Images)*
35. Madonna and her son Rocco perform during the 'MDNA' North America tour. *(© Kevin Mazur/WireImage)*

The Actress and the President

Perhaps the last place Madonna's fans would ever have expected to find her was crouched on the floor of a car racing down a bustling Buenos Aires street. Her destination: the home of the President of Argentina, Carlos Menem. It was Wednesday, 7 February 1996 – just another day in the extraordinary life of Madonna Louise Veronica Ciccone, a woman whose life has been nothing if not unpredictable.

While huddling on the floor of a black Spanish-made car, Madonna was being smuggled to meet the President. Her own rented Mercedes-Benz – surrounded by police on motorcycles – had successfully been used as a decoy moments earlier, confusing the ever-stalking paparazzi who had followed it in hopes of capturing on film whatever they believed Madonna was going to be doing that day, probably shopping. If only they had known the true nature of her plans; *that* would have been a real story.

From the day she arrived in Buenos Aires, Madonna had not been pleased with what she found there: an orchestrated political campaign in opposition of her movie, *Evita*. Much to her dismay, it seemed that everywhere she looked she saw graffiti sprayed on walls, all with sentiments such as: 'Chau goodbye Madonna', and 'Evita Lives! Get Out, Madonna!' Many of those living in Argentina believed that Madonna would desecrate the memory of their beloved Santa Evita. They feared that Evita, as painted by the flagrant Madonna, would be an insult to her memory – and for no good reason other than the fact that Madonna would be the one essaying the role. Perhaps making matters worse for everyone on the

Evita project was the fact that director Alan Parker's cast and crew were comprised mostly of British workers; the 1982 war between Argentina and Britain over the Falkland Islands remained a sticking point for many Argentinians.

Though a replica of the balcony at Casa Rosada, the presidential residence in Argentina, was recreated for the movie at great expense in London, Madonna had longed to film the climax of the movie (when Evita sings 'Don't Cry For Me, Argentina') at the actual location. Standing on the exact site at which Evita gave some of her most dramatic appearances would, no doubt, fill Madonna with genuine emotion, thereby enhancing her performance immeasurably. Originally, Menem had granted the film company permission to film at public buildings such as the Casa Rosada. However, because of the public outcry and controversy, he abruptly changed his mind. He now decreed that locations originally scheduled to be used as sites for filming were off limits.

President Menem, Madonna noted, 'was setting the tone for everything' that was, in her view, ruining her movie. 'He made statements indicating that he agreed the film was an outrage,' she said angrily. ('I don't see Madonna in the role,' he had observed to *Time* magazine. 'And I don't think Argentina's people, who see Evita as a true martyr, will tolerate it.')

It seemed clear that no producer, director or studio executive would be able to change the President's mind. This was a task that would have to be left to the lady herself, the movie's star. It was another one of those times in Madonna's career when a 'handler' would not be able to do her bidding, when she would have to do something herself in order for it to be done to her satisfaction.

Madonna had met Constancio Vigil, a close friend of Menem's, who attempted to arrange a meeting between the star and the President. Menem, however, said that he wasn't interested in meeting Madonna; he refused to see her. Chagrined by his snub, she would not take 'no' for an answer.

After much negotiating, the President relented and agreed to talk with Madonna, but only under the condition that the public not be made aware of the meeting – hence the clandestine manner of her journey on the floor of a car. 'He didn't want people to think he was speaking with the enemy,' explained one government official. When this stipulation was reported to Madonna, she was disappointed by it but also understood that it was the only way she would be able to meet the President. She would simply have to refrain from doing what she, a master public relations strategist, probably really wanted to do: set up a press conference to announce that she and the President were about to engage in a face-to-face meeting.

Before she would sit down with Menem, it was only natural for Madonna to want to do a certain amount of research. A voracious reader, she asked for material about Menem which she would review prior to the meeting so that she could better understand his life and political career. As she put it to one of her associates, 'I want to know who he is. He certainly knows who I am.'

Through her research, Madonna would learn that sixty-six-year-old Carlos Saul Menem was the first Peronist ever elected to national office in Argentina. He was elected governor of La Rioja in 1973, the year Juan Domingo Perón engineered his political comeback. Jailed in 1976 when his wife, Isabel, was forced from power, he was released in 1981. He was re-elected governor in 1983 and again in 1987.

From his early career as provincial governor, Menem rose to the presidency by preaching Peronist politics, the nationalistic style of government formulated by Juan and Eva Perón, which sought to reconcile the interests of industry, business, labour and the poor. Menem's personal charisma and dramatic oratorial style had won him the presidential election in 1989. That election also represented the first transfer of power from one constitutionally elected party to another since 1928. A Roman Catholic convert, Menem was divorced with children. 'Divorced, huh?' Madonna remarked.

'Finally, something we have in common. We're both sinners . . . divorced Catholics.'

When it was clear that they had evaded the press, Madonna and Constancio Vigil were driven to an airport and then flown by helicopter to an offshore island in the middle of the delta in El Tigre. They swooped low, flying directly over what was clearly a large estate in the direction of a nearby small airport. Madonna watched as rolling, green hills flattened out, making way for a concrete landing strip. The helicopter dropped gently.

As soon as Madonna and her friend disembarked, a dignified, elderly, casually dressed man appeared before them. He bowed deeply. They were then escorted to a nearby Land Rover and driven to opulent grounds owned by a business associate of Menem's. There, surrounded by pink flamingos, as if in some magical fairy tale, Madonna would find the President of Argentina waiting for her. It was six p.m.

According to some of his aides, President Carlos Menem had been determined not to be impressed by Madonna. However, like many men before him who had tried to resist Madonna, Menem's cool reserve melted away almost immediately upon meeting her. According to a photograph of her taken that day, she was dressed in a Thirties-style ensemble that was perfectly appropriate for the moment: a black crocheted cotton cardigan and a knee-length silk dress splashed with red, black and white. With black and white leather t-strap pumps on her feet, a sequined tulle clutch bag in one hand and what appeared to observers to be antique French ruby earrings, she looked as if she had just stepped out of a 1930s film. Because her hair was pulled into a chignon and then covered by a Thirties-style black horsehair hat with grey lace overlay, it was difficult to tell if she was blonde or brunette.

As Madonna stood serenely before Menem, perhaps trying to maintain her composure (she would later admit she was nervous), the President began to compliment her profusely. First, he told her that he was amazed at how much she resembled Eva Perón, whom he had met as a young man. Madonna was flattered. She never expected such a compliment from the President of Argentina and, as she would later say, she couldn't help but feel 'ten feet tall'.

It was going well. They walked through a large courtyard. In the middle of a paved quadrant stood a huge carved fountain on which life-sized, bronze sea horses pranced among stone mermaids, octopuses and jellyfish. As they walked by it, Madonna couldn't resist dangling her fingers into the cool water. 'I need one of these in my backyard,' she joked.

As soon as they were seated in the centre of a lovely brick patio, maids and butlers swarmed all about, offering wine and cheese. Then, an attractive and formal looking female interpreter walked over and introduced herself to Madonna. She indicated that she would be assisting in the event of any awkward communication between the actress and the President. While the interpreter spoke, Madonna noticed the President's eyes going 'over every inch of me', as she would later recall, 'looking right through me'. She found him to be 'a very seductive man'.

Once relaxed in her wicker chair, Madonna quickly took stock of Menem, just as he had of her. She noted his tan, his small feet, the fact that he dyed his hair black. She also noted that he could not take his eyes off her.

As ravenous mosquitoes descended upon them, Madonna and the President – followed by his aides – retreated into a parlour furnished with expensive antiques; Madonna was unsure about their age and would later say she thought it 'uncouth' to enquire. In the parlour, the owner of the estate in which the meeting was taking place suddenly appeared with a bottle of chilled champagne in one hand and a small tray of caviar and crackers in the other. After sampling the caviar, Madonna slipped a cassette tape into a player she had brought with her. The song on the tape was 'You Must Love Me', a new ballad from the *Evita* cast album, which Madonna, as Evita, sings when she learns that she is near death. It's an emotionally involving performance, and one of which she was most proud.

Fixing him with a stare to gauge his reaction, Madonna watched Menem rock back and forth, his eyes closed, as her voice filled the room. He then leaned back in his chair and put his hands behind his head as he continued to listen intently. When the song was over, he had tears in his eyes. As Madonna had hoped, the President had been moved. With the moment just right, Madonna then began what she would later refer to as her 'spiel'.

'I so want to make this movie,' she told him, her tone passionate. Small television cameras, mounted on the walls and swivelling soundlessly, recorded her pitch. The interpreter translated as Madonna continued: 'I promise you that it will be fair. I want to be respectful to Eva's memory. You must understand that my intention is good.' She seemed filled with emotion. 'It's all about intention, you know?' she continued. 'And mine is a good one, I promise you.'

'Somehow, I think I believe you,' Menem said as he slowly inched closer to his guest. He reached out and patted her hand, seeming happy to be in the company of an attractive and intelligent woman. Madonna smiled warmly, just a little seductively . . . but not *too* seductively. When she leaned forward, he did the same. While this flirtatious moment was an interesting turn of events, it was not unexpected.

According to one eyewitness – the two were never left alone but were always in the company of a cluster of Menem's aides – Madonna met Menem's gaze with her own. 'You know, you're a very handsome man,' she told him. He didn't need an interpretation to understand the compliment.

'I caught Menem looking at my bra strap, which was showing ever so slightly,' she would later recall. 'He continued doing this throughout the evening with his piercing eyes. When I caught him staring, his eyes stayed with mine.'

Over dinner, Madonna and the President talked about their lives and careers and, as Madonna later recalled, 'our passions'. They spoke of music, politics, mysticism and reincarnation. It must have been difficult for Madonna to come to terms with her circumstances, with how far she had come from her struggling days as a Detroit singer with a New York band called the Breakfast Club. Perhaps it would have been difficult for some observers to reconcile this woman who seemed to possess such a flare for diplomacy with the one who, when she finally did become famous, was often viewed as a temperamental and ridiculously sex-starved pop star. Now, she was the perfect combination of sexuality and brains. But, of course, she had always been just that.

'One always has to have faith in things that cannot be explained,' the President told her as they discussed Catholicism. 'Like God. And the fact that miracles can happen.'

Madonna seized the moment. 'Yes,' she agreed. 'And that's why I believe that you will change your mind and allow us to film on the balcony of the Casa Rosada.'

He smiled warmly. 'Anything is possible,' he said, nodding. 'Anything is possible.'

Five hours passed. It was eleven o'clock. The President took Madonna's face in his hands and kissed her on both cheeks. 'I wish you great luck with your film,' he told her, speaking in English.

'But will you help me?' she asked.

'As I said,' he answered, smiling, 'anything is possible.' With old-world courtesy, he helped her to her feet. Then he stood at the front door and waved goodbye as Madonna and Constancio were driven away.

Once at the airport, Constancio guided Madonna by the arm across the tarmac to a red and white helicopter whose rotor was already beginning to turn. Soon, they were heading back to the city.

Madonna later said she felt swollen with pride over her accomplishment. 'We flew away,' she recounted, 'and I was floating inside the cabin the whole way home. He had worked his magic on me. I only hoped I did the same.'

Less than two weeks later, the Ministry of Culture contacted the film's production company. A second meeting – this time formal and public – was organized and attended by President Menem, Madonna,

Alan Parker and two other stars of the movie, Jonathan Pryce (the Tony award-winning actor from the musical *Miss Saigon* who had now been hired to portray Juan Perón) and Antonio Banderas (Ché, the film's narrator). At that meeting, Menem gave his blessing to *Evita* by making available to the film all government buildings previously off limits – including Madonna's cherished Casa Rosada.

Restless Child

Just who is this person so capable of charming the president of a country into doing something he had no intention of doing, and doing it her way? What is it about this woman – an entertainer who isn't uncommonly beautiful and, while talented, is perhaps not phenomenally so – that has kept her on the top rung of the show-business ladder as the very symbol of success and glamour for more than thirty years? Always comfortable and confident within her limitations, in her 1991 documentary film *In Bed with Madonna* she noted, 'I know I'm not the best singer or dancer in the world. I know that. But I'm not interested in that, either. I'm interested in pushing buttons.'

In the ensuing years since her original success in 1983, many journalists have gone back and explored her past, looking for keys to the mystery of Madonna. However, in her ordinary beginnings there was little to suggest what lay ahead for Madonna Louise Veronica Ciccone.

'I get nostalgic for a time in my life before I was an empire,' Madonna said in September 2000 during an online chat with customers of the Internet server AOL. Like many people who become famous, before she was 'an empire' Madonna just wanted to be a star. A driving, burning ambition to be famous seemed to be born within her, just a part of who she was at the core. When, in fact, she did realize her dream, one of her most celebrated remarks would be 'I have the same goal I've had since I was a little girl. I want to rule the world.'

Though half French Canadian, Madonna seems to most identify with the other half, her Italian heritage. '*Io sono fiera di essere Italiana*' ('I'm proud to be an Italian') she told an audience of 65,000 fans at the Turin football stadium when she performed in Italy in the summer of 1987. Her Italian roots date back to the 1800s in the Abruzzi province of Pacentro. Her paternal great grandfather, Nicola Pietro Ciccone, was born in Pacentro in 1867. At the age of twenty-six, he married Anna Maria Mancini, also from Pacentro. In 1901, they had a son, Gaetano, Madonna's grandfather. Eighteen years later, Gaetano married a woman named Michelina (there seems to be no record of her surname), also from the local village. Shortly thereafter, the couple immigrated to the United States, settling in the Aliquippa suburb of Pittsburgh. Unable to speak English, they forged their way in their new country, Gaetano working in the steel mills of Pittsburgh. They had their first child, Mario, in 1930 and then, four years later, their second son, Silvio – nicknamed Tony – Madonna's father. Four more children, all boys, would be born over the course of the next six years.

Of all the boys, Silvio was the most aggressive, the most intelligent and the most determined to carve his own niche in life; he was the only child to graduate from college with a degree. After graduation, Silvio met and fell in love with a beautiful French-Canadian woman from Bay City, Michigan with the unusual name of Madonna Fortin. Though engaged to another man at the time, Madonna was attracted to Silvio's strong charisma and dark good looks and soon she accepted his proposal of marriage. They married in 1955 at Bay City's Visitation Church. After settling in a small brick home at 443 Thors Street in Pontiac, Michigan – twenty-five miles north-west of Detroit – Tony took a job as an engineer at Chrysler Automotive Corporation.

Madonna Fortin Ciccone gave birth to the couple's first child, Anthony, on 4 May, 1956. Another son, Martin, was born a year later, on 9 August. While visiting her mother, Elsie Fortin, in Bay City, the again-expectant Madonna Fortin Ciccone gave birth, on 16 August 1958, to her first daughter, Madonna Louise (nicknamed 'Nonnie' by her parents) at Bay City Mercy Hospital. She would give birth to three more children over the next three years: Paula, Christopher and Melanie.

'I grew up in a really big family and in an environment where you had to get over it to be heard,' Madonna once recalled. 'I was like the she-devil. It was like living in a zoo. You had to share everything. I slept in a bed for years – not even a double bed – with two sisters.' She also recalled, 'I would even hurt myself, like burn my fingers deliberately, to get attention.'

'She was spoilt from the very beginning,' recalls her brother, Christopher. 'She was the oldest girl, and was the one considered our parents' favourite. That, combined with the fact that she was really aggressive and wanted her way, and got it, made her a spoilt kid. But she was good-hearted. She liked to take care of the bunch. She was also very bossy,' he says. '*Very* bossy.'

While growing up, the young Madonna had always been a faithful fan of classic Hollywood and of its stars. At an early age, she somehow came to realize that many of the world's greatest stars suffered through volatile, early lives rife with mystery and drama. A melodramatic child, she seemed to understand the importance of legend. Years later, Madonna seemed to want to give the impression in interviews that she came from a lower-income family – perhaps hoping to capitalize on the 'good copy' value of the so-called classic rags-to-riches story. While this was apparently the kind of history she wished to claim for herself – one in which she had to overcome great childhood traumas and obstacles before she could ever think of attaining success – it wasn't true.

In truth, her father Silvio was never out of work. He did well, even with the responsibility of so many children and the financial burden inherent in such a large family. Madonna always lived a healthy, middle-class existence.

'Ours was a strict, old-fashioned family,' she has said. 'When I was tiny, my grandmother used to beg me to go to church with her, to love Jesus and be a good girl. I grew up with two images of women: the virgin and the whore.'

As a young girl, Madonna was particularly close to her mother. The two Madonnas shared an intense and special affection, and throughout her career daughter would always speak of mother with great tenderness. 'She was beautiful,' Madonna once recalled, 'and very loving and devoted to her children. Very children-oriented.' Her earliest childhood memories, she has said, are happy ones because they revolved around her mother, whom she has also called 'forgiving and angelic'.

'When I was four and younger, I remember not being able to sleep at night,' Madonna remembers. 'I would walk to my parents' bedroom and push the door open. They were both asleep in bed and I think I must have done this a lot, gone in there, because they both sat up in bed and said, "Oh no, not again!" And I said, "Can I get into bed with you?" My father was against me getting into bed with them. Yet, I remember getting into bed and rubbing against my mother's really beautiful, red, silky nightgown . . . and going to sleep – just like that. I always went to sleep right away when I was with them. I felt really lonely and forlorn, even though my brothers and sisters were in my room with me. So, I wanted to sleep with my parents. To me, that was heaven, to sleep in between my parents.'

Madonna's older brother, Martin, remembers her as a restless, rambunctious child. Though there was the usual sibling rivalry between them, little Nonnie never let her older brother intimidate her. From an early age, Madonna didn't like anyone getting the better of her, and – no surprise – also hated to be told what to do and how to behave, even by her parents. 'When I was a child, I always thought that the world was mine,' she has explained, 'that it was a stomping ground for me, full of opportunities. I always had the attitude that I was going to go out into the world and do all the things I wanted to do, whatever that was.'

Certainly no child likes to be given rules but, repeatedly, people from Madonna's past remark on her particularly rebellious nature as a child. She herself often talks about the defiant personality she possessed from an early age. She started out, and would remain, outspoken about people and matters that rubbed her up the wrong way – even well-meaning children. For instance, one of Madonna's earliest memories is of sitting in her parents' front yard in Michigan, punished by her father as a result of some youthful misdeed. A two-year-old neighbour, wanting to befriend the adorable little girl, waddled up to Madonna and presented her with a dandelion she had picked. Madonna's response was to stand up, face the child, and then push her to the ground. 'My first instinct,' Madonna said years later, 'was to lash out at someone who was more helpless than I. I saw in her innocent eyes the chance to get back at authority.' The fact that the young visitor offered up a dandelion apparently did not help matters for her. The adult Madonna would go on to explain that she detested dandelions because 'they're weeds that run rampant and I like things that are cultivated'.

Even though she was the third of six children, Madonna soon learned how to keep a certain amount of attention focused upon her. For instance, she would use certain tricks inspired by the movies she voraciously watched on television in order to remain the focal point in a busy household – such as jumping on top of a table at a moment's notice and performing a Shirley Temple-type number. At the end of her little impromptu act, she would add 'a personal touch' – she would lift up her dress and flash her panties. This bit of naughtiness was always a success, delighting everyone, young and old. The youngster seemed to be learning that a little flash, mixed with a bit of exhibitionism, could go a long way towards pleasing people. Of course, years later, the adult Madonna would combine these talents to great effect in her professional career.

As is well known by now, the defining moment of Madonna's childhood – the one that would have the most influence in shaping her into the woman she would become – was the tragic and untimely death of her beloved mother at just thirty years of age.

After her mother was diagnosed with breast cancer, little Nonnie and her siblings watched as she slowly wasted away over a period of about a year. Many months before her mother died, however, five-year-old Nonnie began to notice changes in her behaviour and personality, although she didn't understand the serious reasons for such changes. Her mother had always been greatly attentive to detail as a homemaker, but after her diagnosis she grew tired easily and was unable to keep up with housework she had previously maintained with such diligence. Madonna has remembered her mother sitting exhausted on the couch in the middle of the afternoon. The young girl, wanting to play with her mother, just as she always had in the past, would jump on her back; her mother, too tired to move, would be dismissive. The youngster – sensing that something frightening was in the offing – would respond by pounding angrily on her mother's back and sobbing, 'Why are you doing this? Stop being this way! Be who you used to be. Play with me!'

Madonna's mother was, no doubt, at a loss to explain to her frightened daughter the reality of her dire medical condition. Probably scared and helpless, she would just begin to cry, at which point her daughter would respond by wrapping her arms around her tenderly. 'I remember feeling stronger than she was,' Madonna recalled. 'I was so little and yet I felt like she was the child. I stopped tormenting her after that. I think it made me grow up fast.'

Eventually Madonna's mother had to be moved to a hospital. Once there, she attempted to maintain a cheery demeanour, always appearing upbeat for her visiting children and cracking jokes for them. Though she knew she was dying, she didn't want her children to realize it. 'I remember that right before she died she asked for a hamburger,' Madonna has said. 'She wanted to eat a hamburger because she couldn't eat anything for so long. I thought that [she chose a hamburger for her meal] was very funny.' Later that day, though, Madonna's father broke the news to her that her mother was dead. At first, she couldn't comprehend the enormity of the tragedy that had occurred and, as she put it, 'I kept waiting for her to come back. We [she and her father] never really sat down and talked about it. I guess we should have.'

Madonna was just five when her mother died on 1 December 1963, and the impact this loss had on her is almost certainly immeasurable. She lost her mom at a time when, as a young girl, she was forming her personality, her ideals. She needed a mother then, and she would need her ever more.

One theory about childhood loss is that the earlier the age the more profound the influence and the longer lasting the impact. Five is a formative age. A child of five could feel victimized by events, and maybe even think that he or she should have been able to influence them in some way. Certainly, the anger Madonna would feel at losing her mother would be extremely difficult for a five-year-old to handle. Some people never reconcile themselves to such a loss at so early an age, at least not without a great deal of therapy.

After she became famous, Madonna would say, 'We are all wounded in one way or another by something in our lives, and then we spend the rest of our lives reacting to it or dealing with it or trying to turn it into something else'. For Madonna, the anguish of losing her mother 'left me with a certain kind of loneliness and an incredible longing for something'. She has also said, 'If I hadn't had that emptiness, I wouldn't have been so driven. Her death had a lot to do with me saying – after I got over my heartache – I'm going to be really strong if I can't have my mother. I'm going to take care of myself.'

As they grew older, Madonna and her sisters would feel deep sadness as the vivid memory of their mother began drifting further from them. They'd study pictures of her and would come to think that she resembled Anne Sexton, the 1960s Pulitzer Prize-winning poet who wrote about depression and suicide in books like *To Bedlam and Part Way Back* and *Live or Die*. This may have led to Madonna's intense interest in poetry. (Madonna has also cited

Sylvia Plath as a poet she admires – an intellectual reference that goes beyond most people's image of Madonna as being shallow. Actually, many of her songs have roots in art, poetry, philosophy and different religions.)

Not only did the young Madonna learn to take care of herself, she also cared for her brothers and sisters. As the oldest girl, she was happy to take on the maternal role with her siblings. In fact, her brother Martin remembers that Madonna not only fed the younger children but she always made sure that they were properly dressed for school. 'I didn't resent having to raise my brothers and sisters as much as I resented the fact that I didn't have my mother,' Madonna confirmed. Actually, she didn't have to raise her siblings alone since her father did hire a series of housekeepers . . . all of whom eventually ended up quitting rather than having to endure the behaviour of the unruly Ciccone brood. Madonna and her siblings invariably rebelled against anyone brought into the home ostensibly to take the place of their beloved mother. If it meant she could keep other women out of her father's life (and have him to herself), Madonna was happy to continue in the role of surrogate mother. 'Like all young girls,' Madonna would say, 'I was in love with my father and I didn't want to lose him. I lost my mother, but then I was my mother . . . and my father was mine.'

'I see a very lonely girl who was searching for something,' she once said in an interview with *Vanity Fair* in describing her youth. 'Looking for a mother figure. I wasn't rebellious in a conventional way; I cared about being good at something. I didn't shave under my arms and I didn't wear make-up. But I studied hard and got good grades. Rarely smoked pot, though I'm sure I did from time to time. I was a paradox, an outsider and rebel who wanted to please my father and get straight As. I wanted to be somebody.'

The death of her mother had left such deep emotional scars on her, the young Madonna was terrified that she would lose her father, too. As she had done a couple of years earlier with both her parents, she would now crawl into bed in the middle of the night with just her father. The young girl suffered constantly from recurring nightmares and it was only with the assurance that her father was with her could she fall soundly and safely asleep. In time, no doubt because of the devastation she felt, she would never again allow herself to feel as abandoned as she had felt when her mother died. Madonna would have to remain strong for herself because, from an early age, she feared weakness – particularly her own.

Confusing Times

In 1966, three years after the death of Madonna's mother, Tony Ciccone became romantically involved with Joan Gustafson, one of the Ciccone's many housekeepers. Much to Madonna's resentment, the two were soon married. It was, perhaps, at this time that Madonna began to express unresolved feelings of anger towards her father that would last for decades.

Repeatedly, biographies about Madonna have proffered the notion that, because of her mother's death, Madonna has always yearned for her father's approval, and that his apparent lack of approval was the source of ongoing tension between father and daughter. It's true that Tony Ciccone's lack of understanding of Madonna's artistic vision has certainly not enhanced their relationship over the years, and she has definitely sought his approval. However, a close study of Madonna's life clearly shows that another factor in the instability in her emotional relationship with her father has to do with strong anger from her directed towards him. Tony's courage in moving on with his life after his wife died did nothing to elevate him in the eyes of a daughter who felt strongly that her mother could – and should – never be replaced. Or, as one close relative put it, 'It was as if, as a young girl, she was so filled with rage because of her mother's death and the way her father handled it, she had to direct it somewhere . . . and so she directed it at the one person she loved the most, her father.'

Is it possible to be angry with a person and also to seek that person's approval? Most mental health professionals would agree that major characteristics of the human experience are ambivalence and contradictory feelings. It's entirely possible that Madonna was angry at her father for going on with his life after the death of his wife, but underneath that rage she still longed for his approval and acceptance. It was as if she put him to a test she knew he would fail: would Tony accept his daughter under her own terms, even if she acted outrageously? If not, she could continue to be angry at him. If so, she would find another reason to be resentful of him. Certainly, anger just continues to recycle itself until it's finally dealt with, once and for all.

In contrast to Madonna's gentle, olive-skinned mother, the stern, blonde Gustafson was a disciplinarian – or at least she tried to be one. None of the children ever listened to a thing she had to say. The young Madonna also seemed to have a difficult time adjusting to no longer being the female head of the household. She refused, for example, to refer to the new Mrs Ciccone as 'Mother', which her father had requested.

When Madonna's career was just beginning to gain momentum in the early 1980s, she talked a great deal about how her life had changed when her father remarried. She didn't hate her stepmother, she explained, she simply could never accept her in the place of her real mother. True to her sensational nature, Madonna would later embellish any tension between stepmother and stepchild for the press by saying she always felt unwanted and unneeded, 'always like Cinderella'.

Madonna would also tell stories of how the new Mrs Ciccone once bloodied her nose in a physical altercation – although Madonna professed to be delighted by this turn of events since it enabled her to miss Sunday church for a change. ('I most certainly do not remember that,' Joan Gustafson Ciccone once said. 'It never happened. Do you think her father would have allowed such a thing?') Another indignity often recounted by Madonna is that her stepmother supposedly refused to let her wear a tampon when she started menstruating (which, according to Madonna, occurred at the age of ten) because, in Joan's opinion, tampons were the equivalent of sexual intercourse and should not be used until after marriage. ('Oh my God! That *never* happened,' an incredulous Joan said when she heard this story. 'How awful! Did she say that? No, she did *not* say that. Did she?')

According to Madonna, it seems that another major 'wicked stepmother' indignity perpetrated on her by Joan was that she insisted Madonna and her sisters dress in matching outfits, thereby stripping Madonna of the individuality she so valued. Wearing school uniforms was bad enough for Madonna, she said, but dressing exactly like her sisters was pure torture. ('I never did that!' Joan exclaimed when told of Madonna's claim. 'Why would I do that? Are we talking about the same Madonna here?')

Even at this young age, Madonna was learning to be innovative with her wardrobe when attempting to assert her own personality – including wearing her clothes in an unconventional manner by ripping them or even turning them inside out once Joan wasn't around. Madonna would also wear bright, tight pants or tie old rags in her messy hair – anything that would enable her to stand out from her younger sisters. (This quest for fashion individuality would carry itself into later years when Madonna found herself struggling in New York, trying to be a dancer. She would often dress flamboyantly, cutting up her leotard and holding it together only with safety pins. Then, as now, she remained fascinated with the idea of individuality.)

No matter how much Madonna might have resented the situation, it seemed that the new Mrs Ciccone was in her life to stay. Joan and Tony even went on to have two children together, Jennifer and Mario.

Tony Ciccone did his best to make sure his growing family stayed on the right track of life. A hardworking man, he tried to teach his children to follow in his footsteps and focus on their school lessons. There were rules to follow, he would tell them, and they were expected to live their lives within those rules. It was especially important to him that his children attend church regularly. 'I wouldn't call it strict, I'd call it conservative,' Madonna said. 'My father was a stern believer in excelling towards leadership. Maintaining a competitive edge. And be proud of yourself and do good in school and you will reap the rewards of your investment.' Years later, Madonna recalled that her father would tape a 'chore chart' to the wall, assigning each child a task. She never forgot which chores appeared under her name: 'Washing out the diaper pail. Defrosting the freezer. Raking the leaves. Washing the dishes. Babysitting. Vacuuming. Everything.'

Perhaps recognizing the obvious correlation between her ability to achieve success, keep a competitive edge and observe her father's own work ethic, Madonna would often speak of Tony Ciccone with admiration: 'One thing my father was with us was very solid,' she has said. 'Very dependable that way; he didn't confuse me. He didn't preach one thing and live his life another way. He always stuck to his word. He had a lot of integrity. And that consistency, especially not having a mother, was extremely important.'

Always, Madonna enjoyed reaping the rewards of hard work; she liked to win. Tony had a practice of awarding each of his children fifty cents for every A grade they received on their report card; Madonna always got the most As. She was naturally intelligent, a good student who always seemed to have an eye on the importance of preparing for her future. 'That bitch never had to study,' her brother Martin laughs. 'Never. She got straight As. I used to get up there and study all the time but my mind wasn't on it. I did it because I was supposed to, but I didn't like it. She did it because she knew it would take her to the next phase.' Madonna also remembered the rewards she received for her A grades and laughingly added, 'I was really competitive and my brothers and sisters hated me for it. I made the most money every report card.'

As well as their academic studies and household chores, all of the Ciccone children were encouraged to play a classical instrument. Madonna was designated the piano, though she genuinely hated it. The neighbourhood in which she was raised was racially mixed and, with that cultural influence at work, she was more interested in the local Motown sound than she was in classical piano. Her idols were Diana Ross and the Supremes, Ronnie Spector and Stevie Wonder.

'When I was a little girl, I wished I was black,' she said. 'I was living in Pontiac, Michigan, some twenty-five miles north-west of Detroit. All of my friends were black and all the music I listened to was black. I was incredibly jealous of all my black girlfriends because they could have braids in their hair that stuck up everywhere. So I would go through this incredible ordeal of putting wire in my hair and braiding it so that I could make my hair stick up.'

Madonna soon convinced her father to allow her to give up her boring piano lessons and, instead, take on more (for her) exciting activities, such as dance – tap and jazz – as well as baton twirling.

'She was a smart girl, always motivated,' remembers her stepmother, Joan. 'Brilliant. Manipulative, I guess so. Yes. But you knew she would survive. You knew she would never be weak. And you were glad about that.'

It isn't surprising, especially given the religious convictions Tony Ciccone shared with his late wife, that all the Ciccone children were educated at Catholic schools. In the Sixties, the strict rules and regulations of these parochial schools were stringently observed by the nuns in charge, many of whom used tactics that today would be considered child abuse.

'They'd smack you around, for sure,' Madonna has said. 'It was an environment of fear, mixed with these contrasting images of the holy.'

In 1966, she had her First Communion and, when confirmed a year later, she added the name Veronica to her own birth name. 'I took the name of Veronica,' she explains, 'because she wiped the face of Jesus. You weren't supposed to help Jesus Christ while he was on his way to the Crucifixion. She was not afraid to step out and wipe the sweat off him and help him. So I liked her for doing that, and took her name. There was also Mary Magdalene,' she says, when speaking of biblical women who had influenced her. 'She was considered a fallen woman because she slept with men. But Jesus said it was okay. I think they probably got it on, Jesus and Mary Magdalene.'

Catholicism gave her a foundation of faith upon which, she has said, she was always able to fall back, even as an adult. However, the religion's strong emphasis on the notions of guilt and forgiveness has, she's said, 'screwed up many a Catholic person. How many Catholics are in therapy, just trying to get over the idea of Original Sin. Do you know what it's like to be told from the day you walk into school for the first time that you are a sinner, that you were born that way, and that that's just the way it is? You'd have to be Catholic to understand it.'

Early in her career Madonna would playfully make use of religious icons as part of her sexy wardrobe and then distribute juicy comments to journalists, such as the oft-quoted 'crucifixes are sexy because there's a naked man on them'. This is an example of one of her most frequently used and successful 'shock' formulas: taking a respected, sacred image and imbuing it with completely inappropriate sexual connotations, thereby making even the mere thought of the total package completely taboo. She quickly found that making statements combining elements of religion and sex – such as 'crucifixes are sensual because Jesus was so sexy, like a movie star, almost' – was a successful recipe for controversy, got her noticed, and made people talk about her as a sexual revolutionary. While easy to prepare, after the second or third time, it was also a relatively transparent gimmick. Yet, since the public continued to act shocked, and even to express delight and amusement at her observations, Madonna repeated the formula often – on talk shows, in music videos and in some of her songs. (It wouldn't be until nearly ten years into her career, when she published her steamy book *Sex*, that most people would catch on to what she was up to . . . and then begin to reject it.)

One story in her arsenal may or may not be true: 'When I was a little girl, I was at church by myself on a Saturday afternoon going to confession. No one was there, and instead of going out the main entrance, I went through this vestibule off to the side with a swinging door. I opened the door a little bit, and there was this couple standing up, fucking in the church. I thought, "Oh my God!" and shut the door really fast. That's the only sex I've seen in a church. Seems like a neat thing to do, though.'

In fact, many of Madonna's tongue-in-cheek takes on Catholicism (which have been considered blasphemous by some more devout observers) have to do with an intense bitterness towards the church. She had such a strong feeling that the orthodoxy that surrounded her had let her down, she acted provocatively as a way of thumbing her nose at it. It appeared to some that she had rejected God because He had done a terrible thing to her – taking away her mother. Through the years, she seemed to continually dare Him to retaliate against her as she continued to act out in ways that could be considered, at least to a religious person, sacrilegious.

As an adult, Madonna would also blame the church's stringent, puritanical, suffering-based teachings for many of the problems the Ciccone children experienced in life. 'My older brothers were incredibly rebellious,' she said. 'They got into drugs and into trouble with the police. One of my brothers ran off and became a Moonie. Me? I became an overachiever. I had it programmed in my mind – "I don't care if I have to live on the street, and I don't care if I have to eat garbage. *I'll do it.*"'

Adding to Madonna's ambivalence about religion must have been the way she was influenced by the somewhat fanatical – and confusing – devotion she witnessed in her mother. 'Catholicism is a very masochistic religion,' the adult Madonna would declare. 'And I saw my mother doing things that really affected me. She would kneel on uncooked rice and pray during Lent. She would sleep on wire hangers. She was passionately religious. Swooning with it, even. If my aunt came over my house and had jeans that zipped up front, my mother covered all the statues so that they couldn't see such a display. She then turned the holy pictures towards the wall.'

When Madonna was about ten, the family moved to 2036 Oklahoma Street in Rochester Hills, Michigan, an affluent community not far from the exclusive Detroit suburb of Bloomfield Hills. It was then that she began to think she might one day like to become a nun. 'I wanted a pious way of life,' she told me in 1983. 'But I was at odds with the whole thing. The more it repelled me, the more I wanted it, as if I was trying to conquer something. I think the church really screwed me up. It made me competitive. It made me afraid to fail. It caused all kinds of problems, some I probably don't even know about. I'm actually afraid to go into hypnotherapy for fear of what I will learn about my Catholic upbringing!'

Indeed, her rebellious nature being what it was, she couldn't help but turn against the moralistic and conservative school system. In the playground, for instance, the young Madonna would hang upside down from the monkey bars, acting oblivious to her 'performance' but quite intentionally making sure her underpants were exposed for the enjoyment of all the boys. Constantly, she was being chastised by the nuns for flashing her underwear.

Those nuns at St Andrew's Elementary School were always a source of great fascination for Madonna. She would try to sneak glances at them through the convent windows to catch them in their informal, 'natural' setting. She wondered what they looked like *sans* habits and if, indeed, they even had hair. Childhood friend Carol Belager recalls peering through convent windows with Madonna.

'Oh my God, they *do* have hair,' Madonna whispered to Carol as the two girls spied on the unsuspecting Sister Mary Christina.

'Let's go now,' Carol said, nervously.

'No, she's getting ready to strip,' Madonna said, excitedly. 'I want to see what she looks like naked.'

Carol pulled Madonna away before she had the opportunity to see her first nude nun.

These strange, humourless and immensely powerful nuns were, to the young Madonna, beautiful and mysterious. As an adult she would remember, 'I saw them as really pure, disciplined, sort of above average people. They never wore any make-up and they had these really serene faces.' Then, in typical Madonna fashion, she added for good measure, 'Plus, they were very sexy.'

The ambivalence Madonna still feels for the teachings of the Catholic church is especially ironic given that it would seem that Catholicism did empower her with the ability to transcend her own insecurities. The philosophy encouraged her to confront moments of great self-weakness, those times when she suspected that she really wasn't good enough, or talented enough, or pretty enough . . . those times when she most needed to fall back on a foundation of faith in order to conquer feelings of inadequacy. It also imbued her with the strict sense of self-discipline so necessary to challenge the many difficulties she would, no doubt, encounter on the road to stardom.

'I don't talk about it much,' she said in another interview with me in 1985, 'but, yes, I pray. I pray when things are going wrong, like most people, I guess. The key, I think, is to pray when things aren't all screwed up. That's when you know you have a relationship with God. Coming from a Catholic school, though, it's so ingrained in me to pray, that now I do it without even thinking about it. To me, when I say, when I'm pissed off, "Oh my God", well, that's a prayer, in a sense. Even if people don't agree with me that it's a prayer, I don't care. When you're angry and you call out for God's intercession, that's a prayer. And, also, I tend to pray when there's so much bullshit going on that I just need to stop and remind myself of the things I have to be grateful for. So, yes, I pray.'

Losing Her Virginity

Though feeling almost smothered by a strict religious environment, Madonna's talent still somehow managed to blossom and, on occasion, she would find imaginative ways to unleash it. For instance, in a fifth-grade talent show, the eleven-year-old scandalized the school audience, and her father, when, clad only in a coat of fluorescent green paint and a revealing bikini, she did a knock-out imitation of a go-go-dancing Goldie Hawn (*à la* Hawn's early performances on the classic television programme, *Rowan & Martin's Laugh-In*). Madonna's father smouldered at the sight of his pubescent daughter bumping and grinding for all to see. Afterward, he grounded her for two weeks. 'I don't know what she was thinking,' he says today. 'Besides the fact that she wanted to shock everyone.'

Once in Rochester Adams High School, Madonna found various activities with which she could keep herself in the public eye. As a cheerleader, she got a taste of what it was like to be in front of enthusiastic crowds. She then had the opportunity to test some of the tricks she had used as a child in front of her appreciative family, but on a bigger, and maybe even more critical, audience.

Karen Craven, who was on the cheerleading squad with Madonna, recalls the day the squad was to form a typical 'human pyramid' during a break in a game. Madonna 'vaulted up to the top and did a little flip', she remembers. A collective gasp of shock erupted from the crowd when the teenager's skirt flew up. Guidance counsellor Nancy Ryan Mitchell recalls, 'From a distance, it looked like she was nude. However, she was actually wearing a pair of flesh-coloured tights. It was shocking, I must say. But that was Madonna.

'I remember that she would also dance vigorously during some of the plays she was in, using a lot of body movement. It was pretty controversial for the times. Her father wasn't pleased. Anything she could do to shock people, that's what she would do. But, to her credit, she was a bright student, involved in a Big Brother/Sister programme, a thespian group. She was very positive thinking. She was taking dancing lessons after school when a lot of other kids were drinking Cokes. She worked hard.'

Madonna was also involved in the theatre department, starring in productions such as *My Fair Lady*, *Cinderella*, *The Wizard of Oz* and *Godspell*. On the high-school stage, she would learn what it was like to please an audience, to stand in the spotlight and accept a crowd's warm applause. 'She liked it,' says Clara Bonell, a former classmate. 'I saw her in *Godspell*, and I remember that when the audience stood for the curtain call, she was crying. The sense of acceptance, I think now that this is what she most appreciated, most craved. I think she felt that she didn't get it at home from her father, who was just not supportive at all, as I recall it. So, if she could get it from an audience, then that was good for her.'

Beverly Gibson, her drama teacher, adds, 'When the spotlight came on her, she was pure magic. People paid attention to her; you couldn't take your eyes off of her. You often hear about people who become famous being wallflowers. You hear their friends and teachers say, "Oh, I would never have expected her to become famous." Not so with Madonna. There was no way she could ever be anything other than famous at something. I would watch her on stage with that vibrant personality and charisma, and think to myself, "Oh, my, it is inevitable, isn't it?"'

'In high school, Madonna was a nonconformist,' says her former classmate Tanis Rozelle. 'Unlike the other girls, she didn't shave her armpits, and neither did her sister, Melanie. That was considered pretty weird. Both had thick tufts of hair growing out from underneath their armpits. It caused a minor controversy, but after a while people just accepted it. Madonna explained that she didn't shave because she didn't want to be a typical suburban American girl. She said she didn't want to remove something from her body that was natural. It didn't stop her from raising her arms high while cheering, even when she wore a sleeveless uniform,' recalls Tanis. 'And it certainly didn't stop her from being popular with the boys. She was very pretty and the guys really liked her.'

It was during her first year in high school, at the age of fifteen in December 1973, when Madonna lost her virginity to seventeen-year-old Russell Long. Actually, she says she had some sexual encounters prior to this time when she was eight, but not intercourse. 'All of my sexual experiences when I was young were with girls,' she says. 'I mean, we didn't have those sleepover parties for nothing. I think that's really normal, same sex experimentation. You get really curious and there's your girlfriend, and she's spending the night with you, and it happens.'

'She wanted her first time having real sex to be something special,' Russell Long now recalls. 'We had a date – a movie and burgers – and afterward we drove my very cool, blue 1966 Caddy back to my parents' place.'

While Long recalls being nervous about the signals he says Madonna was sending – it was clear that she wanted to be intimate with him – he didn't have to worry about initiating anything. She was the aggressor. 'Are we going to do it, or not?' she wanted to know as she removed her bra.

'I guess so,' Russell said, breathlessly.

'Well, then, c'mon,' she urged. 'Do it!'

Years later, she would observe, 'Even after I made love for the first time, I still felt like a virgin. I didn't lose my virginity until I knew what I was doing.'

After that first time at the home of Long's parents, he says, they chose the back seat of his Cadillac for future rendezvous. 'My friends called it "the Passion Wagon",' he recalls.

'She didn't have a problem with people knowing we were having sex. Lots of girls of that age would have been embarrassed by it, or would at least not have wanted people to know. Not Madonna. She was proud of it, said that it had made her feel like a woman. She was comfortable with her body, didn't mind being seen naked. She just seemed comfortable with all of it.'

'I liked my body when I was growing up,' Madonna once said in a press interview, 'and I wasn't ashamed of it. I liked boys and didn't feel inhibited by them. Maybe it comes from having brothers and sharing a bathroom. The boys got the wrong impression of me at high school. They mistook forwardness for promiscuity. When they don't get what they want, they turn on you. I went through a period when all the girls thought I was loose, and the boys thought I was a nymphomaniac. The first boy I ever slept with was my boyfriend and we'd been going out a long time.'

'She wasn't like most other students,' Russell Long recalls. 'There was a group of kids who were just the odd ones, the ones most of the students thought were sort of creepy. Madonna was in that bunch. She didn't assimilate into the student body, rather she was one of those kids on the fringe, sort of on the sidelines smirking at everyone else.'

'Growing up in a suburb in the Midwest was all I needed to understand that the world was divided into two categories: people who followed the status quo and played it safe, and people who threw convention out the window and danced to the beat of a different drum,' Madonna wrote for *Harper's Bazaar* in 2013. 'I hurled myself into the second category, and soon discovered that being a rebel and not conforming doesn't make you very popular. In fact, it does the opposite. You are viewed as a suspicious character. A troublemaker. Someone dangerous.

'When you're fifteen, this can feel a little uncomfortable,' she continued. 'Teenagers want to fit in on one hand and be rebellious on the other. Drinking beer and smoking weed in the parking lot of my high school was not my idea of being rebellious, because that's what everybody did. And I never wanted to do what everybody did. I thought it was cooler to not shave my legs or under my arms . . . I dared people to like me and my nonconformity.'

Though a rebel at heart, Russell Long recalls Madonna also being 'quite sensitive'. He continues, 'We had long talks about her mother, and how much she missed her. Also, we discussed the tension that existed between her and her father. By the time she was in high school she was rebelling against him in every way, she seemed so angry at him, though I didn't understand why. She would say, "What do you think he'd do if he knew we were having sex? Do you think it would freak him out?" And I would say, "Hell, yeah, it would freak him out." Then she would come back with, "Well, then, maybe I should tell him." I would say, "Madonna, no! He'll kill me." But my safety, or her privacy, wasn't on her mind. If she could blow his mind, shock him, she wanted to do it. Even more than that, if she could piss him off, she wanted to do it.' Long and Madonna continued their relationship for six months.

Russell Long, once a trucker for United Parcel Service, now lives in Seattle, Washington, and is married with grown children. 'I wonder if he still loves me,' Madonna once mused. Then, as if coming to her senses, she answered her own question. 'Oh, of course he does!'

'Sure I do,' said Russell Long. 'Even if she had not become famous, there's no way I would ever have forgotten her. She was one of a kind.'

Christopher & Whitley

In the ninth grade, Madonna joined a high-school jazz dance class. However, with determination and dedication uncommon for a fourteen-year-old, she soon outgrew it. A friend then recommended that she consider the Christopher Flynn Dance School at the Rochester School of Ballet. Once accepted as a student, she was quickly exposed to students who were serious about the art of classical dance, 'which was a real turn-on for me', she has said. In his studio Christopher Flynn stressed hard work and discipline, concepts Madonna had sometimes felt the need to rebel against in her home and at school, but which she now embraced as a dance student. 'He was very Catholic and all about rules,' she recalls. Because she worked up to five hours a day in his class, Flynn was quickly impressed with his new student's remarkable progress. Soon, she quit cheerleading, began to watch what she ate in order to trim her figure, and spoke of little more than her love of dance. Her enrolment at the Christopher Flynn Dance School was the first of several years of serious dance study.

Flynn the dance instructor, thirty years Madonna's senior, was one of the first people to notice the budding 'star quality' in the teenage girl and, as a result, really the first to push her in the direction of a career as a performer. His enthusiasm for Madonna quickly gave her a boost of self-confidence that even the most self-assured youngster needs at that age.

Once, after a particularly gruelling dance routine, a sweaty and exhausted Madonna wrapped a towel around her head 'swami-style', and then gazed moodily out of the window, deep in reflection. Flynn observed his student, so lost in thought. Years later, he would recall the moment with vivid clarity.

'My God,' he said to her, 'you really are beautiful.'

'What?' Madonna asked, wide-eyed and perhaps wanting to hear it again.

'You have an ancient-looking face,' he told her, 'a face like an ancient Roman statue.'

'Why would you say that to me?' she asked.

'Because it's true,' he answered. 'It's not physical beauty I'm talking about, it's something deeper. Know it.'

'I already know it,' she said, speaking frankly. 'I just wasn't sure anyone else did.'

Years later, she would recall, 'I was fourteen, maybe fifteen, and feeling horribly unattractive and unpopular and uninteresting and unfabulous. And Christopher said "God, you're beautiful". Well, no one had ever said that to me before. He told me I was special. He taught me to appreciate beauty – not beauty in the conventional sense, but rather beauty of the spirit.'

Actually, Christopher Flynn's influence on Madonna's life and career cannot be overestimated. 'My whole life changed,' Madonna has said. 'Not just because studying dance with Christopher was so really important, but because he gave me a focus. He took me out of what I considered to be a humdrum existence.'

Flynn was happy to help encourage Madonna to her next level of her growth as a performer. After she became a star he would say of her, 'Madonna was a blank page, believe me, and she wanted desperately to be filled in. She knew nothing at all about art, classical music, sculpture, fashion, civilization – nothing about life, really. I mean, she was just a child. But she had a burning desire to *learn*, that girl. She had a thirst for learning that was insatiable. It was something that would not be denied. She was a very positive young girl, always focused on what she could do to be better. She had this tremendous thirst and, really, it was insatiable.'

Christopher Flynn was also the first homosexual man with whom Madonna became close. Although she was still under age, he allowed her to accompany him to gay bars and clubs. It was there that her education began to expand beyond the scope of classical music, art and sculpture. With Flynn as her guide into the more provocative aspects of Michigan nightlife, Madonna learned a great deal in a short amount of time about eroticism and, as she later put it, 'pushing the envelope to the point where it screams out: "stop!"' It was much more of an education than she could ever have acquired from her home life or at school. Because of her completely uninhibited way of expression through dance, Madonna won over crowds of gay men with her campy, sexy and energetic moves. Her appreciative 'fans' filled her with a sense of self-confidence and energy, making her truly believe that her aspirations to be a dancer were not unwarranted.

Her French teacher, Carol Lintz, recalls that Madonna was so influenced by her experiences at the gay bars, she no longer even needed a partner to dance. 'Something happened to her at this time, and it caused her to no longer think of dance as a social act, but rather an artistic one. There she would be, in the middle of the dance floor at one of those teen dances, by herself, dancing. People would ask me with whom she was dancing. I would answer, no one. Herself. She was dancing with herself, just for the experience.

'I started seeing technique. I started seeing showmanship. It was a fascinating evolution.

'When she graduated, she was given the Thespian Award for her work in the many school plays she did – so many, I can't even remember how many, and she was always the lead . . . she wouldn't have it any other way. She was very proud of that award. I remember, she said, "I always knew I'd get this award one day", as though it was an Oscar. But I never thought of her as an actress. I thought of her as a dancer.'

Christopher Flynn once remembered another conversation he had with Madonna at his dance studio that, he says, 'really clued me in on the kind of entertainer she was becoming'.

While doing stretching exercises in her black leotard, she asked Flynn, 'Why do you think you like men?'

He answered the question by saying his sexuality was something that 'just happened, nothing I can control'.

'Well, I wish I understood it,' she said.

'Why?'

'So that I can tap into it,' she said. 'Look at women like Judy Garland and Marilyn Monroe. These women are gay favourites, aren't they? I wish I knew what it is about them. Is it the glamour? Is it their behaviour?'

'I think it's because they're so tragic,' offered Flynn. 'I think that's what it is. You see them and you want to slit your wrists. Every gay man has wanted to slit his wrist at one time or another. So yes,' he decided, 'it's because they're so tragic.'

Madonna stopped stretching. 'Well, then, forget it,' she said, looking at her dance teacher seriously. 'I will never be tragic. If it takes being tragic to have gay fans, then fuck it. I'll appeal only to straight people, I guess.'*

By the time seventeen-year-old Madonna graduated from Rochester Adams High School in 1976 – a half semester early due to her exceptional studies – Christopher Flynn had become a dance professor at the University of Michigan. Wanting to bring his young protégée with him to the new school, he agreed with Madonna's high-school guidance counsellor, Nancy Ryan Mitchell, that she should audition for a scholarship there. She applied, she got it and so, in the fall of 1976, Madonna enrolled at the University of Michigan in Ann Arbor.

'Our dad was pretty damn proud,' says Martin Ciccone. 'I'm not sure that Madonna knew it, though. Their relationship was strained. If she was in trouble, of course he would be there. But she was never one to admit when she was in trouble, and definitely she would not turn to our father. They argued a lot, there was such anger there from her. She was his daughter; he was an old-fashioned Italian-American man, and family meant a lot to him. But there was always this great divide between him and Madonna. He never understood her. "Break rules?" he would say. "But why? What's wrong with the rules?" When it was time for her to go off to college, I think they were both ready for a break from each other.

'Our father had always stressed education, though. He raised his kids to appreciate a good education. When Madonna went off to college with that scholarship, we all knew she was going to really come into her own.'

It was then, when she enrolled at the University of Michigan, that Madonna Louise Ciccone, middle child of a strict Catholic

---

* Christopher Flynn died of an AIDS-related illness at the age of sixty on 27 October 1990 in Los Angeles. In a statement, Madonna said, 'I really loved him. He was my mentor, my father, my imaginative lover, my brother, everything, because he understood me.'

family, began her metamorphosis into 'Madonna', free-spirited artist.

'I guess my immediate impression of her was a combination of fascination and intimidation,' says Whitley Setrakian, a young, aspiring choreographer who became Madonna's first room-mate at the University of Michigan's Stockwell Hall, and then later at the University Towers. 'She was beautiful. Articulate. Very, very thin. Her hair had been chopped off in a sort of odd way with little bits sticking out on the sides. She wore lots of heavy, dark eyeliner and interesting clothes, baggy T-shirts and tight pants. She was startlingly brilliant with a quick, incisive type of mind. She was very spontaneous, driven and unafraid. She had a way of owning a room when she came into it. I've never met anyone quite like her. Also,' she adds with a laugh, 'her front extensions [a dance technique] were very high, which meant a lot at the time. She was a good danscer with strong technique. She took chances. She was raw, but we were all raw then. However, if one dancer got a lot of attention and she didn't, that made her angry and she would talk to me about it. "What does she have that I don't have?" she would ask. She would think it was unjust that anyone got more recognition than she got. It drove her crazy that others were as good, or better, as if there was a mad race to the finish.'

Setrakian continues, 'She worked well with Christopher Flynn, though a lot of other students didn't. He was a delightful person, and yet scary in ballet class because if he thought you were lazy he would pinch you really hard and leave little blood blisters on you. I had some trepidation about that, but Madonna didn't. She liked it, actually. He was flamboyant and sarcastic, like her.'

Setrakian – who worked at the same ice-cream parlour as Madonna to earn extra money – was struck by the way the seventeen-year-old Madonna gave her all to everything she did, whether it be partying or rehearsing: 'She'd drag me out of bed. I couldn't keep up with her,' says Madonna's former room-mate. 'She was up in the morning and out the door, in class before everyone else, warming up. We'd go out dancing on Saturday nights, up all night dancing very late. She'd be up early warming up if she had a rehearsal on Sunday morning. She was not easy on herself. She lived hard and worked hard.

'She embarked on what seemed to be a calculated campaign to be my friend,' Setrakian recalls. 'I resisted it at first but she won me over. She was determined to break down whatever limits and boundaries I put up. I felt she was being real with me when she would reveal herself in vulnerable ways. But yet, in the back of my mind, I would always think, "Maybe not." I felt that there might be an element of exploitation going on, that she was using our friendship to meet her emotional needs. I felt there was something mercenary about it, but it was vague and unclear to me then. I just knew that she would expect a person to be there for her, unconditionally. However, if you had a problem and you needed her, well, she wasn't always there.

'We had many long talks about her mother,' Setrakian says, 'and about how much she missed her. She envied the relationship I had with my own mother. My mother called a lot and, when I would speak to her on the telephone, I would be aware of Madonna standing around and listening. We also talked about her father, but not much. I sensed anger from her whenever I brought up the subject.

'We became closer after a few months. She was huggy, very touchy. I got used to it. After a while it became a part of the way we related to each other.'

In December, at the Christmas break, Whitley went to the Bahamas on a vacation with her boyfriend. Madonna spent the holiday alone at their apartment, pining for Whitley. When Whitley returned from her trip, she found on her bed a six-page handwritten letter from Madonna. In it, Madonna wrote that she 'missed the hell' out of Whitley. 'I've realized how much I've grown to depend on you as a listener, advice giver and taker and general all around most wonderful, intimate friend in the whole world,' she wrote. She mentioned that she and a female friend had gone to a bar and, because of the way they were dancing, were 'verbally accused' of being lesbians. In fact, wrote Madonna, she wished that she had been dancing with Whitley, not Linda. She also indicated that her rent was due, that she didn't have the money, and didn't know what she would do about the problem. She was so poor, she wrote, that she had taken to rummaging through garbage cans for food. She would just continue dreaming of a career in show business, she concluded, and hope for the best.

Those who knew best at this time agree that Madonna had already made up her mind to be famous for doing *something* and so, as a means to that end, she was completely focused on her dance curriculum. Her inborn instinct for what was right for her, and for finding people who not only believed in her but could also assist in bringing out the best in her, led her to dance professor Gay Delang's 'technique class'. Delang remembers her as a standout from the very beginning. 'She had many qualities that young dancers desire. She was lean. She had a nice edge to her muscles. She was hungry. Great appetite. She was sassy, kid-like. Chewed gum. Lived on butterscotch candies. She was disciplined, hardworking. A pleasure to be with. She was young. Just a kid.'

'All these girls would come to class with black leotards and pink tights and their hair up in buns with little flowers in it,' Madonna has remembered of her days as a dance student. 'So I cut my hair really short and I'd grease it so it would be sticking up, and I'd rip my tights so there were runs all over them. Anything to stand out from them and say, "I'm not like you. Okay? I'm taking dance classes and everything but I'm not stuck here like you."'

In college, Madonna sometimes worked off campus (as in the ice-cream parlour) but, to her, survival meant getting by any way she could. Room-mate Setrakian remembers: 'She taught me how to shoplift. One of us would make a diversion at the counter and the other would place her dance bag under the counter. Then, you'd sort of lean casually over the counter and at the height of the diversion you'd sweep your arm over the counter. Finally, the item would be in your dance bag. We got a lot of cosmetics that way, and lots of food, too. Whatever we needed. She would say, "Who needs it more than we do? When we get famous, we'll give a lot of money to charity to make up for stealing this stuff. It all balances out with God in the bigger picture, don't worry."'

During her year and a half at the University of Michigan, Madonna received decent grades; she was satisfied with her work. However, the notion of graduating soon became less important to her than the idea of finally launching her dance career. She had been studying dance intensely for five years and the response to her work had been positive all around. She had gone as far as the university could take her, and now yearned to go further. Christopher Flynn's enthusiastic encouragement, along with the admiration of her friends and room-mates, served to validate her inner voice, the one that assured her that she had something special – unique – to offer. When she sensed that it was time to move on, she saw no reason to waste time finishing her formal studies. Whitley Setrakian remembers that Madonna 'saw better things for herself if she moved on quickly, without so much as a glance back. She wanted to be a dancer. She wanted to go to New York and get into a good company,' she recalls. 'It was time. She never said she wanted to be a cultural icon or anything like that. She just wanted to dance.'

From childhood, Madonna had wanted to be an actress or, to be more clear, a *movie star*. Now, according to what she would later explain, she reasoned that as a dancer she would eventually find an entrée into the world of dramatics. Of course, in making these decisions, she was working completely on gut instinct. Certainly, she could have migrated to the West Coast, to Hollywood – the so-called entertainment capital of the world. However, she sensed that her immediate opportunities would be found in New York, a city known for its frenetic energy, diverse cultures and pushy attitudes.

Predictably, her father Tony was most unhappy when Madonna told him that she was forsaking her scholarship to run off to New

York and focus on a dancing career. 'He was very, very upset,' says Madonna's brother, Martin. 'Our stepmother backed him, of course. They both agreed that she was making a huge mistake, and they did everything they could think of to talk her out of it. There were some big battles, yes. I recall some pretty bad scenes.'

'You drop out of school, you'll no longer be my daughter,' Tony told her one night over a family meal, according to a later recollection.

'Fine,' Madonna said, angrily. 'But when I'm famous, will I be your daughter again? Is that how this works?'

'We'll cross that bridge when we come to it,' Tony countered. '*If* we ever come to it.'

'Oh, we'll come to it, all right,' Madonna said.

Contrary to what has been reported in the past, however, Tony never discouraged Madonna's show business aspirations. Rather, he just wished for her to graduate from college first, and then, as he puts it now, 'do whatever she wanted to do, but with an education'.

'He would never tell her she was untalented,' says Gina Magnetti, one of Madonna's cousins. 'He wasn't the kind of father to do that. Italian parents, they generally don't do that anyway, especially if they came from the Old Country. They support their kids' ambitions.

'Silvio – Uncle Tony – he wanted the best for her, big things. And, to him, that meant a college degree. Then, after that, she could have done whatever she wanted. She didn't see it that way, however. So they fought. Madonna was so angry all the time.

'I was at their home one night when, right in the middle of dinner, she threw a plate of spaghetti across the room. "Stop trying to run my life," she screamed at him. The plate smashed against the wall, spaghetti and meatballs dripping down all over the floor. Everyone was shocked. Martin was there. I remember his eyes were wide, like saucers.

'I thought Uncle Tony would have a stroke. His face got red, his blood pressure shot up and he looked like he was being stricken. Madonna got scared and ran to him.

'Down on her knees in front of him, she started crying and apologizing. "I'm so sorry," she kept saying. "I didn't mean it. I didn't mean it." An apology to her father? Why, that was a major concession on her part.

'And then he started crying, patting her head, and saying, "No, I'm sorry. I'm the one who's sorry."

'There was always big drama between them, and she was the one who always instigated it. It was as if she felt that she and her father had to have these big scenes in order to validate their love for one another.'

Finally . . . New York City!

Whether it's all true or not – and with the always imaginative Madonna one can never really be certain – the story, or legend, of Madonna's arrival in New York City on that morning in July 1978 is a good one. Intent on her easily saleable image as a modern-day Cinderella, she has often recalled leaving Detroit Metropolitan Airport – her first flight – and arriving in the city with nothing but thirty-five dollars in her pocket, a winter coat on her back, a duffel bag full of ballet tights slung over her shoulder . . . and a determination to do something significant with her life, to succeed. 'Ten summers ago,' she announced in 1988 to a cheering crowd at the premiere of her film, *Who's That Girl?*, 'I made my first trip to New York. My first plane ride, my first cab ride. I didn't know where I was going. I didn't know a soul. And I told the taxicab driver to drop me off in the middle of everything, so he dropped me off at Times Square. I was completely awestruck.'

'The tall buildings and the massive scale of New York took my breath away,' she would say in 2013. 'The sizzling-hot sidewalks and the noise of the traffic and the electricity of the people rushing by me on the streets was a shock to my neurotransmitters. I felt like I had plugged into another universe. I felt like a warrior plunging my way through the crowds to survive. Blood pumping through my veins, I was poised for survival. I felt alive. But,' she also allowed, 'I was also scared shitless and freaked out by the smell of piss and vomit everywhere, especially in the entryway of my third-floor walk-up. And all the homeless people on the street. This wasn't anything I prepared for in Rochester, Michigan.'

Madonna would manage to survive on her wits. As legend has it, she roamed the strange, frenetic city on that first day until finally ending up at a street fair on Lexington Avenue, where she noticed a man following her. Instead of fleeing, as most young women in a new city might, Madonna greeted him. 'Why are you wearing that coat?' he asked her, giving her a cue to launch into her 'story'.

'Hi! I just arrived in town and I don't have a place to stay,' she said. It was a story that had had some rehearsal time; she had already tried it on other disinterested strangers. Still, Madonna's intensity must have made it seem compelling to this particular passer-by because she ended up moving into his apartment and, according to her, sleeping on his couch. Home at last.

Madonna soon learned, however, that a young woman could not always be so trusting of people, particularly of men she might meet on the streets of New York. Years later, she revealed that she'd been raped in Manhattan at this time. 'I have been raped and it is not an experience I would ever glamorize,' she said. The subject came up while she was discussing scenes from her controversial book of nude studies entitled *Sex*. One photograph depicts Madonna dressed in a schoolgirl's uniform while being attacked by two boys. She insisted that the photograph was pure fantasy. 'I know there are a lot of women who have that fantasy of being overpowered by two men or a group of men,' she explained.

At that time, Madonna didn't give any date or details of her own experience, saying only that, 'It happened a long time ago so over the years I've come to terms with it. In a way it was a real eye-opening experience. I'd only lived in New York for a year and I was very young, very trusting of people.'

'I remember her saying something about it,' her longtime friend Erica Bell recalls. 'But it wasn't something I felt she wanted to discuss openly. I think it was a date rape, meaning I think she knew the guy. It was someone who betrayed her confidence, her faith. It must have been devastating.'

Says another friend – a woman who still knows Madonna today and in whom she often confides, 'The date rape was something she never wanted to talk about. But when it did come up, you could tell that she was deeply affected by whatever happened. She cried when she spoke of it, as if she had been traumatized. She said, "I wanted to call my father and tell him about it, maybe go home for a while. But he would have killed me." I felt that she needed her father at that time, but was afraid to turn to him. I know she could have used a mother, as well. These were lonely years.'

Her former manager Freddy DeMann adds, 'I remember a time, long after her first taste of fame, when a girl in one of her audiences was being pushed around by some guys in front, trying to get closer to her [Madonna]. Suddenly, the girl went down, into the crowd. It was as if she was going to get stomped. Then, a couple of guys went down after her, and none of them came up. Madonna was watching the whole thing. She stopped the show, stopped singing, and called security out and told them to help that young girl. "I know what it's like to feel powerless," she said from the stage. "And it doesn't feel good." I'll never forget that night. I felt that she had great empathy for that girl, and a certain amount of fear, too.'

As it turns out, it wasn't a 'date rape' at all. Many years later, in 2013, in an essay Madonna wrote for *Harper's Bazaar*, she said, 'I was held up at gunpoint. Raped on the roof of a building I was dragged up to with a knife in my back.' She told a little bit of a different story to Howard Stern three years later in 2016, explaining that she needed money for a pay phone. A stranger told her she could use the phone in his house across the street. That's where he raped her, she said. Or, she may have meant he raped her on the way to his house. Specific details aside – and one might imagine that she need not be consistent with the public about such an attack – she also said she didn't report the rape because, 'you've already been violated. It's just not worth it. It's too much humiliation.' She blamed her 'stupid friendliness. I trusted everybody. The rest is not worth talking about.' (It's interesting that she has reframed her life at this time in a way that includes the notion of her trusting 'everybody'. In fact, the evidence shows that she was not that trusting a person and, if anything, had a healthy scepticism and even cynicism about most people.)

'I don't want to make it an issue,' Madonna also said about the rape. 'I've had what a lot of people would consider to be horrific experiences in my life. But I don't want people to feel sorry for me because I don't.' She concluded that the experience had made her 'much more street smart and savvy. It was devastating at the time but it made me a survivor.'

Pearl

After a few weeks, Madonna moved out of her benefactor's home – for reasons as unknown now as her destination was then – and she was on her own, again. She moved into a dilapidated fourth-floor walk-up at 232 East Fourth Street between Avenues A and B, truly just barely fit for human occupation.

She survived by taking any odd job available, such as working in a series of fast food chains, or simply by taking the easy way out: asking her friends for handouts. Later she would tell the press that she ate from garbage cans, though some close to her at the time have disputed this memory.* Food did not concern her, anyway. She preferred to eat at irregular hours, a banana for breakfast, an apple for lunch, perhaps some yogurt as a snack. Any hardships she experienced at this time were, in her view, just annoying distractions. After all, as she would explain it, she was in New York to dance – not eat. She didn't waste time on unrealistic planning ahead, or optimistic dreaming, either. She had a goal, and she went after it.

'I was defiant,' she would recall. 'Hell-bent on surviving. On making it. But it was hard and it was lonely and I had to dare myself every day to keep going. Sometimes I would play the victim and cry in my shoe box of a bedroom with a window that faced a wall, watching pigeons shit on my windowsill. And I wondered if it was all worth it . . .'

In November 1978, Madonna auditioned for the highly respected Pearl Lang Dance Company. On that day, she brought with her the emerging 'Madonna persona'. Immediately, Pearl Lang – a former dance soloist with Martha Graham – recognized her as being unique. 'She came in wearing this T-shirt that was torn all the way down the back,' Lang recalls. 'And she had this enormous safety pin – it must have been a foot long – holding it together. I thought if she doesn't poke her partner's eye out, she'll do something with her dancing one day.'

Madonna was one of several people chosen from those who had auditioned for Lang's company. Her freestyle dance was impressive simply by virtue of its wild abandon. After the audition, Lang recalls walking over to Madonna until her face was just inches away from the young girl's. It was as if the instructor wanted to get a closer look. Then, studying her carefully, she stroked Madonna's face: 'My dear, you have something special,' she whispered to her, taking her hand.

---

* As for the garbage-can myth, her old friend Steve Bray says, 'I read several times that this was something she did – I never saw her going through the garbage but I guess it's possible.'

'I know,' Madonna replied.

As Madonna pulled away, Pearl relinquished her hold unwillingly, as if she wanted another moment to study the young woman before her.

'She was an exceptional dancer,' Pearl Lang recalled. 'Many dancers can kick and exhibit acrobatic body control, but that is just run-of-the-mill, taken for granted. Madonna had the power, the intensity to go beyond mere physical performance into something far more exciting. That intensity is the first thing I look for in a dancer, and Madonna had it.'

Clearly, Madonna had won over choreographer Lang just as she had already won over others – such as Christopher Flynn – who would assist her in shaping her talent, guiding her towards her goal and becoming her mentors. As her skills broadened, she became an assistant to Lang. 'I actually started to rely on her quite a bit,' says Lang. 'She was organized, professional and very serious, at first. But then, after a few weeks, I noticed that she was feeling stifled by the regiment of my teachings. She was annoyed when I pushed her for more.'

'I accused her of not wanting to work hard, and she lashed out at me,' Pearl Lang recalled. 'I knew she would have trouble being a dancer in any troupe because she was such an individual. It wasn't really a matter of working hard; she worked hard. But not in a way that gave me hope that she could blend with others.

'When she continued questioning me, well, that was it, really. At one point, after I gave her some advice, she curtsied and, in the most spiteful tone I had ever heard from a student, said, "Why thank you ever so, *Lady Hateful*." I believe it was then that I asked her – told her – to leave.'

Soon after her experience with Pearl Lang, Madonna was accepted for a brief workshop at the world-renowned Alvin Ailey Dance Company. But even with this happy coup, it was becoming clear that all of the determination, desire and pizzazz she could muster would not immediately guarantee her a place in the highly competitive world of New York dance. Though completely dedicated to her craft – mind, body and soul into dancing – Madonna found herself once again counting out change behind the counter of a local doughnut shop in order to make ends meet. She also worked in the prestigious Russian Tea Room restaurant in Manhattan as a hat-check girl.

Gregory Camillucci, former manager of the restaurant, recalls, 'She was a frail girl, very thin. I often thought that the meals she had at the restaurant were probably the only meals she was eating. But she was upbeat, never rude, always on time. At the beginning of her short time there, I caught her staring at the customers. "I watch rich people eating and drinking," she explained, "so that when I can afford to, I can do it right." However, it wasn't long before she became bored by rich people's eating habits. You then had a sense that she wasn't going to last long. "This is not what I came to New York to do," I once heard her grumble.'

After Madonna had been in New York for several months, her father, Tony, paid a visit to the dilapidated walk-up on Fourth and Avenue B.

'I didn't want him to come,' Madonna remembered years later. 'The apartment was crawling with cockroaches. There were winos in the hallway. The entire place smelled like stale beer.'

'What is going to happen if this fool's dream of yours doesn't work out?' Tony asked her, he recollected many years later. Father and daughter were sitting in an Italian restaurant on Eighty-First Street. Madonna was eating spaghetti and clams, and with such fervour it was as if she hadn't enjoyed a good meal in many months. 'Please come back home,' Tony said. 'I miss you so much, Nonnie.'

'I love you, Dad,' Madonna said. 'But I just can't come home.'

'Look at how you're living,' he told her, trying to reason with her. 'In a roach motel. Like a bum, you're livin'.'

'No,' she said, correcting him. 'Like a dancer, Daddy. *Like a dancer, I'm livin'*. Now, just leave me alone.'

The hard fact, of course, was that dancing jobs were really

scarce, even in – and maybe especially in – Manhattan. Competition was stiff from agile, talented dancers whose own intense hunger and drive most certainly matched Madonna's.

'I'd go to the Lincoln Center, sit by a fountain and just cry,' she once recalled. 'I'd write in my little journal and pray to have even one friend. I had been used to being the big fish in the little pond and all of a sudden I was nobody. But never once did it ever occur to me to go back. Never.'

'Oh, please, she never sat by a fountain and cried,' says her brother Martin. 'She never wrote in some diary about her loneliness and pain. And she had loads of friends. She took those years, hard as they were – I mean, she had a lot of despair and I don't want to say she didn't, you know? But she later made it all just a part of the glamorous legend that is my sister. That's what she does best, she creates legend.

'I remember that after my father visited her, he said, "Either she will be the greatest dancer who ever lived, or she will be the biggest fool." She turned out to be neither, of course.'

Busting Out

By the beginning of 1979, Madonna – who would turn twenty-one that year – realized that it could take five more years for her to be accepted into a major touring dance company. She knew that the solution to her dilemma was obvious: she would have to diversify, expand her horizons, maybe even change her vision if she was going to survive in New York.

Ever true to her character, Madonna would not waste much time strategizing her next move. She needed a vehicle that would showcase her extraordinary charisma. She needed a forum, a venue. In order to earn extra money, Madonna began posing in the nude for art classes. She had heard that it was an easy way to make money and, as she later recalled, 'I was so broke and desperate, I would have done almost anything. And I thought it might give me a new thing, that maybe I might become a model. Who knows?'

Anthony Panzera, one of the artists for whom she posed, recalls that he was unhappy with Madonna's appearance when she showed up at his studio on West Twenty-Ninth Street after having answered an advertisement.

'I was hoping for someone a little less boy like,' he said, as he got ready to send her on her way.

Perhaps sensing imminent rejection, Madonna unbuttoned her blouse and exposed her breasts. 'Do boys have these?' she asked. Then, without hesitation, she slipped out of her jeans. Once naked, she blithely asked, 'Now, just tell me where to pose.'

'What's your name?' he asked.

'Madonna.'

'No last name?'

'Do I look like I need a last name?' she said as she stood before him, unclothed. She grabbed her breasts and pushed them up, then out towards him.

'Her answer made no sense,' the artist now recalls, 'but yet, somehow it made all the sense in the world.

'It was basically seven dollars an hour in those days, and that was a lot for her. She needed the money, that's for sure.

'What I most remember about her is that she never seemed to have a place to live that she could call her own. So if you wanted to find her, you'd have to call a series of numbers she had left. "In the morning," she said, "you can reach me here," and she'd hand you one number scribbled on a piece of paper. "Then, at night, try this number," she'd say, and then stuff another piece of paper in your hand. "But sometimes, I'm staying here, and other times, there," and she'd hand you two more numbers. It was absolutely impossible to find her. She was a vagabond. But when you did find her, she was a good model, very cooperative, always willing to do energetic, enthusiastic poses.'

In order to continue making extra money, Madonna then decided to pose nude for photographers who had advertised in the magazines and newspapers she read in order to find work. Martin Schreiber, who was teaching a course for the New School in Greenwich Village at the time, paid her thirty dollars for ninety minutes on 12 February 1979 to pose naked. Upon receiving her payment, she signed the release form with the name Madonna Louise. 'What I recall of that session was that she really wasn't into it,' says Schreiber. 'Whereas some models come in and are raring to go, strip down and pose, I sensed that she was really just doing it for the money, that she really didn't want to give it much thought, and wasn't going to dwell on it. I thought to myself, after she leaves here she will never again think about these pictures.'

Meanwhile, Madonna's combination of style, daring and charisma continued to draw influential people to her, like a magnet. While at a party and spinning around in the middle of the dance floor, she was spotted by graffiti artist Norris Burroughs. 'It was the winter of 1979,' Burroughs recalls. 'I remember she had leopard tights on, and there were people all around her, but she was getting centre stage even though it was a house filled with dancers. It was like some kind of ritual, as if she was dancing in a ring of fire. So there we all were, me and my friends and everyone else, singing and dancing to the Village People's "YMCA", and Madonna was in the middle of it all, holding centre stage. She was this amazing and exciting looking creature with wild hair and loads of sexual energy just waiting to bust out, to make an impression. I was completely taken aback. So I had to approach her.

'If I could rearrange the alphabet,' Burroughs told her, 'I would put U and I together.'

'Screw you,' Madonna said, sizing him up. 'You remind me of a guy on Fifth Avenue who tried to sell me his comb earlier today.' Then, having delivered her sharp dig, she began to walk away. After a beat, though, she turned around and asked, 'Does that offer come with dinner?'

'It does.'

'Fine. But it'll have to be Italian,' she said, 'or the deal is off.'

Still, despite the tentative date, the two didn't get together until a few weeks later after Burroughs finally telephoned Madonna. 'You get your gorgeous Brando body over here,' Madonna told him.

'How could I resist?' Burroughs now asks. 'It was then that our affair began.'

Though the tall and slim 'dirty blond' Burroughs was not Madonna's usual physical type – she preferred darker, more muscular types – she seemed happy in the relationship. He remembers her as a sexual being. 'It was just an animal kind of sexuality,' Burroughs said. 'She wasn't coquettish, or shy, that's for sure. It was all raw, but fun. Lots of disco dancing to Gloria Gaynor's "I Will Survive", her favourite song at the time. She was incredibly self-involved. Everything was all about her, her wants, her needs, her thoughts, her desires . . . but, still, you got swept away by it. She was just so fascinating to watch and to be around.

'During one lunch date, Madonna ordered an ice-cream sundae for dessert, with bananas and chocolate syrup. Then, she poured maple syrup over the whole thing. I was nauseated just watching her lick the bowl clean. Her whole chemistry was always on overdrive; she could never get fat with that metabolism of hers.

'She acted like she didn't care at all about her looks, but I think now that it was all an act, that her whole thing was to make people think she didn't care so that she could be as outrageous as possible,' Burroughs observes. 'I remember giving her a pair of jeans with a thirty-four waist, way too big for her. She couldn't wait to wear them. She had sweaters and shirts with holes in them, and she'd stick her thumbs through the holes, posturing and posing. She always looked cool. She always *was* cool.'

Burroughs says that during the time he dated Madonna there was always a sense of the temporary about the romance. 'I knew it wasn't going to last,' he said. 'She never said it to me directly, but I sensed that she believed that she was going places . . . and that I wasn't. I knew that she wasn't going to be around very long.'

After one love-making session, Burroughs turned to Madonna and said, 'In a year, we'll look back on this time and appreciate it even more, won't we?'

'Hmmm,' Madonna said in her most non-committal tone. 'Interesting,' she concluded with an evasive smile.

Burroughs lay quietly with his arms around her, knowing – he would later admit – that there would not be many more of these tender moments in the future.

So far, the momentum of Madonna's career had been pushed along by a series of random circumstances that had exposed her to certain influential people who could help her achieve her goals. She eagerly took advantage of the opportunities that had been presented to her, then, without much apparent gratitude or sentimentality, she moved onwards and upwards, never once looking back. It was the way it had been up until now, and a pattern of her life that would continue for years to come. Though her relationship with Norris Burroughs lasted only three months, it did take Madonna to the next chapter of her life story. At a party at his home on 1 May 1979, Burroughs introduced her to friends, Dan and Ed Gilroy, who had formed a band called the Breakfast Club.

Madonna hit it off immediately with Dan Gilroy. As the evening wound down, she asked him, 'Well, aren't you going to kiss me?' While he pondered the question, she grabbed him by the tie, pulled him close and kissed him fully on the lips. Then, she smacked him lightly, twice and on the same cheek. After winking at him, she walked away.

Years later, Norris Burroughs would say, 'Before I knew it, she was done with me and was with Dan. Immediately, Dan began teaching her how to play instruments. She learned to play the guitar, she learned to play organ. They put her behind the drums for a while . . . but eventually she wanted to sing.'

Soon, Madonna was living with Dan and his brother in a run-down and boarded-up synagogue in Corona, Queens, which they would use as a rehearsal hall as well as a living space – for she was now a member of the Breakfast Club. Says Whitley Setrakian, 'I remember walking for a long time through what seemed like a bombed-out area of Queens until I finally came to a crumbling synagogue. And I thought to myself, "Oh my God, this is where she is living now?" But when I met with her, I saw further evolution in her personality, more self-confidence about her decisions. I heard the band she and Dan were trying to form, and it was good. It was loud, but it was good. She had the microphone firmly in hand and gyrated a lot. I sat in one of the chairs of the synagogue and watched her and saw that she was really in her element. I knew that she was finished with dancing, even though she never said it. I could tell that she loved this side of performing, as a singer, an entertainer. She and Dan had become romantically involved, and they seemed happy.'

Dan was fascinated by Madonna. 'You make love like a man,' he told her after one love-making session, according to a later recollection. 'You're so aggressive. Uninhibited.'

'Does that scare you?' she asked him.

'No,' he told her. 'It turns me on.'

'I always wanted to be a guy,' she confided. 'I want to just take my shirt off in the middle of the street, like a construction worker. I like the freedom.'

'I like *you*,' he told her.

'I know,' she said as she kissed him.

It was at this time that Madonna wrote her first song. 'It was called "Tell the Truth",' she would recall to Austin Scaggs for *Rolling Stone* in 2009. 'It was maybe four chords, but there were verses and a bridge and a chorus, and it was a religious experience. I had decided that if I was going to be a singer, I had to earn it. I had to learn how to play an instrument. We were living in an abandoned synagogue in Queens, and in return for music lessons I modelled for Dan, who was a painter. I was his muse, and he taught me how to play power chords. While they were off at their day jobs, I'd play drums. I learned by listening to Elvis Costello records. Then one day, I wrote a song, and the words just came out of me. I was like, "Who's writing this?" When their drummer quit, I got to be the drummer, and one night at CBGB I begged them to let me sing a song and play guitar. That microphone position was looking more and more inviting.'

'Dan and Eddie both sang and sometimes she sang, and then they would sing behind her,' Norris Burroughs recalls. 'Eventually she wanted to sing more. She had pretty much given up the idea of dance, I think, once she got into the band, once she got involved with Dan. She soaked it all up, learning everything Dan could teach her about rock music, about playing it and singing it. She just wanted more . . .'

'More' was something Madonna always wanted 'more' of, and it now seemed that she was beginning to wonder if singing was not the way to get it. Producer Steve Bray, who would later become romantically involved with Madonna, recalls, 'With the Breakfast Club, she found her muse medium, she found the best vessel for her drive as a rock performer. She played guitar and fronted the band. I always thought she could have had a great career as a rhythm guitarist. She'd dance on the table tops and break things all around her. She'd pour champagne all over herself. She was just a fabulous, wild child.

'Dan taught her a lot. He loved her. I thought they got along great. But I knew it would just be temporary.'

Each week, Madonna continued to scour the pages of industry publications such as *Backstage*, *Show Business* and *Variety* for job opportunities. She told a writer for *Playboy* (in September 1985): 'I saw an ad in the newspaper for this French singing star, Patrick Hernandez. He had this record called "Born to Be Alive". His record company [Columbia Records] was trying to put together an act to go on a world tour with him, and they wanted girls to sing back-up vocals and dance. It was going to be a big gala performance. I thought it would be great; I'd be dancing and singing and traveling around the world – I'd never been out of America. So I went to the auditions, and after they were over they said they didn't want me for Patrick Hernandez, they wanted to bring me to Paris and make *me* a disco star.'

'But you're a *dancer*,' he argued.

'Since when?' she asked.

Dan didn't want her to leave Queens. Not only was he afraid of what trouble she might get into in Europe, he didn't trust the people financing her trip . . . and was also nervous that she wouldn't come back to him. He cared about her deeply.

'Well, now, I'm a dancer who sings,' Madonna said, flatly, 'if that's what I gotta do to make it in this damn business.'

Madonna explained that she hated to leave Dan so suddenly, and said that he had been one of the most generous men she'd ever known. 'I learned a lot from you, Dan,' she said. 'However, it's time for me to go. And if that makes me a bitch, then I'm a bitch,' she concluded. Hurt, Dan readily agreed with her self-assessment: yes, she was a bitch, he said. He loved her, he would later admit, and thought they had 'somethin' goin' on'. He couldn't fathom that she would leave him, 'especially after all we shared'.

In May 1979, twenty-year-old Madonna was off to Paris with producers Jean Vanloo and Jean-Claude Pallerin, who had promised to treat her well, feed her 'fabulous foods', and 'get me a vocal coach'. To one reporter, she recalled, 'They did all of that. It was a blast. I had a great apartment. I never had it so good. I was chauffeured all over. They were going to develop my talent, find a vehicle for me.'

To another reporter, she changed the story a bit: 'They took me to Paris and introduced me to awful French boys, took me to expensive restaurants and dragged me round to show their friends what they had found in the gutters of New York. I would throw tantrums and they'd give me money to keep me happy. I felt miserable.'

In an interview with me, she continued the story: 'After a couple of weeks, I got bored. They were focusing on Patrick Hernandez and wanted me to wait. Me? Wait? Meanwhile, they were trying to mould me into Donna Summer. I kept telling them, "I am *not* Donna Summer."

'So I went into my rebel mode and gave away my money and started hanging around with bums,' she said. 'Oh, how I missed New York. I hated France and everything French. If they weren't going to do anything for me, then I wanted to go back to New York where I felt I could do something for myself. I didn't have a contract, so I told them I wanted to go home to see a sick friend. They said that was fine, called a limousine and had me dropped off at the airport. "When will you be back?" they asked. I told them two weeks. Then, I just never went back. I heard [in 1985] that they're still waiting for me. Poor dears.' (For years, Madonna collectors have been frustrated that no recordings of any kind have surfaced from this period in her career. There's actually no evidence to suggest that anything was ever recorded.)

It says a lot about Madonna's personality that, even though she had nothing going on for her there, she would eagerly return to New York where she at least felt in control of her destiny. In France, it would have been left up to a couple of record producers she didn't even know very well to make her dreams a reality. However, in New York it was up to her. She was willing to take the gamble, to wager that her own creativity and ingenuity would take her to the next phase in her career.

Before she left Paris for her 'brief stay' in New York, Madonna ran into Patrick Hernandez at the rehearsal hall in which he was putting together his disco act. 'Success is yours today, honey,' she told him, 'but it will be all mine tomorrow.'

'What the hell ever happened to Patrick Hernandez, anyway?' Madonna asked a reporter in 1999.

Certain Sacrifices

In August 1979, three weeks after she returned home from Europe, Madonna and her friend, Whitley Setrakian, talked about her exciting journey overseas. 'She told me this amazing story about how she had gone to Paris on the Concorde, how she hated it there, and turned around and came back,' recalled Whitley. 'She was telling it to me in such a matter-of-fact manner, I was startled by it. To me, this was such a big deal. But she was nonchalant about it. I was so amazed that she was suddenly entering another world and was quite separated from the world that we once shared. The trip may have been an unhappy one for her, but it did inject her with a new confidence. She seemed even more self-assured. Soon after, she saw another ad in *Backstage* for a film role that interested her.'

After having already auditioned for the movie *Footloose* and the television series 'Fame' (and not being cast in either), the twenty-one-year-old Madonna contacted amateur film maker Stephen Jon Lewicki. She was responding to his advertisement in *Backstage* which said, in part, 'Wanted: Woman for low-budget movie. Dominatrix type'.

Recalls Lewicki, 'I was looking for a fiery, sexy, dominant girl in her early twenties who could act. I got about 300 responses, most of which were 8 × 10 glossy photos with résumés boasting of summer stock experience, and all of which were incredibly boring. And as I was getting completely discouraged by the process, I came across this one, last envelope.'

When Lewicki opened the envelope, he found Madonna's résumé, two 3 × 5 colour photographs, one black and white 8 × 10, as well as a handwritten three-page letter, which he still treasures. Madonna, who began by mentioning that she had just 'returned from Europe', further wrote, 'I was born and raised in Detroit, Michigan, where I began my career in petulance and precociousness.

When I was fifteen, I began taking ballet classes regularly, listening to Baroque music, and slowly but surely developed a great dislike of my classmates, teachers and high school in general. There was one exception, and that was my drama class.'

He recalls, 'Suddenly, here was a girl who I thought had some interesting possibilities.' He also noticed that they shared the same birthday, to the year. But it was more than just that particular coincidence – or, perhaps, omen – that interested him in her. Lewicki explained, 'There was something about her photos that made me want to meet her. In them, she was sexy, but not lewd. I had received all kinds of pictures and letters from girls who looked like they were whores who wanted to be actresses, and actresses who wanted to be whores. However, Madonna's photos were different. In one, she was putting on lipstick with her pinkie finger while sitting, I believe, in a bus station. There was something seductive about it, yet it had a certain fragility, an innocence that really fascinated me. I knew I had to meet her. So we set up a meeting in Washington Square Park.'

Madonna showed up in a tight red miniskirt, and with her cocky, self-assured attitude in tow. 'You would have thought she had a great résumé with a lot of experience, judging from the way she acted,' Lewicki recalls with a smile. 'She was tough.'

'Look, I'll do your movie,' Madonna told Lewicki, nonchalantly. 'But there'll be no screwing.'

'Who said anything about screwing?' he asked.

She took out her compact and began applying a pink blush colour to her lips with her pinkie finger, as she had been doing in the photograph that had so fascinated the producer. 'Just know,' she said, seeming bored, 'that you and I will not be screwing. Got it?'

'I didn't realize it then, but now I think she was auditioning for me right then and there,' says Stephen Jon Lewicki. 'I knew she was perfect for the role. She was *doing* the role.'

Lewicki hired Madonna for his low-budget, one-hour movie, the plot of which involved the strange goings-on between a downtown dominatrix named Bruna (Madonna) and her suburban, outcast boyfriend, Dashiel (Jeremy Pattnosh). When Bruna is raped in the bathroom of a diner, she and her boyfriend employ her 'sex slaves' to perform a satanic human sacrifice on her rapist. 'At no time did I ever ask her to take her clothes off,' recalls Lewicki. 'It just evolved as she was doing the scene. She was very comfortable with her body, with nudity. Far from being pornographic, it's very passionate and interesting,' he says. 'We started the movie in October 1979, and we had a lot of fun, she was always up, had a lot of energy, able to improvise. I had a crush on her, actually. We cut each other down a lot, insulted each other. That's sort of how you relate to Madonna. She insults you, you insult her back . . . then, she knows you love her.

'She talked a lot about her life, the death of her mother and how it had affected her,' he recalls. 'I knew that she felt she had to take care of herself because she would never allow anyone else to do so for fear that she would depend on that person, and that he would leave. So, I understood her brash nature. Also, she had a father who she believed disapproved of her. There was a certain scene in the film which was racy, and I remember her saying, "Oh my God, my father will freak out when he sees this." I asked her, "You'll let your father see this?" And she said, "Oh, absolutely." I had the feeling that she wanted to be rebellious just for the sake of rebellion, that she wanted him to see that she had a mind of her own. She was driven by this need, she had to prove she was independent of everyone, her deceased mother, her disapproving father.'

The first low-budget films made by many actresses are seldom memorable, and Madonna's is no different, with its finale featuring a human sacrifice. The script is muddled, the sound mediocre and the acting by everyone, including Madonna, overwrought and amateurish, though perhaps unintentionally prophetic. Still, *A Certain Sacrifice* is well intentioned. It was actually filmed in parts, the first in October 1979, the second in November 1981. (A twenty-four-second outtake of *A Certain Sacrifice* features Madonna singing the song 'Let the Sunshine In' from the musical *Hair*. A short audio clip of this performance has, for years, been circulating on CD in the collectors' bootleg market. Also, the film itself contains an ensemble chant, 'Raymond Hall Must Die'. 'Sunshine' and 'Raymond Hall' are considered by Madonna historians to be two of her earliest recorded vocal performances.)

By the beginning of 1980, Madonna's instincts were telling her that her future was most definitely not in film, at least not yet, and not in dance, either. At this time, she realigned herself with her ex-boyfriend, Dan Gilroy, who couldn't resist taking her back . . . into his life, and also into the Breakfast Club. However, before long, her growing ambition caused conflicts with both Gilroy brothers. While they viewed her as just a group member, she saw herself as the main attraction and thus wanted to sing more leads – especially after another female (Angie Smits) was added to the group as a bass player. Though she liked Angie, she couldn't help but think of her as competition; she didn't like sharing the stage with a woman. As weeks turned into months, Dan became frustrated by Madonna's constant habit of upstaging him and the other band members. 'You're all naked ambition with no talent,' he told her during one particularly bitter argument in front of the band.

'Oh yeah?' she countered. 'Well, screw you, Dan. Screw you.'

'That's when she quit the band. It was pretty tough being her boyfriend, to say the least,' said Dan Gilroy in what seems like a great understatement, 'mostly because you knew there was no way she was going to be faithful. She always had a lot of other guys lined up, and each one had a purpose in her life. When she was done with me that time, well, she was done with me for good.'

Again, it seemed time for Madonna to move on. Dan Gilroy had given her a place to live, the security of being in a relationship with someone who truly loved her, knowledge of certain musical instruments as well as a sense of what it was like to sing in front of an audience accompanied by a back-up band. She now had the idea to start her own band, develop her own sound, and promote her own persona . . . and without Dan Gilroy.

Soon after moving out of the Gilroy's synagogue/studio/living quarters, Madonna partnered up with drummer Steve Bray. The two had met earlier at the University of Michigan in '76. Says Madonna of the dashing African-American Bray, 'the first guy I ever allowed to buy me a drink [a gin and tonic]. He was irresistibly handsome.' After becoming romantically involved with her, Bray allowed Madonna to travel with him across Michigan as he and his band performed in small clubs. When the romance ended, they remained friends. Bray then moved to New York. (In years to come, Steve Bray would write, co-write and produce many of Madonna's greatest hits, including 'Express Yourself', 'True Blue', 'Into the Groove', 'Papa Don't Preach' and 'Causing a Commotion'.)

Now that Madonna had determined that she would have a career in music in New York, she wanted to be immersed in that business twenty-four hours a day. Feeling herself bursting at the seams with imagination and creativity, she would spend the next year writing songs and performing locally around New York with a small back-up band, which included Steve Bray on drums. Because Bray also needed a place to live, the two agreed to move into a Westside Manhattan conglomerate of offices and rehearsal studios on Eighth Avenue called the Music Building, and simply sleep in the offices of any of the tenants there who would agree to such a thing – and some actually did. 'The Music Building,' Bray explains, 'was near Macy's in Herald Square. There were a lot of singers and bands working in rehearsal halls and studios there, just trying to figure out their music. It was a good place, very artistic. You could just taste the creativity there. We loved it, just being in the atmosphere was intoxicating. Our band was hot, and getting hotter all the time.'

There were some problems, though, not the least of which was the solution to a disagreement involving the group's name. Bray recalls, 'We had a lot of names. First, we came up with "Emmy", meaning "M" for Madonna. Emmy was also my nickname for Madonna. Then, we were "the Millionaires". Then, "Modern Dance".' (It should be noted that, in a separate interview, Steven Bray recalled that the name 'Emmy' was actually short for 'Emanon' – 'no name' spelt backwards.)

Despite the uncertainty of the group's name, Madonna's self-confidence and outlook for its future remained unshakable. However, for someone who was not a known performer, she had already developed the ego of a major – and, in some ways, difficult – star. Bray continues, 'She wanted to call the band "Madonna". Well, I thought that was just too much.'

'But it makes a lot of sense,' Madonna told Steve Bray during lunch at Howard Johnson's in Times Square. 'See, there's this group that was called Patti LaBelle and the Bluebells. And when they reinvented themselves, they called themselves LaBelle, after the leader of the group.'

Bray digested this piece of information. 'So, what are you saying?' he asked her. 'That you're the leader of this band?'

'Why, no, not at all,' Madonna answered, her tone sweet. 'You're the brains, Steve. You're the musical genius. Me? Why, I'm just the star.'

'Forget it, Emmy,' he told her. 'It sounds too Catholic, anyway. "Madonna"? No, I don't think so.'

In subsequent years, Madonna had to admit that she was perplexed by the group's reluctance to be named for her. Why didn't her colleagues recognize the clear reality – at least her reality – that she was their meal ticket? While she may have felt she had their best interests at heart as well as her own, it didn't appear that way to the rest of the band, who thought she was just being selfish. In the end, the group did settle on the name 'Emmy', with Dan and Ed Gilroy as front men, Madonna on lead vocals, former Breakfast Club member Gary Burke on bass, Brian Syms on lead guitar, and Steve Bray on drums. Madonna recalls, 'We played, we sang, we went all over New York just trying to make money, which never happened. It got to be less fun than I had hoped.'

Frustrated, Madonna decided that the restrictions of being a member of a band had begun to erode her true identity as a performer, anyway. 'It was too confining,' she would later recall. 'I had ideas. In a band, you can't have ideas. Without being able to express myself, I felt, well, why bother?'

Camille

In early 1981, a woman entered Madonna's life – again the result of happenstance, coincidence and sheer luck – who would go on to become her mentor and, in many ways, her saviour. Her name was Camille Barbone, at the time a musical talent agent with the Gotham Agency and Studios (writing rather than recording studios) at the Music Building. Barbone – who describes herself as 'a tough-talking New Yorker' – is an extremely attractive woman with short, wavy brunette hair, soulful brown eyes and a flawless complexion. Her memory for detail is vivid, especially when it comes to Madonna.

'Madonna and I kept running into each other in the elevators and the hallways of the Music Building,' Camille recalls. 'She flirted with me constantly. For instance, she once opened a door for me when my hands were full, and when I thanked her, she said, "Oh, don't worry. Someday you'll be opening doors for me."

'She was about twenty-two. She was homeless at the time, living in one of the studios in the Music Building. She had just left the group Emmy, saying that she wanted to do other things. She had cut some music, and eventually, I got to hear a demo, which I thought was fair-sounding. I was supposed to see her show at a

Manhattan dump called Kansas City, but I got ill and couldn't go. The next day, she came raging into my office screaming at me.'

'How dare you not show up?' Madonna hollered at Camille, a woman she barely knew. 'This is my *life*. What happened to you? You promised you would be there.'

'I had a terrible migraine headache,' Camille offered by way of explanation. 'I'm sorry. I just couldn't make it.'

Madonna gave Camille a dramatic stare. Then, she asked, 'What? You had a headache? What an excuse! What kind of talent manager are you?'

When Camille promised that she would be in the audience for Madonna's next performance, Madonna told her the date, time and location of that show. Camille began to write the information in her appointment book. Suddenly, Madonna grabbed the book from her and smacked Camille across the chest with it. 'If it's important enough to you, you'll remember,' Madonna said. 'You won't have to write it down because it'll be important enough for you to remember.'

'I should have been outraged,' Camille says with a smile. 'But, instead, I was intrigued. Then, after I saw the show, I knew in an instant what she was about: potential stardom. Her hair was red when I met her but, in a day or so, she had dyed it brown. On stage, she was wearing men's pyjamas, and had this completely original appearance. She had great body–mind coordination. She knew how she looked, and when she was onstage she gave the audience the feeling of being inside her and of knowing what she was feeling. It's a rare quality. She was beautiful, really. What a face.'

Awed by Madonna's raw talent – she was performing a combination of dance and rock and roll music at this time – stunned by her colourful imagination and even a little startled by her brazen *chutzpah*, Camille Barbone's fascination resulted in the quick signing of a management contract between herself and Madonna. In another amazing coincidence, the twenty-nine-year-old Barbone – seven years Madonna's senior – shared birthdays with her new protégée.

It certainly seemed like the stars, karma, the universe, God or simply Lady Luck were always on Madonna's side during these formative years, in perfect alignment with her personal goals and professional ambitions. Over the next twenty months, Barbone and her business partner, Adam Atler, would exhaust most of their company's funds in promoting and developing the burgeoning career of Madonna, whom Camille referred to as 'a nobody who was about to be a somebody'.

During the course of their relationship, Madonna and Camille would become players in a confounding game of wills and emotions. Years later, Camille Barbone would confess that she had probably fallen in love with Madonna. Though Barbone did not admit her feelings to Madonna at the time, surely the instinctive young performer was able to sense their intensity. She would not be able to resist this tantalizing turn of events. After all, by now every step of her career was a seduction – one person after another being seduced by her to do her bidding – and it had been that way for some time.

The truth was that – talent, luck and cunning aside – Madonna was just an extremely ambitious person in a city overcrowded with extremely ambitious people, all of whom were jockeying for the best position to get noticed. Was it wrong for her – she must have reasoned – to realize that she needed people in her corner, pulling for her, pushing her, making the right contacts for her?

In the particular circumstance in which she found herself with Camille Barbone, Madonna would play the role of little-girl-lost to Barbone's sensible and influential mother figure. The older Barbone was more than happy to accept her part in Madonna's real-life drama, first by paying for her to have four wisdom teeth extracted and then letting her recuperate in her Bayside, Queens, house. Soon, she was giving her money for food.

'I thought that the first thing I needed to do was to make her feel secure and safe,' Camille now recalls. 'So I needed to find a place for her to live. She had found a small place that she adored, a one-room apartment across the street from Madison Square Garden on

West Thirtieth Street. The building was called – ironically enough – the Star Hotel. So I moved her in there, paid for it for a few months in advance – sixty-five dollars a month – even though I was frightened to have her live there, it was such a dump. She was there for about two weeks when she got robbed. They only took her photographs, but it was still very upsetting to both of us.

'So I moved her out of there and into a much bigger apartment on the Upper West Side, on Riverside Drive and Ninety-Fifth. My business partner knew a middle-aged guy who lived there, and convinced him to let Madonna move in as a room-mate. We also gave her a hundred bucks a week to live on.'

Because Madonna said that she wanted to act, Camille sent her to an acting coach, a Russian émigré named Mira Rostova, who had taught such notable actors as Montgomery Clift and Roddy McDowell. It didn't go well. After one session, Mira refused ever again to work with Madonna. 'I doubt that this girl will ever be taken seriously as an actress,' she told Camille. 'First of all, she's vulgar. Secondly, you can't tell her anything because she's already decided that she knows all there is to know, about everything. Thirdly, she doesn't listen, and if she doesn't listen now, she never will. If I were you, I'd reconsider representing her.'

It was spring, 1981. 'You are so goddamn selfish,' Camille Barbone was telling Madonna.

As Camille recalled years later, she had been experiencing personal problems with a member of her family and wished to talk to Madonna, as a friend, about what was happening. However, Madonna – often preoccupied and seldom really paying attention when it came to listening to other people's problems – seemed disinterested in Camille's ordeal. It hadn't taken long for Camille to understand that, at this time in her life, Madonna was too self-absorbed to truly care about anything other than her career. 'When you have a problem, I solve it,' Camille said, frustrated. 'But when I have one, you couldn't care less.'

'Look. I pay you to solve my problems,' Madonna shot back, as if Camille was actually making money from her career.

'But what do *you* give, Madonna?' Camille asked, she would recall years later. 'You give nothing,' she observed, answering her own question. 'You're selfish.'

'But I give my all,' Madonna said.

'Bullshit. You give your all to *you*,' Camille said. 'It's all for your career, isn't it? You don't give a fuck about me or my life.'

It was then, as Camille remembered it, that Madonna went on the attack. 'Look at me,' she said, practically screaming, her face instantly red with rage. (She could raise the level of an argument to a full-scale fight in a nanosecond.) 'I'm getting old,' she continued, her eyes blazing. 'And nothing is happening for me. I'm ready to do something with my fucking life, can't you see that? And you promised to help me, Camille. So help me, goddamn it,' she concluded, angrily. 'If you're my friend, *do something for me*. If you love me, *do something for me*.'

Camille reached out and stroked Madonna's face. With an index finger, she wiped away a tear. 'Okay. I'll do what I can,' she told her, trying to calm her down. 'I do love you. Relax. Adam and I have meetings set up next week with record people. I have lots of ideas.'

Taking a dramatic breath, Madonna put the finishing touch on the fight, 'Why, oh why, must everything be such a big deal with you?' she asked, exasperated. 'Now,' she said, shaking off the drama with a shrug, 'tell me, what kind of meetings?'

Years later, Camille would say, 'When the line became blurred between management and friendship, that's when trouble became inevitable. Of course, I knew she was using me. But what could I expect, really, under the circumstances? I tried to set up some boundaries, some rules, but . . . well, forget it . . . Try giving Madonna rules.'

One of Camille's 'rules' was that if any member of the band she had organized to support Madonna musically on stage ever had sex with her, he (or she) would be automatically fired for such indiscretion. Barbone felt strongly that romantic relationships within the band would serve only to complicate matters for everyone involved. Also, no doubt, she just didn't want Madonna being intimate with anyone else. She couldn't help but be jealous, her feelings for her were that strong. However, the cunning Madonna decided to use Camille's regulation to her own advantage. Because she wanted her ex-boyfriend, Steve Bray, to replace the band's drummer Bob Riley, she decided to seduce Riley. 'If you were any more delicious, I'd have to spread you on a cracker right here and now,' she told him with a smack of her red lips. Then, she tumbled into bed with him.

'Now you *have* to fire him, Camille,' Madonna said at a meeting with Riley in Barbone's office the next morning. 'I mean, that's your rule, isn't it? Whoever screws me gets fired, right? And we can bring Steve in now, can't we?'

'My God! I'm not firing Bob just because he screwed you, Madonna,' Camille said, incredulous. 'You set him up! What kind of person are you, anyway?'

'I did not set him up,' Madonna said. 'He came on to me. And I told him what would happen if we made it together. But, no, he wanted to do it, anyway. Now, you have to fire him. Or *you're* the one who will look weak and indecisive.'

Riley looked at Madonna as if he was looking at garbage. 'No one has to fire me,' he decided. 'I quit.'

Madonna blew a big, pink bubble with her gum. 'Fine with me,' she said. 'Suit yourself.'

'I wondered what kind of person would do something like that,' Camille recalls years later, still seeming astonished at just the memory of it all. 'I had created a monster who, I knew, would eventually turn on me. I just couldn't believe she would be so crafty, so mean. Sex, to her, was really just a means to an end, it meant nothing more. I actually became a little afraid of her when she did that to Bob.'

'I love you,' Barbone remembers Madonna telling her one day. The two had just had a meeting with a record industry executive that went well. It seemed that a record deal for Madonna was imminent.

'In what way?' Camille asked, suspiciously.

'Well, in every way, of course,' Madonna said. They embraced. 'How can I thank you for what you've done for me?' Madonna asked. 'I think you're the most wonderful woman in the world.'

There was a beat. Just as it seemed they might kiss, Madonna abruptly pulled away. 'Oh my God,' she exclaimed with girlish enthusiasm. 'I just had the most brilliant, fucking *idea*. Let's you and I call that record guy back and tell him . . .' She had deftly moved the conversation back to business. The mood now altered, the two then began brainstorming about Madonna's 'great idea'.

'She seduced me, psychologically,' Camille Barbone says today. 'I put her first. And, really, that would be my downfall because it was all about her, not about us and certainly not about me.'

'I doubt that she and Camille had more than a business relationship, but true to Madonna's pattern, I am certain that she dangled just the right amount of sexy bait necessary to hook Camille,' noted her brother, Christopher Ciccone. 'As Madonna herself has once confessed, she is a born flirt and automatically turns her flirtatious charms on anyone who crosses her path, particularly if he or she can help her career – which, of course, anyone with whom she flirts naturally ends up doing.'

'There were lots of mixed messages, strange moments . . . and also great ideas as to how to promote her career,' Camille confirmed. 'There was such imagination and fire between us, such great creativity. We never got together without a notepad because there were so many ideas flying back and forth. I had to keep notes just to keep track of all of the stuff we discussed twenty-four hours a day. She was brilliant, really. Constantly, we had this mad banter about what to do, how to do it, and where we would end up. I so believed she would one day be a star. I knew that she was destined to be a great entertainer, a pop star, and I invested everything in her . . . my mind, my heart, my soul, everything.'

'You know what? I promise that we'll always be together,' Madonna told Camille one day over breakfast. Just the night before, she and a female dancer named Janice had had sex with a recording engineer from Queens, much to Camille's utter chagrin. Madonna looked exhausted, a rag tied into her ratty, short, brunette hair, her eyes sleepy.

'Sure, you say that now,' Camille told her, annoyed. 'But wait until you get famous. You won't even remember my name.'

Madonna sighed, shaking her head. 'It's a lousy business, I know,' she said. Her voice was weary with experience, as if she was a seasoned performer.

'Drama Queen'

In August 1981, Madonna recorded a demo tape of four songs, under Camille Barbone's tutelage, at Media Sound (also known as 'Master Sound'), a converted church on West Fifty-Fourth Street in Manhattan in which Barbone had leased studio time. In performances that sound reminiscent of rock singer Pat Benatar's style, Madonna performed 'Love on the Run', 'High Society (Society's Boy)', 'Take Me (I Want You)' and 'Get Up'. The recordings – known by Madonna fans as 'the Gotham Tapes' – were produced by guitarist Jon Gordon who would go on to produce Suzanne Vega. According to Madonna's contract with Camille (signed on 22 July 1981), Madonna was to receive $250 for each unreleased master, and twice that amount for every one that was released, as well as a 3 per cent royalty on the sale of every record.

At one point, Camille Barbone offered Madonna and Sire Records the opportunity to purchase the original studio master recordings, but no deal was struck. Ownership of these songs would eventually become the subject of bitter lawsuits between Madonna and Barbone, in litigation that would drag on for many years. (In March 1993, Camille Barbone played bits of three of the songs during Robin Leach's television special about Madonna, *Madonna Exposed*, on which I also appeared as a guest.)

It took some doing, but Camille Barbone eventually convinced her friend Bill Lomuscio, a band manager and promoter, to give Madonna a break and book her into some local clubs for necessary exposure. Whenever Madonna got up onto a stage, the result was predictable: all of her pent-up yearning to do and be something wonderful – her energy, drive and talent, not to mention her need to be the centre of attention – burst forth in a rush of sheer spectacle. 'It wasn't so much about the music as it was the personality behind it,' Camille Barbone recalls. 'I found that the best way to have a meeting with a record label or a booker was to bring Madonna with me. Once you met her, you either loved her or hated her, but you knew she was fascinating. She was really her own best advertisement.'

'The band I managed was the house band at this particular club, and they were pretty popular,' Lomuscio recalls. 'But out came Madonna, and the band and three break dancers that Camille had picked up in Times Square, and that was the end of anyone's interest in my band. With her act, Madonna proceeded to blow my band off the stage. She really was phenomenal. A great talent. You could see it immediately. And after three songs, she was being called back for encores. My band was having a hard time even getting on the stage.' When the deeply impressed Lomuscio asked Barbone if she'd like a partner in the handling of Madonna, the two began working together as a team.

While her new managers were excited about Madonna's successes on stage in front of live audiences, attempts to impress record executives with her demo tape did not go as well. Most people failed to be sold on Madonna's voice alone. She was a visual performer. The whole package was important, certainly not just the voice which was, at best, no more than average. 'There was a lot of talk that the tape was no good,' Lomuscio says, 'and she'd never go anywhere – one person said she sounded like Minnie Mouse on helium on a song she had recorded called "Get Up" – but that was just not true. All you had to do was come down and see her perform live . . . and that was it.'

Over the next year, as Madonna continued to grow in her New York stage act, she began attracting a cult following, not only of her music but of her funky image (complete with the second-hand street clothes she now enjoyed wearing on stage). Before she even had a record played on the radio, groupies who dressed just like her had begun following her from gig to gig. She didn't have much of a career . . . but she actually had fans!

'These people love me,' she told Camille of her 'fan club'. Then she giggled, 'You know what?' she asked. 'I think I will always be nice to my fans. I think they deserve that.'

Camille smiled. 'Well, that's a nice thought,' she said. 'We'll see how you feel in about ten years.'

Later, in another conversation, according to Camille, Madonna said, 'Some awful person told me today that I was crass, vile, rude and disgusting. What do you think about that?'

'Well, I think that's absolutely true,' Camille said, frankly.

'I know,' Madonna agreed, enthusiastically. 'It is, isn't it? Don't you just love the fact that people know that about me! I mean, that is so *cool*, isn't it?'

'It is,' Camille said. 'It certainly is.'

'Here, I want you to have this,' Madonna said, reaching into her pocket. She pulled out a turquoise rosary. 'It was my grandmother's,' she explained, tears welling in her eyes. She extended her palm to Camille, the rosary in it. The two women sat down over a cup of coffee, and Madonna then told Camille touching stories about her mother.

After about a half an hour, Camille was overwhelmed with emotion. 'I can't take that,' she said, closing Madonna's hand around the rosary. 'I could never take that from you. It's too precious.'

'But I want you to have it,' Madonna insisted. 'I don't want you to think I'm just an ungrateful little bitch. I don't have anything else to give you.'

Camille embraced her. 'Keep your grandmother's rosary,' she told Madonna as she ran her fingers lovingly through her hair. 'You've just given me the best present in the world, and you don't even know it.' Playing out a sexless seduction, Madonna continued to take Camille into her world, teasing her – maybe unintentionally, maybe not – with sentimental stories about her and her family.

It was inevitable that word of Madonna's popularity would continue to spread; soon, those same record company talent scouts who had ridiculed her voice were lining up outside her dressing-room door and waving business cards in her face as she left the club. Geffen and Atlantic Records both passed on Madonna's demo, but it seemed as if Camille had interested an executive at Columbia Records in the songs. However, storm clouds were brewing – though Camille didn't know it yet.

'Unbeknownst to me, Madonna had also started working with another set of people in the record business,' Camille Barbone recalled. 'She had others doing for her what I was doing for her. My company was just four years old, and we weren't moving as fast as she wanted to move. Plus, we were arguing about the direction of her music. She wanted to do more of a black sound, I think. We were doing Pat Benatar-sounding material on her, but we could have changed, and we would have suited her . . . if she had just given me some time to make back some money so that I could reinvest it in new material.'

Suddenly, Camille Barbone's world began to crumble. Just when it seemed certain that Madonna would sign the Columbia deal, she decided that she wanted to end it with Camille. Madonna said that she wanted to terminate the Gotham Agency as her representatives, explaining that she wasn't happy with the music she had recorded while under contract to Gotham. She no longer respected

Camille as a manager, she told her, 'because it's taking too long for you to do anything for me'.

'But I won't let you out of your contract,' Camille Barbone told her while engaged in a tense meeting with Madonna in the recording studio. 'I invested everything in you,' she said angrily, according to later recollections. 'I was doing just fine in my life until you came along. Now, look at me. I'm flat broke. I spent it all on you, Madonna!'

'Oh, fuck you, Camille,' Madonna said, her tone icy and detached. 'That was *your* choice, now wasn't it?'

'Why, you *bitch*,' Camille said, practically sputtering. As she now remembers it, she was so angry she could barely speak. Instead, she plunged her fist into a wall, fracturing her hand. Though Camille was clearly in terrible pain, Madonna walked away from her, shaking her head. 'What a drama queen,' she muttered as she walked out of the studio.

Big Break

'You know what you have?' Madonna asked Camille Barbone on one of the last occasions they saw each other. Madonna tapped her mentor on the chest. 'You have heart,' she said, 'and you really don't need me.'

It was a confusing moment, one that Camille recalls vividly to this day. Her eyes red from crying, she put her palm on Madonna's chest and said, 'If *you* had heart, I don't know that you'd do this to me.'

Tears began to splash onto Madonna's cheeks. 'I have to go,' she explained. 'I love you, Camille. You're such a bitch, like me. We worked well together. But now it's over. So . . . goodbye.'

Madonna then walked, never to look back.

'Sometimes I feel guilty because I feel like I travel through people,' Madonna has said. 'That's true of a lot of ambitious people. You take what you can and then move on. If someone can't go with me – whether it's a physical or emotional move – I feel sad about that. But that's part of the tragedy of love.'

'She seduces people,' Erica Bell observes. 'She'll tell you what you want to hear, she flatters you, kisses your ass, makes you feel a part of her life. She's a smart girl. She knows how to get her way,' says Bell. There is no acrimony in Bell's seemingly harsh assessment of Madonna. 'Then, after she has you set up the right way, she sucks it all out of you.'

'Oh, she's a sponge, all right,' Camille Barbone concurs. 'She soaks up what she can and drains you in every way and then goes on to her next victim.

'I risked my entire career on Madonna and she nearly destroyed me. I begged, borrowed and stole to do what I could do for her. But rules of loyalty and decency that apply to the rest of us didn't apply to her,' she continues. 'She wasn't intentionally malicious, but just incapable of seeing life from anyone else's point of view. She wanted what she wanted, and if you didn't give it she turned her back on you.

'I lost everything in the process because I had focused only on her and spent every time on her. I ended up losing my studio.'

After Madonna had moved on and left her allies behind, Camille Barbone says she felt no malice towards the woman whose eventual success she had helped create – even though she would not be around to share in any of the rewards. 'I don't hate her,' Barbone sighed years later. 'On the contrary, I miss her. And I understand her. It all has to do with her mother, it all goes back to her death. It has to do with Madonna feeling so beat up by what she felt when her mother died, she never wants to connect to her emotions. So, she leaves people before they can leave her, the way her mother did. I knew that when I was going through it with her. And I know it even better now, having had years to think about it. Her mother,' Camille concluded, firmly, 'that's what it's always been about.'

Madonna would say that she left Camille Barbone because 'she had gotten too attached to me'. Also, she said, it was worth it for her not to take advantage of the Columbia recording contract offering because, as she put it, 'the songs they wanted me to sing were crap, and I wasn't going to build a career on them. No way.'

In another interview she further explained, 'I've always been into rhythmic music, party music, but Gotham wasn't used to that stuff, and although I'd agreed to do rock and roll, my heart was no longer in it. Soul was my main influence and I wanted my sound to be the kind of music I'd always liked. I wanted to approach it from a very simple point of view because I wasn't an incredible musician. I wanted it to be direct. I still loved to dance and all I wanted to do was to make a record that I would want to dance to and would want to listen to on the radio.'

So, while she waited for what Camille may have called 'her next victim' to come along, Madonna and Steve Bray moved back into the Music Building where they slept on cots, sat on crates and sustained themselves on popcorn. (Their relationship at this point was platonic, not romantic.) Meanwhile, Madonna again survived by taking odd jobs around the New York City area. This time, though, her 'odd jobs' were music industry related. For instance, she sang back-up vocals for a number of recording artists, including heavy metal superstar Ozzy Osbourne. She could also be seen dancing wildly as an extra in a music video for the group Konk.

Says actress Debi Mazar (*Goodfellas*), one of Madonna's best friends who has known her since those early days (and who appears in the video for Madonna's 2000 hit, 'Music'), 'Neither one of us had any money. We were just young girls trying to do interesting things in New York City. People weren't dying yet of AIDS, and here was a small community of artists and musicians – [Jean-Michel] Basquiat, Keith Haring – and everybody was together: black, white, Spanish, Chinese. It was the beginning of rap, and white people and black people were all together making music . . . [Afrika] Bambaataa was sampling Kraftwerk. Madonna and I used to run around and go to the Roxy, go dancing and to art shows.' She adds, 'At the time, we both had a taste for, you know, Latin boys.'

Without a manager to advance her ambitions, Madonna had no choice but to promote herself. After she and the multi-talented Steve Bray recorded four new songs – 'Everybody', 'Stay', 'Burning Up' ('she has a Joan Jett kind of thing going on with this one,' Bray recalls) and 'Ain't No Big Deal' ('We didn't have access to the vocoder that we wanted for the vocal effect, so Emmy just pinched her nose and pretended,' says Bray) – she began taking the tape to the hottest nightclubs in the city, her goal being to get disc jockeys to play them so that one of her songs would catch on and become a club hit. In the early 1980s, DJs wielded tremendous power on the dance circuit. The songs they chose to play nightly could make an artist. Once a song caught on in the New York dance club scene, its success could easily encourage a major label into signing the artist.

In 1981, one of the hottest clubs in Manhattan was called Danceteria, where Madonna was a regular patron. Madonna had her sights set on the trendsetting DJ at Danceteria, the darkly handsome Mark Kamins. With her eye-catching dancing and sexual aura, she had already become a star in the local club scene. Kamins, who had watched her dance from the DJ booth, was intrigued. He wanted to know her. Apparently, she felt the same way.

One evening, while Mark was playing music from his booth, Madonna strolled over to him, handed him her demo and asked him to play it that evening.

'This is a great song,' she told him. 'It's called "Everybody". People will love it.'

Kamins shook his head negatively. 'What if it's not good?' he said, warily.

She got closer to him. 'Would I just give it to you like this if it wasn't good stuff?' she said. 'Oooh, baby, you are so *fine*,' she added as she stroked his face.

He would remember feeling an urgency as she approached him. Then, as she kissed the disc jockey fully on the lips, he was hers.

While he now says he was 'impressed by her moxie', Kamins still decided that he wanted first to listen to the demo before playing it for an audience. He took the tape home that night, and liked what he heard.

'The following night I threw "Everybody" on and got an amazing response,' Kamins remembers. 'I mean, it was a great song. It was the kind of thing that caught your attention. That voice was so unique, and so perfect for that kind of fun record.'

While Mark Kamins was a DJ by profession, he had hopes of one day becoming a record producer. Although he had already dabbled in music production, he saw in Madonna a chance to further his career, and perhaps further hers as well. He proposed a partnership: he would do the leg work to secure a record contract for her and, then, when the deal was set, she would allow him to produce her first album. Madonna, who craved a record deal and was actually surprised that she hadn't got one by this time, immediately agreed to the partnership. On the edge of tears, her voice faltered: 'Maybe this might work,' she said. 'Or, at least I hope so.' As confident as she was about her future, clearly there was vulnerability beneath all of the bravado.

It seemed only natural – predictable as her life was, in this regard anyway – that the partnership between Madonna and Mark would become intimate: the two become lovers. 'She was always sexually aggressive, and it wasn't just her image,' Kamins said. 'She used her sexuality as a performer, but it's also how she got over off stage. We started hot, and it just got hotter. She was hard to resist.'

With his new lover in tow, Mark Kamins brought her demo tape to Michael Rosenblatt, a young, aggressive executive at Warner Bros. Records who was eager to sign new talent. As Kamins and Madonna sat and studied his reaction, Rosenblatt listened to the four songs on the tape. He then rewound it, and listened again. 'The tape was good,' he now remembers but, echoing others who had shared his view, he adds, 'but not outstanding. However, here was this girl sitting in my office, radiating a certain *something*. Whatever it was, she had more of it than I'd ever seen. I knew that there was this star sitting there.'

Much to Madonna's exhilaration, Michael Rosenblatt decided to offer her a record deal: $5,000 as an advance, plus royalties and publishing fees of $1,000 for each song she would write. It had all happened so fast. All of the years gone by, years of struggling and hoping and plotting and scheming and wondering and worrying . . . and, suddenly, Madonna Ciccone had a record deal. However, there was one signature needed on the contract before it could be finalized and that was Seymour Stein's, President of Warner's Sire Records, the division to which Madonna would be signed.*

Unfortunately, Stein was in the hospital, recovering from heart surgery.

Undaunted – and certainly not willing to sit and wait for someone to recover from a major operation, not after all she had been through up to this point – Madonna pressed Rosenblatt to get the demo to Stein in the hospital. Reluctantly he agreed, probably knowing that there would be no point in challenging his new young artist on this matter. When Rosenblatt told Madonna that he would make sure Stein heard the demo immediately, Madonna took his face in both her hands and kissed it – which must have seemed a little inappropriate but was certainly endearing, just the same.

'I was in the hospital when [Rosenblatt] called me and said, "Seymour, I think you should listen to a one-song demo ['Everybody'] by this girl. Her name is Madonna. I listened to it, and I

---

* Sire Records was formed in 1966 by Seymour Stein and Richard Gottherer. After a decade, the label became a part of Warner Music Group – and Stein helped shape popular music in the 1980s and 1990s, not only with Madonna but also with the Ramones, Talking Heads, the Pretenders, Depeche Mode, k.d. lang, Erasure, the Cult, the Replacements, Ice-T and Barenaked Ladies.

flipped out,"' recalls Seymour Stein, who was in his early forties at the time. 'I said, I want her to meet with me at the hospital. I had my barber come in and cut my hair and shave me – I didn't want her to think she was signing a contract with someone who would be dead in six months. Let me tell you, she was so anxious to do a deal that she couldn't have cared if I was lying in a coffin. She was twenty-three, and I believe she was very poor, but she put herself together great. It was only one song, "Everybody", but there was just a drive, a determination – she was going places.'

Seymour, like so many others, was taken aback by Madonna's aggressive nature, as well as her apparent star quality. 'The thing to do now,' Madonna said, seeming oblivious to the fact that she was talking to a man who was sitting in his underwear, a drip feed in his arm, 'is to sign me to a record deal. Take me,' she said, arms extended, 'I'm yours. Now give me the money!' She was being facetious, but the sentiment was genuine.

'Oh, I don't think so,' Stein remembers saying.

Madonna took a step back, looking confused. After a beat, perhaps to reconsider her strategy, she appeared to marshal her thoughts before jumping back into the game – but now with less aggression. 'Okay, look,' she said. 'Just tell me what I have to do to get a fucking record deal in this fucking town? That's all I want to know.'

'Well, you had one before you even walked in the door,' Stein said, good-naturedly.

'Then why screw with me?' Madonna asked.

'Why not?' asked Stein. It would seem that Madonna had finally met her match in Seymour Stein. Probably relieved, she stepped towards his bed, extended her hand and said, 'Nice doing business with you, Mr Stein.' To her delight, he took her hand and touched it with his lips. Their eyes met. There was something conspiratorial in the moment, a suggestion of intimacy, as if they both knew something about Madonna's future that nobody else knew.

'If the shortest way home was through a cemetery, she would

take it, even at midnight on Friday the thirteenth,' observes Seymour Stein. 'She had an almost ruthless edge to her. I mean that in all the best ways. You could just tell this woman would go far.'

'This is it,' Madonna later told her friend Erica Bell. The two had become the closest of friends at this time, after Erica hired her to work as a bartender at her New York night club, the Lucky Strike, on Ninth Street off Third Avenue. (The job lasted two days.) 'With this record deal, I think I'm finally on my way,' Madonna said. 'I can't believe that it's happened just as I thought it would. This is how I charted my life, for this to happen in it.'

'Tell me. What do you want most in life now?' Erica asked. It was a lazy Sunday morning and she and Madonna were lying on the couch together after a boozy night on the town. Years later, Erica would remember the conversation as if it had just occurred.

'I want to be famous,' Madonna said, quickly. 'I want attention.'

'But you get so much attention now,' Erica said, snuggling closer.

'It's not enough. I want all of the attention in the world,' Madonna said, dreamily. 'I want everybody in the world to not only know me, but to love me, love me, *love me*.'

'Well, I love you,' Erica said.

'That's nice,' Madonna said while gently stroking Erica's hair. 'But it's not enough.'

Roller Coaster Ride

After Madonna was assigned to Warner Bros. Records' dance division at Sire, her first contract was not for an album but rather for two 12-inch dance singles. It was decided that the first release would be 'Ain't No Big Deal', backed with 'Everybody'. However, when the time came to determine who would produce the songs, Madonna wanted her good friend Steve Bray to do the honours.

Mark Kamins, though, felt strongly that, since he had brought Madonna to the label, he should be allowed to produce the single. Both men had been her lovers, so Madonna had a dilemma. 'The deal we had was that, if I got her a deal, I got to produce the album,' Kamins now says, 'and, damn it, I wanted her to honour the deal. I knew that if I let her do it, she would walk all over me.'

An argument ensued, but by the end of it Mark Kamins had the distinction of doing something most people at that time never managed to do when in hot debate with Madonna: he won. Feeling that he had become the latest casualty in Madonna's quest for fame, Steve Bray was so angry with her that he would not speak to her for almost two years. 'It's a shame when stuff like that happens between friends,' he now says. 'But even though I knew her and understood the way she operated, I just never thought I would be next on the list. But I was.'

'Well, it's not like I had a choice in the matter,' Madonna has said in her defence. 'Everyone wanted to work with me by that time. I remember when nobody wanted to work with me, and when it changed everybody got pissed off at one thing or another.'

At this same time, Steve Bray – who got the sole writing credit for 'Ain't No Big Deal' – sold his publishing rights to July Fourth Music. Then, a disco act called Barracuda recorded and released their own version of the song on Epic Records before Warner Bros. Records had selected which Madonna version to release. Consequently, the song was then dropped from consideration. (Years later, a Reggie Lucas production of 'Ain't No Big Deal' would be released on the B side of the 'True Blue' single. The other original versions, however, remain unreleased.)

Instead, Warner issued 'Everybody' (with different mixes on both sides of the record – and a surprising hint of a British accent on the verse vocal) in October 1982, produced by Mark Kamins. (Strangely, 'Everybody' has never appeared on any of Madonna's own albums; a rare remix by Rusty Egan was used on the vinyl 12-inch for the UK release only.) When it charted on *Billboard*'s dance chart on 6

November, 'Everybody' marked the beginning of Madonna's 'new life', or, as she put it most succinctly to Mark Kamins, 'The old me was broke. The old me had no place to live. The old me was someone my father wasn't proud of. The old me was Madonna Louise Ciccone. The new me is *Madonna*.'

Basquiat

Madonna was sitting in a back booth at the Carnegie Deli in Times Square eating a sloppy hot dog and watching as the young artist Jean-Michel Basquiat and his close friend Armon Stewart argued about producing art for money versus the same for pure expression. 'It doesn't make any difference if people buy my art or not,' Jean-Michel said. 'The fact that I have created it is enough. *That's* my reward, the *creation* of it.'

'Nice thought, buddy, but I'm afraid your reward won't pay the rent,' said Armon.

'I ain't worried. Something will come along,' Jean-Michel said, winking at Madonna. 'Something always comes along to save me. Right, Madonna?'

'Yeah, well,' Madonna began with a shrug, 'like my father always says: hope's what keeps you smiling as the ship goes down.'

'What's that mean?' Jean-Michel asked with real curiosity.

'That means you have to be practical,' she said. 'If you're broke, you're broke. Who cares? We're all busted. But don't think something or someone will save you. You have to save *yourself* when your ship's goin' down!'

Jean-Michel looked at her and smiled. 'You know what? Your father's full of shit,' he observed, laughing.

'Yeah, I know,' she concluded. 'But he's right about this one thing, anyway.'

It was November 1982, and Jean-Michel and Madonna were together now, or at least they had been for a week. Prior to this they'd known each other for just a couple of days, having been introduced to one another by Ed Steinberg, who produced and directed Madonna's first video for 'Everybody'. The attraction between them exploded one night when he was high and she was horny. They woke up the next morning in each other's arms and decided then and there that they needed to be together.

Jean-Michel Basquiat's ability as an artist was unparalleled. Born in Brooklyn to a Haitian father and Puerto Rican mother, he would go on to produce iconic work, which was mostly so-called 'graffiti art'. It was abstract, expressionistic and reflective of his conflicted views of living and loving in gritty New York City with all its inner-city joy, sadness and pain. At first, Madonna loved being with him simply because she hoped whatever it was that inspired and motivated him – whatever magic made him who he was – would somehow rub off on her. He was also sexy. Good-looking, tall, dark and lanky, he sported a shocking blonde Mohawk when they first met. He'd dye it back to black, though, in about a week's time saying that 'nothing should be stagnating, everything needs to be evolving.'

'Madonna knows what's up,' Jean-Michel said, now back at the Carnegie Deli. 'You're on your way,' he told her, looking at her with admiration. 'You're a *hit*, girl. You're a star.' She laughed and nuzzled up next to him. 'Okay, fine. *I'll* pay your rent, then,' she told him with a smile – all of this according to Armon's memory of the conversation.

'You mean, you'll save my sinking ship?' Jean-Michel asked.

'Yeah, okay,' she told him. 'This month, anyway.'

'Cool,' Jean-Michel said. He then went in for a full kiss on the mouth.

'Jesus. What a fucking beast,' Madonna said with mock indignation as she pushed him away.

'Jean-Michel thought Madonna was pretty amazing, the next big up-and-coming star,' recalled Armon Stewart who, at the time, had known Basquiat for about three years, having met him through the artist Keith Haring. 'He loved the fact that she truly didn't care what people thought of her, that she was her own woman and that she seemed on her way to great success without kissing ass. As much as he inspired her, she also inspired him. She was two years older and, somehow, seemed much older than that. The problem, though, was all the drugs,' he continued.

'Basquiat. Cocaine. Heroin – the most lethal of combinations. There was only so much a person could take of him, he was that self-destructive. For a woman like Madonna, so focused and directed and determined, his reckless nature was never going to sit well. When he told me they were together, I had my doubts as to how it would all turn out, especially when he told me she wouldn't do coke with him. Coke was the only thing that kept him going, that kept him engaged with the world, the fuel behind the creation of his incredible street art. Without that, I don't think he knew who he was as an artist, or even as a man. Madonna, though, never had illusions that Jean-Michel was well-adjusted. We didn't think like that back then, anyway; all of us had our own problems. She just loved being in his world, hanging out with his friends, people like Keith Haring and Andy Warhol. Like a sponge, she wanted to soak up everything around him.'

After just a couple of weeks, Madonna moved into Jean-Michel's huge loft on the Lower East Side, a place he had been renting for some time from Andy Warhol but, lately, couldn't seem to afford. She kept her own place, though, too smart to abandon it for something that she didn't know for certain would work.

Once she was living with him, Madonna didn't understand Jean-Michel's financial concerns, at least not initially. He was making very good money by selling his paintings through art galleries. When she took a peek into the closet of his loft, it was filled with Armani suits. It made no sense to her that he was always broke.

However, one night at the loft, Andy Warhol told her that Jean-Michel once took a suite at the Waldorf for a weekend using the proceeds from one of his sales, and then never even slept in it. He slept out in the streets, high on drugs. Madonna began to see the problem. Clearly, Jean-Michel was just one of those incredibly irresponsible but totally brilliant artists who made very bad decisions. Also, she learned that he was always giving money away to friends who didn't have it, which actually endeared him to her. Keith Haring would say that Jean-Michel's spending was his 'way of sticking your nose up at people who were looking down on you. Being black and a kid having dreadlocks, he couldn't even get a taxi. But he could spend $10,000 in his pocket.' This lack of responsibility bothered Madonna because she connected it with laziness – a lack of interest in work, in life, in just getting through a New York day, no small feat for struggling artists.

Still, Madonna had to admit that she was surprised she cared so much about Jean-Michel, given that she really wasn't emotionally attached to most people. What was it about him that made her want to nurture him? She didn't know for sure, but she thought at the time it had to do with his brilliant, artistic mind. 'I remember getting up in the middle of the night and he wouldn't be in bed lying next to me,' she would recall to Howard Stern in 2016, 'and he'd be standing, painting, at four in the morning, this close to the canvas, in a trance. I was blown away by that, that he worked when he felt moved.'

For his part, Basquiat was just grateful to have Madonna in his life, and not only because she was able to pay the rent, but because he felt 'blessed', as he put it at the time, that 'our crazy worlds somehow intersected'. Therefore, for the next couple of months, while she was meeting with record company executives and trying to figure out her career, he was at home painting. 'It was actually a very creative time for us,' she would recall. 'Like, there was this kind of magic in the air.'

'I remember having conversations with Keith [Haring] and with

Basquiat about the importance of your art being accessible to people,' Madonna recalled to the magician David Blaine for a feature in *Interview* in January 2015. 'That was their big thing – it should be available to everyone. It was so important for Keith to be able to draw on subways and walls. And Basquiat used to say to me, 'You're so lucky that you make music, because music comes out of radios everywhere.' He thought that what I did was more pop, more connected to pop culture than what he did. Little did he know that his art would become pop culture.'

The couple spent New Year's Eve 1982 in Los Angeles at the beach house of Larry Gagosian, an art dealer friend of Basquiat's. Madonna was frustrated, though. Jean-Michel slept all day while she was out making important contacts in the record business. In other words, he was dozing while she was working. He would then rise at night, have dinner with her and some friends, get stoned and then go back to sleep. Because he was never awake during daylight, Madonna later complained that he never even saw the ocean! One morning, she woke up and decided to pick a fight with him, just to get him engaged and incite him into getting on with his day. However, he was too hung over to even care about her, or anything else. 'But we're in *California*,' she told him, 'I mean, look at this place. How can you not care about this place?' He rolled over and went back to sleep.

That day, Madonna had a full itinerary of meetings with people she knew or suspected were well connected in radio, busily promoting herself and her new record, 'Everybody'. When she finally got back to Gagosian's, she walked into a party. There was Jean-Michel, surrounded by four women who appeared to be hookers, or maybe strippers, Madonna couldn't be sure. 'They weren't choir girls, I only knew that much,' she later said. There were drugs everywhere, little piles of coke on the coffee tables with straws . . . syringes strewn about. 'Out! Out! Out!' Madonna shouted at everyone. 'Just get the fuck out!' Jean-Michel protested that the guests were friends of his. 'What? You don't *have* any male friends?' she screamed at him.

'What is this? Are you *fucking* these bitches?' No, he said. Actually, they were too high to have sex, he explained. All of this was a little more than Madonna could stand; she packed her things and went to a hotel that night. Two days later, she and Jean-Michel returned to New York, but the emotional divide between them was so great the writing was definitely on the wall for this romance.

As it happened, Jean-Michel had an exhibit scheduled in January 1983 at the Fun Gallery; he was extremely nervous about it. A previous exhibit at the same venue had been a massive success for him, impressing art aficionados in the area who chattered about his work amongst themselves for months after. Now, with pressure on him to top that achievement, he didn't think his new work was good enough. This was why he'd acted the way he had in Los Angeles, or so he explained. He was scared.

Really? He was scared? Madonna had no sympathy for self-doubt. 'We're *all* scared, Jean-Michel,' she told him when they were at a local bar with friends. 'You think you're the only one who's scared? I'm scared every fucking day of my fucking life, but I still get up, I still get out of bed, and I still make things happen, and no one knows if I'm scared or not. In fact, they think I'm not! And that's just the way I like it.'

'Oh, fuck you, Madonna,' he said, angrily. 'You don't know what I'm up against.'

Of course, she knew. She understood the temperament of the conflicted artist and what it took to marshal one's strength and deliver the best work, even when it seems impossible. 'Well, I don't know what to tell you,' she said, according to witnesses. 'Paint, Jean-Michel. Just fucking paint! It'll happen. Whatever needs to happen will happen. But not if you don't apply yourself.'

Now very upset with her, he stormed out of the bar. She shook her head in dismay and said it was as if she had suddenly become the mother, and he the child. She wondered how that had happened. 'I don't even *have* a mother,' she said, frustrated, 'and now I'm his?'

'A couple hours later, she called me and was jumping out of her skin,' said Armon Stewart. 'Jean-Michel never came home, and she was afraid he'd been mugged, or worse. Her imagination was running wild. I was surprised; I thought she was more practical, or maybe more thick-skinned. But she really was off the deep end. I told her I'd be right over.'

By the time Stewart showed up, Madonna was in a rage, throwing glasses and dishes against the walls. Her attitude had changed in just the thirty minutes it had taken Stewart to arrive. 'This son-of-a-bitch has the nerve to keep me up at night when I have important things going on,' she exclaimed. 'I'm a very busy person, Armon,' she told him as she shattered one glass after another against the wall. 'Screw Jean-Michel. How'd I ever get myself into this mess?'

'I finally calmed her down, we cleaned up the mess she'd made – shards of glass everywhere – and she went to bed,' recalled Stewart. 'I left thinking, okay, she would probably leave the premises the next day. However, Jean-Michel called me that afternoon, thanked me for coming over and calming her down and told me he'd managed to convince her to stay. He said he promised her that he would stop with the heroin, but not the coke. He thought that was maybe a good start.'

A couple days later, Madonna came home from a meeting with industry execs and found Jean-Michel unconscious in the living room. Frantic, she dragged him into the bathroom and then into the shower and turned on the cold water. Eventually, he awakened and the two collapsed into tears together. However, that one moment made a big impression on Madonna. It was then, in that shower with Jean-Michel – both of them under the cold water, their clothes soaking wet – that her feelings for him changed. There was no way, she knew, they could be together. While she had admiration for him and his talent, she now realized that she had little to no respect for him.

'I gotta get out of here,' Madonna told Armon Stewart that night when he came to see if Jean-Michel was all right. The artist was in a stupor on a couch. 'Look at him! He doesn't care, Armon. He just doesn't give a fuck about me, about himself, his work . . . anything. I can't be around this.'

'Then, leave,' Armon told her. 'Just pack up and leave. You can't save him, Madonna.'

Madonna gazed at Jean-Michel, so beautiful in his sleep yet so pitiful in his condition, shook her head and said, 'You know what happens to saviours, don't you?'

'What?' Armon asked.

'They get crucified.'

'Something else your dad told you?'

'No,' she said. 'That's all me.'

The next night, Madonna and Jean-Michel had another blazing row. According to what they both told their friends, Madonna laid it on the line: either Jean-Michel get off drugs completely, or she would leave him. It wasn't that simple, at least not in his mind. The drugs are what inspired him, he said. The world around him when he was high was the one he wanted to commit to canvas, not the real world with all of its bigotry, anger, racism, hatred. 'Well, guess what?' Madonna told him. 'That's the world we live in! Not the fantasy in your mind. You need to wake up, Jean-Michel. Wake up to the fucking *real* world!' As they argued, she packed her bags. 'I can't be around this,' she reportedly told him. 'I can't be around you.'

He was defeated. 'Okay,' he told her, crying. 'Just go.'

She went into his studio and grabbed two paintings he had done for her and had presented as Christmas gifts. He stopped her. If she wanted to go, fine, but the paintings stayed behind. That was okay with her. 'Fine,' she told him. 'Maybe these paintings will remind you of me and maybe they'll help you figure out *your fucked up life*.' With that, she left.

Madonna didn't feel right about it, though. 'He's such a beautiful soul,' is how she put it to Armon Stewart. 'I don't know if I can leave him. What if something happens to him? Then, that would be my fault.' Unusually, it seems she was actually experiencing pangs of guilt. However, there was just something about the very-wounded Jean-Michel Basquiat that tugged at her heart and made her want to reconsider. Later, with the passing of many years after she'd had time to put it all into perspective, Madonna had to admit that she was probably in love with him. At that time, though, she wasn't sure if it was love, pity, empathy, great sex . . . or whether it was simply that he represented everything she wasn't in terms of work ethic and temperament, and that it bugged the hell out of her and made her want to change him . . . indeed, *save* him. 'This is killing me,' she confessed to Armon Stewart. 'See, this is why I don't care about people,' she concluded. 'It's not worth it. It drains you. Then, you have nothing left for yourself, for what you have to do.'

Three days after their fight, a conflicted Madonna went back to Jean-Michel's loft to check on him. She knocked on the door, but there was no answer. She pounded. Nothing. She then let herself in. The living room was a mess of fast food containers, empty beer bottles, little straws and used syringes. She went into the studio. There she found Jean-Michel, out cold on the floor in the corner, naked. She looked at him with sorrow and pity, her heart going out to him. Then, she took a look around the studio and noticed two easels in the corner with canvases, each nothing but black. She approached and examined them more closely. Beneath the wild, angry strokes of black paint, she could tell that they were the two works Jean-Michel had given to her for Christmas, now completely ruined. She later recalled standing in the middle of the room, looking again at Jean-Michel sprawled out in the corner and back to the paintings . . . and then she did what she knew she had to do: she got the hell out of there.

* * *

Five years later, on 12 August 1988, Jean-Michel Basquiat would die of a heroin overdose at his art studio in Manhattan. He was only twenty-seven.

In 2007, one of Basquiat's paintings would sell for $14 million.

Freddy

Aware that the label was sitting on potential dynamite, Sire Records sent Madonna on the road to polish her act. At this same time, Madonna also began expanding her knowledge of the music business. Instinctively, she realized that no manager, producer, agent or record company would ever have her best interests in mind, not the way she did. No one worked harder for Madonna than Madonna. So, her first order of business would be to strike up friendships with people at the record company who were in positions to assist her. She soon discovered that one of Sire's key dance music promotion men was Bobby Shaw, whose job it was to promote the company's dance records to important clubs. Madonna understood the importance of Shaw's position because she, of course, had done it herself with 'Everybody' when it was still in its earliest, unreleased form.

On Fridays, Shaw customarily held meetings in his office where he played and discussed current music with the local disc jockeys. Madonna convinced Shaw to allow her to sit in on these meetings, which was practically unheard of in the business. 'Leave it to Madonna to break tradition where this kind of thing was concerned,' says Shaw. 'I couldn't say no to her, now could I? Well, I could have,' he added, answering his own question, 'but eventually she would have convinced me otherwise.' Along with the industry experts in the room, Madonna was able to listen to the latest records, learn who produced the hits, what was selling and in which direction the trends in music were headed.

It was at this time that Madonna met John 'Jellybean' Benitez, a disc jockey at the Funhouse in Manhattan. Benitez and Madonna became fast friends, and then lovers. On his arm, she attended record industry functions and, as he recalls, 'for about a year and a half, I loved her very much. She was everything to me, my woman, my favourite artist, the bitchiest, funniest smart-ass I had ever known.

'Yes, she used me to "network" into the business,' he says, objectively. 'But I did the same for her. I think one of the biggest misconceptions is that the people Madonna used along the way didn't also get something out of the deal for themselves. But just by being associated with her, if you played your cards right, you could advance your career. Her position was that if you could get something out of exploiting her – the way she would you – then go for it.'

With more than ample proof that the record company had a money-maker on their hands, Warner was finally ready fully to exploit Madonna's talents; she was given the go-ahead for her first album. While Mark Kamins thought he was going to produce the album, as earlier agreed, he was to be disappointed. 'Madonna decided to go with Reggie Lucas at Warner, which was a bummer,' he recalls. 'I was so pissed off. After all, we had a deal. But that's the way it goes. She went a different way, and that was the end of that.'

With her first album now the task at hand, Madonna could no longer represent herself. There was too much work to do, and she was so busy dealing with her recordings and concert act show there was little time to focus on the business end of 'show business'. It was time for her to find a manager. Experienced at handling her own career, she decided that she would only pass the baton onto someone she considered to be the best in the business. After some research, she set her sights on forty-one-year-old Freddy DeMann of Weisner–DeMann Entertainment, an aggressive and well-respected entertainment manager who, at the time, had the distinction of representing perhaps the biggest music star in the world: Michael Jackson. Seymour Stein arranged an audition for DeMann. Afterwards, DeMann had to admit that he wasn't knocked out by Madonna's act. He asked one of his assistants, 'Who is this girl? And who in hell does she think she is?' Ultimately, it was on Stein's recommendation that DeMann finally agreed to manage Madonna. Again, her timing was impeccable: just before she signed the contract with DeMann, the manager had had a falling out with Michael Jackson and was no longer working for him.

When he heard that DeMann and Jackson had parted ways, Seymour Stein thought Madonna would be disappointed that she would not be sharing a manager with the world's top hit maker. 'I was afraid she would be upset about it, but she wasn't,' he recalls. 'Quite the contrary. She said, "Good. Now he's free to devote all of his time to me." Of course, he had other artists at the time, but . . . that's Madonna.'

Madonna: *The Debut Album*

Madonna's debut album, released in July, could have belonged to any number of dance acts that came and went through pop music's revolving door of 1983. Certainly, the eight-song collection didn't offer even a glimpse of the massive superstardom to which it would be the introduction, but it certainly did give a strong indication as to what the pioneers in the Madonna movement, such as Camille Barbone and Steve Bray, saw in her.

Producer Reggie Lucas had made a name for himself in the R&B music business with songwriting partner James Mtume, producing a series of hit records for such acts as Roberta Flack and Donny Hathaway ('The Closer I Get to You'), Phyllis Hyman ('You Know How to Love Me') and, most notably, Stephanie Mills ('Whatcha'

Gonna Do with My Lovin'', 'Put Your Body in It' and 'Never Knew Love Like This Before'). When Madonna and Reggie Lucas began working on songs for her first album, the process became frustrating. 'She had her way of wanting to do things,' says Lucas. 'And I understood that. So we had to have a meeting of the minds, from time to time.'

Madonna had written a song called 'Lucky Star' (plus two others), which, along with Reggie's composition of 'Borderline', seemed the perfect foundation for the album. However, after recording the three songs, Madonna was unhappy with Lucas's production. 'It's just too much,' she complained at the time. 'Too many instruments, too much stuff going on.'

'You have to let me do what I do,' Reggie told her, according to what he would later remember saying.

She made a long face. 'But I have *ideas*. I have *concepts*,' Madonna argued. 'I've been doing this for a long time, too.'

'I know that,' he said. 'But, Madonna, when you bring in a producer, you have to let him do his job.'

'Well, just don't get in my way,' Madonna told him, her tone threatening.

The next day she apologized.

After he finished the album, Lucas didn't seem interested in redoing it to Madonna's specifications. Instead, he went on to another project as quickly as possible, leaving Madonna to figure out what to do next with her record. She decided to bring in her boyfriend, the talented Jellybean Benitez to remix many of the cuts, including the fluffy, danceable (but forgettable) 'Lucky Star'. Also on the album was a song Jellybean added at the last moment, 'Holiday'.

'She was unhappy with the whole damn thing, so I went in and sweetened up a lot of the music for her, adding some guitars to "Lucky Star", some voices, some magic,' says Jellybean. 'The thing about Madonna is that she has good instincts. You have to listen to her vision. I'm not sure Reggie did. We put together a great album, and I didn't even get co-producing credit for it. But I didn't care. I just wanted to do the best job I could do for her. When we would play back "Holiday" or "Lucky Star", you could see that she was overwhelmed by how great it all sounded.'

At first glance, Madonna's album looked like a rebound project for Reggie Lucas, the kind of job a record producer of some note accepts for the money, and just to stay busy. It especially seemed that way when word got out that he didn't want to finish the album Madonna's way. Upon closer inspection, though, it was clear that the album was armed with hit records. Even if the songs had never become popular, no one could have denied that they were terrific, well-crafted pop songs that deserved to find an audience. However, one would never have known as much judging by the chart performance of the album's first single, 'Everybody'. The rhythmic call-to-party did reach number 1 on *Billboard*'s dance chart – a chart driven more by a song's popularity in dance clubs than by commercial sales – but languished at number 103 on the trade magazine's pop chart, the one, as they say in the industry, 'that really counts'.

The double-sided 12-inch single that followed – the yearning 'Burning Up' backed by the droning but urgent 'Physical Attraction' – didn't make *Billboard*'s pop chart at all, but earned another number 1 position on the dance chart, seemingly defining this young new singer as just another disposable post-disco dance act.

Then, along came 'Holiday'.

Written by young journeymen Chris Hudson and Lisa Stevens (from the group Pure Energy) and produced by Benitez, the festive, infectious anthem caught fire almost immediately, first soaring in dance clubs across the country – where audiences were already hip to Madonna – and then working its way onto R&B and pop charts. Ultimately, the song made it to number 16 on that coveted *Billboard* pop singles chart – a triumph for a new act.

Just when the marketplace had gone on watch for this new 'dance act', Sire mixed things up and released 'Borderline'. Written by Reggie Lucas, the song – as close to an uptempo ballad as you'll ever find – was a sentimental track with a particularly strong melodic lyric about a love that's never quite fulfilled.

Maybe it was Madonna's fluid, loving way with lyrics that had more to say than 'shake your booty', or the fact that listeners had become familiar with her tangy voice; regardless, on 'Borderline', her vocals sounded refined, capable, expressive. The combination – a not-so-great but affecting voice at the centre of Lucas's full, twinkling instrumentation – made the track as close to an old Motown production as a hit could get in the dance-music driven Eighties.

Arguably, 'Borderline', along with 'Holiday', were two of the most important records in Madonna's formative years, and not simply because they reached number 16 and number 10 on the pop charts respectively. Rather, the singles were pivotal because, musically, they supplied Madonna with two distinctively different platforms within the dance music structure. And crucially, they delivered the one-two punch that allowed 'Lucky Star', the fourth single from the album *Madonna*, so ingenious in its simplicity and danceability to glide into the number 4 position.

Later, Madonna, who co-wrote five of the album's eight songs, would refer to this first effort as an 'aerobics album', but the songs were in perfect alignment with the times. In spite of a slow start, the album eventually climbed the charts and, after a year in release, finally found its way into the Top 10. It went on to sell four million copies in the USA, and eight million worldwide.

Shortly after the album broke the Top 10, Madonna and Erica Bell toasted her new success with a bottle of champagne. Years later, Erica remembered the conversation as if it had happened just days earlier.

Seeming contemplative, Madonna said, 'I feel badly about some of the people who aren't with me, the ones I met along the way.'

'You mean, like Camille?' Erica asked.

'Yeah, like her and the others.'

'Well, this is a tough business, Erica observed. 'It's the people hangin' around the moment you become successful who get to celebrate with you . . . not the ones you met along the way.'

Madonna agreed. 'I guess so,' she said, clinking her glass of champagne against Erica's. 'Anyway, sentimentality is a weakness, don't you think?'

Erica didn't respond.

'People hate me,' Madonna observed.

'I know they do,' Erica said.

'Oh well,' Madonna shrugged. 'I did what I had to do. At least I still have you.'

'That you do,' Erica concluded as she hugged her friend.

Perhaps the most perfect timing of Madonna's career was in the seemingly magical way her recording career coincided with the growing popularity of the music video art form. Teenagers at this time seemed to be longing for idols. In the Seventies, the disco era had spawned many hit records but very few memorable artists. Several music performers in the early Eighties, however, would gain popularity for the unique images they showed the television-watching public in videos of their songs: Cyndi Lauper with shocking, orange hair, crazy make-up and thrift-store clothes; Boy George with heavy-lidded mascara eyes and women's wardrobe; Prince with his androgynous sex appeal and 'Purple Rain' ruffles. All three, and so many others, including Michael Jackson – who really helped to pioneer the medium, and even expand it with his long-form 'Thriller' video – benefited from the three-minute star vehicles that allowed them to shine.

No one took better advantage of the medium, though, nor to greater effect than Madonna. Borrowing liberally from the downtown street scene, from night-time clubbing and from icons such as Marilyn Monroe, she added a dash of her own brand of simple sexiness for an early image that was simply unforgettable. Even with her bubble gum-sounding first album, her look fuelled ample controversy as she co-mingled sexuality and religion, belly button-exposing

T-shirts and rosary beads. Many observers felt her use of crucifixes to be sacrilegious, but the religious symbol became a crucial part of the Madonna fashion craze. 'I don't think that wearing the crucifix was an attempt to seek out controversy,' says Mary Lambert, herself a controversial director who would direct several of Madonna's music videos. 'I think that it had meaning for her – religious significance, mystic significance. Madonna is a very religious person in her own way.'

At the time, Susan McMillan of the Pro Family Media Coalition declared of Madonna's image, 'Underwear as outerwear is only there to titillate men. And believe me, some sicko seeing a fourteen-year-old girl walking down the street in nothing but a lacy bra, isn't going to stop and say, "Excuse me, before I grab you, can I talk about what kind of statement you're trying to make?"'

Of course, Madonna loved the outrage she generated in zealots like Susan McMillan. It was what she wanted, what she worked for . . . and what she knew would make her a pop sensation just as much as any music she could ever hope to record. She believed that the more the press dubbed her style 'trashy', the more vociferous the parental objection to her look, it would only encourage rebellious children to emulate her. Young girls, who were soon dubbed 'wannabes' by the press (as in 'wanna be Madonna'), began wearing cross earrings and fingerless gloves. They tied scarves and stockings in their wild hair – again, all introduced to popular culture by Madonna in her videos. Her success most certainly validated the blueprint for attention drawn up by Madonna as a child: do something to shock people and, if it's outrageous enough, it will get them talking. She didn't care what they were saying, as long as they were saying *something* about her.

The image Madonna projected was selfish, vulgar and sexual. More than anything else, the statement she was making with her image and attitude had to do with a hunger for fame and notoriety. It wasn't phony or contrived, that's for certain. It was organic – she just threw her costumes together, she has said, from whatever she had in the closet, from whatever cheap clothing she had picked up at thrift stores – and very timely, as well.

'Do you think my mother would be proud of me?' she asked Jellybean Benitez after her first album was released.

'Oh my God, Madonna, yes,' he remembers answering. 'Look at what you've achieved. Look at all you've done. Any mother would be proud.'

Madonna smiled. 'And my father?'

'Absolutely,' Jellybean said. 'Tony's happy. You know it.'

'Yeah, well,' Madonna concluded, 'not that it matters.'

Two-Timing

While Madonna and Jellybean Benitez enjoyed their new-found success as a result of 'Holiday', the romantic relationship between these two immensely creative and emotionally explosive people soon became combative. 'Egos, man,' Jellybean observes when trying to explain the problems he had with Madonna. 'It happens in show business. She was getting to be huge, and, now, I had my own success going on. Slowly, things changed between us.'

'I never saw fights like the kind they had,' Erica Bell recalls. 'Jellybean is 5 feet 6 inches, a little guy. He wore his hair shoulder length, he was cute. Not a muscle guy, but Madonna didn't go for muscle types anyway. Mostly Latin guys. Still, he was pretty wild, temperamental . . . like her.

'I remember one time he walked out on her, and she just went crazy. She was a heap on the floor, sobbing and moaning, writhing on the floor as if she was having some kind of a breakdown. "What is this about?" I wondered. I know for a fact, because she told me, that she had three abortions, Jellybean's kids, along the way. She wasn't secretive about it. All of her friends knew. She loved Jellybean, but didn't want children at that time. "I can't wreck my whole career by having kids now," she told me. "I'm way too selfish. The only other person I think about is Jellybean."'

While she may have told Erica Bell as much, it seems unlikely that Madonna would have had three abortions in two years. Those who knew her at this time have said that she did use contraception. However, in press interviews over the years, Madonna has noted that the press 'knows every time I have an abortion', implying that she has had more than one such procedure.

Melinda Cooper, who worked as an assistant to Madonna's manager Freddy DeMann, confirms at least one abortion during these early years. 'Madonna loved Jellybean very much,' she recalls, 'but she wanted a career and so did he. So the abortion was necessary.'

Cooper says that Madonna called Freddy to tell him that she was pregnant and had decided not to have the baby. Freddy agreed that the timing was probably wrong for a child in her life, and so he had Melinda make the necessary arrangements. Melinda remembers the pregnant Madonna as, 'scared to death, and I also recall that she definitely did not want her father to know that she was going to have this abortion, or any family member for that matter. I drove her to the doctor's office myself, a long, difficult ride in which she was very quiet, sometimes crying. I know that she had made a conscious decision that the mature thing for her to do at this time in her life was not to bring a baby into her world. "I'm not cut out to be a mother," she told me. "At least not yet." Still, she definitely wanted to be a wife. Jellybean's.'

'We were going to be married along the way,' concurs Jellybean Benitez when speaking of his two-year romance with Madonna. 'But there was no way [this would happen], when you really think about it. I don't know that she could be monogamous, though, at least at this time. I mean, no, to be frank, she couldn't be.'

Says Melinda Cooper, 'Definitely, Jellybean was the man for her. She was crazy about him. I think that the reason she started playing around behind his back was to get his attention. She would do anything to get him to treat her the way she wanted to be treated, even if that meant inciting his jealousy.'

Indeed, while engaged to Benitez, Madonna began dating Steve Newman, the editor of a small-time magazine in New York, *Fresh 14*, after he featured her on the cover.

'I told her that I wasn't going to be into it if she wasn't going to be committed to me,' Newman recalled many years later. 'And she said, "Oh yeah, definitely. I want this relationship more than anything in the world." So I was cool with that, even though I knew she still had a lot of unfinished business with Jellybean. I figured, well, she knows what she's doing. He was out and I was in . . . or so I thought.'

One morning, a frustrated and enraged Benitez broke into Newman's home, where he found the woman he'd been searching for the entire previous evening. It seemed clear that his girlfriend and Steve Newman had just made love. Jellybean turned towards Madonna in a cold fury. He dragged her into another room and became engaged in an argument with her that was so vicious, Newman was stunned by it: 'She was screaming things like, "If it wasn't for me, you'd be nobody today. I fucking *made* you, Jellybean. You were just nothing until I came along and fucking transformed your life." And he was saying the exact same things to her. And it was all about who made who a star.

'I knew then that she was still obviously involved with him, but I loved her. Sure, she was an incredible sexual partner, very imaginative, wild. But more than that, she was seductive, just in her personality. There's something about being with a woman who is that aggressive, and who you know is going to make a success of her life. It's intoxicating to hear her talk, to watch her do the things she does on a daily basis.'

When Benitez finally left Newman's home, Madonna found Steve Newman standing at a window and looking out at the city, probably wondering about his fate in the relationship. She walked up to him and touched his arm. When he turned around, she fell into his arms, tears streaming down her face. 'She hugged me tightly,' he recalls, 'and it was as if time stood still. I was in love. I told her she was not going to ruin me emotionally. I said, "Listen, don't think you are going to do to me what you are doing to Jellybean." And she said, "Oh, no, Steve, you're different."'

She cried and begged for his forgiveness. 'I love you,' she told him, 'and only you.'

'I looked into her beautiful eyes and I saw reflected there all the love we shared,' he now recalls. 'She looked so lost and awful, I felt that I needed to take care of her. So what could I do? Just wait and see how it would turn out, that's all I could do.'

The predicament Madonna has said she faced in her personal life at this time was that, because of her runaway success, she felt she would not be able to find a mate among the men who had been in her circle – all of whom were really still struggling to attain their own measure of success. Even though Jellybean Benitez was making a good living, she didn't think he would ever be able to equal her financial status. Steve Newman, she felt, would probably never even come close to Benitez's financial status. Simply, she was a practical woman who didn't want to be in a relationship with a man who had less money than her. 'I want to be taken care of,' she has said. 'I don't want to be the one doing the taking care of.'

While she may have thought she loved Steve Newman, in another example of her mercurial nature it was only a matter of months before Madonna no longer felt that way about him. One evening during a date, Madonna and Newman were enjoying martinis in an intimate bar in New York. Steve took the moment to address the fact that he sensed her lack of commitment. Many years later, he would recall the conversation. 'I really love you, Madonna,' he told her. 'I mean, I swear to God, you are the woman for me.'

'I know I am,' Madonna said, matter-of-factly. 'That much is clear.'

'So why not just drop that Jellybean character? Let's you and me get together,' Newman said, pushing.

Madonna thought it over for a moment and, toying with the slice of lime in her drink, looked at her boyfriend with a serious expression. 'Steve, face facts,' she said. 'You're this nobody writer making no money. Right? But I'm *Madonna*. I mean, I'm making, what? A quarter million a year? And next year, I'll be making ten times that much. And you? Well, you'll *still* be this nobody writer, making no money, won't you?'

Ignoring the hurt expression on his face, she continued, 'In fact, your magazine will probably even be out of business in a year. So, I'm afraid that this will never work. You and I, we're over, Steve. I'm so sorry,' she concluded, 'but, really, it's over.'

'Is that all it's about for you?' Newman asked, incredulously. 'Success and money?'

'Yeah, it is,' she answered, nodding her head. 'Now that you mention it, it is.'

Anyone who knew her well knew that Madonna – who would turn twenty-six in August – wasn't the kind of woman one might consider a particularly nice person. However, she was also objective about herself and her shortcomings. She would be the first, for instance, to call herself 'a bitch'. In an interview with me in June 1984, she said, 'Yes, I admit it. I'm tough. And I don't use the fact that I'm a woman as an excuse like a lot of other bitches. They say, oh, poor me, I'm a woman, so I have to fight harder. That's true. But that doesn't mean you have to be a bitch.'

She also had a sense of humour about herself.

'How did you get this reputation?' I asked. 'Is it because you want attention, and so you push people around?'

'No, that's not it,' Madonna said.

'Well, then, what is it?'

She mulled over the question. 'Basically, I think it's this: people just tend to *piss me off*. Therefore, I hate them.'

The two of us dissolved into laughter. She was wearing a black lace bodysuit with a plunging neckline. Three crucifixes dangled from her neck: 'One for each of the sins I committed just in the last hour,' she explained.

Later in the interview, Madonna openly admitted that she had been intimate with both men and women, and that often they were people who could advance her career. 'True,' she said. 'And they fucked me to advance their careers, too. Let's face it. It has worked both ways. How many people used me to get ahead? You're a reporter. Make a list and get back to me later.'

I wondered how Madonna felt about comments made by Cher in the media suggesting that she was 'tacky'?

'Now, that's in the eye of the beholder, isn't it?' she answered. 'And who knows tacky better than Cher?'

'She also said that you are "vulgar, aggressive, even mean-spirited".'

'Oh, puh-leeze,' Madonna said, giggling. 'Of *course* I am.'

As her musical career continued to thrive, Madonna turned her sights on one of her earliest obsessions: the movies. She still wanted to be an actress, that ambition had not changed. Obviously, her musical career had begun to be rewarding, financially and creatively. Now, she was seeking a movie role. Once again, timing and Lady Luck conspired to make Madonna's dreams a reality.

At this time, movie producer Susan Seidelman was in the process of casting a relatively low-budget ($5 million) film for Orion Pictures. The script, entitled *Desperately Seeking Susan*, was a good one – a modern, screwball comedy with a New Wave feel about a suburban housewife who, bored with her upper middle-class existence, starts following romance through the personal ads. Enter the 'Susan' of the title, a kooky, scatterbrained 'street girl' who disrupts the sex lives of all concerned and causes the housewife, who was set to be played by Rosanna Arquette, to shed her inhibitions and, after a temporary loss of memory, to 'become' Susan. The character was perfect for Madonna's brash image and in the late summer of 1984

Madonna turned her attention to landing the role, letting Seidelman know she was interested.

Seidelman was also interested in Madonna. She had been having problems casting the role of Susan with an actress who could convincingly convey the character's combined qualities of sexiness, brashness and self-confidence (actresses who were tested included Jennifer Jason Leigh, Melanie Griffith, Kelly McGillis and Ellen Barkin). After Madonna's screen test, it was quickly agreed by everyone involved that she was perfectly suited for the part. She began filming the movie in November 1984.

Though the film had been a vehicle for Rosanna Arquette, it wasn't long before *Desperately Seeking Susan* was being referred to by the media as 'the Madonna Movie' . . . much to Arquette's dismay. The movie was soon structured to showcase the inexperienced pop-star-turned-actress. A song by Madonna, 'Into the Groove', was even worked into the thread of the story line, which prompted Arquette to complain later, 'It was completely unfair. As soon as Madonna came into the picture, the script was changed to suit her. I told them that if *Susan* was going to be nothing more than a two-hour rock video spotlighting Madonna, well, I didn't want to be a part of it. A disco dance movie isn't what I signed on to do. However, I couldn't get out of it . . .' (Ironically, it would largely be because Madonna, described by former *New Yorker* film critic Pauline Kael as 'a trampy, indolent goddess', was in the film that it would go on to become one of the top five grossing movies of 1985.)

Like a Virgin

Back on the pop music scene, Madonna's second album, *Like a Virgin*, was released on 12 November 1984. It was while she was in the studio with that album that her brother, Christopher – who had been working with her as a dancer with Erica and Madonna's other brother, Martin – says he realized that things were again changing in his sister's world. 'Erica, Marty, and I were informed by one of Freddy's assistants that Madonna was dispensing with our services,' he recalled. 'Madonna, of course, assiduously avoided giving us the news herself. I felt a little betrayed. By then, I'd cottoned on at last that if I wanted to continue working with my sister – and I did – I'd need to be prepared for a modicum of betrayal on her part to be woven into the highly coloured fabric of both our filial and professional relationships . . . I still feel slightly abandoned, another emotion I am starting to associate with my sister . . .' (He would continue to work with Madonna for many decades, however, as a dresser, assistant and later, home decorator.)

Like a Virgin is really a portrait of Madonna's uncanny pop instincts empowered by her impatient zeal for creative growth and her innate knack for crafting a good record. With the unqualified success of her debut album, just who and what fuelled the Madonna persona was now clear: she was a street-smart dance queen with the sexy allure of Marilyn Monroe, the coy iciness of Marlene Dietrich and the cutting (and protective) glibness of a modern Mae West. Madonna's first album succeeded in introducing that persona and, now, with the new album, she set out to solidify and build upon the concept. It was a heady time. The work, the dedication – the stubbornness – had paid off. Now, it was time to solidify her future.

'Warner Bros. Records is a hierarchy of old men, and it's a chauvinist environment to be working in because I'm treated like this sexy little girl,' she said at the time. 'I have to prove them wrong, which has meant not only proving myself to my fans but to my record company as well. That is something that happens when you're a girl. It wouldn't happen to Prince or Michael Jackson. I had to do everything on my own and it was hard trying to convince people that I was worth a record deal. After that, I had the same problem trying to convince the record company that I had more to offer than a one-off girl singer.'

Taking control as the record's primary producer, Madonna chose Nile Rodgers, a man of great experience when it came to creating personas in the recording studio. With production partner Bernard Edwards, Rodgers had formed the Seventies band Chic, essentially a studio rhythm section (including two female vocalists and drummer Tony Thompson), who had a string of disco era dance hits, including 'Dance, Dance, Dance', 'Everybody Dance', 'Le Freak' and 'Good Times'.

Because pop and R&B music is a producer-driven medium, Chic's hits quickly put Edwards's and Rodgers's sound in demand. Soon, the duo had written and produced hit records for others, including the sibling act Sister Sledge, who found commercial success with Edwards's and Rodgers's 'We Are Family' and 'The Greatest Dancer', and Diana Ross, who did the same with 'Upside Down' and 'I'm Coming Out'. Indeed, when guitarist Rodgers split with Edwards to work separately, his inventive ability to meld rock and rhythm is what made his production of David Bowie's 1983 hit 'Let's Dance' so spectacular . . . and probably what attracted Madonna to him as a producer. Theirs was – and still is – a mutual admiration society.

'I'm always amazed by Madonna's incredible judgement when it comes to making pop records,' says Nile Rodgers. 'I've never seen anyone do it better, and that's the truth. When we did that album, it was the perfect union, and I knew it from the first day in the studio. The thing between us, man, it was sexual, it was passionate, it was creative . . . it was pop.'

Their collective energy – Madonna wanting to score with a smash second album and Nile Rodgers wanting to be the producer to give it to her – drove the production of the *Like a Virgin* collection with great precision. The album's title track, and first single, offered the perfect continuation of the Madonna persona with sexy double entendres, every step along the way: 'Like a virgin . . . touched for the very first time.' The expensive, lavish video was filmed in Italy, and featured Madonna with a wild lion. When she sang the song on the 1984 MTV Video Awards show – the public's first taste of her in live performance – she wore a knee-length, white wedding dress, veil, bustier, garter belt and plenty of clunky jewellery. She worked the stage like a panther in heat, crawling on the floor seductively, playing right to the camera and flirting all the while with what she knew was an international audience. Recalls Melissa Etheridge, 'I remember thinking, "What is she doing? She's wearing a wedding dress. Oh my God, she's rolling around on the floor. Oh my God!" It was the most brave, blatant sexual thing I've ever seen on television.'

In 2016, Madonna explained to Howard Stern that the performance wasn't a calculation as much as it was an accident. 'I had come down the wedding cake and my shoe fell off,' she said. 'I was like, "Oh shit, I can't dance in one shoe!"' Apparently, the mishap forced her to think fast, which led to her rolling around on the stage. 'I didn't know my skirt was up,' she recalled. 'I proceeded to sing the song lying down on the ground. I was just making the best of the situation.'

She also said that Freddy DeMann told her that she'd just ruined her career with that performance. 'He was white as a ghost,' she said. 'He was very disappointed in me, because I was rolling around on the floor, my dress went up, and you could see my underpants. What was I thinking? It was scary and fun, and I didn't know what it meant for my future. A million things were going through my head.'

Since Nile Rodgers brought musicians from Chic with him to the studio with Madonna, many Chic fans felt that *Like a Virgin* was actually just another Chic album. If that was true, it was certainly armed with better, more durable singles. However, neither Madonna nor Rodgers had a hand in writing the song 'Like a Virgin'. Tom Kelly and Billy Steinberg penned it, and it was middle-aged Mo Ostin (then President of Warner Bros. Records) who found it, then passed it on to the label's fledgling artist. Madonna and Rodgers, who brought the song to life, created a sparse, anxious groove, driven by a big, mechanical snare drum. Madonna crafted a coy vocal that suggested she really was a virgin – excited, sexy and willing. It all worked: 'Like a Virgin' became Madonna's first number 1 pop single and stayed in that position for six weeks. (Nile Rodgers remixed 'Like a Virgin' for the 12-inch dance single; however his version was rejected in favour of the remix produced by Jellybean Benitez.)

With the success of the single 'Like a Virgin', the album then began to show its true worth. Behind the title track, Warner Bros. Records released 'Material Girl', an even funkier musical sound with a New Wave accent. Armed with a great melody and semi-biographical, tongue-in-cheek *ironic* lyric about a girl's love for cash, 'Material Girl' was propelled to number 2 in the pop charts.

In the meantime, two songs from movie soundtracks would further raise Madonna's popularity to fever pitch. 'Crazy for You', a sassy ballad written by Jon Lind and John Bettis and produced by Jellybean Benitez (from the movie *Vision Quest*) would become Madonna's second number 1 single. Then, the uptempo 'Into the Groove', co-written and co-produced by Madonna and ex-boyfriend, musical mentor and cohort Steve Bray (from the soundtrack of *Desperately Seeking Susan*), went to number 1 on the dance charts (even though it was just the B side of 'Angel', the third single from *Like a Virgin*). Both tracks were vital to the public's growing fascination with Madonna; 'Crazy for You' because it provided more proof that she was vocally capable of delivering a serious ballad, and 'Into the Groove' because it demonstrated her continual ability to create infectious dance music. 'Dress You Up', the next single from *Virgin*, added to the successful, commercial streak when it went to number 5 in the pop charts.

Though *Like a Virgin* became Madonna's first number 1 album (and one of the biggest selling albums of 1985), it generated less than enthusiastic reviews ('A tolerable bit of fluff', *People* magazine observed). It's true that, today – and especially when compared to Madonna's body of work since that time – the album seems a bit repetitious and immature. Nile Rodgers confesses, 'As a fan, it wouldn't be what I consider my favourite Madonna album compositionally.'

However, the mere fact that at the time of its release so many couldn't resist commenting on the record was testament to the continuing, growing fascination with the artist who created it. Mick Jagger even threw his hat in the ring by commenting that Madonna's songs were characterized by a 'central dumbness'.

Indeed, maybe it was Madonna's so-called 'central dumbness' that sparked the interest of much of her public, fans hungry for a sexy and provocative star who actually conveyed that she enjoyed the limelight and her celebrity. There really hadn't been a pin-up phenomenon since Farrah Fawcett's reign in the late Seventies, and her role as one of 'Charlie's Angels' had been relatively short-lived before she tired of her bathing-suit-blonde image and sought recognition as a serious television actress.

Madonna, though, had been fantasizing about fame and fortune for years and was more than happy to give to the public the provocative, double-entendre female image that had been absent from the spotlight since the days of Marilyn Monroe. Her new album taunted, with song titles like 'Dress You Up', 'Angel', 'Material Girl', and of course the title tease, 'Like a Virgin'.

Further to fuel Madonna mania and the success of *Like a Virgin*, Warner Bros. Records sent her on a heavily promoted tour. Not surprisingly, the tour was a smashing success; at Radio City Music Hall it broke all attendance records when the show sold out in a breathtaking twenty-four minutes. It certainly seemed that by the mid-Eighties there was no stopping her – Madonna's albums were selling at a staggering 80,000 a day. Although she was looking to the future with declarations such as 'I want longevity as a human being. I want it to last forever', critics like Robert Hilburn of the *Los Angeles Times* were already predicting her rapid decline. 'It's like having a new toy,' Hilburn stated. 'Everyone wanted the Cabbage Patch Doll for Christmas. She's the Cabbage Patch Doll this year.'

Other critics were placing their bets that Cyndi Lauper, with her pure and powerful yet quirky voice, would be the pop diva who would endure. *Billboard* magazine editor, Paul Grein, predicted that 'Cyndi Lauper will be around for a long time; Madonna will be out of the business in six months.'

'In the beginning, I was called everything from a Disco Dolly to a One-Hit Wonder,' Madonna recalled in 1999. 'Everyone agreed that I was sexy, but no one would agree that I had any talent, which really irritated me.'

In fact, if she was going anywhere, it would be straight up. After all, this was the 1980s. In many ways, Madonna was exactly what people wanted at this time. In the previous decade, Andy Warhol had made his famous statement that in the future everyone would be famous for fifteen minutes, and many people seemed intent on making that prediction come true. Many people not only wanted fame, they wanted money, name brands and everything else in excess. On television, ordinary citizens were discovering talk shows as a viable forum to indulge in exhibitionism by exposing their most intimate secrets to a worldwide audience. Cable television brought sex and violence into America's homes as never before. On Wall Street, brokers in their early twenties were becoming rich by selling junk bonds to yuppies eager for overnight millions.

In a sense, Madonna became the human embodiment of a junk bond. People were willing to exploit and sell her in order to make as much money as possible – and she was happy to be exploited . . . if it meant money in her pocket, too. The public, fascinated with fame, was happy to watch.

Not to denigrate Madonna's talent – because she certainly had a great deal of it (most of which hadn't even been explored yet) – but the notion of 'celebrity' has never had much to do with what special abilities a person has, or what he or she has accomplished in terms of artistry. It's always had to do with personal marketing – and never was this more true than it was in the 1980s. With burgeoning cable TV, videos, magazines, billboards, radio and film media, a celebrity could now be exploited twenty-four hours a day: in living rooms, at clubs, in supermarkets or on the streets, the same image projected from every direction, at every turn. Madonna was one of the first artists to understand this cultural twist; Michael Jackson also got it. At the beginning of her career as a singer in the 1980s, she always made sure she had all areas covered for total media saturation. She would gladly appear on any television show, magazine cover, splashy video, whatever it took . . .

Meeting Sean Penn

Perhaps one of Madonna's most popular videos is the one she filmed for 'Material Girl', a modern-day reworking of Marilyn Monroe's most famous vocal performance, 'Diamonds Are a Girl's Best Friend'. Madonna said at the time, 'Marilyn was made into something not human in a way, and I can relate to that. Her sexuality was something everyone was obsessed with, and that I can relate to. And there were certain things about her vulnerability that I'm curious about and attracted to.'

When the time came to film the video (two days in Los Angeles in February 1985), Madonna decided on a clear and obvious homage to her blonde inspiration, Monroe. The video featured Madonna wearing an exact replica of Marilyn's shocking pink gown from the film *Gentlemen Prefer Blondes* (she hated the dress, however, complaining that it constantly slipped down her bosom), singing on a reconstruction of the film's set, complete with staircase, chandeliers and bevy of tuxedo-clad chorus boys. ('I can't completely disdain the song and video, because they certainly were important to my career,' she said later. 'But talk about the media hanging on to a phrase and misinterpreting the damn thing as well. I didn't write that song, you know, and the video was all about how the girl rejected diamonds and money. But God forbid irony should be understood. So when I'm ninety, I'll still be the Material Girl. I guess it's not so bad. Lana Turner was the Sweater Girl until the day she died.')

Freddy DeMann's assistant Melinda Cooper drove Madonna to the sound stage where 'Material Girl' was to be filmed. A photograph taken that day shows Madonna wearing a pink bodysuit and a black velvet shirt, unbuttoned enough so as to reveal her black Chantelle bra. She also wore large dark sunglasses and a wide-brimmed red hat, lest she be recognized.

Because of the enormity of the video production – and the Marilyn Monroe association that was bound to cause a sensation – Melinda Cooper sensed that Madonna's life and career were about to be transformed. It was an exciting notion. 'Do you realize how much things are going to change for you now?' she asked her as they drove to the set.

'What do you mean?' Madonna responded. She had her compact mirror out and was inspecting a pimple. 'Jesus Christ. Of all the days to get a zit,' she said, preoccupied. 'I ask you, can anything else go wrong in my fucking life?'

'I mean, your whole world is going to change after this video,' said Cooper, ignoring Madonna's rhetorical question. 'Do you know that?'

Madonna snapped the compact shut. 'I know that, Melinda,' she said, perturbed. 'Now can we please just get there!'

On that first day on the set, while Madonna was standing at the top of the staircase and waiting for filming to begin, she gazed down and noticed a guy in a leather jacket and dark sunglasses striking what seemed to be a deliberate pose in a corner, looking back up at her intently. He was twenty-four-year-old actor Sean Penn – born on 17 August 1960 – at the time considered the most moody and brooding (and probably most talented) of the young Hollywood actors who made up what was known as 'the Brat Pack'. (Others in the so-called Pack included young actors Charlie Sheen and Emilio

Estevez.) Because he hailed from a privileged background, having been raised in Beverly Hills with both parents in show business (his father was television director Leo Penn, his mother actress Eileen Ryan), Penn didn't have to struggle much to break into the business. However, his privileged lifestyle didn't make him any less angry. He had a reputation for being an intensely private, sometimes violent, and extremely jealous young man – and he was also thought of as a proficient actor thanks to roles in *Fast Times at Ridgemont High*, *Racing with the Moon* and *The Falcon and the Snow Man*. After having expressed an interest in meeting Madonna, Sean Penn had been brought to the set of 'Material Girl' by the video's director, Mary Lambert.

'He was somebody whose work I'd admired,' Madonna has said, 'and I think he felt the same way about me. I never thought in a million years I would meet him.'

As soon as Madonna, still at the top of the stairs and waiting to start her descent, realized that the stranger below was Sean Penn, her heart skipped a beat. Though she fancied actor Keith Carradine at this time (who appeared in the video and with whom she was seen making out in between takes), she knew that she had to meet Penn. Even at first glance, he seemed self-confident and cocky – just her type. When they finally did meet at the bottom of the stairs, he didn't disappoint.

'Well, just look at you,' Sean Penn said to her as he motioned to the gown and wig. Full of swagger, he hooked his thumbs in the belt loops of his jeans. 'You think you're Marilyn Monroe, don't you?' He was joking, but Madonna didn't appreciate it.

'What's the matter with you?' she asked, annoyed. 'You don't even say hello? You just go straight for the insult? Is that what you do? You don't even say, "It's nice to meet you"?'

'Oh, I'm sorry, *Marilyn*,' Sean Penn said, his voice dripping with phony sarcasm. Penn's eyes were a bit glazed, a cigarette dangled from his mouth. He extended his hand to shake hers. 'It's nice to meet you,' he said with a warm smile.

Madonna had to laugh. She took his hand and, putting on a whispery Marilyn Monroe voice, cooed, 'Nice to meet you, too . . .'

Later, she recalled, 'I had this fantasy that we were going to meet, fall in love and get married. Suddenly it's what I was wishing would happen. Why I fell for him that day, I can't say. I have no idea. I just know I wanted him.'

The Affair with Prince

Soon after their first meeting on the set of the 'Material Girl' video, twenty-six-year-old Madonna and twenty-four-year-old Sean Penn began dating. 'After the video shoot, I was over at a friend's house,' he explains. 'And he had a book of quotations. He picked it up and turned to a random page and read the following: "She had the innocence of a child and the wit of a man." I looked at my friend and he just said, "Go get her." So I did.' Complicating matters a bit for Sean, however, was the fact that Madonna was also dating the rock star Prince at this time, whom she had met backstage at the American Music Awards earlier, in Los Angeles on 28 January 1985. He wasn't her type, and it's difficult to know why Madonna was even interested in him, except for the fact that she respected him as a musician and probably just wanted to know what made him tick.

Prince (real name Prince Rogers Nelson) was an eccentric man known for a strangely shy demeanour in private and outrageous sexuality – prancing about in bikini briefs and high heels – on stage. During an interview with me the same year he met Madonna, Prince refused to speak. Instead, he sat silently in his chair in front of a dinner of Chinese food and spent the entire evening playing with shrimp fried rice, all the while with a grim expression on his face. In response to any question, he would either nod affirmatively or shake his head negatively. When the interview was over, he departed without saying goodbye. 'And that, my friend, is Prince,' said his publicist by way of explanation.

As their first date, Prince invited Madonna to accompany him to one of his performances in Los Angeles. Though she was scheduled to leave for New York to begin rehearsals for her own concert tour, she decided to delay that trip a few days so that she could spend some time with the rock star. The night of his concert, he picked her up in a white stretch limousine and took her to the Forum, where he was performing. Madonna later said she was amazed to find that the diminutive rock star smelt so strongly of lavender, 'Like a woman,' she observed. 'I felt like I was in the presence of Miss Elizabeth Taylor. He reeks of lavender. It turned me on, actually.'

Once in the limousine, recalled T.L. Ross, who was a friend of Prince's, 'I heard she was pretty aggressive, that the poor little guy had to fight her off. She was strong. He told me that she had the strength of ten women.' Because he had a performance that evening, Prince didn't want to exhaust himself with Madonna. He suggested that they wait.

After the show, the two ventured out into the Los Angeles night and eventually ended up at the Marquis Hotel in Westwood for a party with Prince's entourage. The gathering turned rowdy when Prince leapt up onto a table and began to undress. Joining him on the table, Madonna engaged him in a sensual bump-and-grind, her shoulders bouncing up and down, her body undulating. The party broke up at five in the morning, after which Prince and Madonna – arm in arm and practically holding each other up – retired to Prince's private suite.

For the next two months, the couple continued seeing each other, though they didn't seem to have much in common other than their status as superstar performers. While she was honest and forthright, he was secretive and bashful. Luckily, they both idolized Marilyn Monroe. When he told her that his home was filled with posters of the blonde movie goddess, Madonna said that she couldn't wait to see his collection of memorabilia.

One romantic evening, Prince leased the entire Yamashiro mountain-top restaurant overlooking Los Angeles, with its breathtaking view of the city lights. Madonna wore a lacy purple skirt with trademark black bra peeking out from behind a sheer white blouse. At the restaurant, they ate Japanese food and then, after three hours of what appeared to some observers to be little conversation, they departed for a nightclub called Façade.

'I've been nibbling around the edges of this thing long enough, because I didn't know where to start or how to tell you,' Prince told Madonna once they were at the club with friends. He was being much more courageous than he'd ever been with her, and in front of witnesses, which made it even more surprising. 'Madonna, I think we should hook up, you and I. I want you to be, you know . . . my girl.'

Seeming surprised, Madonna let the request linger as if anticipating a punchline. But he wasn't joking. He waited for her response. 'Hmmm,' she said while frowning and looking as if she was trying to figure out just how to handle the moment. 'Now, *that's* food for thought, isn't it?' Her words didn't hold much conviction.

When Prince looked deflated, Madonna grabbed his hand. 'C'mon, let's dance!' she said cheerily as she walked him out onto the dance floor.

After about two months, when there really wasn't anything left for them to say to each other, Madonna became bored with Prince. They had recorded a couple of songs in his Minneapolis studio, and one would even be released later. But her friends recall that, while she complained about his passivity, he griped about her aggressive nature.

T.L. Ross said of this period, 'Prince is way too cosmic for Madonna. For him, making love is a spiritual experience. For her – at least at that time – making love was just a physical expression. While he wanted to savour every second of the experience, she was into multiple orgasms. After two months, he cut her loose. Then, she did the scorned woman act.

'After he stopped acting interested in her, that's when the phone calls started. Madonna pestered him for weeks. He said later that she screamed at him, "How dare you dump me. Don't you know who I am?" She was definitely not used to getting dumped.'

'Madonna: A Lonely Life'

After her brief romance with Prince, Madonna began to concentrate on Sean Penn as a potential mate. In spite of her fanatical need for the spotlight and Sean Penn's obsessive desire for privacy, the two began a passionate and exciting courtship that, if nothing else, certainly proved that opposites do attract. Impressed as much by his tough guy reputation as by his acting credentials, Madonna would later admit that he was, as she put, 'completely unable to resist him, not that I ever tried. He was the sexiest, smartest man I had ever known.' Sean was equally fascinated by her. He had been a fan of Madonna's, which is why he had wanted to meet her. Once he got to know her, he quickly realized that she was fun to be with, and also the kind of woman who would, when necessary, meet him at his own level of arrogance. 'I admit it, I was a smart ass,' he says. 'And so was she. It was a relationship made in heaven, two smart asses going through life together. How romantic.'

Of course, the paparazzi were delighted at the pairing of the unpredictable Penn and his exhibitionist girlfriend, Madonna. They were even photographed on their first dates: in New York at a club called Private Eyes, and in Los Angeles where Penn had accompanied Madonna on a pilgrimage to Marilyn Monroe's crypt at Westwood Memorial Cemetery. (Madonna was shaking with nervous tension during the visit to Monroe's grave. When she spotted a red rose left there by her ex-husband, Joe DiMaggio, she was heard to murmur 'Oh, my. He really loved her.')

At this time, with everyone trying to get a piece of her – or at least that's how it probably felt to her – Madonna had said she wanted someone in her life she believed truly loved her. 'She was lonely, the classic victim of stardom in that she was the popular and well-loved celebrity who went home alone at night and cried her eyes out,' said her former producer and boyfriend, Jellybean Benitez. While she certainly wasn't lacking in sexual experiences, missing in her life was a sense of true intimacy with another person. Of course, those in her circle at this time admit that Madonna wasn't an easy person to get to know or to be intimate with on an emotional level. 'She had a lot of barriers up,' says Tommy Quinn, a New York studio musician who dated her shortly before she met Sean Penn.

While Quinn had heard the charge made against Madonna that she was cold, selfish and aloof, he disagreed. 'I found her to be very guarded,' he says. 'Of course, she was brash and – oh, man! – she could be a royal bitch. But beneath it, if you really got to know her, she was a different kind of person, a very insecure girl.

'I remember one night in particular: she was at my place and we made love. It was pretty intense, and afterward, as I held her in my arms, I noticed that she was sobbing. When I asked her why, she refused to open up to me. But every time we made love – which was about a half dozen times – she seemed sadder than she was before. I thought to myself, either I'm pretty bad in the sack or this girl has a problem with intimacy. It was more than she could take when she allowed herself to be vulnerable.'

'What's wrong?' he asked Madonna, touching her tenderly on the cheek.

'Nothing,' she responded quickly. 'I'm fine. Leave me alone, will you?' As he recalled it, she took a deep breath and then let it out slowly, as if being pushed down by an excruciating weight. Then, she pulled away from her lover and slept at the foot of the bed in a foetal position.

'At first, I thought she was crying because she thought having sex made her vulnerable, and then that made her feel weak. But, after knowing her a little better, I decided it was because she was just afraid of being hurt, of letting down her guard, of being truly intimate.'

A few nights later, Quinn decided to ask the question that had been on his mind but for which there had never been an appropriate time. 'Why do you hate your old man so much?' he asked. 'Every time you bring up your father, it's always to say some horrible thing about him. I think that's the source of your anxiety.'

'What are you talking about?' Madonna said, now crying. 'How dare you say that to me?'

She then bolted out of bed, ran into the bathroom and slammed the door behind her.

The next morning, Madonna – her eyes red-rimmed and watery – put on her black fishnet tights and hip-slung miniskirt in preparation for leaving. She slipped into a hand-painted jacket with no shirt underneath. As she was putting on her spike-heeled boots, she looked up at Tommy Quinn and said, 'You know, just because I was crying doesn't mean anything. So don't think you have some kind of hold over me, or that I care about you.' She didn't mention anything about Quinn's having brought up her father.

As he tried to figure out how to respond, she walked across the room and out the door, without saying goodbye.

A week later, Quinn found her staring out the eleventh storey window of his brownstone on East Seventy-Second Street. She looked fetching, wearing his T-shirt and nothing else, certainly putting on a fairly indecent show for the neighbours. 'A penny for your thoughts,' Quinn said to her as he brought her a glass of chilled white wine.

'They'll cost you a lot more than that,' Madonna said with a weak smile. Then, after a sip, she thoughtfully observed, 'It's all a fiction, you know that, don't you, Tommy? I'm just a character in a novel. None of this is real. None of it.'

'What's the novel called?' Quinn asked, intrigued.

'It's called *Madonna*,' she answered. Then, after a thoughtful beat, she added a subtitle: '*A Lonely Life*.'

No different from a lot other people, she wanted to be loved – but she was also afraid to be loved. Or, as her sister, Paula, observed, 'She was a woman, like any woman. She needed someone to hold on to. But it scared her.'

Sean Penn had his own insecurities. His mania for privacy was obsessive, and those who knew him well claim it was because he was never satisfied with the way he looked, always feeling awkward in his own skin and not wishing to be seen by anyone, let alone *everyone*. They say that his bravado and bad temper was – not surprisingly – a camouflage that masked a litany of other emotional issues the explanations of which are probably best left to Sean Penn biographers. However, when he and Madonna began to date, they found something in each other that felt like, as Madonna put it, 'a sense of personal completion'. Also, their sexual chemistry was explosive. After their first date, he threw her to the floor and stripped off her clothes and his own in such a hurry he left his boots on. Then he made love to her. Later, she said, 'We reached orgasm together, and it was as if time stood still.'

'Who's to say how the heart works . . . it just does,' observed Meg Lowery, an actress friend of Sean's who lived in Los Angeles at the time and attended acting school with him. 'Sean told me he was crazy about her. But he was worried about it. "She's nuts," he told me. "And I'm nuts. The two of us together? Man, that's trouble." Plus, he sensed that she wasn't going to be faithful to him. "She's out there, wild and free," he told me. "And I don't think any man will be able to tame her. In fact," he said, "I think the last thing she wants is to be tamed."'

Along with his brooding nature, Sean Penn was also a talented actor and an intelligent man. When she found that he was a voracious reader and wrote poetry, Madonna was even more attracted to him. Soon, she was announcing to any friend, foe or reporter that

Sean Penn was her hero, her best friend, and the 'coolest guy in the universe'. She could tell him her problems, she said. Somehow, he had the instinctive understanding of a man who had suffered himself and knew all there was to know about loss and grief, even though his parents were both still alive. She could talk to him as she could talk to no one else.

The couple soon announced their engagement. As word of this big event spread, publicity about Madonna's life and career reached a new fever pitch. A surprising declaration for some of her fans – but not so surprising for those who knew her – came when the men's magazine *Penthouse* announced it would be publishing nude photographs taken of Madonna years earlier. Not to be outdone, *Playboy* announced its own imminent publication of similarly scandalous photographs. As a media sensation ensued over the idea that photographs of Madonna would reveal her in a new and revealing way, it was just as it had been thirty-five years earlier with news that Marilyn Monroe had also posed nude.

Some observers suggested that these nude photographs of Madonna would somehow damage her career. Reporters pointed to Vanessa Williams who, a year earlier, had been forced to turn in her Miss America crown. It had been discovered that she had posed nude years before she won her title. (Of course, Vanessa Williams would ultimately turn the scandal to her advantage. She is now one of the only Miss Americas whose name anyone can even remember.) The existence of nude pictures, the race between two men's magazines to beat each other to publication, and Madonna's bold declaration, 'I'm not ashamed of anything', only fanned the flames of red-hot publicity.

Tommy Quinn had not seen Madonna in more than a year when, he says, he received a telephone call from her. She asked if they could meet. When he invited her to his apartment, she said, 'No. I'm a trapped animal, now. If I come to see you, everyone will know where you live, everyone will know that I know you, and they'll never leave you alone.' He now recalls, 'In order to protect me, she wanted us to meet in a small Italian restaurant on Second Avenue near Seventy-First Street.'

When he showed up, he found Madonna in a back booth wearing large sunglasses, a floppy hat and an old, worn, flower-print 'house dress'. He recalls, 'She looked like a bag lady. I was astonished.'

'What the hell happened to you?' he asked as he sat down.

'My life. That's what's happened to me,' Madonna responded glumly. She leaned over to kiss him on the cheek. 'So, how do you like my outfit? I'm a millionaire, but this is what I have to wear in public just so that I can have some peace and quiet.'

After ordering spaghetti, Madonna got to the point of why she wanted to see her friend. 'I need your advice,' she said. 'Have you heard about these pictures?'

'Who hasn't?' Quinn answered.

She took off her sunglasses. She looked as if she had been crying. 'I just don't know how to be with this goddamn thing,' she said, sadly. 'I mean, I don't know how to *be* . . . how to act.'

Quinn would recall years later, 'I was astonished. When I first heard about the pictures, I thought she would probably take the position that they didn't matter, that she was above worrying about them. But, sitting with her, looking at how distressed she was, I saw that the existence of these pictures had really bothered her.'

'Oh, screw it, Madonna,' Quinn told her. 'You have to act like you don't care. What choice do you have?'

'But I do care,' she said. 'What about my father? Why should he have to see those pictures? And Sean! What will Sean think?' Her temper rose. 'Parasites!' she said, referring to the media. 'I feel so . . . *misunderstood*.'*

For the next forty-five minutes, over two plates of pasta with meatballs and a bottle of Merlot, Madonna and Tommy finally

---

* '*Penthouse* did something really nasty,' Madonna would complain, years later. 'They sent copies of the magazine to Sean.'

agreed that she had no choice but to act completely unaffected by the existence of the photographs, just as Marilyn Monroe had done before her. 'If they [presumably the public and press] know that I'm unhappy about them, they'll just love that,' Madonna concluded, sounding defeated. 'Oh, who cares, anyway,' she added, with forced cheerfulness. 'I have press agents now, you know?' she added. 'Let them figure the whole thing out. I'll use this thing to my advantage somehow. You know that, don't you, Tommy?'

'Hell yeah, you will,' Quinn agreed, nudging her. 'You're bigger than this, anyway, Madonna.'

He recalls that she forced a sad smile and then, facetiously, made a sign of the cross.

'Are you happy, Madonna?' he asked her. As she rose, hugged him and said goodbye, it didn't seem as if she intended to answer the question. She threw fifty dollars onto the table. 'Look at my life,' she said, arching a brow. 'Who wouldn't be happy?'

'Oh My God! Look at Me!'

Was Madonna really as upset about the nude photographs as she had indicated to Tommy Quinn? Perhaps an example of her mercurial nature was that she could later make light of the predicament in which she had found herself.

'I remember when we were both broke and living in New York, Madonna showed me some of the nude shots,' recalls Erica Bell. 'We were just sort of being lazy, and a little drunk, and she brought out this envelope and spread the pictures on the floor. "Look at me, Rica," [Madonna's nickname for Erica Bell] she said. "I'm as flat-chested as you are!" And we just laughed and laughed, for some reason, thinking the pictures were hysterical. She said, "One day I will be world famous, and *Playboy* will publish these photos, and it'll be the greatest scandal of all time." I asked her, "My God, won't you be embarrassed?" And she laughed and said, "What do *you* think?"'

When the photographs were published many years later, Erica received a telephone call from Madonna.

'Oh my God,' Madonna said, nearly hysterical with laughter. 'It's happened, just as I predicted.'

'I know,' Erica said, giggling. 'I can't believe it, after all of these years.'

Years later, Erica said, 'I don't think she was that upset about the pictures. If she was, I didn't know it. I just know we laughed a lot about them. We thought it was pretty damn funny, the whole thing.'

More of Madonna's past was excavated when film maker Stephen Jon Lewicki decided to exploit his association with her by releasing a home video version of *A Certain Sacrifice*, the low budget movie they had made in 1979. Perhaps hoping that Madonna would pay him to keep the film from commercial distribution, Lewicki was dismayed when her people offered him a measly $10,000, which he flatly rejected. Although Madonna took him to court in an effort to keep the film out of circulation, Lewicki ultimately won the right to release it, making him a millionaire in just a short time – not bad for the producer of a movie made six years earlier on a $20,000 budget.

'I think Madonna tried to stop the movie more as a publicity stunt than anything else,' says Lewicki today. 'It was also an interesting use of her power, really, to get the kind of exposure she wants when she wants it. The *New York Post* had huge headlines on the front page, "Madonna Seeks Nude Movie Ban". I mean, the hysteria she whipped up over this film was amazing. But in the end, when it came right down to it, she really didn't put a wholehearted effort into suing me. I think even the judge realized that all that was happening was a certain amount of posturing, and just for publicity. So he threw the case out, and I released the movie.'

At this point in her career, Madonna really didn't need to seek out publicity – it came to her in tidal waves. She had a love/hate relationship with the press: for the most part, she loved seeing herself in the media, but at the same time she pretended to hate the attention. Once at a birthday party in her honour she stood up to model a green silk pants ensemble. 'I like it,' she told her guests, 'because it's green, the colour of envy. I envy all of you,' she continued melodramatically, 'because you all have your privacy . . . and I don't.' Madonna, however, did nothing to stop the media's attention – on the contrary she almost always courted it.

In May 1985, Madonna made the cover of *Time*, with the accompanying headline: 'Madonna – Why She's Hot'. Though she seemed to some observers to be blasé about much of her newly acquired fame, this particular tribute from such a well-respected publication was not one that she took lightly. According to one of her manager Freddy DeMann's assistants at the time, 'Madonna waited by the front door for the messenger to arrive from Freddy's office with a first copy of the magazine. I remember the day so well. She was wearing black mesh stockings, a short skirt and brief top, with four crucifixes around her neck. Because she was working, she also had on her herringbone glasses. When the magazine arrived, she ripped the envelope apart trying to get to it. Then, when she saw it, she let out a shriek.'

'Oh my God, look at me!' Madonna said, dancing around the room in her Gucci flip-flops, magazine in hand. 'I am on the cover of *Time* magazine! Can you believe it? Just look! Can you imagine it?' Earlier in her career, she had said, 'I won't be happy until I'm as famous as God.' Maybe now she was beginning to feel that she was on her way to that goal.

Truly awed by Madonna's appearance on the cover of one of the most respected magazines in the world, the incredulous assistant said, 'No, I just can't believe it.'

Suddenly, Madonna stopped dancing. Whipping around to face the employee, she said, 'What do you mean, you can't believe it? Why *shouldn't* I be on the cover of *Time*?'

'I didn't mean . . .' the secretary began to stumble over her words. 'What I meant was . . . I'm sorry.'

'Oh, stop your grovelling,' Madonna said, exasperated. 'You're so *weak*. Just get Sean on the phone. I want him to see this.'

When the assistant telephoned Sean to ask him to come by Madonna's home to see the magazine, Sean indicated that he was busy. He asked that she send the magazine to his home, by messenger. Madonna, pacing the room and staring at the magazine cover, overheard the conversation between the assistant and her boyfriend. She went to the employee and grabbed the phone from her. 'You get over here, now, Sean,' she said into the phone. She had an angry, imperious edge to her voice. 'How many girlfriends have you had on the cover of *Time*. One! Me! Now, get over here.'

Penn showed up thirty minutes later.

The fact that Sean Penn was also such a combative person only added fuel to the bonfire of image-making and publicity that seemed to erupt on a weekly basis for Madonna. On 30 June 1985, he was charged with assault and battery after he beat up a couple of journalists outside a hotel in Nashville, Tennessee, where he was filming a movie.

That morning, he and Madonna had received a bouquet of balloons delivered to their room, sent by someone in the media and with a card that read, 'Madonna and Sean. Congratulations Mom and Pop. How about an exclusive?' Penn, who was annoyed by the constant scrutiny, as well as rumours that Madonna was expecting, bolted out of the room, heading towards some waiting journalists.

Lori Mulrenin, who witnessed the ensuing attack, recalls, 'He was screaming at them like he was going to break open their heads. Then, when one of the journalists took his picture, he blew up. He picked up a rock and threw it carefully and precisely at the photographer. Then he ripped the cameras off the photographer's back and slammed them against the photographer, who fell down. He then picked up the rock again as the other newsman tried to step in. Sean hit that one in the eye with his fist, and also hit him on the head with the rock. Madonna, who had been in the background when the fight started, pulled her hat over her eyes and then ran back into the hotel.'

Sean Penn would enter a no-contest plea to charges that he assaulted the two journalists. He received a ninety-day suspended sentence and was fined fifty dollars on each of two misdemeanour charges.

While some of Madonna's publicity ploys seem fairly unsophisticated in retrospect, they always worked. For instance, when the time came for the planning of her wedding to Sean Penn, she insisted that she wanted it to be a private affair with no publicity. She acted as if she did not want the kind of international attention she knew was bound to be generated by such an event. Besides simply going to Las Vegas where she and Penn could have quietly and quickly married, there were any number of ways Madonna could have ensured an intimate wedding, if such a thing was what she really desired. However, savvy as she is, she no doubt realized that the air of secrecy she pretended to foster only made the press more determined to cover the event . . . and the public more determined to read about it. Of course, to make matters even more tantalizing, Madonna banned the press from the wedding.

The only thing Madonna could not control was Sean, and his ambivalent feelings about the impending nuptials. Two nights before the ceremony, he threw his bachelor party in a private room above Hollywood's Roxy nightclub. Among others present at the party were his brother, Chris, actors Harry Dean Stanton, David Keith, Tom Cruise and Robert Duvall. Stripper 'Kitten' Natividad, who entertained at the party, recalls, 'Those guys were pretty drunk. They had a good time. But Sean didn't fall on his face, or anything. When he talked, he made sense. Sort of.'

Sean told his friend Isaac Benson, also at the party, 'Man, I don't know that I can go through with this thing.'

'Do you love her?' Benson asked.

'Hell yeah, I love her,' he said, sipping a Bacardi and Coke. 'But we're gonna tear each other apart. We're nuclear, together, man. *Nuclear.*'

'So maybe you shouldn't marry her,' Benson suggested.

'Oh yeah? And then what?' Penn asked, raising an eyebrow. 'She'll kill me for embarrassing her in front of the whole world, that's what. No,' he decided after tilting back a beer. 'I love her. So, I'm marrying her. God help me. Look, if the whole thing falls apart,' he offered, trying to be optimistic, 'at least I'll have acting, right?'

Then, the two friends toasted the upcoming nuptials. 'Hopefully, no one will find out where the wedding is gonna happen,' Sean said. 'That's what Madonna wants. A nice, quiet ceremony.'

The Remaking of Apocalypse Now

It would seem that Sean Penn actually believed that Madonna wanted 'a nice quiet ceremony', the location of which was to be kept a closely guarded secret, even though such a concept was at odds with everything everyone else believed they knew about the publicity-hungry superstar. No address, location or telephone number was given on the invitations, written by her brother Martin and printed on shocking pink paper. ('Please come to Sean and Madonna's Birthday Party. The celebration will commence at six o'clock. Please be prompt or you will miss their wedding ceremony.' Those on the select list realized that the bride would turn twenty-seven on her wedding day; the bridegroom twenty-five the day after.) Guests were to be informed of the location by telephone at their homes or hotels less than twenty-four hours before the ceremony. Only key employees at the caterer, chair rental firm and florist were to know of the location of the ceremony. Delivery drivers were to be given the address only when their trucks were loaded and ready to go. Also, supervisors were to follow the trucks just to be certain that no driver stopped on his way to the ceremony to make a telephone call that (for a few bucks) would tip off any press people to what was happening, and where.

Of course, it didn't take long for word to get out that the Penn/Madonna wedding would take place outdoors on the very visible Point Dume, Malibu, hilltop property of real estate developer Don Unger on 16 August 1985, at six p.m.

In the days before the ceremony, there was a great deal of acrimonious discussion regarding Sean's refusal to sign a prenuptial agreement. Madonna's handlers were adamant that she should not marry without first having a 'prenup' in place with her fiancé, and they pestered her until she finally – and, one might speculate, with some hesitation – asked Sean to sign one. He was adamant that he would do no such thing. 'I equated it to a death warrant in a marriage,' he explained, years later. Perhaps he knew that the request wasn't coming from Madonna; it was coming from attorneys and managers (whom he later referred to as 'a bunch of pathetic idiots who were accusing me of trying to cash in, move in on Madonna's money. It was completely ridiculous, and it really pissed me off.') Sean must have quickly become concerned about what would be in store for him as Madonna's husband. 'She had become a one person megacompany,' he said, 'and all of those people were on the telephone with her every day, to make sure I wasn't looking for cash, as if I didn't have my own career. Buncha' chumps.'

'Look, Sean, just sign the goddamn papers,' Madonna told him in front of one of her attorneys.

'Fuck you, Madonna,' he said, his tone acrid. 'I ain't signing nothing.'

'Then, I ain't marrying you,' she told him.

'Fine,' he said. 'Fuck you, anyway.'

'No,' she countered. 'Fuck you, Sean.'

'No,' he responded. 'Fuck you, Madonna.'

And on it went . . .

In the end, after all of the screaming and shouting, Sean did not sign a prenuptial agreement. The wedding plans were finalized, though to some observers it seemed that these two people barely liked each other, let alone loved one another. There wasn't much warmth between them. Sean was distant; Madonna aloof. They seemed to annoy each other. Still, the marriage was on. Perhaps in their quiet moments alone, out of the public eye, they shared something no one else was aware of, something that they may have interpreted as genuine love and trust: a foundation for a life together.

There was simply no way to ensure that the news of this marriage ceremony wouldn't somehow be leaked, despite the 'precautions'. Some of her friends joked that Madonna probably sneaked into a guest room and called the *National Enquirer* herself. In a matter of an hour, it seemed that practically every tabloid reporter in the Los Angeles area – more than a hundred of them in any case – congregated in front of Unger's $6.5 million estate, scheming to find ways to get a closer look, bribing caterers so that they could sneak onto the property. Media outlets began making deals with the locals to rent neighbouring houses so that cameras with telephoto lenses could be implemented for exclusive photographs.

The wedding ceremony – complete with a celebrity-driven guest list of more than two hundred (including Andy Warhol, Tom Cruise, David Letterman and Cher) – turned out to be a highly publicized fiasco. Not only was the property surrounded by press, but photographers were hanging from the trees. Earlier, Sean had tried to convince Madonna to allow the press a few quick photographs in private just to let some of the steam out of the event, but Madonna would not allow such a 'photo op'.

At first, the helicopters stayed 500 feet above the wedding. However, as soon as Madonna walked out of the house, they came dangerously close to the ground, whipping the hair of the female guests with the power from their rotating blades. A cursing Sean Penn ran around the perimeter of the seaside mansion with a gun, shooting at the eight helicopters circling above. Madonna looked stunned. The naked hatred etched on her groom's bitter face must have been a startling sight. 'I would have been very excited to see one of those helicopters burn and the bodies inside melt,' he later declared. 'They were non-people to me. I have never shot a firearm at anything I considered to be a life form.'

'I realized then,' Madonna would remember years later, 'that my life would never be the same.'

Madonna looked stunning in a strapless, white $10,000 wedding gown (created by her 'Like a Virgin' tour designer, Marlene Stewart), on the arm of her father, Tony, who gave her away. For some unknown, odd reason, under her veil – which she had to hold down to keep it from flying away – Madonna wore a black-rimmed hat. Under the hat, her hair was spun into a French twist. Sean wore a double-breasted $695 Gianni Versace suit. His tie was clumsily knotted. He had missed a few patches while shaving.

With their long dresses flying up, female guests began screaming as Madonna furiously shook her fists at the helicopters. 'Welcome to the remaking of *Apocalypse Now*,' said Sean Penn to the windswept guests. Then, the angry-looking bride and groom began shouting out their vows to Malibu judge John Merrik over the roar. In the middle of 'I do take you', Madonna jabbed her middle finger upwards. Sean's mouth was grimly set throughout the service.

The ceremony lasted five minutes, during which time the couple exchanged plain gilded rings. Penn then lifted his wife's veil, and to the accompanying theme from *Chariots of Fire*, he kissed her, as the guests stood and applauded. Afterwards, on a balcony a few feet above the guests, Sean toasted 'the most beautiful woman in the world'. Then, he was to remove his wife's $700 custom-made garter. Delicately, Madonna raised her gown so that Sean could find it. But, just as indelicately, Sean completely disappeared under the billowing skirts, where he acted as if he was scrambling about and having a difficult time finding the garter. Finally, he emerged with it. Madonna, her eyes twinkling, threw it out to the crowd, where it was caught by her sister, Paula, who was also her maid of honour. (She handed it over to the young daughter of Madonna's manager.)

The wedding dinner – lobster in a white cream sauce, swordfish and a mixed vegetable side dish – was then held under a large tent on the front lawn of the home (of course!), catered by Los Angeles chef (and owner of the famous Spago restaurant) Wolfgang Puck. Three fully stocked bars, each eight feet long, kept the guests distracted from the continual noise of the circling helicopters. No live band played at the wedding reception – much to the amazement of some of the guests such as Cher who, in a shocking purple spiked wig, said, 'What? She couldn't afford live entertainment? We have to listen to records? I could listen to records at home! And without helicopters!'

At the reception, Madonna danced with the guests to records by Prince and Michael Jackson. Meanwhile, Sean seemed glum and depressed, much as he had seemed at his bachelor party.

Later, acting as if she was in a sour mood, Madonna called the wedding a 'circus', as if that were a bad thing – a thing she hadn't counted on. 'Damn them,' she told one associate when speaking of the press's intrusion. 'Damn them all to hell for ruining my special day.'

'Really?' the associate asked her. 'You didn't expect all of this to happen?'

'I didn't say that,' Madonna answered, sheepishly. 'But damn them, anyway,' she concluded, with a smile. (Later, demonstrating either her sense of humour about the ceremony, or the fact that she really wasn't that upset about the way it turned out, she spoofed it hilariously on a *Saturday Night Live* sketch.)

In fact, Madonna had staged the ultimate press event. 'What better to get on the cover of *Time*. And *People*, and *Life*. And every other magazine,' Madonna's brother Martin Ciccone said. 'It was all calculated. She's a marketing genius, no question about that.'

'I thought it was a lovely affair,' observed her father, Tony, fifteen years later. Perhaps only a father would be able to overlook the fracas in order to see the beauty of his daughter, in white, marrying the man of her dreams. He recalled that, just before she married Sean, Madonna asked him, 'Are you proud of me, Daddy?'

'I have always been proud of you,' he told her.

'Daddy, that's not true,' she said. 'Just be honest with me, for once.'

'But why won't you just believe that I am proud of you?' he asked her.

Tony would later recall that Madonna had tears in her eyes as she answered, 'Because you never wanted any of this for me. You didn't even want me to be a dancer, let alone what I became. You just wanted me to stay home, go to college, get married and have children.'

It was difficult for Tony to comprehend the reasons for his daughter's statements. While it was true that he had wanted her to go to college, he had simply never shown as much indifference to her career as she had repeatedly maintained he had. It was clear that something else was wrong, that Madonna had feelings of anger towards him about another matter. However, because father and daughter had never truly communicated their emotions in an honest, direct manner, the real source of Madonna's resentment towards Tony would have to remain unaddressed.

'Well, you're getting married now, aren't you?' Tony Ciccone concluded. 'That's gotta count for something, doesn't it?'

Shanghaied

After the wedding, the newly-weds moved into a Spanish-style canyon villa in Malibu with a stunning view of the ocean. The estate chosen by Penn sat on fifty acres; surrounding hills shielded it from prying photographers. Just to be on the safe side, Penn hired contractors to build a wall around the property, topped with spikes. 'We're also going to have gun towers,' Sean said, and only half joking.

Ensconced in her safe haven, Madonna then tried her hand at married life, even making half-hearted attempts at doing housework. Sean was bemused to come home with friends and find the Queen of Pop washing dishes. Laughingly, he would introduce his sponge-wielding wife as one of the richest women in America.

Like most young couples, the Penns had their share of first-year challenges. Of course, the difference between their relationship and those of most others was that Sean's and Madonna's was played out in the public eye. Because they were, arguably, the most famous young couple in the world, their spats – many of which took place in front of strangers outside the privacy of their home – always made for splashy headlines. Young, glamorous, exciting to watch, and unpredictable in every way, they were constantly followed by the press, spied on in restaurants and reported about as they went about the business of screaming at each other in public, which seemed to be a commonplace occurrence. Madonna seemed to take the scrutiny in her stride. 'Well, you have to expect a certain invasion,' she said, 'such as people walking up to you on the streets. But I draw the line when I get to my house. People hang out at the bottom of our driveway a lot and ring our bell constantly. They want to see us. They think we're going to invite them in for a cup of tea or something.' Such intrusions drove the fiercely private Sean Penn to exasperation. In one interview, he scornfully observed, 'I hate it. I hate those people. I hate the whole goddamn thing.'

At this time, Sean entertained several ideas that would team him up with Madonna in a film. She wanted to be a movie star; he was already one. It seemed natural that he would help her to achieve her goal. Eventually, the couple settled on Beatle George Harrison's movie *Shanghai Surprise*. The film – about a missionary in China – seemed doomed almost from the start. The script was lousy, and soon after filming began (Madonna and Sean had to fly to Asia for the production) the Penns started making changes to the story. At first they had great faith in their director, but they soon grew to despise him.

'We had the wrong script, the wrong director [Jim Goddard] and the wrong stars,' George Harrison now says of the film. Of the Penns, he says, 'Don't ask.'

There was trouble off the set as well, as the Penns continued to engage in almost daily battles with the press. Although they were both highly paid stars who relied on the public's interest and support for their livelihoods, Sean Penn seemed determined to keep himself and his wife from the media; he regularly brawling with and spitting at reporters and photographers, she looking on, beaming and seemingly bemused. They were already being tagged 'the Poison Penns' by the time they flew to London for more work on the film.

Once back in America after the movie's completion, and against a backdrop of anger and hostility – towards each other as well as the outside world – the couple attended the premiere of Sean's latest movie, *At Close Range*, for which Madonna wrote and recorded a song for the soundtrack entitled, 'Live to Tell'. At the premiere, Madonna sported a new, gamine look: short hair, softer make-up and a short black cocktail dress. As they rushed into the theatre, a reporter asked Penn, 'Does your appearance tonight have anything to do with you trying to sort of patch things up with the press? Is that part of why you're here?' Sean stopped walking. He watched with a disgusted face as photographers jockeyed for position to get the best shot. Meanwhile, Madonna smiled broadly . . . this way . . . then that way . . . then this way, again . . . at the cameras that were pointed towards her. All about her, fans cheered and waved.

Considering the hoopla and interest surrounding the couple who had starred in it, the real surprise of *Shanghai Surprise* was that no one was interested in seeing it. *Rolling Stone* declared the film 'Madonna's first flop', after the $17 million film grossed an embarrassing $2.2 million. Producer George Harrison blamed Penn and Madonna for the film's failure. Both of the movie's stars had refused to breathe life into the anaemic box office by doing any publicity for it, and Madonna had even badmouthed it. 'The director turned out to not know what he was doing,' she complained. 'We were on a ship without a captain and we were so miserable while we were working on it that I'm sure it shows . . .'

'I had just gotten married,' she would say years later when talking about *Shanghai Surprise*. 'It was still really new to me, and my ex-husband was really kind of railroading his way into the whole project. Because I was in such awe of him, I kind of let him make a lot of the decisions that I shouldn't have allowed him to make. I was so green. I just found myself in a situation where I felt completely bullied and out of control, and I didn't know what was going on, and it was not pleasant.'

Of George Harrison, she observed, 'He's a sweet, hapless kind of character without a mean bone in his body.'

Sean was blunt about the experience, telling *Playboy*'s David Rensin, '[During filming] I just said, "I don't give a fuck." I just stayed drunk the whole fucking time. I was so pissed off and preoccupied with other things that it's the one time I took a movie entirely for the pay cheque.'

Friends noted that the failure of the movie marked the beginning of Madonna's ambivalence about her marriage to Penn. 'The fights were incessant,' says Todd Barash, a friend of Penn's at the time. 'She stuck around, I think, because she thought there might be an "up" side with the movie. But when the movie tanked, she began wondering what she was doing married to a temperamental guy who hated publicity.'

What Sean didn't know at the time – but found out many years later – is that Madonna would often have her press agents call the media ahead of time to alert them of dinner or movie plans the couple had made. Then, when they arrived at their destination to find themselves surrounded by photographers, Madonna would act chagrined.

'My understanding of the direction that Madonna was choosing was a misunderstanding,' Sean told David Rensin, choosing his words carefully. 'And to the degree to which she would be choosing, and chosen for, such an intense spotlight was not something that I had seen in the cards. So that was a surprise. It was a big surprise. I started to get the idea very shortly after we were together, but by then there's that heart thing that gets involved, you don't walk away so easily just because something is a little difficult. And you don't know how long certain things are going to last. That might have passed. It could have just neutralized itself.'

'When it all would blow up into a physical altercation between Sean and the media, she would become infuriated with him,' said Todd Barash. 'I was at their home the day after Sean had spat on a reporter, and he was still fuming about the incident. He was going on and on and, at one point, he said, "What I don't understand is how the hell these guys know our every fucking move. Everywhere we go, there's a sea of fucking cameras!"'

Madonna was preoccupied with something else, on her knees organizing books on a bottom shelf ('They must be in alphabetical order,' she had said, 'or how will we find anything?') when, under her breath, she observed, 'Well, look at who we are.' The tone of her voice was distant and bored, as if she had said these words to Sean many times in the past. 'We're stars, Sean. People take our picture. So, what's the big deal?'

According to Barash, Sean turned on Madonna. His face instantly crimson, he shouted, 'And you love it, don't you, Daisy? [His nickname for her was 'Daisy Cobb', which he had tattooed on one of his toes.] You can't get enough of it. You don't care how much it interferes with our lives, do you?'

Never one to back away from a good fight, Madonna stood and faced him. Immediately, she seemed to be trembling with rage; it never took long for her to meet Sean at his level. 'Look, I worked hard to get to a place where people care about me, and damn it, I'm going to enjoy every moment of it. So what? Get used to it, or get the fuck out!'

'One of these days, you're gonna have to choose,' Sean countered, glaring at her. 'It's gonna be me. Or them.'

Her eyes blazing, Madonna reached out and grabbed Sean's arm. She dug her nails into his skin. He twisted away from her and yelped. 'Jesus Christ, Madonna!' Sean took a breath and shook his head. 'You bitch,' he said, massaging his arm. 'I'm bleeding here. Look at this.'

Ignoring his small wound, Madonna narrowed her eyes and opened her mouth to say something, but then checked herself. She returned his angry look with a steady, unblinking gaze. Suddenly, the mood changed. Madonna sidled closer to Sean and ran her finger down the side of his cheek. She nuzzled his neck. 'I'm sorry, Sean,' she said. 'I choose you. Not them. You. I will always choose you.' She dropped her voice to a confidential whisper, her manner unexpectedly conciliatory, and said something in his ear. His face lit up with a grin. They embraced.

True Blue

It's been said that the third album is actually the most important one in an artist's career. Generally, recording companies aren't run by sentimental people. If a label asks an artist to record a third album, it is usually only because the first two were a success, not out of a sense of duty or loyalty. The debut album that finds an audience creates the need for a second album, which then serves to feed a suddenly acquired appetite. The role of a third album, however, is tricky and not so easily defined. The third time around, the artist can simply give his or her audience more of what was found on the last two albums and risk boring them, or explore new musical terrain and risk alienating them. Or, the artist can do what Madonna did with 1986's *True Blue*: build on the musical theme she'd already established in such an honest and creative fashion that the results actually reflect legitimate musical growth and maturity. She was getting a lot of attention because of her exploits with Sean Penn. However, there was more to Madonna than her headlines, and she wanted people to know as much. She was an artist and not a tabloid cartoon, though it was admittedly sometimes difficult for some of her public to reconcile the two.

In creating the recordings that were included on *True Blue*, Madonna again turned to Steve Bray, who obviously knew his ex-girlfriend's musical tastes well, in part because he actually helped to develop them. Of course, she knew his musical strengths too, which is why she turned to him when she wanted to create uptempo songs with a classic Top 40 commercial sensibility.

Madonna's other collaborator on the album was keyboardist/songwriter Patrick Leonard. Leonard had collaborated with her on 'Live to Tell'. Pleased with the outcome of that track, she decided that Leonard would be a great new musical voice with which to work. For the most part, Madonna worked with Bray and Leonard separately, with the three minds meeting only on one track.

One could sense that *True Blue* was a vehicle of growth for Madonna simply by looking at the cover artwork. The washed-out colour photograph of Madonna with her head tossed back and eyes closed in seductive meditation is understated, especially when compared to the sexier poses with which she had been associated in the past. The album's inner sleeve didn't feature any photographs at all, devoted instead only to song lyrics and production credits, an indication that Madonna may have wanted to be best represented by just her work.

'Papa Don't Preach', the album's opening track, began with an odd, classical-sounding synthesized string arrangement that gave way to an urgent, driving beat. The song was written by Brian Elliot with additional lyrics by Madonna. How incredible it must have been for an unknown songwriter like Elliot to one day answer the telephone and hear that Madonna wanted to record one of his songs. Even though she contributed some lyrics to the tune, according to the credits she didn't even take a percentage of the song's lucrative publishing points.

'Papa' tells the story of a young girl who suddenly finds herself pregnant and insists to her stern father that she is 'keeping my baby' and marrying her teenage lover. (The staid string arrangement at the beginning of the song might have been specifically designed to symbolize the parental authority of this girl's strict, doting father.) 'Papa Don't Preach', as produced by Madonna and Bray, succeeded in telling a dramatic tale in the time-honoured tradition of Top 40 tragic songs from the 1960s – such as Diana Ross and the Supremes's 'Love Child' and 'I'm Living in Shame', or either of pop/country artist Bobbi Gentry's hard-luck songs 'Ode To Billie Joe' or 'Fancy' (later recorded by country artist Reba McEntire). These kinds of records were usually about working-class people faced with simple but dramatic circumstances, songs that have the listener sitting on the edge of his seat while following the story and hoping for a happy ending. Madonna was rewarded for her skill at delivering such an intriguing tale – 'Papa Don't Preach', the first single from *True Blue* went to number 1 in the pop charts. ('Live to Tell', also featured on the album, had gone to number 1 before 'Papa', but it was from the soundtrack of Sean Penn's latest movie *At Close Range*.)

Before 'Papa Don't Preach' was even issued, Madonna alerted the media that the song was bound to be an eyebrow-raiser by announcing that it was 'a message song that everyone is going to take the wrong way'. The storm of publicity that Madonna had predicted occurred, of course, but in a way that may have surprised her. Conservative groups like Planned Parenthood, who had previously spoken out against Madonna's image, now applauded her for what they thought of as an anti-abortion song. Meanwhile, her liberal supporters blasted her. Other groups like 'NOW' attacked the song for (as they saw it) condoning teenage pregnancy. Magazines put her on the cover with headlines asking 'Should Papa Preach?' and 'Does Madonna's Hit Encourage Teenage Pregnancy?'

'It just fit right in with my own personal zeitgeist of standing up to male authorities, whether it's the pope or the Catholic Church or my father and his conservative, patriarchal ways,' Madonna would say of 'Papa' years later in 2009. 'There have been so many fallouts, they all get confused. But for "Papa Don't Preach" there were so many opinions – that's why I thought it was so great. Is she for "schma-smortion", as they say in *Knocked Up*? Is she against abortion?'

After two rather solemn singles, Madonna and Warner Bros. Records brightened matters for the fans by releasing the album's title song, 'True Blue', one of two light-hearted, fun tracks for the project written and produced by Madonna and Bray, that had a retro 1950s feel to it ('Jimmy Jimmy' was the other). 'True Blue' soared to number 3 on the pop charts, clearing the way for another number 1 for Madonna – Leonard's big, anthemic production of a song she penned (with writers Gardner Cole and Peter Rafelson), 'Open Your Heart'.

Madonna may not be remembered in the annals of pop music history for having the greatest singing voice ever to grace a recording. That voice, however, will most certainly be noted for its emotional quality. In her own way, Madonna sold 'Open Your Heart' as convincingly as Aretha Franklin sold 'Respect'; as heartfelt as Barbra Streisand rendered 'A House Is Not a Home'. The record couldn't help but go to number 1; it was a tune people could understand and latch on to – which is what makes a pop song memorable, when audiences adopt it and apply it to whatever they're going through every day.

Nevertheless, the pride of *True Blue* would turn out to be another collaboration with Leonard (and Bruce Gaitsch), the exotic 'La Isla Bonita'. An enchanting, uptempo Spanish-themed song with an equally enchanting melody, 'Bonita' was unlike any song Madonna had written or recorded before, its tropical attitude able to bring warmth even to the synthesized production. This romantic number went to number 4 in the pop charts. (The music track for this song, composed by Leonard, was originally intended for Michael Jackson, but he rejected it.) 'I don't know where that came from,' Madonna would say of 'La Isla Bonita. 'I don't know where San Pedro is. At that point, I wasn't a person who went on holidays to beautiful islands. I may have been on the way to the studio and seen an exit ramp for San Pedro.'

True Blue was rounded out by the dynamic groove 'Where's the Party', which harked back to her dance-floor roots and turned out to be the only track collectively produced by Madonna, Bray and Leonard; the confection 'Love Makes the World Go Round' and the uptempo 'White Heat' (dedicated to screen legend James Cagney).

For her 'True Blue' video, Madonna displayed a new look – leaner and blonder than ever before. Always searching for ways to improve herself, she had hired a personal trainer to assist her in a relentless exercise programme. With trainer and bodyguards in tow, she would run ten miles a day, no matter what the weather conditions, in the hills when in Los Angeles and through Central Park when in New York. After the run, she would continue her exercise regime by working out for another hour. She also took her diet seriously, sticking to a strict vegetarian menu with pasta and nuts, no junk food. Because of her gruelling schedule, her trainer tried to include foods in her diet that allowed a protein and carbohydrate base.

In the end, *True Blue*, which went to number 1 on *Billboard*'s album chart and would go on to become Madonna's most internationally successful album (selling five million copies in the USA alone, and another thirteen million worldwide) wasn't a great album. A less intriguing artist might not have survived it. Even the organic percussion work of the legendary Paulinho da Costa could not help the record's musical identity rise above the cold, synthetic sound so typical of the 'drum machine records' of the era. Nevertheless, several of its songs showed considerable artistic growth and fortitude on Madonna's part, keeping the Madonna phenomenon musically humming along.

Trouble in 'Paradise'

By mid-1986, twenty-eight-year-old Madonna's musical career was nothing if not monumentally successful; she couldn't have been happier by the results of her *True Blue* endeavour – artistically and commercially. Her personal life, however, was not as stellar; her marriage had fallen further into disrepair. The couple seemed to argue over everything, including her refusal to be tested for the HIV virus. At this time, there was much less known about the HIV virus, and also a great deal of discussion about the pros and cons of being tested for it. Today, Madonna – an AIDS activist – would most certainly suggest that a sexually active person be tested for the HIV virus, and often. However, in 1986, she seemed just as confused about the dangers of deadly HIV as most of the population.

'But why should I get tested?' she asked Sean in front of two people from her management company. She was preparing to take 'test shots' of the wardrobe that would be seen in a new video. Frustrated, she ran her hands through her new platinum pixie cut. 'What if I'm positive?' she asked. 'What then? I'm dead, right?'

'Well, if you're positive then at least I'll know, won't I?' Sean said, clearly annoyed at her.

'So, what are you saying?' Madonna pushed on. The two witnesses present became more uncomfortable by the exchange. 'Are you saying that you won't make love to me if I'm [HIV] positive?'

'Hell, yeah, that's what I'm saying.'

Madonna vanished. A few minutes later, she reappeared wearing a black corset tied tightly in the back with gilded breast cups, mesh stockings and high heels. She looked stunning. She could always manage to make the trashiest of outfits look classic. A designer's assistant walked out clutching what appeared to be a Norma Kamali fake leopard coat. 'Is this what you wanted?' he asked her, his tone tentative. Madonna ignored him.

'Well, then, all the more reason for me *not* to get tested,' Madonna said, picking up the argument as if she had never left the room.

Sean Penn took a beat to stare at his wife in her unusual wardrobe, perhaps admiring her elegance, her elusiveness, her impeccable style. She studied him, as well. Then, without releasing her gaze on him, Madonna snapped her fingers twice. A subordinate ran to her and placed a freshly lit cigarette between her lips. She puffed away. Sean smiled. 'That's my wife,' he said, dismissing the futile discussion in a tolerant fashion.

'Oh, screw you, Sean,' Madonna said from the corner of her mouth.

'Yeah, well,' he muttered, 'not until you get tested.'

In the summer of 1986, the epidemic hit home when artist Martin Burgoyne, a good friend and former room-mate of Madonna's from her New York days, was diagnosed with AIDS. Madonna was devastated. Earlier, as a surprise, Sean had flown Martin and Erica Bell out to Malibu from New York for a party to celebrate the release of 'Papa Don't Preach'. Madonna immediately noticed that Burgoyne was not himself. A few weeks later, he called her with the tragic news.

'She was beside herself,' says Melinda Cooper. 'From that point on, whenever Martin's name was mentioned, she would just begin to cry. She leased an apartment for him on Twelfth Street, so that he could be closer to St Vincent's Hospital, where he was being treated. She also arranged to take care of all of his medical bills, which would come to more than $100,000.'

As a last-ditch attempt to save Burgoyne, Madonna asked Sean to fly to Mexico to purchase an experimental drug there, one that was not available in the United States. She hoped the drug would 'cure' her friend. Of course, it didn't. Martin, only twenty-three, died in November 1986, just before Thanksgiving. At his bedside, Madonna held his hand until he passed away. She paid $4,000 for his memorial service.

Sean did what he could to console Madonna after Martin's

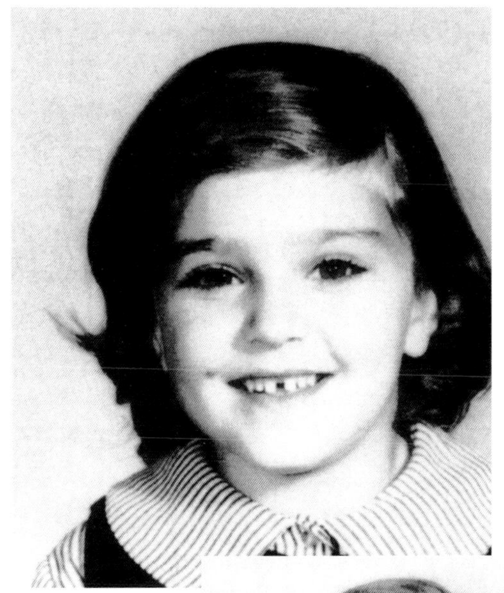

Madonna Louise Ciccone in 1963 at the age of five. This was the year she suffered the loss of her beloved mother.

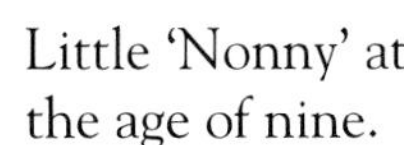

Little 'Nonny' at the age of nine.

Madonna at twelve.

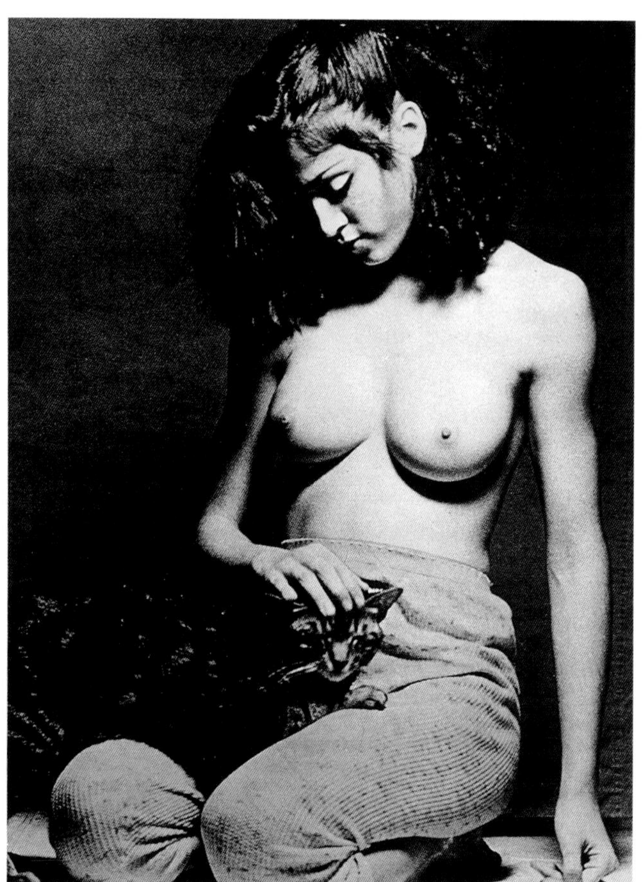

Left: Once in New York, Madonna posed in the nude for art students and photographers in order to make ends meet.

Below: Madonna's first film, *A Certain Sacrifice*. The first low-budget films made by many actresses are often not memorable and Madonna's is no different . . . with its finale featuring a human-sacrifice number.

Right: Working on the showbiz image . . . still a long way to go.

Below: Early, and innovative, Madonna. 'I just threw my look together,' she has said, 'with old rags and anything else I could find around the house.'

Above left: Madonna on her first major concert tour, spring 1985.

Above right: A thirty-year-old Madonna trying to collect her thoughts on the set of the 'Like a Prayer' video in 1988.

Left: Madonna performs 'Like a Virgin' at the MTV Music Awards, September 1984.

Above left: Perhaps a more conservative approach to image-making?

Above right: Getting the star treatment on the set of *Who's That Girl?*

Right: 'I've always loved performing,' Madonna has said. 'The give-and-take with an audience. If it's not about that, then, really what good is it?'

They became known as 'the Battling Penns' because of their turbulent marriage. Still, the love Madonna felt for Sean Penn was strong and certainly resilient.

With husband Sean Penn and George Harrison on the set of the doomed film, *Shanghai Surprise*, in 1986. Madonna played a missionary on a dangerous errand of mercy in China during the turbulent thirties.

Having fun with Sandra Bernhard. In 1988 the two stars enjoyed tantalizing the public with rumour and innuendo about their relationship. Sadly, Sandra is today hostile towards Madonna.

Just a simple girl at heart?

On stage during the 'Blond Ambition' tour, 1990.

death, demonstrating a tender, sympathetic side. However, his all too frequent jealous outbursts had become a significant problem.

One of the first signs that Sean's sometimes violent temper could be directed not only towards photographers but also towards his own wife had occurred before their wedding when he learned that she had once dated Prince. An argument about the rock star resulted in Sean punching a hole through the wall. Madonna has since said that she was stunned and frightened by the incident. 'That's when I first saw the appearance of the demon,' she said. 'I should have known then that there would be trouble.'

However, Freddy DeMann's assistant, Melinda Cooper, remembers a different story. 'I went over to their apartment one day to pick her up for a recording session, and there was this huge hole in the wall,' she says. 'So I asked Madonna what happened.'

Madonna told the story as if she was recounting the plot of an exciting soap opera on television. 'Oh my God, Melinda,' she said. 'Sean found out about me and Prince, and we had this amazing fight. I told him to fuck off, that I can do whatever I want. He was so mad, he left the house, and then I slammed the door behind him. Then, he came back in,' she continued, breathlessly, 'and, I swear to Christ, Melinda, he was so mad at me, he punched this hole in the wall. Look at that? Is that cool, or what?'

'That's cool?' Melinda asked, examining the hole. 'Madonna, that is not cool. That's scary.'

'What are you talking about?' Madonna enthused. 'I mean, how much must he love me, to punch a hole in the wall like that.' (A couple of days later, Madonna telephoned Prince and told him to come to her home and fix the hole, 'because you're responsible for it, after all'. As instructed, Prince showed up with plaster, and repaired the hole.)

Now that they were married, Madonna didn't think Sean's violent streak was so 'cool'. When he became angry, he would grab one of his guns and fire off a string of shots at rabbits or birds. He walked around the house with a loaded .22 tucked into the back of his pants, which seemed, to Madonna's concerned friends if not to the lady herself, a form of emotional abuse.

One close friend of Sean's recalls what happened at a dinner party at the Penns' home. 'We were at the pool. Sean had a little too much to drink. Madonna did, too. There was a guy there who had been eyeing her all night. Madonna went over and started flirting with him.'

'What's this all about?' Sean said bitterly as he walked over to them.

'Oh, get lost, Sean,' Madonna told him. 'We're just talking.'

Without a second's hesitation, Sean picked up his wife and, in one quick motion, threw her into the pool. The crowd of about thirty seemed stricken. As they watched, Madonna swam leisurely to the shallow end of the pool and then climbed its few steps. Dripping wet and without saying a word, she walked across the patio and into the house. 'She never came back out,' recalls the friend.

Earlier in 1986, Madonna and Penn were dining at Helena's, one of their favourite restaurants in Los Angeles, when an old friend, David Wolinsky (from the group, Rufus Featuring Chaka Khan), approached her at their table, bent over and gave her an innocent kiss in greeting. Immediately enraged by the gesture, Penn leapt from his chair and attacked Wolinsky, beating and kicking him. The attack ended only when shocked onlookers managed to restrain Penn. Madonna was humiliated. 'She looked like she wanted to crawl into a hole,' recalled one witness. 'I remember watching her as she glared at Sean and thinking to myself, she's starting to hate him.'

'He was a hothead,' says David Wolinsky. 'I did nothing but greet his wife, someone I knew before he had married her. It was completely unprovoked. I wondered what she was doing married to that creep.'

Though her marriage with Sean seemed to be falling apart, she wasn't able to focus completely on repairing it for she was a busy woman with a thriving career. Constantly, she was distracted by the business at hand. 'There's no time to figure out how to handle Sean,' she despaired. 'I barely have time to sleep.'

Sean Penn had bounced back after the *Shanghai Surprise* fiasco and was busy at work on a gritty cop film, *Colors*, with Dennis Hopper. Meanwhile, Madonna was considering several scripts for herself. Influenced by her love for old Hollywood, she was keen to do a remake of Judy Holliday's smash 1950 comedy *Born Yesterday*, or Marlene Dietrich's star-making role in the 1929 drama *The Blue Angel*. As for new scripts, she was offered something called *Blind Date* and an early version of *Evita* (which would remain in development for years). However, she was most eager to appear in a film that had a Carol Lombard screwball-comedy flavour to it. Called *Slammer*, it was about a madcap blonde, Nikki Finn (Madonna), who, after being released from jail for a crime she did not commit, sets out to find the man who framed her. The usual screwball complications ensue, including chase scenes, mobsters and a 160-pound cougar. A deal was made; filming began in New York. Perhaps because Sean was now awaiting sentence on the assault charges, the name of the movie was changed from *Slammer* (which, her handlers reasoned, was where Penn was destined) to *Who's That Girl?*

Meanwhile, in Los Angeles, Sean's volatile temper continued to get him in trouble when he attacked a thirty-two-year-old actor on the set of *Colors*. As the young extra knelt on the sidelines with a camera, hoping for a good shot, Sean appeared from seemingly nowhere. He knocked the camera from the extra's hands. 'You bastard,' Sean snarled, 'don't take any pictures of me between takes.' Then, he punched him in the face.

Who's That Girl?

Although Madonna would publicize the movie heavily, posing for many magazine covers *à la* Marilyn Monroe, *Who's That Girl?* would go on to become another box-office bomb, no doubt because its star was trying so hard to be so many different things she was not. By appropriating a Judy Holliday voice, along with Marilyn Monroe's hair and make-up for a movie that seemed somehow designed for Carole Lombard, Madonna proved she was not up to any of the tasks at hand. *Variety* called the film 'a rattling failure', while most of the other reviews were no better.

So far on the screen, Madonna had been most successful in *Desperately Seeking Susan*, a film in which she had exploited so many of her own personal characteristics – in essence playing herself. Had she continued to brand her performances with her own unique and, by now, identifiable persona (at least until she was more skilled at developing characters), her movie career might have ignited in the same way as her musical career. However, in trying to create a popular character for *Who's That Girl?* by imitating her movie idols rather than using her own personality, Madonna just came across as annoyingly cloying. 'I don't like that movie,' she would say in February 2000. 'Don't like my performance in it. Any other movie I did, I would say there are things in it that are good. Or I think my performance was good, but the movie wasn't. *Who's That Girl?* I think all of it was pretty bad.'

If Madonna was worried that the failure of the movie meant that her star was fading, she needn't have been concerned. After all, she still had that amazing recording career.

As soundtracks go, 1987's *Who's That Girl?* was not much of one in the conventional sense, but rather a collection of nine songs from the movie. While Madonna only had four songs on the album, each was important because, conceivably, it meant the album could sell on the strength of Madonna's presence, alone. After three hit albums, her presence was certainly formidable. Still a fresh commodity and successful at her career, twenty-nine-year-old Madonna was not only one of the hottest artists in popular music, but one with obvious and incredible staying power. *Who's That Girl?* was a relatively low-budget film with a cast of actors who weren't going to be receiving Oscars anytime in the near future, so to Warner Bros. Records, the soundtrack was at least as important as the film.

When Madonna was presented with the challenge of writing and producing the film's title song, she got together with Steve Bray and Patrick Leonard, her co-writers/producers, and went to work. Meanwhile, other slots in the album were filled mostly by obscure Warner Bros. Records' acts, like Club Nouveau, Michael Davidson and Scritti Politti.

It was of course Madonna who delivered the hits that kept the *Who's That Girl?* soundtrack out of record-store bargain bins. The title track and first single, written and produced by Madonna with Leonard, were quintessential Madonna music – funky, sassy and melodic, with a Latin accent. It wasted no time in going to number 1 on the *Billboard* singles charts.

The soundtrack's second single, Bray's party 'groove', 'Causing a Commotion', did just that on both international dance floors and the US singles chart, climbing all the way to number 2. The other two Madonna tracks – 'The Look of Love', an exotic Madonna/Leonard ballad, and the uptempo dance number, 'Can't Stop', another Madonna/Bray creation – were strategically left on the soundtrack album to induce LP sales. It worked. The *Who's That Girl?* album ended up selling more than a million copies in the United States and five million worldwide.

Riding on Madonna's coat-tails proved profitable for everyone involved, including Warner Bros. Records, which notched up big sales with a compilation that was basically a showcase for its marginal artists; the artists and producers themselves, most of whom were never involved in a project as successful, before or since. For Peter Guber and Jon Peters, the film's producers, the album's brisk sales served as the bright spot in a film enterprise whose overall success could be deemed modest at best.

Meanwhile, it was during 1987's 'Who's That Girl?' tour that the public first saw Madonna's new updated, sleek look in concert – a look uncluttered by bangles, jewellery and other accessories (although Mr Blackwell would still add her to his infamous list of worst dressed women that year).

The 'Who's That Girl?' tour was musically and technically superior to Madonna's first concert appearances in that she incorporated multimedia components to make the show even more compelling. For example, huge video screens projected images of the Pope and Ronald Reagan as she belted out 'Papa Don't Preach'. She had more confidence in her stage presence, her music was showing a deeper maturity, her voice was fuller, and the show was expertly choreographed with complicated numbers. She was mobbed in London and in Japan a thousand troops had to restrain a crowd of 25,000 hysterical fans who turned up to greet her at the airport.

Many artists become difficult and unreasonable when they reach superstar status, and Madonna was no different. For instance, during some of the 'Who's That Girl' tour, she wouldn't allow crew members to talk directly to her; they had to talk to her representatives lest they distract her from the business at hand. She has, to this day, a difficult time giving names to faces and so, rather than struggle to do so, she'd rather not meet anyone she's not going to have to know for a long period of time. (Early in her career, there were times when she wasn't able to remember the names of lovers the morning after. One assistant who accompanied Madonna during evenings on the town would be sure to place a note on her kitchen counter with the consort's name written on it, just in case she forgot.)

Her dancers too were told never to address her directly, a far cry from the rapport she would establish with her troupe later, on the 'Blond Ambition' tour; they were told to direct any requests to her 'people'. Her musicians were not permitted even to look at her, unless they were on stage with her. Moreover, when coming on and off the stage, Madonna asked that her road managers hold sheets around her in order to shield her from the eyes of those backstage who she felt couldn't help but stare at her. Her dressing rooms at each stop along the way had to be redecorated to her specifications with new carpeting, fresh paint (always pink), new furniture and so much Mexican food it would have taken an army to eat it all. 'She has a way of demanding that compels you to give her your undivided attention,' Freddy DeMann says, diplomatically.

One evening, at a very late hour, DeMann's assistant, Melinda Cooper, received a telephone call from Madonna. She was expecting a limousine to take her to a party, and it hadn't yet arrived.

'The goddamn car isn't here, yet,' Madonna said, fuming. 'It's, like, fifteen minutes late, Melinda.'

'It'll be there, soon,' Melinda recalls replying patiently.

'Why, you idiot,' Madonna screamed at her through the telephone. 'It's your job to get the limousine here on time, Melinda! Do you know how much I have to do?' she asked, her temper rising. 'I have a lot to do, Melinda, and all you have to do is get the car here on time. And can you do it? No you can not. What in the world is wrong with you, Melinda?'

'But, Madonna . . .' Melinda began.

'Don't "But Madonna" me,' she said, interrupting her. 'Look, here's the deal: if the fucking car isn't here in five minutes, you're finished.'

Madonna hung up.

Melinda Cooper burst into tears.

You Can Dance

In November 1987, Warner Bros. Records quickly followed 'Who's That Girl?' with the one-two punch of *You Can Dance*.

In any business, there's nothing quite like the windfall created by being able to sell something to somebody twice and, in the recording industry, popular music is the gift that keeps on giving. At the major record labels, greatest hits and catalogue sales packages (the various albums in an artist's career) have always accounted for a good portion of annual profits. In the 1980s, something else came along to enhance the companies' bottom lines: the 'remix album'. Thanks to the popularity of post-disco dance music, many fans now wanted to hear how some of their favourite songs would sound if the music was reworked, or 'remixed', to enhance the song's danceability.

Remix albums – collections of already popular songs enhanced in the studio to alter their tempo and sound – are common today, but in the 1980s it was a revolutionary concept.

By the Eighties, with post-disco dance music in full swing, the remix concept had truly come into its own. By then, several artists' tracks were being remixed and compiled to make up an album. Madonna, the most important dance artist of the period, led the charge with *You Can Dance*, a compilation of remixes of six of her more uptempo songs.

How does one bring more 'danceability' to songs that were crafted specifically to get people on to dance floors in the first place? Probably by hiring remixers who are most familiar with the material, in this case, Jellybean Benitez. Also on board was Shep Pettibone, a popular remixer who'd earlier engineered more dance rhythm into Madonna's single, 'True Blue'.

You Can Dance made one point clear about Madonna. While she was evolving into a serious pop star, musically she still knew how to host the best party. The new and pumped-up versions of 'Holiday' (two different versions), 'Everybody', 'Physical Attraction', 'Over and Over', 'Into the Groove' and 'Where's the Party' took *You Can Dance* to number 14 on *Billboard*'s pop album chart. To further entice music fans, *You Can Dance* also featured 'Spotlight', a previously unreleased track recorded during the *True Blue* sessions. The album's performance both in the charts and in the clubs served as a testament to the quality of the material and the enduring appeal of Madonna.

With *You Can Dance*, Madonna may not have initiated a trend but she certainly played her part in jump-starting it. Soon, major acts of the day were following suit with remix LPs of their own, including Bobby Brown's 'Dance . . . Ya Know It!' and New Kids on the Block's 'No More Games/Remix Album'.

'I don't know that I like it,' she would say, 'people screwing with my records, remixing them. The jury is out on it for me. But the fans like it, and really, this one was for the fans, for the kids in the clubs who like these songs and wanted to hear them in a new, fresh way.'

At the time of the release of 'You Can Dance' in November 1987, Sean Penn had disappeared from Madonna's life for a number of days. She was frantic with worry. Then, he turned up unexpectedly at her New York apartment, expecting to spend Thanksgiving with her there. She probably didn't know whether to be furious or relieved. She chose the former. 'You're not spending Thanksgiving here,' she told him. She then informed him that she had already instructed her lawyers to draw up divorce papers. (Her attorneys filed those divorce papers on 4 December 1987. Twelve days later, though, Madonna would withdraw them.)

'She was completely distraught,' said a friend. 'She could see that the marriage was over, and she was really starting to get scared. "I don't want a divorce," she told me, "but I don't know what else to do. I'm starting to really hate him. You know that saying that there's a thin line between love and hate?" she asked. "Well, I think I've crossed it. It's very ugly on the other side, too."

Perhaps one of the reasons Madonna had such a particularly strong reaction to the problems caused by Sean was that her nerves were frayed by the discovery of a lump on her breast shortly before Thanksgiving. Because of her mother's death, Madonna has always been conscientious about self-examination for signs of cancer. When she found the lump, she feared the worst and called Dr Jerrold Steiner, a respected Beverly Hills specialist, to make an appointment. She was so upset that she was unable to drive herself to his office and asked her secretary to take her. After examining her, the doctor told her to watch the lump and look for any changes in texture or size. He also suggested seeing her in two weeks to conduct tests. Madonna couldn't help but be frantic. Two weeks seemed an eternity to wait to handle something that so frightened her. Yet, she was so scared that she cancelled the appointment and decided just to, as she put it to one friend, 'sit still and try to figure out how to handle this'.

No doubt, her troubled marriage did little to ease her nerves at this time. Madonna spent Thanksgiving with her sister, Melanie, in Brooklyn while Penn flew back to Los Angeles, where he indulged in a drinking binge. While she didn't say much about the scary lump during the holidays, Madonna did confide to friends that she was confused as to how to handle Sean and his erratic temper. Neither was really mature enough to be able to understand, or help, the other deal with the anger, hurt and insecurities that had turned them into the so-called 'Battling Penns'. 'I'm ashamed of how we turned out,' Madonna told her friend. Then, perhaps romanticizing the past, she added, 'I think back on our wedding and how wonderful that was. Then, I look at today, and I think, it's all turned to shit, hasn't it?'

Kennedy

All artists are inspired by others, but perhaps no modern-day entertainer has borrowed as much from so many and with so few alterations as Madonna. Although her hard-as-nails personality, ambition and canny sense for publicity and business are all her own – her 'reinventions' of her persona were more often than not inventions created by someone else and then borrowed for a Madonna makeover. In various points in her videos, movies, interviews, and photo sessions of the 1980s and into the '90s, we saw heavy traces of Marlene Dietrich, Judy Holliday, Twiggy and Lana Turner in her looks and attitudes. Even lesser known performers such as Edie Sedgwick, Andy Warhol's decadent star of the Sixties who starred in his underground films and died of a drug overdose at an early age, had a big influence on Madonna's various projects. But perhaps the biggest influence on early Madonna's career was Marilyn Monroe, the sex symbol from a generation earlier. Fans of both stars couldn't help but notice the impact Monroe had on Madonna's career, in everything from hair and make-up, expressions and poses for the camera – some of Madonna's most famous photo sessions are exact replicas of Monroe's – all the way to paraphrased quotes she gave in interviews.

Some critics commented that during the filming of *Who's That Girl?* Madonna looked as if she had stepped right off the set of *The Seven Year Itch*, one of Monroe's most famous movies – although Madonna did add a contemporary element to the look with a leather jacket. Sandra Bernhard, who was at one time close to Madonna, went as far as saying that 'she thinks she *is* Marilyn Monroe'. (One of Madonna's funniest and most clever moments on television occurred in 1993 during a sketch on *Saturday Night Live* when she spoofed Marilyn's 'Happy Birthday' song to President John F. Kennedy, complete with skin-tight gown and bouffant blonde wig.)

Through the years, John F. Kennedy Jun. – son of the late President of the United States – had also expressed his own interest in Marilyn Monroe, with whom his dad had famously indulged in an extramarital affair. When John started his own magazine, *George*, he astonished many observers by featuring Drew Barrymore on the cover of one of the issues dressed as Marilyn in a replica of the gown Monroe wore the night she sang 'Happy Birthday' to his father at Madison Square Garden in 1962. Many people were surprised that Kennedy would pay homage to a woman who had been so linked with his father, but he felt the imagery was fair game because the assignation had become such an indelible part of American iconography.

Madonna and John either met at a party in New York in December 1987, as John had said, or at a 'fitness salon' that same month, as Madonna has recalled. What we do know is that after an early date, the dashing, dark, muscular Kennedy gave her a set of keys to his apartment. According to what Madonna once told a friend, John walked into his new apartment shortly thereafter to find her lounging on the couch wearing nothing but sheets of clear plastic wrap, the kind purchased in the supermarket. He said later that he couldn't believe his eyes. After a beat, Madonna smiled lasciviously at him and purred, 'Dinner's ready, John-John.' (The press always referred to him as John-John, but family or friends never did.) That night, they laughed and danced and drank great quantities of wine.

Later, another oft-told story would have it that, while making love to her, John would apply peanut butter to her legs, and then lick it off. 'Nonsense!' Madonna said when asked if this story was true. 'Do you know how many calories are in peanut butter? Low fat whipped cream, yes. But not peanut butter.'

She may have found him fascinating, but she was not yet close enough to John Kennedy Jun. to discuss the troubling lump in her breast that had ruined her holidays. No doubt it was on her mind. To whom could she turn?

One lonely evening, she picked up the telephone and called the one person she felt closest to, despite the shattered state of their relationship. Though there was such acrimony between them – and had always seemed to be, even before they were married – she still sensed that the one person who knew her best and could tell her what to do about this dizzying scare was Sean.

'Sean was distraught to hear about the lump,' says his friend, actor Stephen Sterning. 'He told her that she simply had to have it looked at, have a biopsy done. He later said that she was crying on the telephone, saying she was frightened and didn't know what to do. So he offered to go with her, and that's what he did. They went to the doctor together. She had the biopsy. A few days later it came back negative. She was fine.'

Said Sean at the time, 'Nothing sobers a man like knowing your wife might have cancer. I finally got the message that I had to get serious about my life, about Madonna's life, about our marriage.' He now believed that if they could only recapture the sexual passion they had felt for each other at the beginning of their relationship, she might change her mind and not divorce him. Still, he was not naive. He knew they had problems. 'Ultimately, we had different value systems,' he would say to writer David Rensin.

However, for Madonna, it was too late in 1988 to recapture anything with Sean. As much as she appreciated his support during a tough time – perhaps one of the most difficult in her recent memory – she felt that it would take more than the occasional medical crisis to keep them together. He had been the only real love of her life, but she was no longer comfortable being with him. She understood him all too well. Says Sterning, 'She told Sean that she loved him, still, but because of their differences, there was no way they should be together. She said that the cancer scare made her see even more clearly that life was too short not to be completely happy. Sean had to agree, actually. I think that little crisis made them both see the light . . . and, ironically, maybe in seeing that light it somehow brought them closer together as it pushed them closer to divorce.'

'Will you look at how handsome Johnny is,' Madonna asked a friend over a martini lunch. She was holding a colour photograph of Kennedy – a close-up – which she had carefully clipped from a gossip magazine. His face was raw-boned and lean. If ever a person had 'bedroom eyes', this was the guy. 'Have you ever seen a man this handsome? Look at his face. Look at his hair.'

Many years later, her friend ('Don't use my name or Madonna will kill me') would recall Madonna saying, 'He's unbelievable. A perfect specimen. And look at that body. Who has a body like that? He's a god,' she concluded with a sigh.

Again, her friend had to agree.

'Finally, I'm dating someone respectable, someone the public loves, someone I can be proud to be with,' Madonna said. She signalled the waiter to bring her and her friend another round. 'Can you see John Kennedy beating someone up and humiliating me in public. Now *that* would never happen.'

'But what about Sean?' her friend asked. 'You're still married.'

Madonna's smile quickly faded. She folded the magazine photograph into quarters and put it away safely. 'I don't know what to say about Sean,' she said with a frown. 'I love him. I'll always love him. He's the one person who knows the real me. But it's over. Oh,' she concluded, wistfully, 'to be a Kennedy. Do you think they have the kinds of problems I have?'

It seemed that 'Johnny' felt the same about her. After a few months, as the relationship continued, he pinned posters of Madonna on to the walls of his Manhattan bachelor apartment, and began to shed his Ivy League wardrobe for a look that he thought was more punk, and one that she would prefer: leather jackets, ripped jeans, spiked hair. He even grew a goatee, which looked terrific and just a bit edgy. After a few months, John seemed to become all but consumed by his fascination with Madonna. He told Thomas Luft, a college friend from Hyannisport, that he couldn't stop thinking about her. 'It's like she put a spell over me,' he said. 'I'm a little obsessed with her.'

Madonna acknowledged that she now couldn't help but fantasize about divorcing Sean and marrying into the affluent and influential Kennedy family (a fantasy that the troubled Marilyn Monroe had often related in the last few years of her life). 'To have a Kennedy baby was a goal Madonna had set for herself,' says her former manager, Camille Barbone, 'and I heard from good sources that she did what she could to interest John in the proposition.'

Sean had been a lot of trouble. She loved him, but how much more could she take, she must have reasoned. John was smart, sophisticated and . . . sensible. However, there would be one major stumbling block to the continuation of any romance between her and the heir to so-called Camelot – and, as it happened, it would come in the form of the same woman who had put the kibosh on the President's affair with Marilyn Monroe: Jackie Kennedy Onassis. Indeed, any woman in John Jun.'s life prior to this point had always been measured by a formidable standard: his mother's.

Steven Styles, a good friend of John's who attended Brown University with him, recalled: 'He telephoned me one day and sounded uncharacteristically depressed. He eventually confessed that he had fallen in love with a married woman who was a very celebrated personality. Conflicted, he said he didn't know what to do. He was torn by his desire for this woman and his need to conform to societal pressure that he find the so-called "right girl", someone of whom his mother and the other Kennedys would approve. And he said, "Believe me when I tell you that this is not the right girl." I asked him who she was. When he told me, you could have knocked me over with a feather. It was Madonna.

'He asked me if I wanted to be with him when he told his mother. I told him, "John, I actually would prefer to be almost anywhere else."'

Jackie Refuses to Meet Madonna

Jacqueline Kennedy Onassis was already well aware of the whisperings that something romantic was going on between her only son and Madonna. She used to purchase all the tabloids and other papers at a news-stand in the lobby of the publishers Doubleday's Fifth Avenue offices (where she worked as an editor) to keep up on current events, and that's where she first read about the growing romance. She quickly made it clear to John that she did not approve.

Thomas Luft, whose mother was close to Jackie, said, 'He couldn't decide if he was intrigued by her because he liked her, or because Jackie *didn't* like her – not that Jackie ever met her. He said, "I don't want to string her along if I'm really just rebelling against Mother." His therapist had told him that Madonna represented insurrection to him, not romance.'

For her part, what most fascinated Madonna about John was his complete lack of pretence. 'We were exercising with her, running through Central Park one day,' recalled Stephen Styles. 'She had four bodyguards trailing her. John, of course, had none. It was so ludicrous, I said to him, "Why is it that she needs all of that security and you don't need any?" He laughed and facetiously answered, "I may be a Kennedy but she's *Madonna*!"'

'He always introduced himself as just John, never John Kennedy, Jun.,' another college friend, Richard Wiese, remembers. 'The word "Kennedy" never came willingly off his lips. He downplayed it as much as possible . . .'

'Johnny, do you know how big a star you could be if you only acted like a Kennedy instead of just any other person?' Madonna told him. She was nearly unrecognizable in a baseball cap, scruffy hair, and a T-shirt belted outside cycling shorts. She was chewing gum, as John liked to say, 'like it's going out of style'. She said, 'I mean, my God! You could be absolutely huge!'

'Oh, don't worry about me. I'm huge enough,' John said, with a grin. He, too, was in tight biking shorts and a simple white T-shirt. A baseball cap was turned boyishly backwards. His chiselled cheeks were shadowed by two days' growth of beard. 'I don't want to be a star,' he said, dark eyes dancing. 'I'm just me.'

Madonna seemed stunned. 'But how could anyone not want to be a star?' she asked.

'Count me out,' John said, still jogging. 'You can be the star in this family.' Then, with a grin back at her, he sprinted off.

When John finally told Jackie that he had fallen for Madonna, she made it clear that she was unhappy about it. If Madonna had been single, perhaps Jackie would have been better able to deal with the relationship (though, no doubt, she would still have been unhappy with Madonna's sexually charged image). She didn't want to have to deal with the scandal it would have caused if word had got out that John was dating a married woman. Also, according to those who knew her, she had heard stories – many of which were probably true – about Sean Penn's temper. She feared for her son's safety. But, says Thomas Luft who witnessed the scene, John told Jackie, 'Mother, I can take that loud-mouthed little punk Penn blindfolded and with one arm tied behind my back.' 'And he could have, too,' said Luft. Jackie shivered at the thought. 'Oh, great! That's all I need, John,' she said, 'seeing you led away in handcuffs for getting into a fight with that hooligan. Don't you dare!'

'I was there at her home on Martha's Vineyard when Jackie told John, "I need you to think about this, carefully. Madonna may be a nice girl, but until she is single, she will be nothing but trouble,"' says Thomas Luft.

'But I like her,' John said, trying to reason with Jackie. 'She's intelligent. You should know her, mother. You're an editor! She's just the kind of woman you would find fascinating.'

Luft says that Jackie rolled her eyes and shook her head in dismay. 'My goodness, there are millions of intelligent women on this planet, John,' she told him. 'And you have to go out with the only one who calls herself a "Material Girl"? I just don't understand it. I mean, really!'

'John got angry,' says Luft. 'Even though I was standing right there, and he never talked back to his mother in front of others, he shot back, "Mother, let me ask you this: who in this world has been more materialistic than you?"'

Luft recalls that Jackie shot him a look. Then, without warning, tears came to her eyes. She rushed from the room. John was immediately overwhelmed by regret. 'Mother, please, I didn't mean that,' he said, following her. 'I'm sorry.' Then, for the rest of the day, he was angry with himself. 'How could I be so stupid and mean,' he said. 'Stupid, stupid, stupid,' he muttered, chastising himself.

With Sean Penn in Asia filming *Casualties of War*, Madonna was free to explore a number of life options. In her personal life, there was the possibility of a long-term relationship with John Kennedy, though that seemed a long shot. As adorable as he may have been, she would later have to admit that something was 'missing'. She liked strong-willed, powerful men. John seemed too reliant on his mother, his family, for strength. She needed time to marshal her thoughts, but it did seem that her future with John had its limitations.

Professionally, Madonna was considering a Broadway show which, she hoped, would allow her to shine so brightly that she would be able to eradicate the memory of the many bad reviews generated by her last two films. She wanted to prove that she could act. Film director Mike Nichols had mentioned to her a part in David Mamet's *Speed the Plow*. Madonna was a huge fan of Mamet's earlier works and has said that she went after the role in his new play 'with a vengeance'. She personally called Mamet and requested an audition.

The plot of *Speed the Plow* involved a plain, seemingly naive secretary, Karen (Madonna), who comes between two movie moguls (Joe Mantegna and Ron Silver) known for their production of surefire, commercial Hollywood films. Mantegna bets Silver $500 that he can bed Karen. However, she turns the tables by seducing him. She then tries to convince him to put up the money to turn a brainy, pretentious book she has been reading, one with absolutely no commercial appeal, into a film. Mesmerized by the dynamic woman masquerading as a plain office worker, he agrees to her request – almost enabling Karen to destroy the commercial deal that Mantegna and Silver virtually have in the bag. Madonna described her character as, 'honest, sincere and naive, and hungry for power, like everybody else'. Her observation proved that, at first,

Madonna didn't even realize that her character was not what she seemed to be; she was anything but naive. 'It was a real mind-fuck of a script,' she discovered midway through rehearsals. 'Little did I know that everyone else involved saw me as a vixen, a dark evil spirit.'

Whether or not Madonna agreed with the interpretation of the role, her name on the marquee meant big business for the show. It sold out for six months in advance, which meant millions of dollars in ticket sales. Although the three-character play did much to confirm Madonna's drawing power, it did little to reverse critical reaction to her acting skills. Madonna's opening night on 3 May 1988 at the Royale Theater in New York City attracted celebrities such as Brooke Shields, Jennifer Grey, Jennifer Beals, Tatum O'Neal, Christie Brinkley and Billy Joel.

While the critics praised the play, they panned Madonna. 'She moves as if she were operated by a remote control unit several cities away,' said Dennis Cunningham of CBS, adding that 'her ineptitude is scandalously thorough'. John Simon of *New York* magazine complained that 'she could afford to pay for a few acting lessons'. The *Washington Post*'s David Richards said simply, 'she's the weakest thing in it'. Madonna, though, was happy with her performance. 'It's like having really good sex,' she said of the experience.

'I hated to love it and I loved to hate it,' she said, later. 'It was just gruelling having to do the same thing every night, playing a character who is so unlike me. I didn't have a glamorous or flamboyant part. I was a scapegoat. That's one of the things that attracted me to it. Still, night after night, the character failed in the context of the play. To continue to fail each night and to walk off that stage crying, with my heart wrenched . . . it just got to me after a while.'

Also in that first night audience, perhaps to check out her son's latest romantic interest, was Jackie.

'John told me that Jackie thought she was "fascinating",' said Stephen Styles. 'I asked him, "What does that mean?" and he laughed. "That's mother's way of saying that Madonna isn't her cup of tea," he said.'

'Madonna didn't know Jackie was in the house [the theatre],' said Diane Giordano. 'If she had known, as fascinated as she was with Jackie, she might have had trouble going on, she would have been that nervous.'

After the show, when Madonna *was* told that Jackie had been in the audience, she waited backstage for an hour, hoping the former First Lady would come back and say hello. She had applied a pale, almost white foundation to her face, which contrasted dramatically with her bright red lips. Carefully she pencilled her eyebrows and then shaded her beauty spot. She pulled her dark hair back severely and dressed in a natty, grey, pinstriped Armani trouser suit with a white silk blouse – buttoned all the way to the top. Three friends joined her. Someone fixed martinis. Then they waited . . . and waited. Jackie never showed up.

Later, Madonna would say that Jackie's absence backstage 'ruined' her opening night. 'The only reason a person doesn't come backstage after a show is if they didn't like what they saw and don't know how to tell you that,' Madonna said, sadly. 'If I had only known she was out there, I swear to God, I would have been much, much better. I would have tried so much harder. Why didn't Johnny tell me she was coming?'

Madonna loved a good icon, always had. She was such an admirer of Jackie's, she desperately wanted her approval, especially now that she was dating her son. She was certain, she told friends, that she would be able to convince Jackie that she wasn't as notorious as the former First Lady believed her to be. However, Jackie steadfastly refused to meet her. 'How can she not take my calls?' a perplexed Madonna was reported as having said. 'Doesn't she know who I am?'

In July 1988, Madonna pleaded with John to arrange a meeting with his mother. How fascinating it was to anyone who knew Madonna that this young woman, who had achieved so much in such a short time and who did not seem to be intimidated or impressed by anybody, was now so fixated on the notion of meeting Jackie. It was as if nothing else in her life mattered if she couldn't have the approval of this one person.

Two other people were present at John's Upper West Side apartment in New York with John and Madonna while they engaged in a conversation about meeting Jackie. John was in red sweats and a black T-shirt with the words 'Man Power' emblazoned across his chest in big, white letters. In an odd contrast of fashion, Madonna wore a slinky, short black dress that appeared to be designed by Yves Saint Laurent, with heels. She was smoking. John never smoked. He asked Madonna why she was so certain his mother would be interested in meeting her. His tone, the witnesses recall, was sarcastic and inconsiderate.

Madonna, as per usual, was unruffled. 'She'd want to meet me because I'm Madonna,' she said, exasperated. 'Who *wouldn't* want to meet me? After all, John,' she concluded, 'your mother is probably the only woman on earth more popular than I am.'

'Can't happen,' John declared. 'Mother would make sure we never see each other again if she meets you. I can guarantee it.'

The fact that Jackie refused to meet her tapped into Madonna's deep inferiority complex. Beneath all of the bravado, she'd always been insecure – it wouldn't take a psychiatrist to have discerned that much about her. During this time, she kept saying to friends, 'His mother would love me, if she gave me a chance.' Jackie's refusal even to give Madonna 'a chance' quickly became a source of hurt for her.

Besides the Jackie factor, another issue in her relationship with John was her communication with him. One had to know how to deal with John when he was angry. He was a shouter. If he was angry, he'd scream at full volume, his own face just inches from the object of his aggression. Though such a thing could be daunting to some people, it certainly wasn't to Madonna. She was equipped with the skills to handle this kind of explosive personality, simply because of who she was married to and what she put up with on an almost daily basis. However, for some reason, she didn't seem to be able to meet John at that hot level during a disagreement with him.

A defining moment in Madonna's relationship with John occurred when, in the summer of 1988, he thought she had told someone else something personal about him – and that this person had then gone to the press with it. When Madonna denied having done it, he didn't believe her. 'What the hell is wrong with you?' he screamed at her at full volume in front of friends. Everyone in the room who knew Madonna held onto his chair for dear life. However, instead of firing back, Madonna was quiet. Her startled expression indicated that she was stunned by John's outburst. She dropped her eyes, unable to meet his accusatory gaze. Then, she ran from the room. This was odd behaviour from a woman used to taking as much as she could dish out. Mystified, John turned to his friends and sputtered, 'What'd I say? What'd I say?'

After that incident, Madonna seemed to lose interest in John. Some intimates believed she now viewed him as a 'hothead', and since she already had one of those at home she didn't need another. Others said that the intensity of the physical intimacy they shared had waned and it now wasn't worth her tolerating him and his mother. Madonna didn't say much about any of it. To one friend, she called the situation with Kennedy 'toxic and sad', and said 'I needed out of it'. She asked that friend, 'Don't you think the need for companionship is a weakness? Because I do. And I refuse to be weak.'

After a two-week cooling-off period at the end of July, John invited Madonna to dinner at a trendy West Side restaurant to discuss their relationship. According to law school classmate Chris Meyer (whom John brought to the dinner because, as he put it, 'I don't want to be alone with her. She scares the hell out of me') John told Madonna that he was sorry for all that had happened in their relationship concerning his mother. He hoped that they could still be friends. He also indicated that there could be nothing more than that between them because Jackie would never approve, 'and her approval means everything to me'.

'Madonna was annoyed by the whole thing,' said Chris Meyer. 'He thought he was letting her down easy, but she was clearly finished with him anyway. In her mind, she had already given him the heave-ho.'

A week later, Chris Meyer had an appointment with an attorney at the same New York high rise that housed Doubleday. He happened upon John in the men's room; John was probably visiting Jackie at work. As they stood beside each other at adjoining urinals, Meyer asked Kennedy about Madonna. 'How's it going, buddy?' he wanted to know. 'Is it really over with her?'

Staring straight ahead, John smiled thinly and said, 'She's great, but, yes, it's over between us, Chris.'

'Because of your mother?'

John shrugged. 'Not really,' he said, sounding vague. 'But any excuse will do, I guess. That's as good as any other when you're trying to break it off with someone.'

'Wow,' Chris said. 'Too bad.'

Without a reaction, John zipped up, walked over to the basin and washed his hands. As he dried off with a paper towel, he turned to Chris who was finishing up at the urinal. 'We had some good times,' John observed. 'I like her a lot. Oh well. Easy come,' John said while crumpling the towel, 'easy go,' he concluded as he tossed it into a trash can.*

---

* John Kennedy Jun. and his wife of nearly five years, Caroline Bessette (along with her sister, Lauren), were killed when the private plane he was piloting plummeted into the Atlantic Ocean in the summer of 1999. John, Caroline and Lauren were all buried at sea on 22 July 1999.

Dinner with Warren

Despite her phenomenal success as a recording artist, Madonna still dreamed of critical respect as a film actress. She no doubt realized that her stint on Broadway had done little to make her more marketable as a Hollywood actress. Typically, she kept her eye on her goal and instructed her film agents to continue the search for properties in which she could appear, roles for which she might be suited. In the fall of 1988, a part came her way in a film she knew she couldn't resist, a new Warren Beatty movie which was in the process of being cast. The film, *Dick Tracy*, was based on the popular comic strip character and had all the makings of a top-grossing film, something Madonna wanted in her career about as badly as she wanted anything at this point in her life. The role of sexy femme fatale Breathless Mahoney seemed tailor-made for her.

The problem was that the quality of Madonna's acting work in past screen endeavours did little to warm Beatty to the idea of her playing opposite him as the film's Mahoney. He favoured Kathleen Turner, whose sultry voice had added steamy dimensions to the character of Jessica Rabbit in *Who Framed Roger Rabbit?*. The beautiful Kim Basinger had also been smashing in a similar fantasy movie, *Batman*, and Beatty thought she could contribute the same kind of sexual glow to the female lead role in *Dick Tracy*.

When Warren Beatty wanted to go out with Madonna to discuss the movie, she put him off. 'It took me weeks to get a date with her,' he once recalled.

In her book *Sex*, published in the 1990s, Madonna explained that, in her view, 'The best way to seduce someone is by making yourself unavailable. You just have to be busy all the time and they'll be craving to see you. Then, you don't fuck them for the first five dates. Let them get closer and closer, but definitely don't fuck them.'

When Madonna allowed Warren to take her out for dinner at the Ivy restaurant in Los Angeles, she finally turned on the charm in order to get him to see her in the role. Wearing a sleek, black leather jumpsuit – unzipped in a revealing manner – with a matching leather cap, she asked a lot of questions. She was clearly trying to find out new information about him, weaknesses, anything that could prove helpful. He did the same. According to Beatty's later recollections to friends, Madonna said, 'I know you've heard a lot of terrible things about me, and I'm here to tell you that they're all true.' She laughed. 'How about you?' she asked. 'I've heard a lot about you? True?' Warren didn't answer. 'Just as I thought,' Madonna said. 'All true.'

Warren later said he was instantly struck by Madonna's humour. She was entertaining, and sexy – perfect for the role for which she was auditioning. He kissed her on the doorstep, after he dropped her off. 'Houston,' he reportedly said, after kissing her, 'we have lift-off.'

'He thought she was pretty great,' said a friend of Beatty's. 'He hired her on the spot.'

The truth is, however, that both Kathleen Turner and Kim Basinger were unavailable at this time. Beatty could have continued looking for his Breathless Mahoney or he could just hire Madonna. He clearly didn't think she was worth much as an actress, though, because he asked that she essay the role for Screen Actor's Guild scale wages of just $1,440 a week. So, in effect, Madonna's participation lowered the film's budget considerably, since neither Turner nor Bassinger would ever work in a $60 million budget film for less than $2,000 a week – nor would any popular actress, except one smart enough to know that such a decision could be a brilliant career move. After all, *Dick Tracy* boasted top production values and, along with Beatty, an all-star cast including Al Pacino, Gene Hackman and Mandy Patinkin, with cameos by Dick van Dyke, James Caan and Charles Durning. As a splashy, summer-released Disney film, it was almost guaranteed to do big business. Madonna realized that if, by some fluke, the movie flopped, it could hardly be blamed on her since she was only one star in an ensemble piece. However, if it was a success, she would be credited for having had her first screen bonanza, and she could use it to demonstrate her box office appeal. Also, Madonna's deal had it that, in return for her small fee, she would receive a percentage of the film's profits. For Madonna, therefore, *Dick Tracy* presented a win-win situation. She was savvy enough to see it just that way and eagerly accepted a contract that was viewed by some observers in the industry as an insult, especially considering her status in the entertainment field.

Malibu Nightmare?

By Christmas 1988, Madonna's marriage to Sean Penn was more than three years old. To say that the forty months since their 16 August 1985 union had been difficult would be an understatement of epic proportions. Penn's drinking and his violent temper had been more than Madonna could handle, and by the end of 1988 the marriage was all but over. She said that it was as if she had married a child in a man's body, someone who operated on the emotional level of a ten-year-old.

By this time, of course, Madonna fully understood that Sean Penn had a drinking problem, and that this made it impossible for him to focus on saving their marriage. His temper was more unpredictable than ever. For instance, after one bitter argument, he threatened to drown their dog, Hank. Somehow, Madonna managed to change his mind. The next day – at the suggestion of actor Robert Duvall – she personally drove Sean to Palm Springs to the Betty Ford Center where, she hoped, she could convince him to dry out. They signed in as 'Mr and Mrs Victor Cobb', but after speaking to counsellors, they realized that the chances of keeping Sean's presence there from the press were negligible. They weren't even half way back to Los Angeles on the two-hour drive home when calls began coming in on their car telephone from Madonna's manager, Freddy DeMann, telling them they had been recognized at the Betty Ford Center. 'But how did anyone know?' Madonna remembered asking Freddy. 'Someone must have told someone.'

'The press is psychic when it comes to you,' he told her.

Once back in Malibu, Madonna didn't know what to do about Sean. 'I have to help him, I know. But he doesn't want any help,' her friend, the comic Sandra Bernhard, would later recall her saying. Sandra had flown to the West Coast to spend the Thanksgiving holiday with Madonna.

'I don't know what to do,' Madonna continued. 'His drinking is wrecking our marriage. He pushes me away. I'm miserable.'

'Let me ask you a simple question,' Sandra asked her. 'Do you ever have fun?'

'What do you mean?'

'Fun, Madonna. Do you and Sean ever have fun?'

Madonna looked dispirited. She had answered her friend's question, and without saying a single word.

'Then he's got to go,' Sandra decided.

Madonna said she agreed, even though she and Sean had been thinking about having a baby to save their marriage. She had promised him that 1989 would be the year that they would start a family. She feared having Sean's child, she said, because she didn't want a baby to be raised in a broken home, 'and we are nothing if not broken,' she added tearfully.

'You're crazy if you bring a kid into this mess,' Sandra said. 'I'm telling you, he's got to go.'

After another fight, Madonna asked Sean to move out. He moved in with his father, director Leo Penn. A few days later, on the morning of 26 December, Sean telephoned Madonna to discuss the state of their relationship. During the conversation, Madonna told Sean that she had decided not to have his baby. In signing a contract to appear in *Dick Tracy*, she explained, she would have to postpone a family for another year.

According to documents she would later file with the Los Angeles County Court House, Madonna said that Penn was 'disgusted and pissed off' with her after that conversation, and they engaged in a heated argument.

'It's over,' Madonna told Sean on the telephone, she later remembered. 'I want a divorce. I *need* a divorce.'

When she hung up the telephone, she must have been shaking.

That afternoon, Madonna telephoned John Kennedy in New York. Recalls Stephen Styles, 'By this time, John and Madonna had cooled their own romance, but she was still depending on him for emotional support. She asked him to fly to the West Coast and help her solve some problems related to her marriage.' According to Styles, Madonna further explained to Kennedy that she needed 'moral support to get through this time in my life'.

John decided not to fly to California. 'I think he didn't want Madonna depending on him,' said Stephen Styles. 'He was afraid that if he came to her rescue every time she called, they would end up back in a relationship – which would only upset his mother, and he didn't want to do that. He felt badly about it, but he also felt he shouldn't just drop everything and be at Madonna's beck and call.'

(Adds Stephen Styles, 'John told me that he ran into Sean Penn at a party a couple years later. Penn wanted him to apologize for sleeping with his wife while she was a married woman. John told him to take a hike, and then left the party before a fight could break out. Madonna apparently found out what had happened because the next day, John received a funeral wreath at his home. The message on it read; "In Deepest Sympathy, from Madonna." He thought that was pretty funny.')

Although Madonna was perceived by her public as strong and independent, at this point in time she was actually frightened and vulnerable, causing some of her friends to wonder what was really going on in her marriage. Doubtless, Sean Penn was angry that

Madonna was engaging in what appeared to him to be an extramarital affair with Warren Beatty. 'He would follow her at night and, always, they would end up at Warren's,' says a friend of Penn's. 'He'd sit in his car in front of Beatty's gate, waiting for her to leave. Often, she wouldn't do so until the sun rose. This was driving Sean crazy, along with her decision to not start a family with him. It was all building up in him, a fury that was bound to explode.'

Madonna's telephonic declaration of independence from her husband that December morning was her first step at regaining her identity. However, it wasn't that simple. Nothing with Sean was ever simple.

In the late afternoon of 28 December 1988 Sean Penn allegedly scaled the wall surrounding the Malibu house and burst in, finding Madonna alone in the master bedroom. She had given the live-in help the night off to attend a holiday party. What happened then remains the source of great controversy. For decades, it had been published that Sean Penn was violent with Madonna that night, and that she filed a police report against him. In 2015, though, Penn filed a massive law suit against the TV producer, Lee Daniels, for just vaguely referencing the story in an interview. Madonna then gave a written declaration swearing that there was no incident of violence. 'Sean has never struck me, "tied me up", or physically assaulted me, and any report to the contrary is completely outrageous, malicious, reckless, and false.'

Why after years of ignoring the accusations had Sean taken action and what are we to make of Madonna's statement? Who knows for sure, but it may be that Sean had finally just got fed up with it and decided to set the record straight. If all of the previously published reports of Sean having struck her really were erroneous you could hardly blame him. That seems the most logical explanation, especially since Madonna has such a strong responsibility to feminism, having been a beacon for it for most of her life. It's a given by her loyal admirers that she wouldn't cave in to a request to sign a document denying spousal abuse if that document didn't state the truth. The suit was settled with an undisclosed payment from Lee Daniels.

The chilling effect of Sean Penn's lawsuit is that the media now isn't able to report the allegations previously made without fear of similar reprisal. In other words, it's as if Penn has pretty much cleaned the record by striking fear in the hearts of anyone who now seeks to report a story which had been published and re-published countless times over the last almost thirty years, or question why he left it so long to take a stand; no writer with any sense would want to tackle it now, especially since all of the police reports filed with the Los Angeles county were, apparently, expunged after 1992. It hardly seems worth the trouble to tangle with Sean Penn over it.

Here's what Sean told *Playboy* about the night in question:

After a typical argument with him, Madonna stormed out of the house to cool off. He hollered after her that if she dared return, he would cut all of her hair off. He says that as a result of his threat, 'she developed a concern that she would get a very severe haircut'. If Sean's story is true, it's understandable that the image of her infuriated husband coming at her with a pair of shears or clippers would be a terrifying one to Madonna. 'So, she took this concern to the local authorities, who came back up to the house,' Sean said. 'She felt the responsible thing would be to inform them – since they were coming up there ostensibly to keep her from getting a haircut and to let her gather some additional personal effects – that there were firearms in the house.' He admits that, indeed, he did have weapons in his home. Penn was in the kitchen eating Rice Krispies cereal when the authorities arrived, brandishing bullhorns and handcuffs. Sean says that the police, fearing that he had a gun, 'suggested I come out of the house. They did what they had to do, the way they had to do it. I was cool with that.'

In the divorce, Sean didn't want any of Madonna's money, though by California law, he could have been entitled to half of her fortune. Instead, he wanted Madonna to keep the entire $70 million her career had generated for her in the three years she was a married woman. 'I could have gone any way I wanted,' he said later. 'There's community property in California. But I would never, even under the worst of circumstances, take a penny of somebody else's change.'

Instead, Sean Penn walked away from the marriage with the approximately $5 million he had earned (while being paid $1 million a film), as well as the couple's $2 million three-bedroom, Spanish-style villa. Because Penn's personal investment in the joint property was only $880,000, he made $1.2 million on it. He also got to keep the south-western and Santa Fe-style furniture in the home, including a log-built four-poster bed. Madonna took all of the art deco and art nouveau paintings and sculptures. Oddly, she did leave behind, at least according to one court document, a mutilated doll with pins through it. Madonna kept their New York apartment, but gave Penn $498,000 – the equivalent of his investment in that property. (She purchased for herself a $2.9 million seven-bedroom home in the Hollywood Hills which, in itself, was worth more than Penn's total reported assets.) According to legal papers filed, she also handed over $18,700 in 'short-term paper' investments and another $2,300 in cash (both sums from a joint financial account).

The divorce was finalized on 25 January 1989. Because the necessary documents had been prepared and then filed away so many times in the past, they were updated and ready to be signed by Sean Penn within days. Madonna had loved Sean and truly intended to honour her marriage vows, so she was deeply affected by the divorce. She hadn't been happy for some time, so she may have thought that she wouldn't miss Sean. She was wrong. She was actually surprised at the sense of loss she felt in the months after the final decree, as she would later admit. On a deep level, as she would explain to friends, she felt that she and Sean were 'soulmates'. It was difficult for her to fathom the way it had all turned out for them.

Today, according to those who know her best, she still looks back on the union with Sean with a certain amount of regret. She can't help but romanticize her marriage to him, retrospectively viewing it through a filter that obscures the darker aspects of the relationship. Perhaps to her credit, she only seems to want to recall the happier times with Sean. Of course, some of her friends have wondered when those happy times occurred since most people never actually witnessed her and Sean being happy, at least not after their wedding ceremony – and Sean didn't seem too thrilled that day, either. However, it's true that no one really knows what happens in a marriage when two people are alone, other than the two people to whom it's happening.

Madonna feels, or so she has said privately, that perhaps she could have been more tolerant of Sean's feelings where Sandra Bernhard was concerned. Also, she wonders if perhaps she should have been more proactive in forcing him to stop drinking. She has said that she felt guilty because, 'I should have made him stop. Every time we ever had a drink together, I felt guilty about that.'

Perhaps some of her guilt stemmed from her Catholic upbringing. 'Once you're a Catholic, you're always a Catholic – in terms of your feelings of guilt and remorse and whether you've sinned or not,' she explained in an interview. 'Sometimes I'm racked with guilt when I needn't be, and that, to me, is left over from my Catholic upbringing. Because in Catholicism you are a born sinner and you're a sinner all your life. No matter how you try to get away from it, the sin is within you all the time.'

It could be argued that Sean and Madonna did the best they could with what they had available to them, in terms of common sense and maturity. The fact that both were so famous at such a young age did nothing to enhance their marriage, either. Certainly, today, Madonna would never be as publicly antagonistic to her partner as she was with Sean. While still a complicated, often temperamental, and sometimes difficult person to understand, she's obviously not the same woman she was a thirty years ago.

Madonna would also later admit that the break-up with Sean made her 'more suspicious of people. You imbue men with characteristics you want them to have,' she observed. 'Then they're not what you expect, at all. But it's your own fault too for not having done the homework, the investigating. I'm more cautious now. But I'm still a hopeless romantic.'

Since his marriage to Madonna, Sean Penn has worked to clean himself up – he's not 'sober', still drinks, but hasn't had a display of public drunkenness in years. He has gone on to be a contented and productive person. When asked if he thought the marriage to Madonna could have worked, Penn replied, 'No fucking way. Not with what we had to deal with.' In years to come, he and Madonna would continue to hold strong feelings for each other.

Some years later, in 1995, Sean suddenly appeared on stage unexpectedly before a stunned audience as Madonna was receiving a VH1 Fashion and Music award. While Madonna enjoyed shocking others, but rarely – if ever – enjoyed it when the tables were turned, she seemed genuinely happy to see Sean. The two embraced lovingly. When he left the stage, she walked to the microphone and said to the audience, 'Now, that was really dirty.'

Perhaps her brief 1995 reunion with Sean Penn stirred something in Madonna that had lain dormant for some time. The next day, she tucked her hair under a hat, threw on a leopard-skin coat and rendezvoused with the low-key, baseball-cap wearing Penn in Central Park. 'I miss you so much, baby,' she was overheard saying to him. 'Don't you miss me, too?' The ever-present and stirred-up paparazzi feverishly snapped pictures of the couple formerly known as 'the Battling Penns'. This time, Madonna and Sean, lost in each other's company, didn't seem to mind.

'She was in the process of becoming the biggest star in the world. I just wanted to make my films and hide,' Sean said many years later about his marriage, trying to put it into perspective. 'I was an angry young man. I had a lot of demons and don't really know who could have lived with me at the time. I was just as badly behaved as her, so I can't point the finger of blame.'

He also said, 'She was a phenomenon, but nothing could have

told anybody what would happen next, I describe that marriage as loud. That's how I remember it. I don't recall having a single conversation in four years of marriage. I've talked to her a few times since, and there's a whole person there. I just didn't know it. I was just living in my own head. Who was it that said, "Men are vain, particularly young men?" That was me. Plus, I liked to drink a lot . . .'

Like a Prayer: *The Album*

In March 1989, the commercially prudent thing for Madonna to do would have been to release another dance album of new material. After all, based on the sales performance of the recent *You Can Dance*, her public would have been happy just to keep dancing. However, Madonna – who was now thirty – had certain matters on her mind, personal thoughts about her troubled relationship with her ex-husband, her family, the world and even with her God. So, while she still wanted her fans to party, with her fourth album she also wanted them to think. To that end, Madonna began to develop lyrical ideas that, until then, were personal meditations never to be shared with her public so openly and pointedly. Thoughtfully, she sifted through her personal journal and diaries and began considering her options. 'What was it I wanted to say?' she recalled. 'I wanted the album to speak to things on my mind. It was a complex time in my life.'

As Madonna considered her alternatives, producers Steve Bray and Patrick Leonard individually began to tinker with various instrumental tracks and musical ideas to present to her for her consideration. Though the two producers knew one another well and had even worked together on songs with her, there was always quiet but fierce competition between them as they vied to see who could get the most songs on one of her albums. Since Madonna had become a franchise, songwriting royalties from albums that sold millions of copies globally had already made Bray and Leonard wealthy men. The stakes remained high.

Both producers brought their own special style to the project that would go on to become the *Like a Prayer* album. Though Bray had a penchant for kinetic pop-dance songs, while Leonard was more melodic in style, both proved indispensable to Madonna's ever-developing sound. In fact, the versatility of both producers unwittingly saw to it that there was no real Madonna 'sound' to speak of, no way for critics or fans to pigeonhole her. Thus, while Madonna was well aware of the sometimes contentious dynamic of the relationship between Bray and Leonard, she never did much to deter them – the tension was good for creativity and business. 'I like it when people go up against one another,' she has said. 'I even like it when they go up against me. If you want creativity, you have to have sparks. I'm all for that.'

Moreover, Madonna's own music tastes and ideas have as much to do with who she is artistically as anyone else's. Ultimately, she's the one who decides for which tracks she'll write lyrics.

When *Like a Prayer* was released, music journalists took note of Madonna's artful, mature way of expressing herself. She had become a proficient songwriter and was credited with co-writing ten songs on the album, and writing one on her own.

'Like a Prayer', written by Madonna with Leonard, deserved every bit of the curiosity it generated. Like the startling music video that would accompany it, the song is a series of button-pushing anomalies, filled with references to both the spiritual/religious and the carnal – a joyful celebration of love . . . but for whom? In a twist so typical of Madonna's clever way with words, the lyrical theme of devotion could either be for a lover, or for God. For instance, throughout Madonna sings 'Prayer' with a measure of devotion and reverence, as if to a higher power. Yet the lyric about being 'down on my knees', and wanting to 'take you there' evokes distinct images of . . . something else.

Indeed, double entendres and ironies abound in 'Like a Prayer'. While devilishly danceable, the music is interrupted by a quiet break during which Madonna offers a loving homage against a backdrop of heavenly, angelic voicings. While the song feels distinctively religious, the underlying sexual tension is undeniable. The jubilant voices of a gospel choir conducted by André Crouch heightened the song's spiritual nature while a stingingly secular rock guitar kept it dark and mysterious. Like the legendary Marvin Gaye (whose music she greatly admired), Madonna has the uncanny ability to inspire strong, conflicting emotions during the course of a single song, leaving the listener scratching his head for answers – and craving more. This is certainly one of the woman's great gifts.

'Express Yourself', one of two tracks Madonna produced with Bray, was a funky dance anthem and a female call-to-arms in communication and self-respect. 'I think it's one of my better songs,' Madonna has said. 'We had fun in the studio with it.'

In three songs on the album, Madonna sought to purge herself of certain personal demons. 'Till Death Do Us Part', her sad, harsh, open letter to Sean Penn, revealed her feelings of hopelessness for their marriage. As would any artist intent on exposing herself through her music, she transformed personal experience into art, making clear to anyone interested how she felt about what had happened. Likewise with 'Oh Father', Madonna revisited the pain and confusion that had characterized her relationship with the most important man in her life. Some critics felt it was a love letter to Tony Ciccone, while others saw it as an indictment. 'That's fine,' Madonna said. 'It is what the listener thinks it is, all open to interpretation. I just write the songs, it's up to others to interpret them to mean what they want them to mean.'

She countered the sombre moments with songs such as 'Keep It Together', the other Steve Bray track, which is an uptempo romp about the trials and tribulations – and the joys – of family.

'Cherish' was a particular triumph for the Madonna/Patrick Leonard partnership. A delightful confection of radio-ready proportions, the song had it all – strong, positive, remarkably dysfunction-free lyrics about love; a memorable, singalong vocal melody and a tight, punchy, rhythm arrangement. It remains, quite simply, one of the best songs Madonna has ever written; sweet and happy but by no means corny, it's a perfectly constructed pop song which Madonna delivered beautifully, and with undeniably sassy charm. Indeed, if 'Cherish' had been released in the Sixties, it would have most likely emanated from Detroit's Motown or the New York songwriting Mecca, the Brill Building, both sources for some of pop music's most enduring classics.

Madonna and Patrick Leonard created much of the *Like a Prayer* album, with the exception of 'Love Song', a duet co-produced and performed on the album by Prince. While they were dating, the two superstars had tried writing together, but never came up with anything that ever saw the light of day. Perhaps 'Love Song' should also have been kept where light couldn't find it. A potentially fabulous collaboration is wasted on a meandering mid-tempo song that goes nowhere – an exercise in Prince excess. Though she shared the production credit with him, Prince played all the instruments and Madonna's role was reduced to sitting in on her own album and trying to sing like Prince. Her guest star might have even inspired 'Act of Contrition', an experimental mess that has Madonna mumbling a prayer over edgy, solo rock guitar while a choir's background chants are played backwards, a recording tactic used by the Beatles and Jimi Hendrix for psychedelic effect some years earlier. Like any art, sometimes what Madonna comes up with works . . . sometimes it doesn't. (Of course, who's to say what works and doesn't, all criticism being subjective.)

Every important artist has at least one album in his career whose commercial and/or critical success becomes that artist's magic moment. For Madonna, *Like a Virgin* was just such a defining moment. *Like a Prayer* was another. For better or worse – usually better! – Madonna pushed onwards as an artist, using her creative wit to communicate on another level, musically. '"Like a Prayer" is about the influence of Catholicism on my life and the passion it provokes in me,' she explained. 'In these songs I'm dealing with specific issues that mean a lot to me. They're about an assimilation of experiences I had in my life and my relationships. I've taken more risks with this album than I ever have before, and I think that growth shows.'

Goodies

When production began on Warren Beatty's new film *Dick Tracy* in February 1989, it seemed inevitable to some Hollywood observers that a romantic relationship had developed between the longtime Hollywood rogue and pop music's current, publicity-mad temptress. Now that she was working alongside him, Madonna, a longtime movie fan, probably couldn't resist the idea of a relationship with Beatty, a film icon who cultivated women with astonishing success. She told friends that she was determined to move forward with her life and remain as distracted as possible, so as not to focus on Sean or her failed marriage. What better distraction, one might muse, than a relationship with a man who had romanced many of the biggest and most glamorous names of his era, including Natalie Wood, Joan Collins, Julie Christie, Carly Simon, Cher and Barbra Streisand?

While still certainly easy to look at, at fifty-two Warren Beatty's sex symbol status in Hollywood had long ago faded. Now, around his still-handsome face was the faint suggestion of discoloration – thin white lines that were nearly concealed by either a tan or maybe even pancake make-up. (Some who got close enough for an inspection would wonder if these marks could have been the result of cosmetic surgery.) Perhaps realizing that his 'Old Hollywood' image would be bolstered by becoming linked with the young, leading sex object of the day, Warren seemed dumbfounded by his good fortune.

'Sometimes I look at myself in the mirror and say, "Man, I am with Madonna!"' he told a reporter. 'She makes me young.'

From the beginning, Warren provided loads of fun for Madonna. For instance, one day Madonna came home to find her living room full of packages: perfume, make-up, and dozens of expensive dresses, both formal and informal – all her size. There were also boxes of lingerie in a variety of colours – again, all her size – and a dozen black lace Lejaby brassieres – her favourite. (One might wonder how Warren would have known, or even remembered, the brand name of her favourite bra.) There were also eight pairs of expensive Italian designer shoes. She was astonished when she read a card that had been propped on a large hatbox: 'From Warren'. Had he really selected all of these clothes just for her? Had he spent that much time making certain of the sizes? And why would he do all of this?

As she pondered those questions – and who knows how many others – Madonna and two of her female assistants enjoyed a wonderful afternoon with Warren's exquisite presents. After putting her *Like a Prayer* CD into the player, she slipped in and out of each new dress while dancing and preening in front of the mirror, admiring her reflection. She and her friends enjoyed 'a silly girls' day', as one of the assistants called it. They pinned up their hair, let it back down, sampled the new lingerie – tags dangling – and tossed aside the garments Madonna decided were 'tacky'. At the end of the fun day, Madonna gave the two girls the clothing and make-up she thought flattering on them, and kept the rest for herself – including all of the shoes.

The next day, Madonna telephoned Warren to ask about the gifts. He explained that buying for himself was a bore since, as he put it, 'a man can only wear pants and a jacket. What fun is that?' He said that he enjoyed shopping for women and, if Madonna didn't mind, he might send over an assortment of 'goodies' whenever the mood struck him.

Madonna was ambivalent about such generosity. As she would

later say, she was, at first, annoyed. 'I'm not some little starlet that you can buy things for and control,' she told him. 'I'm a very wealthy person. I can buy my own underwear.' However, she was also impressed. 'What girl wouldn't be?' she had to admit. After what she had been through with Sean, perhaps she decided that she deserved a bit of pampering. She decided to keep the gifts, but on the condition that the next time Warren Beatty had such an impulse, he would take her along so that she could help select 'the goodies'.

As well as his passion for beautiful and famous women – and for buying them 'goodies' – Warren Beatty's other great love was for film making. On *Dick Tracy*, he would act as star, producer and director. Madonna could learn a great deal about movie-making and screen acting from him. She needed his credibility and experience as much as he needed her youth. To her restless child, he would play the indulgent adult, slightly abashed but definitely enchanted by her whirlwind lifestyle. Some people in her circle went so far as to say that Madonna looked to Warren as a father figure.

After Sean Penn, Warren Beatty must have seemed like a breath of fresh air for Madonna. For one thing, she would soon learn that he could be pushed around. He would take a lot, get angry, and then disappear . . . to cool down. Unlike Sean, he wouldn't lash out. It had always been Madonna's nature to bully the man with whom she was romantically involved. Whereas Sean had been emotional and explosive about her daily defiances, Warren would usually just be resigned and philosophical about them. For the most part, he was tolerant of her; he thought she was amusing.

As we've seen, it had been Sean Penn who first introduced Madonna to Warren Beatty, and on the night of Penn's first date with her, 'Sean took me to Warren's house,' Madonna said. 'I guess he wanted to show me off – I'm not sure. I didn't know LA at all. I remember meeting a lot of movie stars that night like Mickey Rourke.'

Warren was intrigued by Madonna from the first time he laid eyes upon her. 'I understand rebellion,' he observed when speaking of his new consort. 'So I understand Madonna. She's all about rebellion, basically.' (If that's all she was 'about' in his view, maybe he didn't understand her as well as he thought he did.) To *Vanity Fair* writer Kevin Sessums, though, Warren was a bit more forthcoming when asked what he thought of Madonna's artistry: 'I think she's courageous in the areas that she explores artistically. I think that's what she wants to explore. If you mean what do I think are the resonances of that or the personal motivations for that, I don't know that I would address myself to that. Off the top of my head, her generous spirit would be the thing I think that informs her work the most. As she goes on, she will gain the artistic respect that she already deserves.'

Diane Giordano recalled the way Madonna described a date with Warren at the Sushi Cove, a trendy restaurant in Los Angeles on Mullholland Drive, less than a mile from Warren's estate, in January 1989: 'He wore a black silk suit, black shoes, a white shirt and a black silk tie. He also wore tinted glasses. She suspected that he was trying to hide crow's feet. She said she felt awkward because he was so nattily dressed and she had on a funky jeans outfit. They had a nice dinner and then the waitress came and asked if they wanted dessert. The only choice was chocolate or vanilla ice cream. Madonna wanted both.'

The next day, Warren telephoned Madonna at her home. In talking about the date, he went on about how Madonna had wanted both flavours of ice cream. 'You seem to like to try everything,' he told her, teasing her. 'So, have you ever made it with a woman?'

At this time, with Madonna's friendship with Sandra Bernhard flourishing, she was still teasing the public with the possibility that she was a lesbian. With Beatty now apparently questioning the validity of 'those stories', Madonna suddenly became the model of discretion. She refused to answer his enquiries and, instead, attempted to turn the tables. 'Have you ever done it with a man?' she countered. Beatty, it is said, ignored the question.

'Do you want a woman?' he pressed on. 'Because if you do, it will be my present to you. I'll get you a woman.'

'And all this, just from ordering two kinds of ice cream?' Madonna asked with a laugh.

The next night, Warren and Madonna – in a black vinyl jumpsuit with high heels (a strange fashion choice for beach restaurant dining) – again dined at the Sushi Cove, this time joined by Sandra Bernhard, at Warren's request. 'All I remember about that date was that Madonna and I ordered one plate of sushi for the two of us. And I said something like, "Warren, you know that Madonna and I share *everything*, don't you?" And his eyes lit up like a kid in a candy store. A wild ride, I thought to myself. A very wild ride.'

Differences

Although Madonna told reporters – such as one for *Cosmopolitan* – that she didn't want to 'belittle the relationship by talking about it', she was intrigued enough about what was going on with Warren Beatty to want to discuss it with close friends. When the two finally made love, Madonna had confided, it wasn't the kind of passionate experience she had known with Sean Penn. Nothing could compare to what she had with Sean, she had to admit. However, Warren was much more generous as a lover than Sean had been. Warren politely apologized for the brevity of his performance in bed, and then made sure that she, too, was completely pleasured. He sought out her needs, her preferences, her desires. 'He knows a woman's body better than most women,' Madonna said. 'He can pinpoint the day of your cycle.

'He's into all aspects of sexuality. This is why he's so perfect for me,' she added. 'He has no restrictions. He says to me, "If you misbehave, I'll just have to spank you." I love that. Everything to him is living out his sexual fantasies.'

'I don't know that he's ever slept with a man,' she later said to a reporter for the gay magazine the *Advocate*. 'But he's certainly not homophobic. I asked him once, "Would you ever sleep with a man?" and he said he was sorry that he hadn't but that now because of AIDS he felt it was an unsafe thing to start experimenting with.'

After she felt she knew him well enough to do so, Madonna suggested that Warren retrieve his former trim and youthful shape by exercising with her. When he told her that he wasn't interested, she was perplexed as to why a person would not want to 'better himself'. Rather than let it go, she pushed on, suggesting liposuction. He was either hurt or insulted – only he would know which. The two then became embroiled in a heated debate about whether she had a right to have an opinion about his body, the matter playing out in front of friends at the Los Angeles nightclub, the Club Nouveau.

'You're the one who is always telling people that they shouldn't judge others by outside appearances,' Warren said to her. 'How dare you judge me? It works both ways, you know?'

'Oh, please,' Madonna said as she sipped a cocktail, looking terrific in velvet hot pants. 'You older guys are too sensitive,' she said, taking a drag from a cigarette. 'I'm just being helpful. If you want to be fat and flabby, Warren, fine with me. Go right ahead.'

To whom did she think she was talking? Sean Penn? It was as if Madonna hadn't learned much from her experiences with her former husband, at least in terms of diplomacy, discretion and sensitivity. It now seemed to observers that she was being purposely cruel to Warren, maybe continuing an explosive theme in her relationships, whether consciously or subconsciously.

Warren's eyes turned as cold as granite. He began to say

something, but stopped himself. Typical of him – he was *not* Sean Penn – he probably didn't want to make a scene in front of so many witnesses. Instead, he sniffed his brandy as if a connoisseur before quickly downing it. Nodding pensively to himself, he then walked away, careful not to make eye contact with any observers. 'Now what was that about?' Madonna asked no one in particular. 'I hate it when he does that to me. That is *so* like my father. He is *so* like my father!' She then began biting on her knuckles, as if suddenly nervous or fearful.

The argument may have continued the next day in a Hollywood restaurant. 'Keep your stupid remarks to yourself,' Madonna said to Warren in front of other diners.

'Oh, Christ! Grow up!' Warren countered, this time visibly exasperated.

'No. *You* grow up,' Madonna said, petulantly. She then reached into her bag and pulled out a Snickers candy bar, which she threw at Warren's chest. Both were apparently unaware that their display had stopped all conversation around them. Finally, ice-hockey star Wayne Gretzky charged over to them, 'Hey, you two,' he said, 'knock it off, will ya?'

After five minutes, Warren began cutting Madonna's fillet of sole into little pieces, and then delicately placing each into her mouth with his fork. (Though Madonna was said to have been on a strict vegan diet at this time, which prohibited fish, she did indulge now and then.)

Madonna declared to a reporter, again for *Cosmopolitan*, 'What I'm doing this time is starting out being good friends with somebody.' She loved Beatty's self-confidence, she said. 'I used to want to be President,' Warren told her. 'But Hollywood is better than Washington. Here, I have more power, and I don't have to put up with the bureaucracy. I'm the President of Hollywood.'

Madonna also enjoyed the manner in which Warren continued to pamper her. For instance, on the set of *Dick Tracy* he paid for a masseuse to wait on her at all times. He sent her flowers every day of shooting. One night, after a tough day of filming, Warren took Madonna out to dinner to an expensive Italian restaurant. Wearing a sheer black and red polka-dot blouse, black bra, black hot pants and a red bowler hat – and chewing on a wad of gum – she sat down and promptly demanded a Diet Pepsi, a drink not on the menu. Diet Coke, yes. Diet Pepsi, no. 'Well, we're leaving,' Madonna decided. Warren then asked the waiter to go to a convenience store and purchase a can of Diet Pepsi.

When the waiter returned, Warren peeled off five $100 bills from a wad and handed them to him. He then waved towards the Diet Pepsi as if he had just conjured it up out of thin air. 'There you go, my dear,' he said to Madonna, 'the most expensive soda in the world, and it's all yours.' As Madonna laughed gaily, the waiter popped open a can and poured its contents into a glass of ice. After dinner, Warren and Madonna held hands under the table. Later, Beatty would say, 'Because she's surrounded by so much stuff, I don't think people quite realize how much fun Madonna is. She's an enormous amount of fun to be around and certainly to work with.'

Warren thought that the fact that Madonna had tried to have her breasts insured for $12 million was 'hilarious'. During the filming of the movie in late winter and into the spring of 1989, make-up artist John Cuglione literally had to glue Madonna into some of the skin-tight gowns. 'I was terrified that she'd have an allergic reaction to the glue,' he recalls. 'If I'd discoloured a breast or inflicted permanent damage, she could sue me for a fortune. Worse yet, I'd be known as the schmuck who destroyed a national treasure.' When Madonna had the idea to have her breasts insured – interesting considering the history of breast cancer with her late mother – she asked Warren for the name and number of his agent. The agent told her that the amount she was asking for her figure to be insured was too high. 'But I think each one is worth $6 million, don't you?' she asked Warren. He had to agree.

Madonna tried to be realistic about the relationship with Warren. She said that she didn't want to be swept away by the excitement of being with him. 'Sometimes I'm cynical,' she said wistfully to one reporter, 'and I think it will last as long as it lasts. Then I have moments when I'm really romantic and I think: My God, we're just *perfect* together.' Indeed, hope does spring eternal . . .

Working with Warren as her director was not as difficult for Madonna as some thought it might be. Warren is known for directing his actors to film a scene twenty, sometimes thirty, times before he is finally satisfied. Many observers thought Madonna would be intolerant of such demands. 'Even I thought it would be a problem,' Madonna observed at a press conference for *Dick Tracy* after the film was released. 'Because of our close friendship, I thought there would be problems. But there weren't. I respect him. He's been in the business for so many years, how dare I question his judgement about anything?'

To Kevin Sussums, for *Vanity Fair*, she said, 'I think you want the approval of anybody you're having a relationship with, and even if I wasn't with Warren, I would want his approval because he's a brilliant guy.'

Warren was equally as generous in his public comments about his new consort. Again, to Sessums: 'I don't know that there are many people who can do as many things as Madonna can do, as well, people who are in a positive frame of mind, who bring as much energy and willingness to work as she does.'

While there may have been harmony on the set of *Dick Tracy*, there were growing problems backstage as Madonna and Warren hit upon important differences in their personalities. For instance, while Madonna was the ultimate party girl, Warren was a 'homebody'. One night in the spring of 1989, Madonna took Warren to a dance club in a seedy part of Los Angeles called the Catch One, a notoriously popular gay hustlers' hangout in the ethnic South Central district. Woefully out of place in his tailored Versace three-piece suit, Warren declined to get up and dance with Madonna.

'Hey Pussy Man, come on out here,' she shouted at him from the dance floor. Wearing a hooded sweatshirt under a blue denim jacket, shorts, boxer's shoes and a leather cap, backwards, she laughed, tossed her head back and beckoned to him. 'Let's have fun!'*

I – observing Madonna for a feature about her – watched as Warren stuck out his lower lip and shook his head. 'No, I'm just fine,' he said with a weak smile. He then took a small bottle of allergy nasal spray from his jacket pocket and sprayed the medicine into his nose. 'I can't even breathe,' he complained, 'let alone dance.'

'Oh my God,' Madonna hollered back at him. 'Quit your whining, will you?'

Clearly exasperated by Warren's conservative demeanour, she danced with a couple of shapely young women. Beatty sat on the sidelines, watching, wheezing and looking as though he was truly feeling his age.

'I shoulda' come here with Rob Lowe,' Madonna shouted out at Warren, referring to the young actor she was also rumoured to be dating at the time. 'Now, he's a guy who knows how to party-hearty.' (The two were not in a serious relationship.)

Warren just shrugged.

The next morning, Madonna was at the Johnny Yuma Recording Studio in Los Angeles recording the vocals to the Stephen Sondheim songs that would appear on the album *I'm Breathless (Music from and Inspired by the Film Dick Tracy)*. Wearing a low-cut, pink, satin minidress over leggings, she stood in front of the microphone and sang the song beautifully while a room full of people, including Warren watched, apparently agog.

Recalled one studio technician, 'Madonna and Warren were

---

* Madonna's nickname for Beatty was 'Pussy Man' because, as she explained to the *Advocate*, 'When I say pussy, you know what I mean. He's a *wimp*. I enjoy expressing myself, and if I think someone's being a pussy, I say it.'

happy together, but mismatched just the same. I remember the night she recorded the vocals to "Hanky Panky" – which is about Beatty's favourite sport, spanking. The atmosphere was so charged and intimate, I felt like I was intruding on something private. She was flirtatious. He lapped it up. She definitely knows how to keep a man interested. Plus, she was proud to be there with Warren. She wore him like a badge of honour. Some people whispered that he was only using her to help promote his movie. That seemed possible to me. But she was definitely using him, as well.'

Later that day in April 1989, Warren accompanied Madonna to an audition for the futuristic video of her song, 'Express Yourself' (inspired by the 1926 Fritz Lang classic film, *Metropolis*). She had twenty dancers (some were only models who could also dance) in a line-up, finalists for the $1 million production (only Michael Jackson's long-form 'Thriller' cost more). Marching down the line, a gum-chewing drill sergeant, she sized up each candidate. To one long-haired fellow, she said, 'Now, there's no problem with cutting your hair, is there?' When he hesitated, she said, 'Oh, give me a break. Yes or No!'

Then, on to the next dancer. 'What's with that posture?' she asked. 'Stand up straight,' she ordered. 'Do you want this job or not?'

Then, to the next one. 'Oh my God,' she said. 'Look at you.' She paused for a moment to scrutinize him. Then, she turned to Warren and said, 'Look at the bulge in this guy's tights. What's *that* all about?'

Warren didn't respond. Instead, he just looked on with a bemused expression. 'Man, she's rather a bitch, isn't she?' Warren observed to one of the choreographers.

'Yeah, well . . .' answered the choreographer, his tone exhausted.

'Or maybe she's just showing off for me?' Warren wondered aloud. Looking troubled, he took out a silk handkerchief from his breast pocket. Then, he blew his nose.

'Blond Ambition'

After they finished *Dick Tracy*, Warren and Madonna would have some time away from each other while busying themselves with other career matters. As he focused on editing *Dick Tracy*, she concentrated on her 'Blond Ambition' concert tour

On Friday 13 May 1990, Madonna kicked off 'Blond Ambition' in Tokyo. With complete control over virtually every aspect of this extremely theatrical presentation, from music to sets to dancers to gowns, she would see the four-month tour through a total of twenty-seven cities worldwide. It was a truly spectacular show, the tour during which she wore the well-known gold cone bra designed by Jean-Paul Gaultier (who had been designing such exaggerated bras since 1984). 'With Madonna, it always comes down to clothes and shoes,' says her friend, background singer and dancer on the show, Niki Haris. 'Cone bras, bustiers, platforms . . . anything she could do to make it bad, she went for it.' Brazenly sexual dance numbers and moments of religious imagery commingled in a fast-paced, tightly choreographed, unforgettable extravaganza. Choreographer Vincent Paterson recalls that Madonna's goal was that the cast 'break every rule we can. She wanted to make statements about sexuality, cross-sexuality and the church. She did it.'

Madonna brought her sexual image to a new, more controversial plateau, by casually throwing in quips relating to sadomasochism. After performing the Forties-inspired 'Hanky Panky', she joked, 'You all know the pleasures of a good spanking, don't you?' Then, in what may, or may not, have been a double entendre, she told the audience, 'When I hurt people, I feel better, you know what I mean?'

To add new life to classic numbers from her repertoire, such as 'Like a Virgin', Madonna lay on a scarlet bed attended by two male dancers, both wearing the cone bras strapped to their bare chests which they lovingly caressed throughout the number, reorchestrated somehow to sound Middle Eastern in melody. Then, to bring the song to a rousing climax, Madonna frantically humped the furniture while rubbing her body in a frantic, *faux* masturbation scene. If she was a 'virgin' before the song started, she seemed determined to lose her maidenhood before it was through.

At the time of the 'Blond Ambition' tour, Madonna was at the peak of her popularity. (When HBO broadcast the show on 5 August 1990, she reached her largest American TV audience: 4.3 million households tuned in, giving HBO its highest ratings ever for an original programme. For those who thought the special was too racy for television, Madonna had a message during the broadcast. 'You know what I have to say to America,' she said, employing a tough New York accent. 'Get a fucking sense of humour, okay?' Then, pointing directly to the view: 'Lighten up!')

While she was still in rehearsals for 'Blond Ambition', Madonna decided to market a video vehicle tie-in to the concert tour. While the public had not so far been eager to accept her in an acting role, it did seemed constantly transfixed by the Madonna character she had created. Certainly the outrageous, sensational, sarcastic and petulant side of the Madonna persona was based in truth. It's part of who she really was at the time. Her vulnerable side, though, is what she usually kept from her fans, and when she allowed that aspect of her personality to be exposed it was usually in a calculated attempt to generate sympathy. Her concept now was to produce a documentary of her life while on tour. Although she would soon be seen as the character Breathless Mahoney in *Dick Tracy*, perhaps she reasoned that if the role didn't interest her fans, they would, hopefully, enjoy seeing Madonna playing Madonna – on and off stage in the self-produced documentary. 'May St Jude, the saint of lost causes, find a way to bring that girl to her senses,' the privacy-obsessed Warren Beatty said when informed of Madonna's new idea by a mutual friend.

To direct the documentary, Madonna chose Alek Keshishian, a

young film maker who had directed music videos for Elton John and Bobby Brown. A Harvard graduate, he had directed one small film – a rock opera based on *Wuthering Heights* (his Harvard senior project) which Madonna had seen and enjoyed. In all probability, Madonna's gut instincts told her that the handsome, long-haired film maker with fresh ideas was the kind of hip, cool artist who could lend the film the right edge. 'There was a mutual attraction,' Keshishian now says, 'but it wasn't necessarily sexual.' That attraction would soon bring Keshishian into Madonna's trusted circle; he would become one of her best friends. He flew to Japan, where she was kicking off the tour, and began filming her in March 1990 for what would become a documentary entitled *In Bed with Madonna* (or *Truth or Dare*, as it is known in the United States).

Madonna gave Keshishian full access to her world, complete entrée to her life during the tour's four months. He and his camera crew would follow Madonna's every move, while on stage and off, while in make-up and without, while being nice . . . and not so nice.

I'm Breathless

By the time Madonna began working with Alek Keshishian on her 'Blond Ambition' documentary, she had already finished her next album.

No doubt, Warren Beatty had realized that hiring Madonna as an actress would have an added bonus attached to *Dick Tracy*: the possibility that she would participate in the soundtrack of his movie. To a film studio, the release of a Madonna record several weeks in advance of a film in which she was involved would automatically amount to millions of dollars' worth of promotion. When Warren Beatty gave Madonna the role of the gold-digging Breathless Mahoney, Disney (the film's distributor) got the benefit of a hugely popular pop star on the soundtrack, and Warner Bros. Records a good reason to release Madonna's seventh album, *I'm Breathless (Music from and Inspired by the Film Dick Tracy)*, in May 1990.

Once upon a time, a soundtrack album was just that: a theme or love song from the film among a collection of incidental music also heard in the movie. They were usually only marginally successful in the marketplace. Then, in the Seventies, the unprecedented success of the biggest selling of all pop music movie soundtracks, *Saturday Night Fever*, inspired film producers and record labels to rethink the soundtrack album as a viable, money-making concept. By the Eighties, and into the Nineties, record labels had embraced a different kind of 'soundtrack' LP, in which just a couple of songs included were from the film, with the rest of the music provided by various artists not heard in the movie, singing songs that had absolutely nothing to do with the film.

Madonna's album would feature three songs she recorded from the film. However, her real challenge would be to write and produce new songs for the album as well, songs that would have an authentic lyrical/musical connection to the film. Hence, the album's subtitle, *Music from and Inspired by the Film Dick Tracy*. It would be a difficult job because the three songs Madonna sang from the film were written by theatre legend Stephen Sondheim. So, the new songs Madonna chose to record would have to be at least comparable in style to his. In Madonna's favour, she would have a hand in producing the entire album – including the Sondheim songs – and her participation would at least ensure some measure of continuity. To help her with this ambitious project, Madonna brought along Patrick Leonard (who had become her most reliable ally in the studio), and recording engineer-turned-producer Bill Bottrell (whose work with Madonna would serve him well in securing production jobs with Michael Jackson and pop rocker Sheryl Crow).

Madonna and Leonard toiled to create music that would fit the style and attitude of the film, set in the Untouchables days of prohibition. On the album, Madonna and Leonard set the pace with the opener, 'He's a Man', a big, intense, vamping, bluesy song, which Madonna sings as if she's a hooker stalking the boulevard. Vocally, she's magnificent. 'I want people to think of me as a musical comedy actress,' she said at the time. 'That's what this album is about for me. It's a stretch. Not just pop music, but songs that have a different feel to them, a theatrical feel.' Indeed, she tackled the Sondheim selections – the moody, determined 'Sooner or Later', the modified ragtime of 'More' and the quiet, sentimental wonder, 'What Can You Lose' – with the verve of a Broadway veteran. Particularly during 'What Can You Lose', a duet with Mandy Patinkin, Madonna holds her own, her voice making its first appearance on the song like a flower opening at dawn, warming to the mission at hand. Her performance truly was sublime.

Comparably, Andy Paley's 'I'm Going Bananas' is sweet taffy, a Ricky Ricardo kind of song that Madonna performs totally in Breathless character. Then, as if to say, 'Hey, I can do that, too', she and Leonard crafted 'Cry Baby', a playful, Roaring Twenties ditty which Madonna sings as Betty Boop. Both tracks, pure fun and games, are left seeming like so much filler when Madonna and Leonard roll up their sleeves to create 'Something to Remember', which is complex and bittersweet, sailing on a wave of gorgeous, melancholy chords and rambling melody that quietly make it the most compelling thing to which Madonna has ever lent her voice. Should anyone ever query the lady about musical integrity, she can always point to the composition for 'Something to Remember' – it would silence even the most accomplished composer.

Madonna also managed to bring a certain dimension to what seemed like the lightest moments. The steamrolling 'Hanky Panky' simply sounds like a silly innocent romp until you realize what she's going on and on about is ('Warren's favourite pastime') . . . being spanked! It's difficult to listen to the songs on *I'm Breathless* and not be compelled to try and find the real Madonna in each song. She is, no doubt, more intelligent than Breathless Mahoney, but both possessed the drive and tenacity required to get exactly what they want. Consider: in 1983 Madonna was just a fledgling dance music star looking to do great things. In less than ten years, she was the co-star of a major movie, performing on its soundtrack album, singing a playful duet – 'Now I'm Following You' – with Warren Beatty!

As fine as *I'm Breathless* turned out, it still needed a musical hook: a hit song. To that end, Madonna and Shep Pettibone (the brilliant engineer/songwriter/producer still standing in the shadow of Madonna's steady cohorts Steve Bray and Patrick Leonard), dreamed up a sleek song which Madonna would co-write and produce, 'Vogue'. It's a funky, uptown anthem celebrating the art of 'voguing' – a then-popular dance that was more about posing like a high-fashion model than breaking a sweat. Actually, voguing had been around long before Madonna sang about it; like Michael Jackson and his 'Moonwalk' dance, Madonna simply introduced to the rest of the world another hot, urban trend. The knock-out, pulsating dance track was a masterful dance tribute to 'Ladies with attitude, fellows who were in the mood' (with an accompanying, memorable black and white video that was, no doubt, inspired by classic photographs of Hollywood legends taken by Horst). The 'Vogue rap' is still one of Madonna's greatest camp, musical moments ('Greta Garbo and Monroe, Dietrich and DiMaggio . . .').

Madonna historian Bruce Baron notes that 'Vogue' was first planned as the B side of the 'Keep It Together' single. When Warner executives heard the song, however, it was decided to issue it as an A side. Baron points out that Madonna had to alter some more suggestive lyrics because the song was to be included on an album connected to a Disney movie. In 2016, Madonna would say that it only took her a couple hours to write 'Vogue', and that, in fact, her best songs were the ones that took about that long to write. 'I thought it was a very cool dance, very presentational and elegant and all about vanity,' she said about the song and the choreography it inspired.

'Vogue' did what Madonna and Shep Pettibone hoped it would do; it went to number 1. (Her grand performance of the song on the MTV Video Music Awards in 1990, dressed as Marie Antoinette in a giant hoop skirt outfit with lots of cleavage, a bouffant wig and white-powder make-up, was a classic, camp show that elevated the standards of future performances on that programme.)

Then, after 'Vogue', 'Hanky Panky' did a respectable climb to number 10. Both singles served to push *I'm Breathless* to number 2 on *Billboard*'s album chart. It sold two million copies in the US and five million globally.

I'm Breathless is one of Madonna's greatest musical moments, a fairly heady proclamation considering her prolific recording career. 'I worked so hard on that record,' she later said. 'In its time and place, it's important to me.' Also, Warren Beatty could not have been more pleased with it and, as her friends have recalled, she wanted nothing more than his approval when it came to all of her work in the film, acting and singing. 'He meant a lot to her,' confirms Freddy DeMann. 'She wanted him to be proud.'

Perhaps an indication of Warren's feelings about the album came when he co-hosted a party at his home with Madonna shortly after its release. He asked her to 'dress down' for his Hollywood friends, such as Jack Nicholson, Michelle Pfeiffer and Al Pacino, as well as the studio heads of various movie companies, the so-called movers and shakers of the business.

Madonna had often commented on Warren's 'people skills'. It was true in 1990 – and is still true today – that his warm, firm handclasp the moment he turns his attention to someone often leaves that person with the feeling that he or she has been touched by something special. Madonna noticed the way people felt quickened by any encounter with Warren, sincerely happy to be in his presence. With her, it was a different story: unless they were real fans, most people were generally fearful of her upon meeting her, worried about what she might say or do to them. Indeed, usually when she walked into a room, people swarmed about her not because they wanted to touch her, but rather because they wanted to see what outrageous event might occur as a result of her presence, who she might insult, what swear word she would utter while doing it. She said that she wanted to learn from Warren how to be more gracious. Therefore, parties at Warren's were always thrilling for Madonna; she enjoyed the company of his influential show-business friends, and appreciated the way they treated her, accepting her as one of their own.

For the *Dick Tracy* party, Madonna wore a simple, bare-back black gown by Halston, her golden hair in a sophisticated twist. She appeared feminine, tailored, graceful and elegant. Smiling, touching, kissing and moving through the crowd, she looked like an experienced socialite. She was breezily conversant with people who usually bored her. She laughed gaily at Warren's jokes. She didn't swear. Did she ever dream she'd come so close to the magic, power and glamour of true Hollywood, and fit in so well? Probably, yes. 'She was delightful,' recalled a guest, 'the perfect hostess.'

During the party, Warren played 'Something to Remember' from the *Dick Tracy* soundtrack and asked his guests to stop talking long enough to listen to the song. Everyone obliged. Certainly, during these few minutes, Madonna must have felt at least a little awkward as she stood with a martini in one hand, a cigarette in the other . . . and all eyes on her. Even the platoon of tuxedo-clad waiters, stationed like toy soldiers with trays of crudités, pâtés and other appetizers, stopped serving long enough to take notice.

When the song was over, Warren walked over to Madonna and said something to her. She responded with a surprised smile and a nod of what seemed like appreciation. Then, with a flourish, he turned from her and began to applaud. Following his lead, his guests joined in, showering Madonna with cheers, smiles and words of congratulations. For her, it must have been a moment like no other. As Jack Nicholson later remembered, 'She stood there and just accepted it all graciously . . . this beautiful, unpredictable, amazing, young woman with tears in her eyes, and I thought – Jesus! What a star.'

Warren Asks for Madonna's Hand in Marriage?

It was 1990. In a few months, Madonna would turn thirty-two. Seemingly incapable of true intimacy, she somehow always managed to attract men, like Sean Penn, John Kennedy and now Warren Beatty, all of whom were equally incompetent. Her love life was about to become even more entangled . . .

On 16 May, over a romantic dinner at a Hollywood restaurant after a hard day's dubbing in the studio, Warren Beatty made a surprising move. Either he asked for Madonna's hand in marriage (which is what she told her friends) or he asked her to agree one day to become engaged to marry him (which is how he vaguely described the offer to his friends). Whatever his proposition, he presented her with a six-carat, $30,000 diamond and sapphire ring.

Madonna – wearing a long straight blonde wig parted in the middle and what appeared to be a man's classic pinstripe suit with a bustier – slipped the ring on the middle finger of her left hand, ostensibly to conceal the fact that it signified a promise of marriage. After Warren signalled the waiter to refill their glasses of Cristal champagne, the couple toasted the moment. So excited was he that Madonna had accepted his ring, Warren tipped the waiter – one of the sources for this story – $500.

Most of their friends had to agree that the promise between Madonna and Warren – whether it was an actual engagement or, rather, an agreement to one day become engaged – didn't seem to bring them any closer as a couple; they continued in their argumentative way.

'Keep your stupid opinions to yourself,' Madonna said to Warren over dinner one night at the Ivy in Los Angeles just days after the 'engagement'. The reason for the fight remains unclear. Appearing somewhat angry, Beatty tossed a handful of bills onto the table. He got up. He walked out. A chagrined Madonna was left to sit alone and stew – with about fifty bemused patrons gawking at her. 'Stop staring at me,' she loudly called out before storming off.

When the couple went to San Antonio, Texas, to fulfil a weekend studio publicity commitment, Warren and Madonna stayed at the expensive La Mansion del Rio Hotel. In between press responsibilities, Warren let off steam by golfing while Madonna enjoyed daily facials and other such pamperings. Bill Hollerman, a golfing buddy of Beatty's, remarked, 'Warren spent the weekend on the telephone to Jack [Nicholson] complaining about Madonna, that she and Sandra Bernhard were planning a big wedding, that Sean Penn was calling him every fifteen minutes screaming at him to leave his wife alone. It went on and on. Beatty said that she wasn't happy unless she was fighting with him. He told me, "She's a nice girl, but you can't take her out. You don't know what she's going to say, or do, next. You don't know what the next big fight will be about. I'm too old for this."'

'But you're not old,' his friend told him.

'Well, I'm old enough to not want to look foolish,' Warren said.

Hollerman also reported that Barbra Streisand, one of Beatty's ex-girlfriends, was also on the telephone to Texas telling him that he was 'crazy for falling for a young floozy'. A former business associate of Barbra's concurs, 'When she heard about Warren and Madonna, she became a great instigator. She and Warren had little to do with each other prior to that news, then suddenly she was his great protector, telling him that Madonna was only using him to advance her film career.

'Also, his elderly mother Kathleen, still a big influence on his life, did not approve of Madonna. No matter how much Madonna tried to impress the older woman, she was not able to do so.' ('It's no wonder,' Madonna said, privately. 'Look at how many women she has seen with her son. She probably didn't approve of any of them, either.')

An unpredictable breaking point came when Madonna presented Warren with an expensive oil painting as a gift. After politely thanking her, he stashed it behind the couch where he probably intended for it to remain, for it did not match his decor. After three days, Madonna took it upon herself to hang the painting on a wall in his living room. When he saw it displayed without his permission, Warren exploded at her, accusing her of trying to 'control' him. The battle raged on from there. It was a small incident but, as often happens, it triggered something in Warren and Madonna that caused a fight big enough to lay ruin to any future plans they may have had.

Dick Tracy premiered in June 1990 and, after all the attendant hype, it seemed as if it would be the box-office success Disney had anticipated. It opened to big box-office receipts. (In the end, though, the film would prove to be a financial disappointment, with US sales of only $104 million.)

Madonna was unhappy with the way her production numbers were edited; she has said that she refused to watch the entire movie because she couldn't bear to see the way her routines were cut. Warren thought she was being silly, which only inspired more arguing between them. Matters became especially tense between the couple when Warren would only agree to a cover of *Newsweek* magazine on the condition that he be featured alone. When *Newsweek*'s editor-in-chief Rick Smith informed Disney studio head Jeffery Katzenberg that without Madonna there would be no cover profile, he ordered a photograph that included Madonna be immediately sent to the magazine. Still, Madonna thought it disloyal of Warren to try to cut her out of a major magazine cover, and the two engaged in yet another argument, this one about that matter of publicity.

One business associate and friend of Beatty's says, 'I was in Florida with Warren [for further *Dick Tracy* promotion] when a call came in from Madonna. "I'm working," he told her. We were golfing. That, to me, told the story.'

'Do you love her?' Warren's friend asked as the two played golf.

Warren seemed confused by the question. 'She's fun,' he said. 'But what is love, anyway? I really don't think I know. My problem,' he admitted, 'is that I'm easily bored.'

His associate now says, 'I wasn't encouraged by his answer. I knew then and there that they would not be getting married, though he did tell me he had asked Jack Nicholson to be his best man if he ever married her. He also said she had asked Sandra Bernhard to be her maid of honour. I thought to myself, well, that sounds like a pretty good show, but maybe not such a good marriage. I knew it would never happen, just by his attitude.'

While the relationship was clearly doomed, Madonna seemed determined to hang on to Warren Beatty, anyway. At the time, she was known by people in her circle to have an addictive personality when it came to men. She seemed to become 'hooked' to the drama of whatever relationship she was in at any given time. The fact that she and Warren engaged in such terribly acrimonious fights is what, apparently, tied them together. It was the same kind of drama that had kept her linked to Sean Penn long after their relationship should have been history. While it may not have been a good relationship, it was, at least, still some sort of relationship . . . her way of hanging on to Sean. Now, Madonna wanted to save whatever she had with Warren.

The End of Warren

In August 1990, after *Truth or Dare/In Bed with Madonna* was finished, Madonna showed Warren Beatty and some other friends of hers a rough cut in the screening room of Beatty's home. One friend of Beatty's who was present recalls that she brought popcorn for everybody – a dozen people – and served it with sodas saying, 'I want this to be like an old-fashioned movie.' (For her own enjoyment,

Madonna brought a bottle of soy milk along with Cheddar Lites – fat-free cheese crackers.) Then, as the movie got underway and it became clear that Madonna's salty language would be as it is in real life, Warren said to his friends, 'My definition of old-fashioned and her definition of old-fashioned seem somewhat at odds.'

'Oh, Christ, when did you get to be so stuffy?' Madonna asked Warren while the film played on and he winced and grimaced at certain scenes. 'Don't you remember when you were young and free, and rebellious? Don't you remember when you walked a thin line?'

Beatty smiled wearily. 'Barely,' he said.

'My old man,' Madonna said lovingly as she put her head on his shoulder. 'He'd rather be home looking at his "Hollywood Ladies of the Eighties" girlie calendar.'

Beatty turned away in dismay while watching Madonna teach her dancers how to give oral sex by using a water bottle as a prop. During another scene, when Madonna calls Warren an 'asshole' and hangs up on him, he shook his head with disapproval. Perhaps he was wondering if his girlfriend could tell the difference between her personal life and show business. Certainly, to a man as conscientious about privacy as Warren Beatty, the delineation must have seemed blurred in this documentary.

Later in the film, a conversation between Madonna and Beatty over a room-service meal was caught on camera. 'It was completely innocuous,' says the friend of Beatty's who was present at the screening. 'It wasn't so much what the two of them were saying, it was the way they were saying it. Madonna was being bitchy, as usual, and Warren was tolerant, as usual. You could see him tense up as the scene played out in front of everyone, making him look as if he allowed her to walk all over him. There were other scenes with Warren, too, that I suppose he was unhappy about.

'Afterwards, as the credits rolled, there was a lot of applause for Madonna. Warren seemed happy but, if you knew him, you knew he was just acting. She kept prodding him, asking what the problem was. "What's the matter? You didn't like my movie?" she kept asking, like a child wanting Daddy's approval. Finally, he said, "You know what? I just have a headache. I'm fine." Then, she started rubbing the back of his neck saying things like, "My poor Daddy, so tense. So much on his mind." I thought to myself, my goodness, either she really loves this guy, or she thinks he's her father.'

The next day, Madonna received a letter by messenger from Warren Beatty's attorney. In it, the demand was made that certain scenes with Warren be deleted from the final version of the film, or she would be sued. Most of her friends would have predicted a volatile reaction from Madonna. However, there wasn't one. If there was an argument between Madonna and Warren about the legal threat, no one heard about it.

'She didn't say anything to anyone about any of it,' said Niki Haris. 'However, I felt a deep sadness in her. But one thing about Madonna that people around her well know is that if she doesn't bring up a sore subject, you don't bring it up, either. The fact that she didn't say a word about the matter said, at least to me, that she was very bothered by it.'

In the end, the scenes in question were excised from the movie.

Later, Madonna complained to writer Don Shewey, 'There were phone conversations I thought were really moving and touching and revealing, but Warren didn't know we were recording. It wasn't fair, plus it's a federal offence. He, more than anybody, was reluctant to be filmed. Ultimately, I don't think he respected what I was doing or took it seriously. He just thought I was fucking around, making a home movie.'

Upon the film's release (in May 1991), some viewers were amazed that Madonna had left intact another surprising and genuinely candid moment. Because she was having throat problems, she visited a throat specialist. When Madonna was asked if she wanted the consultation filmed, Warren Beatty, also present, observed, 'She doesn't want to live *off camera*, much less talk.' Upon the movie's release she explained, 'I think what Warren was trying to say is that he is very shy and private and he doesn't understand my lack of inhibition because he's the opposite of me. What's so intimate about my throat? I mean, my God, everyone knows when I'm having an abortion, when I'm getting married, when I'm getting divorced, who I'm breaking up with. My throat is now intimate? Anyway, the cameras didn't follow me around twenty-four hours a day. They weren't in the room when I was fucking.'

There were some incidents, however, that Madonna decided should not be seen by her public. For instance, during the three nights of concerts in Boston, she caused so many problems for the staff of the Boston Harbor Hotel, she's not likely ever to be forgotten there. She and her entourage had taken over thirty rooms on floors nine to eleven, at a cost of $48,000. Making matters difficult for the kitchen staff was that all of her food had to be flown in from Hong Kong.

'She would be absolutely infuriated if she had to wait more than twenty minutes for a specially cooked order,' said Diane Demitri, who worked in Guest Relations at the hotel at that time. 'We didn't know how to cook those foods, and so the poor chefs were in the kitchen frantically looking up directions in Asian cook books while Madonna was phoning down every ten minutes screaming, "Where's my fucking noodles? Where's my fucking noodles?"'

Madonna also insisted that none of the staff ask her for autographs, or attempt to chat with her if they saw her in an elevator.

'No employee who came into contact with her was allowed to address her or even act as if they recognized her,' said Diane Demitri. 'She had registered under the name of Kit Moresby [a character from one of her favourite books, *The Sheltering Sky*] and, even though you knew it was Madonna when she called for room service, you had to address her by the other name.

'Housekeeping called me one morning and said, "Ms Moresby is upset because she says her bath water is a funny colour." I told them to send someone up to her room right away. When he got there, he found "Ms Moresby" in a white robe, pacing the floor, livid. Sadly, she was right. The pipes had apparently rusted and the water was slightly off-colour. When he apologized, "Ms Moresby" took the towel that had been wrapped around her head, rolled it into a ball, and hurled it at him. "How is a woman supposed to bathe in that muck?" she screamed at him. "I have a show to do tonight. Do you know how much stress I am under? Do you know how torturous my life is?"

'When she and her staff checked out of the hotel, everyone breathed a sigh of relief,' said Diane Demitri. 'When we went into her suite, she had left on the room service tray a card with her name embossed on it. In it, she wrote, "What a dump!"'

After Warren Beatty's warning that he might litigate against Madonna over her documentary, nothing seemed the same between them – not that it had been good between them prior to his threat. He had already begun to distance himself from her and, despite her apparent desire to do so, Madonna was powerless to salvage the relationship. It was actually Warren's decision that they end the relationship. Madonna had no choice in the matter.

Most of the public seemed unaware of the particulars of the romance between Madonna and Warren, and why it was that she seemed to be so angry whenever asked about him. It was difficult to separate the sensational reports from the truth, and there were so many conflicting tabloid reports that most sensible people simply disregarded all of them.

Madonna spent a couple of days crying over Warren, about how cruel he had been to lead her down this road, only to drop her. He again explained that the ring he had given her had only been a friendship ring, not one that signified an engagement.

To Madonna, it may have been like losing a father, as well as a lover, and for no reason she could understand. Warren simply could not commit to a relationship – which is why he stayed single for so long, until Annette Bening finally tamed him. Madonna had her issues, but he had his, too. It could never have worked.

Moreover, Warren Beatty had shown Madonna a side of elite

Hollywood she'd never before known, and one that she didn't yet want to abandon. His was a rarefied, exclusive world, one in which he encouraged standing ovations for his girl from big stars at glamorous cocktail parties. It wasn't easy letting go of all of that. How she had enjoyed melting into the elite company of his friends, if only a few times during parties at Warren's. She told intimates that she hated him for having aroused not only emotion in her, but for introducing a new way of life, as well – one in which people carried themselves with grace and dignity rather than with rock and roll arrogance – only then to force her to have to walk away from it. True to her often melodramatic nature, she felt cheated and used. Also true to her personality, Madonna privately said that she was annoyed at herself for not having had the strength to be the one to end it with Warren Beatty, before he ended it with her. Everyone in her circle, though, viewed her relationship with Warren for what it had really been: a simple dalliance between two film stars that was not meant to amount to much.

After it was all over, Madonna attempted to downplay the significance of their romance in press interviews, probably because she was truly hurt by him and does not like to portray herself in the public eye as ever having been sad or vulnerable. For his part, Warren has said next to nothing about how or why the relationship ended.

'I guess I meant nothing at all to Warren Beatty,' Madonna said sadly to one person on her management team. 'He used me and then tossed me aside like a piece of old meat.'

'I don't know about all of that,' says her friend Erica Bell. 'I always wondered how serious she really was about him. They didn't have much in common, let's face it. But the heart wants what it wants, I guess. And she wanted him. Was it really that Warren was just a big conquest for her? Could be,' Erica Bell concludes, answering her own question. 'I think she went after him because she could, because he was good prey. But then, as it sometimes happens, the hunter got captured by the game.'

The Tony Ward Epiphany

On 16 August 1990, Madonna's thirty-second birthday, she received a package at her home, a gift from Warren Beatty. When she opened the box, she found a brooch that probably cost about $300. It seemed like a cheap gift; unimpressed, she dismissed it with a quick flick of the hand. 'I need to take a drive,' she said, looking sombre. She then got into her car with a friend who happened to be with her when the package was delivered. 'If Warren and I weren't finished before, we sure are now,' Madonna said. She kicked off her high heels and began driving barefoot. As she steered her black Mercedes 560SL around a sharp curve of Mullholland Drive, she tossed the brooch out of the window.

Annoyed by the way her romance with Warren Beatty had turned out, Madonna began to take stock of her life. At thirty-two, she looked back on the years – as she would later recall – and began to realize that she could only remember her life by what she was doing in her career at the time. She enjoyed her fame, still, and her career was thriving. She couldn't stop now. She wouldn't think of it. However, she was beginning to feel pangs of regret. 'What had she given up to get where she was now? That was the question,' recalled one of her brothers. Though not ready to address such concerns fully at this time, Madonna did what many unhappy people do when they feel desperate and lonely . . . especially at the end of a relationship – even a mediocre one, such as the one she had with Warren Beatty: they transfer their emotions to another person in what is then known as a rebound relationship.

Young, handsome Tony Ward was Madonna's rebound from Warren Beatty. While smoking a Marlboro cigarette and, perhaps, looking for love, Madonna spotted the twenty-six-year-old Tony on Malibu beach. His body was slender and coltish. His eyelashes were long and dark. His skin translucent. Though he had appeared as an extra in her 'Like a Prayer' and 'Cherish' videos, Madonna paid him little attention then. Now, it was her thirty-second birthday, and she knew immediately that Tony should be her special gift. She went over to him and – who knows why – proceeded to grind out her cigarette on his back. She then reached around him and pinched one of his nipples so hard, he cried out, 'Fuck!' Rather than be angry, Ward was fascinated. His good-looking face broke into a grin. 'I think I can balance my glass on your ass,' she told him. 'You know, I just love a man with an ass like yours.' She patted his butt softly; he closed his eyes, like a puppy. Then she traced his lips with her fingertip. The attraction between them was immediate.

After they got to know each other, Madonna found Tony to be kind, gentle and understanding. Though she didn't speak much about what had occurred with Warren Beatty, Ward would later say that he sensed an underlying unhappiness in Madonna's personality. 'I'm not a woman who likes to admit to needing anyone or anything,' Madonna told him. 'I've always thought of that as being a weakness.' It was as if she needed someone in whom to confide. However, any shared confidences would have to wait because, that night, Madonna and Tony shared her bed.

Afterwards, Madonna couldn't stop talking to friends about Tony's body, so hard and firmly muscled. 'A nice change from Warren,' she cracked.

Says Erica Bell, 'Madonna was essentially holding casting calls for a boyfriend, and this was the guy she chose. Physically he was perfect for her. If you had a computer dating service, and you fed all her preferences into the computer, Tony Ward is what would come out. Five-foot-six, about 170 pounds, dark and sexy with the most beautiful brown eyes.'

The couple didn't waste much time in moving forward with their relationship. They actually had a lot in common, including their love of movies. 'When I fell in love with film as a kid, I was emotionally affected,' Tony Ward said. 'When I was a kid, I watched *Grease* fifty-plus times. I watched *Hello Dolly* fifty times. I watched endless Lucille Ball and I was addicted to Danny Kaye movies, Abbott and Costello, Katharine Hepburn and Jimmy Stewart. I wish I could have done a film with Danny Kaye,' he says. 'He was my favourite actor, the one I most related to.'

Tony moved into Madonna's Hollywood mansion in September 1990.

'It was so weird because he always fantasized about making love to Madonna,' recalls fashion designer Jayme Harris who was one of Tony's many girlfriends at the time. 'He also used to wish that he could have sex with me and have Madonna there watching. Tony wanted to do everything – to play my love slave and, also, my maid. For instance, he wanted to cook, do the dishes, take the trash out and make the bed. He liked high heels and thigh-high boots.'

Not surprisingly, given that both had a penchant for the outrageous, Madonna and Tony had an unusual, unconventional relationship. They enjoyed playing 'role games', and, she later admitted, few men were as accommodating as he was when it came to making her fantasies come true. Tony was bisexual, a cross-dresser and a nude model for homosexual magazines and leather pin-ups. Using the name Anthony Borden Ward, he was most known by some factions of the gay community for his nude six-page layout in a magazine called *In Touch for Men* in 1985. 'He was such a hit with our readers that the issue completely sold out within a few weeks,' recalled Keith Saltar, an editor at the magazine.

To entertain herself, Madonna would make up Tony and dress him in women's clothing – including underwear – and then go out on the town with him as her new 'girlfriend'. Ward also enjoyed playing a subservient role in Madonna's fantasies. For instance, when she took him to a birthday party for photographer Herb Ritts, she told him that she wanted him to wear jeans, and nothing else. When he insisted on adding a black leather vest to the ensemble; she allowed it. (For her part, she wore a black Chanel jacket, black tights, black sunglasses and black ankle boots.) She then proceeded to 'humiliate' him in front of the guests by forbidding him to speak even a word in her presence. He seemed to enjoy the game. When she demanded that he shave off his Fu Manchu moustache in front of the partygoers, he obeyed. Later, Madonna organized a game of Truth or Dare. During it, she dared Ward to strip for the crowd. He eagerly complied. When she further dared him to pull down his briefs and expose himself to the guests, he did that as well. That night, the two went back to her place – perhaps excited by their party antics – and enjoyed another 'wild ride' together. If she felt powerless about the way in which her relationship with Warren Beatty had ended, she was certainly balancing the scale with Tony Ward. In this relationship, she was the one calling the shots.

'I don't like being controlled,' she told him one day. 'To be free, you need a lot of money, and power, which I have,' . . . and which Tony didn't have.

On 10 December 1990, Madonna learned that she was pregnant with Tony's child. As she had been feeling queasy for a few days, she had told him that she suspected she was expecting, and asked him to accompany her to Cedars-Sinai Medical Center for the necessary tests. She had hoped it was true that she was pregnant. He wasn't sure what to hope for, 'except to just hope for the best'. When her physician, Doctor Randy Harris, confirmed that she was expectant, Madonna was jubilant. 'I want this child more than anything else in my life,' she told a friend the next day on the telephone.

'Will you marry Tony?' the friend wanted to know.

Madonna sighed deeply, as if acknowledging defeat in the marriage department. 'I doubt it,' she said, sounding weary. 'But I guess I can raise the kid on my own. In fact, I know I can do it.'

She must have realized that Tony was not husband material for her. Still, she was happy about the pregnancy. Perhaps she reasoned that if she could not have a satisfying relationship with a man, at least she could have one with her own child.

However, just a few days after the good news came the bad. Because of gynaecological complications, the health of Madonna's baby was already in jeopardy. In what must have been a heart-wrenching consultation, Harris recommended to Madonna and Tony that she terminate the pregnancy. This was crushing news. Madonna had undergone a number of abortions in the past, and had vowed to bring to full term any other baby she conceived. However, it was not meant to be. On 14 December Tony accompanied her to Cedars for a dilation and curettage (D&C) which took just fifteen minutes, but which also took a toll on Madonna.

Tony, who had been pacing the floors while the surgery was taking place, recalled, 'When I came back to the room, she was crying. It was very upsetting. She wanted that baby, and it seemed unfair that she couldn't have it.'

Madonna was impressed by the way Tony Ward cared for her. He was supportive in every way, determined to show her that he could be a good mate. He loved her, that much was clear to any observer, and hoped for a future with her. Tony, for whatever his faults, was different from the men Madonna had recently known. He seemed really to want to be with her, and to have no ulterior motives. 'I've been with a great many men and women,' he told her. 'But none that I've really loved. Until now.' For her part, she said she felt 'safe' with him. However, there were problems: Ward was confused and immature in ways that were impossible to deny. He had a secret: he was a married man.

Four days after Tony met Madonna, he and his girlfriend Amalia Papadimos were wed in Las Vegas. After the ceremony, Tony was ambivalent; he didn't know if he wanted to be with his wife, or with Madonna. Two weeks later, he told his wife that it wouldn't work out between them.

'We never really spent time together,' Tony explains of his marriage. 'She was shocked that I would change my mind like that. But I love her, still. She's my buddy. Obviously, being married for two weeks and then saying, "I can't do this", put her in a really bad spot.'

He also didn't know whether or not to tell Madonna of his marriage, and opted not to do so immediately. Instead, he moved into her home and, perhaps, hoped 'for the best'.

'It was just before Christmas, I believe, that Tony told Madonna that he was a married man. I guess that was a big hurt for her,' says Tina Stanton, who also dated Tony at this time. 'I once overheard Madonna tell him, "Guys like you usually bounce right off my radar screen. I'm not even sure why I ended up with you, except that I couldn't resist you." Plus, she saw something in Tony, a naiveté, an innocence, a good heart.'

The fact that Madonna would tell Tony Ward that a man such as himself would 'bounce right off' her 'radar screen' indicates that she didn't understand herself as well at this time as she may have thought. If anything, she was *attracted* to men like Tony, welcomed them into her world . . . and, inevitably, paid the price for such poor judgement. Not only was Tony emotionally unavailable – like Sean Penn, John Kennedy and Warren Beatty – he was married.

It was at a Christmas party at her home in December that Madonna and Tony became embroiled in an argument that would be the subject of discussion among her intimates for years to come.

Dressed for the festive and formal occasion in a black Gaultier halter-top dress, Madonna's hair that evening was short and blonde. One would never know from her easy composure that she'd had such a bad day. A household employee had poured the wrong bath essences into her hot tub at home, turning her hair green while she relaxed in it. (One can only imagine her reaction upon making this discovery in the mirror on the morning of a big party!) It took her hairdresser four hours to restore her 'natural' blonde colour, at a cost of $750. Now, she looked terrific. White-coated waiters circulated among the guests – the usual relatives, friends and business consorts mixed with the publicity seekers and hangers-on who hoped to be mentioned in the gossip columns the next day – with trays of chilled champagne and warm hors d'oeuvres.

A pretty girl who couldn't have been more than sixteen – her eyes heavily veiled by drugs – threw herself into Tony's arms, asking to be taken. Madonna glared for a moment, then shrugged and turned away.

Later, Tony spotted Madonna dancing with a man he had long viewed as a rival for her affections. As he watched them cuddle on the dance floor, he seethed until he could take it no more.

'Hey, you're *my* woman,' Tony suddenly hollered. 'Knock it off.'

'Oh yeah?' Madonna countered as she broke away from her dance partner. 'You have your nerve. I'm my *own* woman.'

Angry, Tony grabbed an expensive Chinese vase and threw it to the floor, shattering it.

In retaliation, Madonna hurled an antique lamp at him. He ducked. Everyone watched with horrified fascination as the lamp hit the wall and smashed to bits.

In response, Tony took a silver tray of crudites, pâtés and olives, and threw it to the floor with a crash.

Then, in the finest tradition of melodramatic frustration and rage, Madonna said, 'Out! Everyone, get the fuck out. The party's over.' Turning to Tony, she further clarified, 'And that includes you. Get out!' Then, she turned and walked out of the room, leaving everyone to fetch their wraps and jackets.

The next day, Ward apologized profusely and presented Madonna with a new vase filled with white roses. It was a sweet gesture yet one that would not change anything. After all, how many more hair-raising scenes could she tolerate in affairs of the heart?

Bingo. It was at this time that she had an epiphany.

Unwittingly, the existence of Tony Ward in Madonna's world had provided a transformative catalyst, one that would alter her life. Something in her had been adjusted by the holiday confrontation with Tony and she made a decision about what she expected from the men in her life. It was likely the cumulative experiences of Madonna's doomed romances up until this point, all of which, finally, brought into clear focus what she wanted in a relationship. As Madonna put it to Sandra, 'I feel as if my disorganized mind has just been organized.'

'Tony, you're just not enough for me,' Madonna said to him, as Tony later recalled. 'I'm finally at a stage in my life where I realize that I have to have more than what you can offer. I see that now.'

Tony was thrown. It was startling, he would later say, to hear Madonna suddenly so certain about what she wanted, what she deserved. The pain of it, of course, was that her newly painted picture didn't include him.

'If that's how you feel about it,' he told her in a crushed voice, 'then I guess there's nothing I can do but leave.

'It was really hard for me to take, to hear her say that to me,' Tony recalls. 'It was a very powerful statement. I was feeling very hurt, very abandoned and all of these "poor me" things. It took me a long time to understand. I still have a very strong love for Madonna, and it doesn't matter to me whether she's here with me, or somewhere else. If I never see her again, I will still always love her. I know that if she's in a pinch, if the chips are down and she needs a friend, that she realizes she can call me and I'll be there.'

'I don't want us to hate each other,' Tony Ward remembers Madonna telling him as she hugged him goodbye. 'I'm just so exhausted,' she said, perhaps referring to her most recent romances. 'After people break up, they say terrible things about each other. I'm not going to do that to you, Tony' she concluded. 'I'm not going to let anyone else do it, either.'

'Madonna, if people knew the real you, I think they'd be surprised,' Tony Ward told her.

'Well, let's just hope they never find out,' she said with a grin. 'After all, I have an image to protect.'

Years later, Tony would put the relationship into perspective: 'That lady!' he exclaimed. 'I was never a fan. I saw her in that silly "Lucky Star" video in the early days of MTV, and I knew I would be reunited with my mother/lover/teacher/friend/bitch/cheater/liar/goddess/student/poetess/angel/pain/tears/broken-heart/inspiration/intrigue/and human awe. We fell hard immediately, too much, too soon for the both of us. In the end, when you love something, let it go.'

In another interview he summed it all up this way: 'I love you *always*, lady.'

The Immaculate Collection

By the end of 1990, a new Greatest Hits album from Madonna was ready for release from Warner Bros. Records, *The Immaculate Collection*. Actually, this was much more than a mere collection of Madonna's biggest-selling and most popular songs. It served as a proud landmark for a career that, from its professional inception, had moved in only one direction: up.

Released in November, with its title a clever play on the biblical reference to Mary's Immaculate Conception of Jesus, the album contained more genuine hits than a Top 40 radio station usually plays in an hour. It was an audio chronicle of Madonna's wild ride thus far, starting at the beginning with three of her first singles – 'Holiday', 'Lucky Star' and 'Borderline' – and moving on to the present day. Detractors could say what they wanted about the woman being a flash in the pan with little talent (and, believe it or not, there were actually sceptics who still expected Madonna to have a short-lived career), but *The Immaculate Collection* crystallized the reality of the Madonna success story: 'Like a Virgin', 'Material Girl', Crazy for You', 'Into the Groove', 'Live to Tell', 'Papa Don't Preach', 'Open Your Heart', 'La Isla Bonita', 'Like a Prayer', 'Express Yourself', 'Cherish' and 'Vogue' – fifteen hit records in all. Some of the most successful pop stars in the world have come and gone without ever having even a single number 1 record. It is the ultimate goal of any pop artist to top the record-selling charts – *The Immaculate Collection* contained eight of Madonna's chart-toppers.

Madonna's success as a recording artist wasn't really difficult to fathom if one understood what she represented. Someone like Pat

Benatar was cool, but she was a rocker, not a pop star. Madonna was the kind of female artist who didn't come along often in pop culture – a white girl with attitude who could keep a beat.

Madonna's music always had something for everyone. While not too funky for the white kids in suburbia to embrace, it was still rhythm and blues and hip hop enough for inner city kids – her core black audience – also to endorse. After all, several million records ago, Madonna was a dance act, an artist whose energy and inspiration emanated from the streets.

Before Madonna, the last singer to meld so effectively dance and pop influences was Donna Summer and her songwriters/producers Giorgio Moroder and Pete Bellote (and later just Summer and Moroder), whose brand of Europop successfully transcended mere disco. But Summer, however successful, was not armed with Madonna's uncanny musical sense of self and of the marketplace – instincts integral to creating the hit records that were compiled for *The Immaculate Collection*. By 1990, the production on some of those hits might have sounded a little dated (the drum machine was both one of the best and worst inventions of twentieth-century pop music), but the songs themselves were timeless.

Unlike most young artists who came along when she did, Madonna could redefine her identity at will. While she could easily create party music such as 'Into the Groove' and 'Express Yourself', she could also appreciate a cute pop ditty like 'Cherish'. She could also completely relate to serious, soul-bearing love songs such as 'Live to Tell' and 'Crazy for You', and do so without exhibiting even a trace of the cynicism required to make smart, self-deprecating records such as 'Material Girl' and 'Like a Virgin'. (Prince could also be as versatile, but not until much later in his career was he able to take himself less seriously on record. Michael Jackson could never do it. To him, record making was such serious business, there was no room in it for irony.) For Madonna, the reward for such versatility came in the form of a string of enduring hit records. *The Immaculate Collection* reached number 2 on *Billboard*'s album chart.

It eventually sold an amazing eighteen million copies worldwide, nine million of that number in the United States and five million in the United Kingdom. The marketplace spoke loud and clear in its acknowledgement that the music was as enjoyable the second time around as the first.

Of course, *The Immaculate Collection* had assistance in getting the attention of record buyers with the inclusion of two new Madonna songs. 'Justify My Love', which would serve as the album's first single, was written and produced by fledgling rocker Lenny Kravitz with keyboardist André Betts serving as associate producer. (Later, Ingrid Chavez, a muse of Prince's signed to his Paisley Park label, came forward to claim and – also end up receiving – a share of the credit for writing some of the lyrics.)

On paper 'Justify My Love' must have sounded rather simple – a funky, drum pattern under a droning, aural synthesizer pad, with Madonna speaking sexy verses over the music, Kravitz casually moaning a melody in the background. The result was one of the few songs in Madonna's career on which she didn't actually have her creative imprint. Except for adding a few words, she let Kravitz shape the track. The finished mix oozed pungent sex, it was just that passionate. The single would hit number 1 on the *Billboard* chart, but not without the controversy that somehow always seemed to surround a new Madonna project.

Since *The Immaculate Collection* album was to be issued just before the release of her *In Bed with Madonna* documentary, Madonna was determined to keep the public's interest in her at a peak level. She decided – no surprise here! – that the creation of a good controversy could only work to her sales advantage. The problem was that she had crossed the line of what most people would consider good taste so many times in recent years, it had now become more difficult for her to shock the public. She needed a new idea, and it came to her when, during an interview, a journalist asked if any of her videos had ever been banned from MTV.

The 'Justify My Love' video – directed by Jean-Baptiste Mondino

– seems to have been made with the specific intention of having it be banned from television broadcast. In order to create the necessary outrage, Madonna incorporated into the video many of the themes that had generated headlines for her in the past. The concept is a simple one: Madonna, once again donning her Marilyn get-up, stumbles into a hotel room where an orgy seems to be taking place. Intrigued, she watches as topless and butch-looking lesbians fondle one another, transvestites cuddle, a voyeuristic and drugged-looking Tony Ward leers. Later, Madonna deep kisses an androgynous lesbian, and then runs out of the hotel, giggling mischievously.

Whether MTV was an unwitting participant or a co-conspirator in Madonna's scheme to create a sensation is unclear only to those who don't understand show-business commerce. The convenient chain of events ran like this: after heavily advertising an 'All Madonna Weekend', of which Madonna's 'Justify My Love' video was to be the main attraction, the station suddenly announced with great fanfare that the video could not be broadcast because it was 'religiously and sexually offensive'. On 29 November 1990, MTV announcer Kurt Loder explained to the channel's international audience that, 'When MTV programming executives got their first look at the video's steamy bed scenes, gay and lesbian snuggling, S&M and briefly bared female breasts, they decided they couldn't air it.' (Certainly few people who watch MTV would be uninterested in such a video with that kind of description.)

Suddenly, Madonna had scored a coup that had previously eluded her: a banned video.

As soon as the video was banned, Madonna's publicity juggernaut once again began to roll. There was much protestation from Madonna, who talked a great deal about censorship and how 'unfair' it all was to her. By this time, though, the media and public had long ago caught onto Madonna's game of 'controversy before product'. Still, Sire Records executive Seymour Stein seemed to buy into the game, or at least act as if he did: 'When she went in to make the video for "Justify My Love", she didn't make a video for the purposes of having it banned, so it couldn't be shown . . . I think she just believes in what she is doing.'

When ABC-TV's respected late-night programme, 'Night Line', decided to air a special devoted to the controversy, and then show the video in its uncut entirety, Madonna agreed to be interviewed for the programme on 3 December 1990. 'There was this enormous hoopla over a music video,' recalls Forrest Sawyer, her interviewer. 'It was all kind of astonishing.' During the interview, Sawyer pointed out the obvious: as a result of the controversy, the video – available in stores within a week of its ban, and just in time for Christmas at $9.95 – would most certainly make even more money for all concerned. 'Yeah,' Madonna said, shrugging, 'So, lucky me.' The first ever video single sold over 400,000 copies.

While 'Justify My Love' was controversial, breaking all the rules, by comparison, the second single from *The Immaculate Collection*, the uptempo 'Rescue Me', written and produced by Madonna with Shep Pettibone, was standard, pulsating dance fare. It rocketed itself to number 9 on the pop chart, inducting itself into the exclusive club formed by sixteen other number 1 and Top 10 hits that made *The Immaculate Collection* a project both to behold and respect.

Ingrid

In the spring of 1991, Madonna met a fascinating woman who was to become one of her closest friends, Ingrid Casares. Casares, an attractive and stylish Cuban-American, was introduced to Madonna by Sandra Bernhard. At the time, she was working as a model booker at Wihelmina Modeling Agency in Los Angeles when her lover, Sandra, took her to Madonna's birthday party.

With her boyish, short dark hair and contagious personality, Ingrid appealed to Madonna who, after meeting her, said that she wanted to get to know her better. The two became fast friends, much to the dismay of Sandra Bernhard.

Photographer Chita Mavros was a friend of Ingrid's at the time. She recalls, 'Ingrid and Sandra were having certain relationship problems. Sandra asked Madonna to talk to Ingrid, to intervene and help her work things out. However, in the course of doing that, Madonna and Ingrid became very close, very quickly. Suddenly, all Ingrid could talk about was "Madonna, this" and "Madonna, that". Sandra was upset.'

Since that time, Sandra has said she could have solved her problems with Ingrid if only Madonna had stayed out of it. 'She felt that Madonna – with her show-business lifestyle and wild days and nights – was a complete distraction to Ingrid,' said Chita Mavros. 'Then, she accused Madonna of sleeping with Ingrid, though Madonna denied it.

'Madonna and Sandra had some horrible fights about Ingrid. One day, Sandra went to Ingrid's apartment, and who did she find coming out of the shower in nothing but a towel? Madonna. Sandra went berserk, screaming and hollering and accusing Ingrid of cheating on her with her best friend. There was no controlling her, she was that irate. After that, she and Ingrid broke up, and she and Madonna were no longer friends.'

The irony, at least according to Chita Mavros, was that Ingrid and Madonna were probably not involved in a sexual relationship. Ingrid had said that Madonna wasn't her 'type', and that she just appreciated her friendship. Certainly, both women deny the relationship went any deeper.

When I once asked Madonna what happened between her and Sandra, she said, 'I can only tell you this: there was a huge misunderstanding about something, and she went off the deep end and never returned. That's all I will say on the subject.'

In Bed with Madonna

In May 1991, *In Bed with Madonna* was finally released. In 'pushing the envelope', as she would put it, this movie, along with several upcoming projects, would prove that even Madonna could push too much and go too far . . . until finally crossing the line between good taste and bad.

In Bed with Madonna is fascinating to watch, not so much because its star is particularly witty or clever in it but rather because of what happens around her – the way her dancers fawn over her and vie for her attention, her manager Freddy DeMann is mistreated by her, and how she alternately rides roughshod over and mothers everyone about her. It is truly a camp 'performance'.

It's also intriguing to watch a woman in action who is, apparently, narcissistic enough to believe that everything she says or does has great importance and relevance. Why otherwise would she want herself committed to film while having her make-up applied, or while talking on the telephone, or even visiting her mother's grave for the first time since she was a child – in a limousine, her eyes hidden by big and round Jackie-O sunglasses? ('I wonder what she looks like now?' she mused of her deceased mother, her voice a monotone. 'Probably just a bunch of dust.')

As the cameras rolled, Madonna bickered with Warren Beatty, whispered secrets to Sandra Bernhard, and recalled a sexual encounter with a high-school girlfriend, who later turned up in the proceedings to say with a mixture of embarrassment and astonishment that she had no recollection of the incident. 'But she *did* finger-fuck me,' Madonna insisted. 'I remember looking at her bush!'

Shrewdly, she also showed her soft side by playing mother hen to her brood of vulnerable, pampered back-up dancers and singers – some of whom were so young they were leaving home for the first time. Madonna led them in a prayer before every concert, she advised them on their love lives and refereed their arguments. In the film, she explains that she selected dancers and singers who were 'emotionally crippled' so that she could 'mother' them. She said, 'This was the opportunity of their lives. I wanted to impress them. I wanted to love them.' At one point, when twenty-two-year-old dancer Oliver Crumes – who kept insisting that he was the only heterosexual dancer in the troupe – was rumoured to have become sexually involved with her, and the story made the front page of one of the tabloids, Madonna counselled the others as to how to deal with their jealousy of Crumes. During a scene when she learns that Canadian officials may shut down her show because of its alleged indecency, she prays to God because 'all of my babies are feeling fragile'. At the end of the movie, she cavorts in bed with all of them, in various stages of undress. 'Get out of my bed and don't come back until your dick is bigger,' she orders one giggling dancer. Her manner was one that suggested cruelty and humour at the same time.

'I see a huge paradox in me,' she told the *Advocate*, in talking of her impression of the film, 'the intense need to be loved and the search for approval juxtaposed with the need to nurture other people, to be the mother I never had. I didn't realize how matriarchal I am, how maternal I am, until I watched this movie.'

Further, she told *Vanity Fair*, 'People will say, "She knows the camera is on, she's just acting." But even if I am acting, there's a truth in my acting. You could watch it and say, I still don't know Madonna . . . and good! Because you will never know the real me. Ever . . .

'I think the impression of me will be twofold,' she said. 'People will think, "Oh she isn't just a cold, dominating person." I think that's the world's perception of me, that I'm power-hungry and manipulating. I think a great deal of the movie shows a gentler side of me.'

When a journalist asked her if the movie was shocking, Madonna became defensive. 'Is what shocking?' she asked. 'Me giving head to a bottle? You see people doing it in movies all the time. It's a joke. What's shocking? Why don't *you* know if it's shocking or not? Don't you know your own feelings? It's a joke.'

Her manager, Freddy DeMann, felt that the movie would damage Madonna's reputation. As she later recalled, he tried to convince her to cut several scenes.

'The one where you stick your finger in your mouth to indicate that Kevin Costner makes you want to vomit, that has to go, Madonna,' he told her during one meeting.

'No. It stays,' she said, shaking her head.

'Well, the one where you say that woman finger-fucked you, that has to go. It's disgusting.'

'It stays,' she said. 'There's nothing disgusting about it.'

'Okay, but the one where you are a bitch to everyone . . .'

Finally, Madonna cut him off. 'Fuck you, Freddy,' she said, according to his memory of the meeting. 'Everyone knows I'm a bitch. Who cares? People think I'm Saddam Hussein. They compare me to Hitler. Leave my fucking movie alone! It's not telling people anything they don't already know.'

Apparently, one aspect of her life that Madonna did not want revealed in the film was any that involved the running of her business affairs. While she is known to be open, revealing and forthcoming, on matters of business she chose then (and still does today) to remain an enigma. So, cameras were forbidden in business meetings, even though director Alek Keshishian tried to force his way into them. 'Get out!' she screamed at him.

Rather than have her public understand that a good deal of her immense celebrity had to do with her genius for public relations as well as her talent, it seemed that Madonna wanted the public to believe that it stemmed only from her talent. So, when magazine editors scheduled articles that were to focus on her extraordinary business savvy, she refused to discuss profits, revenues or business strategies. Likewise, Madonna instructed her staff and friends not to talk about those matters, either.

In 1991, Madonna's revenues from her assorted music, film and commercial projects were around $60 million, including the $36 million generated by the 'Blond Ambition' tour. She put in long hours managing her holdings and investments, seldom delegating important responsibilities to others. She also set up a number of lucrative companies: Boy Toy, Inc., for music and record royalties; Siren Films, for film and video production (taking the place of Slutco, a video production company that she dissolved soon after starting); Webo Girl, for music publishing; and Music Tours, Inc., for live performance contracts.

Madonna was – and still is today – involved in all negotiations that relate to her career, always walking into meetings with a legal pad, a pencil and a great many questions. Says her former boyfriend, John 'Jellybean' Benitez, 'She has a lot of people feeding her the information she needs, and she looks at it more creatively than other artists do. She absorbs everything, and she asks a lot of questions.'

In 1991, Freddy DeMann received up to 10 per cent of her annual earnings. Her accountant, Bert Padell, had his services capped at $1 million, annually. Her legal negotiations were handled by Paul Schindler of Grubman Indursky Schindler, a company who used a system called 'instinctive billing' where fees are negotiated with clients *after* a deal had been struck, depending on how lucrative the outcome. Madonna felt that the attorney was worth the curious billing method.

Her fans, however, didn't really care what went on with Madonna behind the scenes, as long as she delivered to them on stage. Truly, the most wonderful part of *In Bed with Madonna* is the concert footage from the 'Blond Ambition' tour. The dancers, the sets, the music and, of course, Madonna, all are visually spellbinding. While watching her perform, one marvels at her level of commitment to her act and her audience. Certainly, few entertainers work as hard as Madonna to please a crowd. Few have even an inkling of Madonna's expansive imagination and vision.

Also captured in the video is the moment when Madonna brought her father Tony onto the stage in Detroit so that her audience could sing 'Happy Birthday' to him. Genuinely touching, it shows the daughter paying homage to father by literally bowing down to him in front of her fans, but only those closest to her and her family saw the real significance of the gesture. 'She was saying, "I love you, Dad. I want you to accept me. Look at all of these people. Look at how they love me",' says Niki Haris, who was on stage with Madonna at the time as one of her two singers. 'It was a genuine moment.'

Besides the jarring reality of how talented Madonna is as a performer, perhaps the one thing the viewer of *In Bed with Madonna* is left with is that – at least at this time – she was not someone most reasonable people would ever welcome into their lives. Certainly, she gave definition to the phrase 'high maintenance'.

Sex

On 21 October 1992, Madonna's notorious book, *Sex*, was published by Time-Warner. When the book finally appeared – after months of speculation and hype – the public discovered that Madonna's foray into the publishing world would be in the form of an oversized and overpriced ($49.95), 128-page volume, spiral-bound between embossed, stainless-steel covers, aptly titled, simply, *Sex*. As if to make certain that the public fully recognized the controversial nature of this publishing endeavour, the book arrived in book shops wrapped in silver Mylar (which also ensured that only paying customers were privy to what lay between its covers). Also included was a CD of Madonna's new song, 'Erotica', in a silver Mylar Ziploc bag. 'Warner Books is shitting in their pants about it,' said Freddy DeMann in assessing the publishing company's nervousness about distributing such a work.

Some might say that the genesis of Madonna's *Sex* shows a typical side of her character and the way that she, as she has put it in the past, 'takes a little of this and that and turns it into my own'. Earlier, in the fall of 1990, Judith Regan, then an editor of Simon & Schuster Pocket Books, had an idea for a book of erotica and sexual fantasies which she felt would be ideal for Madonna. 'I felt that it was right in line with what she was all about at that time,' says Regan. 'So I sent a box of material to her manager's office, which included erotic photos that I thought would interest her, as well as the kind of text I thought would be appropriate. It was colourful and imaginative, if I do say so myself. I was happy with it, anyway. As it turned out, she, too, was impressed and thought it would be a good idea. The next thing I knew I was in Los Angeles sitting with her and her manager, Freddy DeMann. I was pregnant at the time, and the first thing Madonna said to me was, "Well, you know, I don't have any children." It seemed odd that she would think that I wouldn't know such a thing about her, one of the most famous women in the world.'

'I just want you to know that I won't even think of doing this thing if you've offered it to even one other celebrity,' Madonna cautioned Judith Regan during their meeting.

'Why is that?' Judith asked. Of course, she knew the answer, but still wanted to hear it from the woman herself.

'Because it has to be unique to me,' Madonna said, predictably. 'It has to be for me, and for me alone.'

'Well, I started at the top. With you,' Judith assured her. 'If you're not interested, then I'll go elsewhere. But I hope that you will be interested. I think this could really work for you.'

Madonna seemed satisfied. During the rest of the meeting, she made it clear that she would only do such a project if she could exert complete control over it. 'She has amazing instincts, I learned that right away about her,' says Regan. 'She knew just what she wanted to do, and how to do it. She asked intelligent questions about publishing. Not surprisingly, I found her to be very eager, very smart. Shrewd.'

Perhaps Madonna was even shrewder than Judith realized. By the end of the meeting, she had agreed, 'in principle' says Judith, 'to do a book we would call *Madonna's Book of Erotica and Sexual Fantasies*. She said that her manager would call me and we would work out the details. I never heard from her, and decided that she just didn't want to do it. Then, six months later, I learned that she was doing the project for Warner Books. She had obviously taken my concept, my photos and ideas and used it as a proposal to secure a deal with another publisher. I never heard from her, not a word of gratitude, or an apology, or anything,' concludes Judith Regan. 'Frankly, I thought it was in poor taste.'

The contents of *Sex*, when finally published (by Warner Books in the United States and Secker & Warburg in the UK), consisted of visual and verbal essays by Madonna (as herself but also in the role of a character named Dita, borrowed from screen goddess Dita Parlo of the Thirties) regarding her personal, sexual fantasies – or, at least, what she wanted the public to believe were her sexual fantasies. 'This book does not condone unsafe sex,' she hastened to add in one of her missives to the reader. 'These are fantasies I have dreamed up. Like most human beings, when I let my mind wander, I rarely think of condoms.'

Photographed beautifully in black and white by Steven Meisel – who has photographed her throughout much of her career – Madonna was seen hitchhiking in the nude, posing lasciviously while clad in leather S&M outfits, brutally dominating a pair of butch lesbians, happily sucking somebody's toe, brazenly shaving someone else's pubic area, receiving oral sex from a biker, being viciously raped by skinheads (while dressed as a schoolgirl). She is at least partially nude in most of the photographs, and completely nude in many of them. In one, she is posed in a sexually suggestive position with a dog. 'It turned out to be a lot more salacious, I think, than what I would have wanted to publish,' says Judith Regan. 'She went over the top with it. I wanted it to be imaginative, erotic . . . but not quite so prurient.'

Indeed, much of the book reads like a letter in a pornographic magazine: 'I love my pussy, it is the complete summation of my life,' Madonna wrote. 'My pussy is the temple of learning.' A lot of attention is also paid to the joy of anal sex, 'the most pleasurable way to [have sex], and it hurts the most, too'. Many graphic paragraphs are devoted to the ways she enjoys making love, each position described in vivid detail, a great deal of it having to do with sadomasochism. She also waxes rhapsodic about the first time she masturbated.

Much of *Sex* is surprising, if not shocking. Rather than an 'adult' book, it is really childish and impetuous. Though Madonna insisted that she was trying to demystify sexuality in all its many facets, knowing who she was and how she operated made it clear to any keen observer that what she was really just trying to get away with was as much naughty-girl text and as many pornographic photographs as she could because . . . well, because she could get away with it. She was being a brat, not a revolutionary. That much is clear if one reads between the lines in an interview she gave to MTV in 1998. 'I thought, "You know what, I'm going to be sexually provocative, I'm going to be ironic, and I'm going to prove that I can get everybody's attention and that everyone's going to be interested in it . . . and still be freaked out about it."' One might ask: Why? Hadn't she already proved her ability to be sexually provocative, ironic and attention-getting?

Those who knew Madonna well knew what was really going on with her at this time: the *Sex* book – and the outrageous antics that preceded it and would follow it – was really just something she used as a barrier between her and the rest of the world.

For years, it had seemed to Madonna that every moment of her life had been exposed to the world, her every word and mood flashed across the newspapers for comment, often biting and critical. She felt hunted, even though it was she who had started the hunt. By her own doing, she had become one of the most watched and most criticized women in the world. She had never let her public down, always at the ready with a provocative comment, a salacious anecdote, a shocking photograph. Now, because she was just who she had created, she was having trouble relating to 'normal' people. She felt that they didn't understand her. And she certainly didn't understand *them*. She seemed to have lost herself somewhere in all the headlines. Terrible isolation was her ironic fate, isolation that came from being such a sensational public figure. Her relationships with men had been abysmal. Was some of that also due to her fame?

To prevent herself from having to be a part of the masses, either consciously or subconsciously, Madonna created a persona that no one could begin to understand . . . one so outrageous as to defy explanation, one found objectionable by most people (at least those who were not pornographers). 'She was losing touch,' said one of her public relations handlers. 'The barrier she put up between herself and the rest of the world was the notion of crazy, wild sex. Pure and simple, and trashy and controversial, sex.'

Tony Ward, Naomi Campbell, Isabella Rossellini and rappers Big Daddy Kane and Vanilla Ice all made guest appearances in the *Sex* book in photographs which showed them in various stages of undress.

The photographs were taken during the eight-month period during which Madonna and Vanilla Ice (real name Rob Van Winkle) were romantically involved. Ice, whose song 'Ice, Ice Baby' was, in 1990, the first rap song to top the *Billboard* charts, says that the relationship with Madonna was difficult, 'because she would change personalities a lot'. He also says that he now regrets having posed with her for the book. 'It kind of cheeses me out,' he says. 'It makes me look like I'm like all the other people in there, a bunch of freaks. I'm no freak.'

Also prominently featured was Madonna's friend, Ingrid Casares, who would later complain that her participation in the project would fuel years of far-fetched gossip about her own sex life. 'I'm actually quite conservative,' Casares states flatly. Casares and Madonna were photographed in male drag, kissing passionately.

Though initial fascination for the book pushed it to number 1 on the *New York Times* bestseller list, the reviews were generally negative. Richard Harrington of the *Washington Post* called it 'an oversized, overpriced coffee table book of hard-core sexual fantasies sure to separate the wanna-bes from the wanna-be-far-aways. Is *Sex* shocking? Not really. Mostly because it's Madonna, and in a way we've come to expect this from her. Is *Sex* boring? Actually, yes.'

With all the sexual posturing, it was ironic that in the summer of 1992 Madonna was seen in Penny Marshall's light comedy romp, *A League of Their Own*, about a women's baseball league in 1943. As part of an all-star cast including Geena Davis, Tom Hanks and Rosie O'Donnell, Madonna would again not have the burden of carrying an entire film on her shoulders. The movie was top-grossing in the summer of 1992, an added bonus to Madonna's acting résumé – though she was only fair in the role and most don't consider it memorable. However, any observer who thought that the movie would mark the emergence of a tamer Madonna knew he was wrong as soon as *Sex* was published. (Prior to this film, she was seen making a brief appearance in Woody Allen's black comedy, *Shadows and Fog*, a box-office failure that quickly disappeared from cinemas.)

Erotica

To tie in with the publication of *Sex*, Madonna released a new album, aptly entitled *Erotica*.

It is unfortunate that *Erotica* has to be historically linked to other less memorable ventures in Madonna's career at this time because, unlike *In Bed with Madonna* and *Sex*, *Erotica* actually had much to recommend it. Coming on the heels of the two previous adult-orientated projects, the album seemed like more of the same to most observers, and yet this record should be considered on its own merit.

Madonna has often said that in her view – one shared by many cultural historians – one reason pop music is so powerful in society is because it often serves as a mirror to our culture. If one wants to know what's going on in the world, perusing the *Billboard* Top 40 might be a good place to start. For instance, one might not find any songs about peace, love or changing society in the Top 40; if so, their absence speaks volumes. It could mean that society is looking the other way at the moment, that it would rather trade its woes for a pretty pop ditty about good times and romance. Apathy or hopefulness, optimism and good cheer – wherever pop culture is at the moment, so, usually, is its music.

It is clear that few singers have their fingers on the pulse of society like Madonna. At the time of *Erotica*'s release in October 1992, much of society seemed to be re-examining its sexuality. Gay rights issues were at the forefront of social discussions in the West, as was an ever-increasing awareness of AIDS. A generation seemed increasingly curious to explore, without guilt, shame or apology, a different slice of life, something more provocative, maybe darker . . . which is reflected in the themes of *Erotica*. A concept album of sorts, its music boldly and openly focused on sexuality, more so than any previous Madonna album.

Erotica wasn't a complete surprise to anyone who had been paying attention to Madonna's recent music. She had shown her hand earlier with *Breathless* when she sang 'Hanky Panky', the song about spanking, with just a little too much authority. Then there was her single, 'Justify My Love'. *Erotica*, though, was the full-blown musical exploration, an *exhibition*, of what we were to believe was Madonna's sexual reality.

For this album, Madonna again turned to producer/writer Shep Pettibone, with whom she had written and produced 'Vogue'. After having to work within the musical constraints of *Breathless*, Madonna wanted to do a clear and obvious dance record and Pettibone was proficient in this genre. Indeed, judging by the music they've created together, it would be safe to say that Pettibone is by far her best dance music collaborator. After he laid down the musical tracks, Madonna would shape the vocal melodies and write the lyrics. Often (as on *Erotica*), she has ideas for the music tracks as well; she's that versatile. They work well together, mostly because he understands her. 'She's the opposite of calm,' says Pettibone. 'Her patience level is incredibly low, so you have to make things run smoothly. It's better to bring out the angel in her, because the beast ain't that much fun.'

One didn't really need to hear the music to understand Madonna's intention with *Erotica*. If the title itself wasn't a tip-off, the CD's cover artwork certainly made the point clear. In pictures lifted from *Sex*, one photograph shows Madonna in S&M garb, toying with a riding crop and licking her arm; in another shot, she sits bound and gagged. The back cover features Madonna engaged in 'foot worship' – blissfully sucking on someone's big toe. Before her *Sex* book, her public would have been surprised by the poses; on the heels of that published work, however, these photographs now seemed redundant.

The title track, also the first single to be released, consisted of an irresistible house music beat, over which Madonna, in her 'Mistress Dita' persona, spoke in a hypnotic, orgasmic style about the correlation between pain and pleasure and how it relates to sex. The spoken lyrics are separated by the hypnotic, teasing chorus, 'Erotic, erotic, put your hands all over my body.' The song could easily have been the theme to a Fellini film.

The 'Erotica' video was quickly put into 'heavy rotation' by MTV . . . after midnight, of course, to protect the kiddies. On the screen, Madonna appears as a masked dominatrix, complete with a gold tooth and slicked down hair. She tongue kisses a girl and does her S&M shtick, but it is too quickly edited to be really revealing. The video seems to be more about creating a montage of images designed to shock. Looking incongruous in leather and sunglasses, the usually clean-cut MTV announcer Kurt Loder tantalizingly explained that, 'Some people have no objection to such role-playing games as long as they're consensual. Others find such practices repellent, which is why MTV is not airing this video in regular daytime or evening rotation.'

Wrote columnist Molly Ivins, 'You could tell you're out of touch with your fellow Americans when the reigning sex goddess is someone you wouldn't take home if she were the last woman left in the bar.'

This time, a more tamed Madonna did not act as if she objected to MTV's restriction of air time for her video. 'MTV plays to a huge audience and a lot of them are children,' she said in an interview on that cable network. 'And a lot of the themes explored in my video aren't meant for children, so I understand why they can't show it.'

True to course, Madonna's public was all the more fascinated by the song and video thanks to the controversy. It reached number 3 on the *Billboard* singles chart.

'Deeper and Deeper', the second single from *Erotica*, was a change of pace from the title track. A straight-ahead house groove in the tradition of the funkiest New York clubs, the track had Madonna singing mainstream lyrics about falling hard for a lover. It worked its way up to number 7 on the chart.

Erotica could have been ahead of its time. Madonna's song 'Secret Garden', with its lyrics spoken over a jazz combo, is akin to the cool soul music acts such as the Roots and Erykah Badu would champion almost a decade later, under the banner of 'Neo-Soul'. Musically, *Erotica* was actually a melting pot of Nineties urban music – burgeoning hip hop and house, partnered with a more conventional synthesizer-based rhythm and blues. Madonna's most sexually promiscuous record was also her most R&B-sounding.

However, it was the spectacle of the artist's sexuality on parade that seemed to have her fans and critics alike gasping for breath. *Erotica* was the first Madonna CD to carry a warning on its cover: 'Parental Advisory: Explicit Lyrics.' Obviously, Madonna didn't invent the images of S&M and bondage she so valiantly exploited, but it could be argued that *Erotica* was a soundtrack for the era's sexual liberation as people struggled to still find ways to enjoy their sexuality despite the threat of AIDS. Unlike her book, this music was an art form of which her public would not tire . . . and to which it could repeatedly return for entertainment. However, *Erotica* would become the least commercially successful of Madonna's releases, selling just over two million copies.

'Most people want to hear me say I regret putting out my *Sex* book. I don't,' Madonna told *Time* magazine a couple of years later. 'What was problematic was putting out my *Erotica* album at the same time. I love that record, and it was overlooked. Everything I did for the next three years was dwarfed by my book.'

Bad Career Moves

By the end of 1992, many of her fans, as well as critics, were asking if Madonna had gone too far. The release of the *In Bed with Madonna* film, the *Sex* book and the *Erotica* album and video served to answer that question for some with a resounding, 'Yes!' Who was this woman, anyway? Was she a sexual renegade, or just a spoilt and internationally known brat who liked to take off her clothes and talk dirty? No one could answer the question with much accuracy, as she had so clouded her true identity with scandal and sensationalism. Even when she tried to explain herself ('I love my pussy, and there's nothing wrong with loving my pussy') she sounded like a lusty porno star no one could take seriously.

'After the *Sex* book came out,' she has recalled, 'there was a time when I could not open up a newspaper or magazine and not read something incredibly scathing about myself.'

Had she foreseen the negative publicity that would be generated by *In Bed with Madonna*, *Sex* and *Erotica*, Madonna might have chosen a different direction for her next film, perhaps continuing with light family oriented movies like *A League of Their Own*. Instead, she chose a lurid thriller, *Body of Evidence*, as her next movie release – the final of the four unwitting steps in the dismantling of her image.

In the movie, which premiered on the heels of *Sex* in January 1993, Madonna plays Rebecca Carlson, a gallery owner accused of murdering a wealthy older man when he dies after having sex with her (raising the perplexing question of whether or not a sex partner's body can be considered a lethal weapon if the act results in a person's death). She ends up becoming sexually involved with her defence attorney, played by Willem Dafoe.

At the end of the movie, Madonna's character is murdered, causing some disgusted moviegoers to cheer at her demise. 'She's a powerful lady,' says the film's director Uli Endel, of Madonna. 'Sometimes you feel like a tamer with a she-lion in a cage. You have to force her to jump through this burning hoop, and there are just two possibilities. Either she'll jump through the ring of fire . . . or she'll kill you.'

'In all the movies of the Forties, the bad girl has to die,' Madonna has said. 'What I originally loved about the role [in the first script] was that she didn't die. And in the end, they killed me. So I felt that I was sabotaged to a certain extent. For some reason, when that movie came out, I was held responsible for it entirely. It was my fault, which was absurd, because we all make bad movies. I mean *Diabolique* came out [in 1996] and Sharon Stone was not held responsible for the fact that it was a crap movie.'

Indeed, critics 'murdered' Madonna in reviewing the film, declaring *Body of Evidence* a third-rate rehash of every murder mystery of the past twenty years (and particularly of *Basic Instinct*, the box-office blockbuster of the year before). Reviewers were quick to compare Madonna unfavourably to that movie's leading lady: 'It's not just that Madonna does not make an effective Sharon Stone,' a critic for *Rolling Stone* complained. 'She doesn't even make an effective Madonna. Instead of emoting, Madonna strikes poses and delivers stilted lines that sound like captions from her book *Sex* read aloud in a voice of nerve-jangling stridency.'

Bad notices and the condemnation of religious groups had certainly never hurt Madonna's career before this time, but when it was reported that movie audiences had been laughing out loud at Madonna's supposedly serious characterization in *Body of Evidence*, it seemed she had pushed the envelope as far as it was going to be accepted. It was becoming clear even to her that a new reinvention would have to be in the offing, that is if she was going to be able to sustain a career – especially when another film, *Dangerous Game*, was released (in 1993) to terrible reviews and dreadful box-office receipts. In this one, Madonna plays an actress with limited skills who has sex with practically everyone in her life. The sex is violent – Madonna gets to strip several times, and does so with great zest. In one scene during *Dangerous Game*, actor James Russo says of Madonna's character, Sarah Jennings, 'We both know she's a fucking whore who can't act.' Again, it was all more than critics – or her public – could bear. What a disappointment this movie was, especially considering that it was directed by the highly respected Abel Ferrara (known at the time for *The Bad Lieutenant* starring Harvey Keitel, who also co-starred in *Dangerous Game*) and that Madonna had financed much of it with her own money.

Meanwhile, happily for her, Madonna's recording and performing career still had enough momentum to overcome the slump that had resulted from such exploits as *Body of Evidence* and *Dangerous Game*. Facing the barrage of publicity, Madonna chose not to hide. Instead, she decided to do what she had always done best: she took her act out on the road.

In the last quarter of 1993, Madonna forged ahead with a limited twenty-date, four-continent world tour – her first in four years – which she called 'The Girlie Show'. Wisely, she realized that a complete about-face in her career would be transparent, and at the same time would probably minimize much of what she had done prior to this time. She really had expanded the consciousness of much of her public, even if the way she'd gone about it was sometimes questionable. Now, if she was going to come up with a new image, the transformation would have to come about slowly. As a result 'The Girlie Show' was a transitional tour. While still sexy, it was more of an innocent burlesque rather than a blatant attempt to shock. Gone were the hardcore S&M images and the blasphemous religious iconology of the previous two years. Rather, this concert had the feel of a racy Barnum and Bailey circus, even revealing a softer, gentler Madonna.

Time described it as, 'At once a movie retrospective, a Ziegfeld revue, a living video, an R-rated take-off on Cirque du Soleil – opens with Smokey Robinson's "Tears of a Clown" and closes with Cole Porter's "Be a Clown".' The critic concluded that Madonna, 'once the Harlow harlot and now a perky harlequin, is the greatest show-off on earth'. 'The Girlie Show' enabled Madonna to end the difficult year 1993 on a successful note. Many observers and fans considered it to be her best show to date, reaffirming that, as a singer and stage performer – if not a movie star – Madonna could still please her audience. Still, she was now more sensitive than ever to criticism, probably because she'd had to endure so much of it in recent times. Even the slightest negative tone to a review would send her reeling. 'No one understands me,' she complained to one close friend. 'I'm breaking the rules. Why don't people get that?'

'Maybe because people are sick to death of you and all of the sex nonsense,' said the friend. 'Even toned down, it's still too much.' Madonna didn't speak to that person again for six months.

Tupac

Madonna's assignation with Tupac Shakur in late winter of 1993 was brief. They met at a party in Los Angeles and had an instant sexual chemistry neither could deny. When she got to know him a little better, what fascinated her almost as much as his mammoth artistry was his serious interest in acting. He'd just finished a role in *Poetic Justice* with Janet Jackson and he had some very good ideas as to how he and Madonna might work together in a film. She thought it could be a worthwhile and maybe even historic collaboration and, while she didn't necessarily like anything he had in mind, she felt that if they put their heads together they could probably come up with a project. He was always so rageful, though – not at her but just about life in general – that, after a few months of dating Tupac off and on, Madonna felt he was, as she put it to one of her associates at that time, 'maybe too toxic for me'.

One friend of Tupac's, a Las Vegas musician named Devon 'Pooch' Arnold, recalls being at a party with Madonna and Tupac in Vegas in the spring of 1994 at the recently opened Luxor Hotel. 'It was in a private room Tupac had reserved,' he remembered. 'The place was packed with rappers and tough chicks, most of them African-American. I remember there was this one white chic in the middle of all of it. I said to myself, "Wow. What is *that* girl doing here?" I looked closer and, sure enough, it was Madonna, surrounded by people, talking, drinking and seeming very accessible, really kinda cool. I asked Pac about her. He said, "Yeah, she's with me." I was surprised. "What's she like?" He said "She's smart, man. Shrewd. I like her a lot. I'm thinking about maybe doing something with her, some music or a film or a video or somethin'." "It could be a cool thing, for sure." I said, "Bruh, she's kinda old, ain't she?" He nodded and said, "You know what they say: with age comes wisdom."' (Madonna was thirty-six at the time; Tupac was just twenty-three.)

Arnold says that Tupac went over to get Madonna to introduce her. With his arm around her, he walked her to Arnold. 'She seemed meek to me, like she felt she didn't fit in. I was surprised this was *the* Madonna; she was much smaller, much more vulnerable than I expected. She had an edge though. After we spoke for a minute, Pac wanted to introduce her to someone else and she said, "Fuck you, Pac. I'm not your trophy. Get me a drink." He ran off to get her a cocktail. She winked at me and said of him, "He's kind of a pussy, huh?" We shared a laugh knowing that if he ever heard her say something like that about him she'd be dead on the ground, right then and there.'

About a month later, Arnold saw Tupac and asked about Madonna. 'Nah. I had to cut her loose,' Tupac said.

'Why?'

'We look at life in different ways,' he said. 'She's white, she's a woman . . . she doesn't get it, or me. It's no big deal.' Then, with a grin, he added, 'Hot as fuck in bed, though. Seriously, bruh. I ain't kiddin'. The bitch is *hot as fuck!*'

'He didn't give her a chance,' said someone who knew both Tupac and Madonna at the time. 'She actually could have been a good influence in his life. He was angry at the world and, to a certain extent at that time, so was she. However, she knew how to channel it, he didn't. She told me that she once said to him, "How do you get through the day all pissed off about every goddamn thing?" He said, 'There's a lot to be pissed off about, girl.' He gave her a long list of things that he was raging against at that time, society . . . the industry . . . his personal life . . . I mean, he ticked off the list one by one and, the way I heard it, she said, "You can just live with all of that anger if you want, or you can live a good life. Your choice, Pac." She felt he was too young, that maybe he wasn't enjoying his success, that he would get old and look back and wish he'd had more fun with it – not that Pac didn't have fun. Obviously, he did. But his anger was a big part of his persona.'

At the end of the day, though, she was too smart to let her rage become misdirected. 'I'm too busy to be that pissed off all the time,' is how she put it. 'She can't be distracted, even by her own rage. She's too directed, too focused. It wasn't a big loss when Pac ended their friendship. I think she realized it was to her advantage, that she was better off without him.'

After he stopped seeing her, Tupac made a few comments about Madonna he later regretted. 'I was letting people dictate who should be my friends,' he would say to *Vibe* reporter, Kevin Powell. 'So, I dissed her, even though she showed me nothing but love. I felt bad because when I went to jail, I called her and she was the only person that was willing to help me.'

Two years later, Tupac Shakur was gunned down in Las Vegas. As he lay dying, a cop asked who'd shot him. Tupac looked up at him and, according to that officer, had only two words for him: 'Fuck you.'

Bedtime Stories

What was she to do now? After all, she had practically trashed her image in recent years with one scalding controversy after another. According to one of her managers at this time, Madonna realized that she needed to make some dramatic changes in her career or, despite her huge record sales, she soon might not even have one. Always a smart woman, despite some recent bad decisions, she now realized that she needed to grow up, soften her image, and reconnect with her public. For the next few years, she would try to do just that . . . and her album *Bedtime Stories* would go a long way towards achieving that goal.

Bedtime Stories would also be the second of her albums to be released on Maverick, her own record label, funded by (its distributor) Warner Bros. Records with $60 million (the first was *Erotica*).

For years, Madonna had wanted to release her own music on her own label and, expanding that vision, she wanted the label to be a full-service entertainment company, specializing not only in music but also in television, film, book and song publishing.

Since Madonna was still very much a best-selling recording artist by the early 1990s, the existence of her Maverick Records was an anomaly. One of the first female artists to have a *real* label, and one of the few women to run her own entertainment company, Maverick wasn't just a company in logo only, but a genuine venture for her with a staff and executives in place, all of whom were, at the time, governed by Freddy DeMann, who served as President of the company. The enterprise had its headquarters in a sleek, anonymous single-storey office building in West Hollywood, close to one of Madonna's favourite shopping haunts, the chic Fred Segal department store on Melrose Avenue. Madonna had discussed such a venture with Warren Beatty on several occasions. He had encouraged her to do it, and was said to have been proud to hear that she'd finally launched the company.

'My goal, of course, is to have hits with the new company,' she said. 'I'm not one of these dumb artists who is just given a label to shut her up. I asked for a record company. So, I'm not going to be invisible or simply phone in my partnership. There's no honour or satisfaction in palming the work off to someone else.'

That 1994's *Bedtime Stories* would follow the soft porn of *Erotica* might have seemed a bit odd to the untrained ear or to the casual Madonna fan. After all, though *Bedtime* was considerably more tame in tone than the ethereal-sounding, sexually charged *Erotica*, it demonstrated that, as always, Madonna had a keen instinct about where pop music was headed. By the early Nineties, hip-hop music had completely permeated the national music sales charts. It was the 'dance' music of the day, the 'new' R&B of a generation of kids in fashionably sagging anti-designer designer jeans and backpacks. It was a trend, and, not surprisingly, Madonna wanted to be a part of it.

Bedtime Stories would be one of Madonna's most unique recordings so far. It marked the first time since Nile Rodgers and 1984's *Like a Virgin* album that she had worked with well-known producers. (For reasons that were as much about creativity as they were about control, she had chosen to work with relative unknowns on her recent recordings.)

For the tracks that would be included in *Bedtime Stories*, Madonna sought out the hottest young producers working in urban/hip-hop music. At the top of her list was Dallas Austin, the twenty-two-year-old songwriter/producer from Atlanta, Georgia, who'd found fame and fortune producing, among others, male vocal group Boyz II Men, teen R&B singer Monica and, especially, the young female hip-hop trio TLC. Freddy DeMann was also instructed to place a call to another prominent name in pop/R&B, songwriter/producer Kenny 'Babyface' Edmonds. Edmonds was black music's *hitmeister* of the moment, having penned chart recordings for Whitney Houston and Toni Braxton, among other R&B acts.

Austin's and Edmonds's names among the CD's production credits would have proved the seriousness of Madonna's intention to enter the world of R&B and hip hop proper. However, she also rounded out her team of collaborators by pulling in Nellee Hooper, once the creative core of a British studio tribe called Soul II Soul, who had enjoyed 1989 hits with the singles 'Keep on Movin'' and 'Back to Life (However Do You Want Me)'. She also added Dave 'Jam' Hall, then one of urban soul's most solid rising young songwriter/producers who had scored hits with, among others, the R&B girl group Brownstone. 'She knows how to man a project,' says Freddy DeMann. 'She knows how to surround herself with the biggest and the best, and I think that has been one of her greatest achievements. She's not like a lot of people who feel they have to do it all themselves. She wants assistance, but from only the most qualified people.'

When 'Secret', the first single from *Bedtime Stories*, was released, it surprised many Madonna fans, as well as her critics. It isn't a big sounding dance track or a twinkling melodic ballad, both of which have been Madonna's style. Instead, it begins with just the sound of her voice singing over a rhythmic folksy guitar, before opening up to a sparse, retro rhythm section. Madonna's tangy voice remained at the centre of the production. 'My baby's got a secret,' she sang, though she never shares with the listener just what that secret may be. She and Dallas Austin wrote the clever song which, no matter how many times one listens to it, never ceases to intrigue. It rode the *Billboard* singles chart up to the number 3 position.

'Take a Bow' was the second single from the collection, a melancholy and beautifully executed ballad written by Madonna with Babyface. 'Take a Bow' is a sombre, sarcastic all-the-world's-a-stage song about unrequited love (a recurring theme in Madonna's lyrics) whose phoniness might have fooled everyone else, but not her. 'Take a bow,' she implored, for rendering a great, transparent performance in life and love. (The picturesque video was filmed over seven days in Ronda, Spain, with a bullfighting theme – using three bulls – and featuring popular bullfighter, Emilio Muñoz. It was partly because of the Forties look of the video that Alan Parker thought Madonna might work in the part of Evita.)

Though he isn't listed in the credits as a performer, Babyface also sings on the track, vocally co-signing Madonna's lines in a way that makes their performance practically a duet. It proved to be a winner. 'Take a Bow' put Madonna back in the place on the *Billboard* singles chart to which she'd become accustomed – number 1.

Something to Remember

'So much controversy has swirled around my career this past decade that very little attention ever gets paid to my music. The songs are all but forgotten. While I have no regrets regarding the choices I've made artistically, I've learned to appreciate the idea of doing things in a simpler way. So without a lot of fanfare, without any distractions, I present to you this collection of ballads. Some are old, some are new. All of them are from my heart.'

So wrote Madonna in the liner notes accompanying her tenth album, *Something to Remember*, issued at the end of 1995. Perhaps no truer observation has ever been made of Madonna or of her musical career, and made by the lady herself. Like so many of the strong female entertainers from Hollywood's past who have inspired her, Madonna's personal life has often left her professional accomplishments sitting in the shade. Of course, she neglected to add that she has usually been at the very source of the distracting madness. After all, she was the one who had practically ruined her image with her maddening, one-track-mind sexual outrageousness.

'She knew it was time to make a change,' said one member of her management team who insisted on remaining anonymous. 'She would have to be pretty stupid not to know it, and you could never say that Madonna was stupid. She was upset, a little frantic about what people were saying about her. That's why she put together the *Something to Remember* album, to remind people that there was more to her than just the controversy that had surrounded her almost from the beginning of her career.'

Madonna was also correct when she wrote that some of her songs have many times been overlooked in favour of the current gossip and innuendo. Her savvy as a serious pop songwriter has attracted even less attention. For instance, the tabloids don't report that she has written most of her songs and publishes them. 'She hasn't shouted about her musical abilities,' notes French electronica star Mirwais Ahmadzai, a star of France's burgeoning electronica scene who would go on to produce Madonna's 2000 album, *Music*. 'She is the consummate songwriter,' he says. 'She listens to classical musicals a lot. Not just the obvious ones, like *Singin' in the Rain*, but the lesser ones. She loves them. I remember one time we all had dinner in Germany, and somebody brought up old musicals, and she was the one who knew all the verses. Things our mum and dad watch, she's into it all. Really solid, melodic stuff like that. And she writes really solid, melodic stuff.'

While such facts don't make exciting headlines, Madonna's interest in publishing is significant, especially in a business where, everyday, famous singer/songwriters create valuable copyrights that they don't own. Nor is much made of the fact that Madonna is one of the few hands-on female record producers in the music business – and one of the most successful of either gender. She is certainly able to hold her own with such legends as George Martin, producer of the Beatles (whose chart performances Madonna's hits have challenged), and Quincy Jones.

So, whether Madonna released *Something to Remember*, a collection of previously released love songs, because she had a point to prove or simply to keep a contractual obligation, the fourteen-track recording did make a statement. That statement began with the CD's packaging. On it, Madonna looks deliciously cosmopolitan in a form-fitting white cocktail number. On the front she's posed in meditation; on the back photograph she is coy, playful and just a bit sexy.

As she wrote in her notes, not all of the songs were re-releases; four of them were new. It's interesting that even though Madonna profits greatly each time she records a song she has written, she will gladly and eagerly perform a new song by another writer, or, if she feels she can bring something new to it, even redo a classic. Such is the distinction of an artist more concerned with the whole of the project as opposed to how much money she can deposit in her current account as a result of its sales.

Long a fan of Marvin Gaye's 1976 classic, 'I Want You', Madonna recut the song with the British dance music unit, Massive Attack. (It was also released on *Inner City Blues – The Music of Marvin Gaye* by Motown Records in November 1995.) The track was produced by Nellee Hooper. Whereas Marvin Gaye's version of the song, penned by veteran R&B writer Leon Ware and T-Boy Ross (younger brother of Diana Ross), is more elaborately produced, Madonna's is pared to basically just her voice and Massive Attack's club beat. The result is a bit sexier than Gaye's version; one can almost imagine Madonna crawling seductively across the floor, after her prey.

'I'll Remember', another new cut, is just the opposite of Madonna's take on Gaye. Written by Madonna, Patrick Leonard and singer/songwriter Richard Page, the beautiful, million-selling song was the theme from the 1994 motion picture *With Honors*. It sounds like a flick theme, too, equipped with smart chords and big emotion. It is reminiscent of another movie theme of Madonna's, 'Live to Tell', also featured on the album, only better.

Also included were two new sentimental and expansive ballads, 'You'll See' and 'One More Chance', both written by Madonna with songwriter/producer David Foster. The working universe of a star as big as Madonna is small. At some point, she had to end up working (or consider working) with those who have had success with her peers, even competitors in the pop music world. Foster had produced Barbra Streisand and had written hits for Al Jarreau and Earth, Wind & Fire ('After the Love Is Gone'). It was interesting that, with all of his exciting musical ability from which to draw, he and Madonna would come up with two of the most sombre songs she had ever recorded – but such is the excitement of collaboration: one never knows what will come from it.

'Madonna was great to work with because I never really understood her mystique although I always liked her music,' David Foster has said. 'We met in New York, had dinner to discuss the album. And there was something so intoxicating about her. We were just the two of us at dinner and I was looking at her going, "Wow, she totally sucks you into her world. It's like there's nobody else in the restaurant." She had a great work ethic. A lot of artists, they want to be co-producers just because they can. She wanted to be a co-producer, but she earned it. She really knows her way around a studio. She works hard.'

The rest of *Something to Remember* consisted of some of Madonna's most important ballads, including 'Crazy for You', 'Oh Father', 'Take a Bow', 'Forbidden Love', a remix of 'Love Don't Live Here Anymore', 'This Used to Be My Playground' (a melancholy performance heard in *A League of Their Own*, and which went on to become her tenth number 1 record in 1992, making its Madonna album debut here) and 'Something to Remember', from the *Dick Tracy – I'm Breathless* collection. That she made the *Dick Tracy* ballad this CD's title track might indicate how she felt about the song she and Patrick Leonard had written – perhaps wanting it to have the attention it did not receive first time around.

In any case, perhaps all that *Something to Remember* lacked was a bow around it. It was a valentine, a love letter from Madonna to her fans and music lovers alike. Like any Madonna project, it seemed to say just a little more than the obvious. In this case, the collection seemed to nudge teasingly at her contemporaries, '. . . And *these* are just my ballads.'

Perfect Casting?

She had wanted it for years, but never had she *needed* it as much as she did in 1995.

From the first moment in early 1995 that Madonna learned she had won the prized role of Eva Perón in Andrew Lloyd Webber's film interpretation of his musical *Evita*, she sensed a major shift about to occur in her life and career. 'I really want to be recognized as an actress,' she had once said. 'I've learned that if you surround yourself with great writers and great actors and a great director and a great costumier or whatever, it's pretty hard to go wrong. In the past, I've been in a really big hurry to make movies and I haven't taken the time to make sure all of those elements were in line and good enough. It's a waste of time to do something mediocre. Unless you absolutely believe in every aspect of it then you shouldn't waste your time.'

For over a decade, much of the press and the public had speculated that Madonna was the perfect choice for the role of Evita. However, because her movie career had never really ignited, as a result of box-office disasters such as *Shanghai Surprise*, *Who's That Girl?* and *Body of Evidence*, a number of other actresses were considered for the part. It was a search that nearly rivalled the casting of Scarlett O'Hara in the classic *Gone with the Wind* back in the 1930s.

Patti LuPone, who had masterfully created the part on Broadway, was under consideration and was said to have wanted the movie role badly. Glenn Close, who had caused a sensation starring on the stage in another Andrew Lloyd Webber musical, *Sunset Boulevard*, was also vying for the part. Meanwhile, Meryl Streep diligently took lessons to better her voice for her own *Evita* audition. There were also sporadic announcements that genuine singing divas such as Bette Midler, Mariah Carey, Olivia Newton-John and Gloria Estefan were all interested in starring in what promised to be a big-budget, highly publicized movie musical. Not to be outdone, Liza Minnelli and Barbra Streisand – performers respected for their acting ability as well as their singing talent – were also associated with the project at different points along the way.

After years of announcements, denials, rumours and speculation, most Hollywood observers believed that Michelle Pfeiffer had finally been chosen by the film's director Alan Parker (*Bugsy Malone*, *Fame*, *Pink Floyd – The Movie* and *The Commitments*) to star in the movie. Pfeiffer had, indeed, expressed an interest in the project. However, it had taken so long for decisions to be made that, while waiting for the wheels to turn, Pfeiffer had a baby. When Parker met her just before he was to make his final casting decision, it was clear that her motherhood status now presented a problem. With two small children in tow (an adopted daughter as well as the new baby), the actress wasn't eager to tackle the long, difficult shooting schedule Parker had in mind. So, she was out. But who would be in?

It was upon hearing of Pfeiffer's rejection that Madonna, her uncanny instinct for perfect timing at work, just as always, sent Parker a handwritten, four-page letter. In it, she explained why she would be the perfect choice to play the role of Evita.

In her letter, Madonna promised that she would sing, dance and act her heart out if Parker would only give her the opportunity to do so. She would put everything else in her life and career on hold in order to devote her time and energy to *Evita*. She may have felt that she had no choice; Madonna was that desperate to do something worthwhile in films. In 1995, and then again in 1996, she would appear in supporting roles in movies of which most people didn't even know she was a part, just for the experience of doing them. The first had been 1995's *Four Rooms*, a series of vignettes, one of which featured Madonna as a witch named Elspeth. *Blue in the Face*, also released in 1995, was a sequel to the popular *Smoke*, in which Madonna is featured briefly, mooning Harvey Keitel after delivering a singing telegram. In 1996, she would appear in Spike Lee's *Girl* 6 in which she appears briefly as the owner of a telephone sex service.

'When I was chosen to make *Evita*, I knew I wasn't Andrew Lloyd Webber's first choice,' she would later say. 'I don't think he was particularly thrilled with my singing abilities. I knew I was going in with odds against me. That's an awkward position to be in. You feel everyone's waiting for you to stumble.'

Of course, there are clear similarities between Madonna and Eva Perón. Eva was a Latino-looking brunette who found fame as a dyed blonde, as did Madonna. Eva was strong willed, as is Madonna. Eva was emotional, dramatic and sometimes self-pitying, as is Madonna. The story of Madonna's rise to fame – a legend partly of her making and partly that of the media's – also parallels Eva Perón's in that both women exploited a series of relationships with men in order to survive early years of struggle and then, ultimately, clawed their way from obscurity. Perfect casting, then it would seem . . . and exactly what Madonna needed most to boost her career during a time she was trying to refashion her image. However, there would be a few challenges when it came to aligning Evita's story to Madonna's vision of it.

One major problem Madonna faced was that the story of Eva Perón was not completely in alignment with the new, softer and uncontroversial image she wanted to project to her public at this time in her life. The story of a manipulative woman who really slept her way to the top – Eva's true story – may have worked better for Madonna in the Eighties when all she could think about was how to shock the world, but not in 1995. Before she went into rehearsals, she spent hours going over the script, listening to the music, reading up on the history, and suggesting to the producers changes to what was historically documented. Not to say that Andrew Lloyd Webber had been completely accurate in his own version of Eva Perón's life, but he was a lot closer to the truth, in tone and intention, than the version Madonna wanted for her breakout movie. Her desire was to rewrite history – even if just in a subtle way – in order to create a softer, more vulnerable Eva Perón. She wanted to craft an Evita more to her liking and, by extension, a Madonna more to her public's.

The real story was that the canny and intelligent Evita influenced an entire nation by aligning herself with a man who would become the country's next President, Juan Perón. Before her relationship with Perón, Eva Duarte was a minor actress in film and radio who had secured equally minor acting roles by virtue of other romantic relationships. However, as the protégée, and then wife, of the most powerful man in the country, the real-life Eva was able to turn her attention to politics, which was where her true talents lay. Ultimately, Eva became as important to Juan Perón's future as he was to hers. She instinctively knew she could endear herself to the country's working classes, thus endearing her husband to them.

She perfectly understood the masses. After all, Eva also came from an impoverished background.

While established Argentinian charities shunned her as the wife of the President, Evita had the power to establish her own charity foundations which brought in enormous sums of money. Though she did a lot of good for the people of Argentina, she also spent lavishly on herself. She dazzled all by spending millions of dollars on jewels and haute couture. Born poor and illegitimate, she understood that the image of a woman who had attained great success against all odds was her most important weapon in reaching working-class people. The masses wanted her to succeed because her success meant the possibility of their own. 'I'm one of you,' she would say, throwing her arms forward and becoming a symbol of what an illegitimate child from an impoverished family could attain.

Fame, money and glamour were not enough for the ambitious Evita. She also craved power on a major scale and had ambitions to be the first woman elected to the office of Vice-President. Sadly, her dreams would go unfulfilled. Cancer took her life in 1952 at the age of thirty-three, thereby assuring that she would forever remain, at least in her adoring public's eyes, a saint.

It was a terrific story just as it was . . . and certainly the story to which Madonna had originally been attracted. But now she felt it was in need of some tweaking.

'It's just not me,' Madonna told director Alan Parker.

'Indeed, it's not,' he shot back. 'It's Evita Perón.'

'But my public will think it's me. And it's not.'

'But it's Evita Perón!'

And back and forth they went . . .

It seemed that Madonna was most offended by the implication of Evita having used so many men in her climb to the top, perhaps because the press and public had often implied just that about her. 'It's a way envious people undermine your strength and your accomplishments,' she observed in a *Vanity Fair* interview. 'I didn't use any man who didn't want to be used,' she said. 'If anything, *I've* been used. I'm the one who has been used.' Of course, Madonna was really not as blind to her past as that observation seemed to indicate. Anyone who knew her well would remember that she had admitted to having used people in the past – both men and women – and that her conscience had bothered her about such manipulations, going all the way back to feeling regretful for not having Camille Barbone at her side when she finally became successful with her first album in 1983. However, now was not the time for true confessions.

'I thought it [the original take on Evita Perón] was a male chauvinist point of view, that any woman who's powerful is a whore or slept her way to the top,' she stated. 'There's that implication right through the musical and it's ludicrous. You can't sleep your way to the top,' she concluded. She then stopped abruptly, perhaps thinking about what she was saying, and quickly revised it: 'Well, in Hollywood, maybe, but she [Evita Perón] influenced an entire nation.'

'I hate that she looks like such a bitch,' she complained, making clear her intention to tweak things. 'I'd like it if she was . . . nicer, I guess. More dimensional.'

'Well, a lot of people may have liked it if Madonna was nicer, more dimensional,' said chagrined film critic Gene Siskel when the film was eventually released. 'But, at least from what I hear, she's not that nice, and she's not that dimensional. What's true is true . . .'

As seen through Madonna's eyes, Eva Perón would no longer be a political animal. Gone would be the brilliant, scheming, conniving climber who used sex as a weapon to demolish anyone who got in her way – the truth of Evita's story, and maybe even of Madonna's, depending on how one chose to look at it. In her place would be a shy, reserved, ethereal Eva Perón who had been pushed around by men but who – by using her brains and will power – would eventually rise to the top of the political ladder. Because she was so beautiful and persuasive, she would also go on to become a legend.

After her death at the end of the movie, the viewer would weep, that's how much he would respect and love Eva Perón. 'A couple of years ago, no one would have cried if I died, people were so sick of me,' she said, privately. 'I only hope that will change with this movie.'

Once Madonna was able to fashion the role in *Evita* to her liking, it was time to prepare herself to become Eva Perón. As had always been her style, the moment she was sure she had her goal in sight, she would make sure not to stumble. Throwing herself into the project, she began with a plan first to improve her singing range.

Being a filmed musical, all of *Evita*'s cast members would be expected to sing their parts themselves and not rely on other voices. Madonna's ability to do so – she was, after all, a singer – was at least one of the reasons the producers chose her for the starring role in the first place. However, the reason Madonna was thought to be ideal for the job could also have been the very reason she would have been terrible at it. Yes, she was a singer . . . but a *pop* singer.

Madonna immediately went into vocal training with respected New York vocal coach Joan Layder. 'She had to use her voice in a way she's never used it before,' observed Layder. '*Evita* is real musical theatre – it's operatic, in a sense. Madonna developed an upper register that she didn't know she had.'

Ironically, one of Layder's clients was Patti LuPone. Always competitive, Madonna feared falling short when being compared with the bombastic-voiced LuPone. Layder joked that Madonna felt that LuPone had her ear to the door during the lessons.

Vocal training for the film was difficult. Madonna was forced to stretch herself vocally in ways she had never before attempted. However, even she was amazed at her own vocal dexterity, once she became accustomed to using her 'tool' (as Layder called it) in the proper way – singing from her diaphragm rather than her throat. Whereas she had often sounded tinny and thin on her recordings prior to this time, suddenly – after just a few weeks of training – her voice was full-bodied, rich and theatrical. Every time she opened her mouth to sing, she was amazed to find herself accessing elements of her voice she never knew were there. It was as if she had gone to bed and, magically, awoken a real *singer*. 'Where did *that* come from?' she would ask Layder of her new sound. 'God,' she told her. 'God!'

'I suddenly discovered that I had been using only half of my voice,' Madonna later told *Los Angeles Times* pop music critic Robert Hilburn. 'Until then, I had pretty much accepted that I had a very limited range, which is fine. Anita O'Day and Edith Piaf had very limited ranges, too, and I am a big fan. So I figured I'd make do with the best I had.'

As it happened, she wouldn't have to 'make do' with a limited vocal range. At the end of each lesson, she would excitedly telephone friends and say, 'You won't believe this! Listen!' Then, she would sing into the telephone at full volume, completely amazed at her own proficiency.

When, in September 1995, Madonna arrived in London with Antonio Banderas and Jonathan Pryce to start rehearsals for the recording of the *Evita* soundtrack, she was ready.

Alan Parker was delighted to hear the 'new' Madonna. Since all the filming would consist of the actors lip-synching to pre-recorded vocals, the making of *Evita* was double the work for all involved. First, the actors were required to perform their roles in the recording studio, and then they would have to repeat the performance in front of the camera on a film set.

On the first day of actual recording, though, it became apparent that special considerations would have to be made for the film's female star. 'I'm used to writing my own songs and I go into a studio, choose the musicians and say what sounds good or doesn't,' Madonna later explained. 'To work on forty-six songs with everyone involved and not have a say was a big adjustment. It was difficult to go in, spill my guts, then say, "Do what you will with it."' Moreover, Madonna was not comfortable laying down a 'guide vocal' simultaneously with an eighty-four-piece orchestra in a huge studio. She was used to singing over a pre-recorded track and not having musicians listen to her as she made mistakes natural to the recording process. 'Three worlds were colliding,' Parker observed, 'musical theatre, pop, and film.'

Despite all of her hard work, the first day of recording was a disaster. She had to sing 'Don't Cry for Me, Argentina' on that day, and in front of Andrew Lloyd Webber. Believing that she had done a terrible job, she stormed from the studio, tears rolling down her face, pale as porcelain. ('How can I go on?' she lamented. 'I can't work like this. I'm an *artist*. Not a puppet.') Later Parker would dub that first day 'Black Monday'.

'I was so nervous,' she recalls, 'because I knew that Andrew had had reservations about me, and here I am singing the hardest song in the piece. All of a sudden there, with everybody for the first time, it was really tense.'

An emergency meeting was held between Alan Parker, Andrew Lloyd Webber and Madonna. The entire eighty-four-piece orchestra was fired, and Webber also brought in a new conductor. It was also decided that Madonna would record all of her vocals at a more contemporary studio in which she would be more at ease, while the large orchestrations would be conducted and recorded elsewhere. It was also decided that Madonna would sing only in the afternoons, and every other day. Days off were allocated for her to rest her voice. Still, regardless of the accommodations for her, the recording of the soundtrack was an arduous task. The cast and director worked for four months putting in over 400 recording hours – and that was before a single foot of film had been shot.

Making Evita

In early February 1996, Madonna left Los Angeles for Buenos Aires. After recording the soundtrack to *Evita*, she may have thought the worst was behind her. However, Madonna was still in for a bumpy ride. When she arrived in Buenos Aires a few days before she was scheduled to begin filming, she realized that life wasn't going to be easy for her in 'this godforsaken place' (as she referred to the city). Plastered all over the city was graffiti screaming, 'Madonna go home'. It was apparent that some Argentinians were unhappy with the notion that a brazen pop star would be portraying their beloved Evita.

To make matters worse, living conditions were, at first, a lot more challenging than those to which Madonna had become accustomed during the last twelve years of being a superstar. 'No gyms! No decent food!' she groused. 'I can't live like this,' she shouted at one of the film's production assistants. 'I need Evian. Do you hear me? *Ev-i-an!*'

Soon, though, Madonna was ensconced – at least on weekends – in a lavish $12 million mansion, renting it for $70,000 a week. Of course, as would be the nature of any diva, she made a couple of demands deemed outrageous by some observers – such as floating gardenias in the bathroom bowls, and white orchids in all of the other rooms – as well as some other less unreasonable requests: a blender, apple and mango juices, popcorn, Gummy Bears, Special K cereal, oatmeal, potato chips, assorted fresh vegetables, teriyaki chicken, and a CD player in every room. She also asked that one room be transformed into a gym equipped with a treadmill, Life Cycle, Stair Master, Versa Climber and free weights. Of course, there was always shopping to keep her busy, as well. On one Sunday, she went on a shopping spree at the sprawling San Elmo flea market, where she stayed for three hours. Then, it was off to Antigona, a vintage clothing store where she bought fifty hats, ten pairs of gloves, a dozen dresses and ten lace mantillas. Bodyguards, chauffeurs and assistants waited to open doors for her, write out cheques for her, or compliment her on her good taste.

Despite her comfortable lifestyle, there was still the nagging problem with which Madonna was so well acquainted: the burden of fame itself. Those fans who had migrated to this strange land 'tormented' (her word) and 'stalked' (again, her word) her when she wasn't at her weekend home but at her hotel, closer to the set, turning it into a virtual prison. A group of young, determined admirers kept a steady vigil outside the window of their idol's second floor suite, chanting and serenading the object of their obsession. 'I slept like shit,' Madonna complained. 'The children outside my window came at two-hour intervals all through the night to beckon me to my balcony and profess undying love . . . Shakespeare this was not.'

The stress, however, didn't dissuade Madonna from sticking to a strict agenda in order to continue to better herself during production. Since she would be called upon not only to sing, but to dance and, of course, act, she worked diligently to be at peak form in all three areas.

As for her acting, in order to become absorbed by the complicated character of Evita, Madonna travelled about Argentina meeting people who had known the real Eva Perón – diplomats, intellectuals, ministers and even a few of her childhood friends. 'Of course, some refuse to meet me,' Madonna said at the time. However, to those who would agree to talk to her, Madonna asked dozens of well-thought-out questions about the way Evita looked, the food she ate, the manner in which she behaved and what she enjoyed doing in her spare time. So grateful for the information she was receiving, she would kiss some of her interviewees on the nose, others gently on the lips. 'It was fun to be the interviewer for a change,' she laughed. As a result of this kind of research, Madonna began to understand subtle character traits she sensed would be necessary to guarantee her best performance of Eva Perón.

Filming of *Evita* began on 13 February 1996. In the first days of production Madonna became aware of the reality of how excruciating it was going to be to put all of her hard-earned, new-found acting skills to the test on the *Evita* set. It was swelteringly hot in Buenos Aires in February and on the first day of shooting, Madonna, as the fifteen-year-old Eva in her period costume and uncomfortable wig, was required to do take after take while saying goodbye to her family on the way to the big city. An ancient train billowed out a steady stream of noxious smoke and hot winds blew dust into her mouth as she lip-synched to her pre-recorded song. It was a miserable experience, and only a foreshadowing of things to come.

In the days that followed, Madonna was required to spend long days in the intense sun alternating between waiting around for the proper light to film and performing in complicated song and dance numbers. 'I was dying from heat exhaustion and being made a meal of by ants and flies and hornets,' she said later.

Madonna was shooting six days a week and rehearsing on her day off. As filming dragged on in Buenos Aires she began feeling more and more lonely and alienated. 'My family and friends are the people in the movie,' she said at the time. 'They have seen me bare my soul and yet they know nothing about me.' She was also feeling dizzy and nauseous every day, conditions she blamed on the incredible heat.

Her moodiness aside, Madonna continued to prove herself the consummate professional while actually doing her job in front of the cameras. Cast and crew members, some grudgingly, couldn't help but admire her total commitment to the project. Even Jonathan Pryce – who played Evita's husband Juan Perón and who said after the first few days of working with her that he had never worked with anyone quite as rude – eventually found good things to say about her. 'She's a strong dynamic force and I can only admire that,' he admitted. 'I've grown to like her a lot. People have preconceptions about her due to the media but you soon learn she's a regular person. True, she doesn't discourage the media too much, but there's a lot of myth created around her.'

Adding to Madonna's turmoil was the fact that Antonio Banderas' girlfriend, the actress Melanie Griffith, had become an annoyance. As soon as Banderas was cast as the movie's narrator, Ché, Madonna began hearing from certain associates of hers that Melanie Griffith was unhappy. Because Madonna was widely viewed as a 'man killer',

Melanie was concerned that her boyfriend would fall prey to her, especially since Madonna had made it clear in her *In Bed with Madonna* film that she fancied Banderas and thought he was 'very sexy'. (She also hastened to add, 'He must have a really small penis because no one is that perfect'.)

'What I don't need right now is a jealous girlfriend,' Madonna told Alan Parker, according to one of Parker's associates. 'I'm not even interested in Antonio. That crack in *Truth or Dare* [*In Bed with Madonna*] was just a stupid joke. Antonio is too strait-laced for me.' She was clearly upset. Alan Parker rested his forehead against Madonna's in an attempt to comfort her. Then, he kissed her on the nose and walked away. She stood in place, probably feeling that she had just been treated in a condescending manner.

Later, when Madonna was told that Melanie would be accompanying her boyfriend to Argentina, she couldn't believe it. 'How could a woman be that insecure?' she asked. 'If it were me, and he was my boyfriend, and I was worried about another woman – I'd say, "Hey, go get her tiger . . . and then get the fuck out." And that would be the end of it.'

Shortly before filming began, Madonna took matters into her own hands and decided to call Melanie Griffith.

'I understand that there have been some rumours,' she reportedly told her, 'and I just want you to know that they're completely ridiculous. I actually can't wait for you to get here, Melanie. We'll have fun!' Melanie's reaction to the call is unknown. After she hung up, though, Madonna turned to an associate and said, 'Well, that should take care of *that*. And if it doesn't, I guess I'll just have to deal with her when she gets to Argentina with her hen-pecked boyfriend.'

Despite having received the conciliatory telephone call from Madonna, Melanie was still distant towards her when she finally did arrive on the set. 'It seemed as if she didn't trust her,' said Louise Keith, a Los Angeles-based friend of Griffith's. 'Madonna was certainly flirty towards Antonio, but I think it was harmless and just the way Madonna is. However, Melanie didn't like it. She told me that Madonna did everything she could do to win her over, but Melanie wasn't giving in to her. "I don't want to socialize with her, not really," Melanie said when asked by one of Madonna's "handlers" if she might like to join Madonna for lunch. Well, that really pissed off Madonna. Actually, I don't think they said two words to each other the whole time Melanie was there, a couple of weeks. Instead, they just shot each other frosty glares whenever they were in each other's company.'

A crew member later recalled, 'Madonna couldn't contain herself and she blurted out, "Melanie hates me". She told Parker, "She won't accept an invitation if I'm in the same room. I don't know what Banderas sees in her but she's got him by the balls."'

For publication, Madonna made light of the Melanie Griffith situation. In writing about the incident in *Vanity Fair*, Madonna refused even to mention Melanie's name: 'The press is trying to make a big deal about my competing with his [Banderas'] girlfriend,' she wrote, 'which is ludicrous because everyone knows I would never date a man who wears cowboy boots.'

For her part, Melanie remained diplomatic with the media. In fact, Griffith told me that she was instrumental in smoothing the working relationship between her husband and Madonna. 'They say she can be difficult, but I understand her,' says Melanie Griffith. 'In fact, I think I understand her better than Antonio, being a woman in this business. I know that she wants things perfect but that some men don't want to listen to her opinion precisely because she is a woman. Do you know how frustrating that is? I told Antonio to listen to her instincts. She has very good instincts. He did.

'Of course, they never had an affair,' Melanie said. 'Would I tolerate such a thing? No, I would not.'

Madonna's enthusiasm for the *Evita* project re-emerged when the production moved to the location of her dreams – the balcony of the Casa Rosada – the shooting location for which she had pleaded with the President of Argentina, Carlos Menem, for permission to use. To make the scene as visually dynamic as possible, the production used every extra available, a total of 4,000. When Madonna walked onto the balcony, she couldn't help but gasp in awe of her surroundings. Looking down from the balcony, as far as the eye could see were . . . people. True, they were hired hands, but they must have seemed like fans just the same. When she began to mouth the words to the pre-recorded 'Don't Cry for Me, Argentina' this audience erupted into unbridled cheers.

After the all-night shoot, Madonna was so exhilarated by her work she could barely speak. As the sun rose, the cast and crew quietly hugged each other. In spite of the difficulties they had been experiencing, on this morning they seemed to feel a keen sense of triumph. The filming of the many difficult Buenos Aires segments of the movie was finally coming to a close and, now, after the emotional night of shooting at the Casa Rosada, everyone felt as if they were actually accomplishing what they had set out to do. Maybe things would work out after all. Maybe they really were working together to create something extremely special. After having sunk to such a desperate low only a few days earlier, everyone's morale was now suddenly elevated to a new high.

However, *Evita* was far from complete. After a few days of rest, the entire company would move to Hungary for many more weeks of gruelling work. Once there, a new problem would arise, and it would be one that no one could have anticipated . . . and which, at least for the moment, only the leading lady suspected: Madonna was pregnant.

Carlos Leon

In mid-March, with the filming of the Argentina scenes of *Evita* completed, Madonna flew back to America for a few days of rest before continuing on to Budapest. In Miami, she sailed, rode her bike and watched the Mike Tyson fight on television while lounging around in her nightgown, eating ice cream and reading Shakespeare sonnets. Then, she headed to New York for a couple of days of shopping. All of this she dutifully reported in the 19 March entry for her 'diary', published in *Vanity Fair*. What she did not report is that she also scheduled a visit to her doctor, who then informed her that she was pregnant. 'I was stunned when I saw on the ultrasound a tiny living creature spinning around my womb,' she later recalled. 'Tap-dancing, I think. Waving its tiny arms around and trying to suck its thumb. I could have sworn I heard it laughing. The pure and joyful laughter of a child. As if to say, "ha-ha I fooled you".'

Actually, she had been talking about wanting a baby for years, but at the time of her marriage to Sean Penn, with her career progressing at a rapid pace, she kept postponing a pregnancy with her temperamental husband.

In newspaper articles throughout 1995 Madonna had spoken longingly of having a baby, but she was careful to add that she didn't want to focus on becoming pregnant until after she finished her dream role in *Evita*. The thirty-seven-year-old Madonna then began hinting that she was contemplating getting a sperm donor to help her have the child. She had joked to reporter Forrest Sawyer on the American television programme 'Prime Time Live' that her biological clock was ticking so loudly that she was going to put an ad out for a suitable man to sire her baby, to 'take care of the fatherhood gig,' she said.

On Wednesday 10 January 1996, Madonna had a rendezvous with Sean Penn at the Carlyle Hotel in New York. The two stayed in the room together for twenty-one-and-a-half hours, according to reporters waiting for her finally to emerge. Those closest to Madonna and Penn now say that she was trying to talk Penn into having a baby with her. 'I've had a lot of men since our marriage ended, but you're the only one I want as a father to my children,' she said, according to a friend of Penn's. 'You're the only man I've ever truly loved, Sean, and you know it.'

Penn, who already had two children by his second wife Robin Wright, is said to have 'really considered it', but declined Madonna's offer.

However, she seemed more determined than ever to have a baby. 'It's the one thing she wanted more than anything else,' says her ex-friend, Sandra Bernhard. 'I think she would do anything to have one.' It's true that anyone who knew Madonna knew that once her mind was set on a goal, it was unlikely that she wouldn't find a way to achieve it.

It would be her darkly attractive, handsome new boyfriend, the six-foot-tall Carlos Leon, who would assist Madonna in achieving her goal of motherhood. Madonna met Carlos in September 1994, while jogging in Central Park. As he cycled through the park, she watched intently, impressed by his well-toned body and the way his sinewy arms and legs filled out tight, black spandex. After asking her bodyguard to stay at a safe distance, Madonna approached the strapping stranger with finely chiselled Latin features. She asked him to join her for a cappuccino at a local coffee house. Over coffee, Madonna learned that the New York-born Cuban-American was raised in Manhattan and educated in parochial schools. He had aspired one day to become a professional cyclist, with aspirations of winning such races as the Tour de France. However, in order to earn a living, he was now a personal fitness trainer who received $100 an hour for his work, mostly at the gym, Crunch. Still, he dreamed of one day making the Olympic cycling team.

Impressed by his seductive looks and contagious personality, Madonna asked Carlos to stay in touch. Of course, what is probably most amazing about the story of how the internationally known superstar performer met the anonymous fitness trainer is that, at this stage of her life and career, Madonna would actually pick up a stranger in Central Park. One can only imagine the practically unbelievable story Carlos Leon had for his buddies over drinks that evening. Shortly thereafter, they began dating.

Sometimes referred to in press reports as a 'New York dancer', the amiable Carlos was soon seen hand in hand with the happy and animated Madonna at functions in New York, Miami and Los Angeles. 'We plan to start a family,' Madonna suddenly announced at her thirty-seventh birthday party, 'but we're waiting until I finish making *Evita*.' Of course, this proclamation of hopeful motherhood made little sense to interested observers, who couldn't figure out exactly who Carlos Leon was, or his purpose in Madonna's life.

It seemed that she felt she was unable to have a fulfilling relationship with a man at this time in her life, and simply didn't want to wait to find one before she had a child. Madonna is an impatient woman, as anyone who knows her will admit. After Tony Ward, she had raised the stakes when it came to the kind of man she would allow in her life. So far, no one measured up. However, it was now time for her to have a child . . . the ideal relationship would have to wait.

During Carlos's visits to Buenos Aires, he and Madonna seldom slept in the same bedroom, causing speculation among the cast and crew about the state of their relationship. What was not known at the time, though, was that Madonna had been suffering from nightmares ever since she began the movie. 'I was constantly being chased, caught and mauled in these awful nightmares,' she later confided to a friend. 'Every night, I would have these dreams. I would wake up exhausted.' Madonna slept in the master bedroom of her suite, while Carlos slept in a guest room. (Often, the two would start the night in the same room, before Carlos then withdrew to the smaller one.)

After experiencing the joy of hearing her baby's heartbeat, Madonna became concerned about the future of the movie, only adding to her stress. What would happen to *Evita* now? Her doctor had informed her that she was approximately ten weeks pregnant. She estimated that she could hide her condition for, perhaps, another seven weeks. However, a number of major dance numbers had been scheduled for the end of the shooting. 'Of course they could always get a body double for all my dance sequences [like

Jennifer Beals in *Flashdance*],' Madonna mused, 'but the idea of someone else doing my dancing is repulsive.'

While trying to figure out how to proceed, Madonna decided to reveal the news only to her immediate circle: her trainer, her assistant, and the child's father, Carlos. She chose not to tell her sisters, or any of her other friends. 'Not because I was ashamed of anything,' she later explained. Her biggest fear, she added, was that the story would somehow be leaked to the voracious press. She knew that the notion of Madonna-as-unwed-mother would become instant, worldwide news and cause a sensation that would, in her view, make her life a living hell. 'They will send their camera crews to torture me,' she said at the time, 'and I am desperate to finish filming in peace.'

Finally, when she realized that she had no choice but to inform Alan Parker, Madonna picked up the telephone.

'Are you sitting down, Alan,' she asked by way of greeting. Then she blurted, 'I'm pregnant.'

'How much?' the stunned Parker asked, dazed. 'I mean, when is it due?'

A Race to the Finish

Alan Parker tried not to panic but, as he would later recall, he couldn't help but do some quick calculations after learning that his star actress was expecting a baby: how many shooting weeks were left on his $59 million film, against how many more weeks she would look slim and trim. What could he do but to congratulate Madonna, and agree with her that they would both just have to 'see what happens next'. They also agreed to keep the pregnancy a secret, again for fear of the disruption the media's reaction might cause the film. Madonna would later say that she felt like a frightened adolescent trying to keep an unwanted pregnancy from her strict parents.

It wasn't long, though, before some of the crew began wondering about the unexplained and dramatic changes Parker began to make to the shooting schedule, especially where the dance sequences were concerned. 'They started to wonder if I had finally lost my marbles,' Madonna recalled. So, she and Parker had no choice but to fill the other producers in on the secret. Madonna, however, continued to keep her pregnancy from her friends and co-stars, realizing that the fewer people who knew about it, the greater her chances of keeping it out of the news. 'I feel like we are all in a race against time,' she said at the time. 'How will I do all those glamorous photo shoots to promote the film when I can't even fit into my costumes?'

Alone in her hotel room at night, Madonna brooded. Being pregnant should have cheered her up, but it didn't. She had a nagging feeling that she was about to destroy what she and the crew had worked so hard to accomplish. But was success at this film really so important, she would recall wondering to herself. 'All I want, really, is some peace in my life,' she remembered saying aloud to no one in particular. 'Is that so much to ask?'

The days were long, filming scenes outdoors in freezing temperatures, marching up and down the streets while leading torch-carrying masses, who were singing for Perón's freedom. On some days, she was on her feet for hours at a time, mostly dancing.

Back at the hotel, gazing at herself in the mirror, she did not see the happy glow of pregnancy. Instead, her reflection revealed an exhausted woman with an imperfect complexion. Clearly visible was a network of lines around her mouth, a web of wrinkles at the corners of her eyes. Sitting at her dressing table, she would begin the careful application of make-up. Her eyes would not leave her image until she was satisfied that her public mask was perfect. However, as she would later recall, it would take longer, with each passing day, for her to achieve that goal.

Constantly feeling chilled, she just couldn't seem to warm herself. She felt panicked, on edge. Later, she would have to admit that she couldn't shake the sick feeling that she was experiencing the unravelling of her carefully constructed life, that everything she had worked so hard to attain was about to be irrevocably lost.

No Big Thing?

On 13 April 1996, Madonna's manager Caresse Norman telephoned America's premiere gossip columnist, Liz Smith – always a big supporter of Madonna's career – and confirmed the news of Madonna's pregnancy. Smith's article was published in newspapers around the world the next day. 'Surprise, surprise, the stork couldn't wait,' she wrote. 'The happy news from Budapest has just arrived – that Madonna is indeed pregnant.'

'Madonna doesn't want this to be a big thing,' publicist Liz Rosenberg told Liz Smith in a follow-up call, 'though I don't know how she thinks it won't be a big deal. But she is deliriously happy, and so is everybody close to her. I hate to resort to a cliché, especially about Madonna, but she is radiant!'

Just prior to the phone call that was made to Liz Smith, Madonna telephoned her father, Tony, with the surprising news. During the filming of *Evita*, she had developed a closer relationship with her family, ironically enough by long-distance telephone communication. Each time Madonna called her father from Argentina to let him know how she was faring, he was thrilled to hear from her. He was proud of her, he said. The frequent conversations he had with her about her life and career at this time were certainly more civil than talks they'd had in recent years. Inadvertently, Tony had always seemed to rub Madonna up the wrong way.

'She was homesick,' says her brother Martin, whom she also

called periodically. 'She was calling all of us, her brothers and sisters and even some cousins.' Tony told one relative, 'We've been talking, and not fighting. I don't know, maybe things are changing.' It was as if, in some ways, Madonna was actually transforming herself into a gentler, more reasonable person – the kind of woman she had been trying to convince her public she really was at this time. 'Not that she was a saint,' says Alan Parker, 'but I did notice that as time went on with the film, she seemed to mellow.'

When Madonna learned she was pregnant, she said that she didn't want her father to read about it in the press. She telephoned him with the news, and also confessed to him that he was the most important person in her life – and that she hoped her child would not let her down the way she had let him down so many times in the past. Of course, Tony was concerned that Madonna was unwed and didn't seem at all eager to marry Carlos Leon. However, he was also elated and filled with genuine emotion by her call. 'We cried on the phone,' he recalls. 'I knew my kid was growing up. And she was nice to me,' he says, laughing. 'No smart cracks.'

Perhaps along with her pregnancy finally came a sense of acceptance and recognition for Madonna that she had only one surviving parent, and that she should at least try to be good to him. If she had directed her fury about her mother's death at Tony – and it certainly seemed to most people that she had done just that over the years – maybe she now realized how unfair she had been to her father. Or, maybe she had just grown to accept her mother's death as a terrible tragedy for which no one was responsible, and that her father's ability to move on with his own life was an act of strength and courage, not a betrayal of her mother's memory. Certainly, if a similar tragedy were to ever befall Madonna she, too, would somehow carry on with life, as difficult as it would be to do so. The Ciccone spirit – as passed from father to daughter – is strong and unwavering. Or, as the saying goes, the apple doesn't fall far from the tree.

The expected media frenzy about Madonna's pregnancy was not a surprise to anyone in her camp; the news travelled across the globe as rapidly as a war bulletin. Her characteristic flair for the dramatic at work, Madonna complained about the attention: 'Well, the world knows,' she said at the time. 'And I feel like my insides have been ripped open. The front page of the *Post*, CNN, even Hungarian Radio. What's the big deal?' she asked. 'I wish everyone would just let me do my work.' At this important time of filming *Evita*, Madonna couldn't help but feel that the public and media's focus on her pregnancy was a nuisance. What she really wanted, she claimed, was privacy and peace of mind, so that she could finish her movie.

Carlos's mother, forty-nine-year-old Maria Leon, rose to Madonna's defence. 'Everything people say about her is not true. When you get to know her, you know she's very affectionate, very warm. She's a real person, like you and me.' His father, Armando, who owned several Manhattan cheque-cashing stores, added, 'She loves Carlos very much. And we love her, too.' (Armando has said that when his son first showed up at a family gathering with Madonna for what they would later learn was her favourite meal of black beans, 'we couldn't believe it. We thought it was a lookalike, or something. We played Cuban music and talked all night.')

Making matters more interesting for the media to report, the jibes at Carlos Leon began instantaneously. He had been visiting Madonna in Buenos Aires because she wanted him at her side for moral support when she announced her pregnancy, but he quickly grew bored waiting around for her as she worked long hours on the set. On arriving home, he experienced aggressive media interest. 'It's great to be back in New York,' he snarled when a photographer snapped his picture as he sat on a bench in Central Park. Much to his dismay, the press now dubbed him 'Madonna's Top Seed', and her 'Baby-Making Beau' (both headlines courtesy of the *New York Post*).

The press immediately learned that he was a native New Yorker who had grown up on West Ninety-First Street, in a very different neighbourhood from Madonna's ritzy Central Park co-op (into which he had recently moved). Some sources hinted that Carlos hoped that meeting Madonna might provide the opportunity for a better life for him. Loyal friend Michael Gacki quickly came to Carlos's defence. 'He's not riding her coat-tails,' he reported to the *New York Post*. 'He's up at six a.m. every day working twelve or thirteen hours a day as a personal trainer to make it himself. He's been with her for a year and a half, and in my opinion it hasn't changed him one bit.' Gacki went on to explain that he and his pal Carlos were both involved with women 'more successful' than themselves but, he explained, 'we both wanted to make sure that we paid our own way'.

Patrice Gonzalez, who had a platonic relationship with him, said of Carlos's relationship with Madonna, 'He liked her from the time they first met. He was amazed that she was as timid as she turned out to be.'

Gonzalez was at the home of Carlos's parents when he and Madonna came to visit. As they were getting ready to leave, Madonna turned to Carlos and, in a rather abrupt tone, said, 'Get my coat.'

'Get it yourself,' he snapped back at her, his eyes flickering with annoyance.

'What's the matter with you?' she asked. 'You can't get my coat?'

'Carlos, go get her coat,' his mother, Maria, said, trying to keep the peace. 'Be a gentleman.'

'Look, I'm not your personal assistant,' Carlos told Madonna, ignoring his mother's request. It seemed clear to most observers that, for Carlos, a bigger issue was at stake than just the retrieval of his girlfriend's coat. Perhaps he and Madonna had engaged in previous discussions about similar matters. 'If you want me to get your coat, say "please",' he told her. 'I don't work for you. I'm not on the payroll, you know?'

Madonna rolled her eyes and shot him a cool look. 'My God,' she muttered.

'Oh, now I understand,' Carlos said. 'You see, I had completely underestimated your capacity for being . . . *a bitch*.'

Though Madonna looked angry, she somehow held her temper in check. Perhaps trying to tone down the moment because Carlos's mother was watching, she acquiesced. 'Carlos, can I ask you to get my coat?' she said, before adding, sweetly, '*Por favor.*'

As Carlos helped Madonna with her coat, his mother said, 'Now, now. See how nice?'

When Madonna finally told Carlos she was expecting, he realized, according to Patrice Gonzalez, that this child would create a bond with her that he would live with for ever. 'This was a big adjustment for him,' says Gonzalez, 'and forced him to look at her another way, as a woman who would be in his life for the long run.'

Betrayal

Two years earlier in 1994 – before the filming of *Evita* – Madonna had begun dating Dennis Rodman, a basketball star two years her junior who had an eccentric reputation – on and off the court. With his outlandish appearance – bleached blond hair, tattoos and various piercings – as well as his flamboyant behaviour, he relished the celebrity spotlight as much as Madonna did. In fact, borrowing a page from her career handbook, he often made controversial moves just for the sake of titillation – such as the time he announced his wedding and then showed up at the resulting press conference in full drag, complete with wedding dress and veil. He then declared that he was marrying himself.

The games between them began when Madonna first met Dennis and asked him for his telephone number. Instead of his phone number, he gave her his fax number. 'Your trying to fuck with me,' she faxed him the next day. 'You gave me a number that's for your damned machine. What's your problem?'

It wasn't long, though, before playful and sometimes sexy love messages were flying back and forth between the two. 'I want to have six kids,' Rodman faxed Madonna, 'what do you think?'

She faxed back to Rodman that six children would be fine with her, but they would have to get to work on it immediately. 'You think I'm joking, but you'll see that I'm not,' she wrote. She also mentioned that she would still be interested in Dennis even if he were broke and working at a car dealership. 'Lie in your bed, close your eyes and fuck me at some point today,' she concluded.

Perhaps because he was at the height of his own notoriety, Dennis Rodman seemed unimpressed with Madonna's fame or money, which only served to make him more interesting in her eyes. A friend of Dennis's recalls being at a party with Rodman and Madonna. 'He and I were flirting with some girls,' he says. 'Madonna kept trying to interrupt, but he just ignored her.' Not one to be ignored, when Rodman finally did give Madonna his number (not his fax number) she began a campaign to win him over. 'She called ten to fifteen times a day,' Rodman's friend reveals. 'She kept asking him, "What's going on? What are you doing?"'

In early 1995, Dennis confided in friends that Madonna was 'a lot of fun'. Meanwhile, Madonna told her own confidantes that she loved Dennis, though it seems difficult to imagine that any of them would have believed as much – or that she believed it herself. It's more likely that she was just carried away by the sexual chemistry between them. When he was unavailable and she couldn't reach him on the telephone – perhaps he was screening his calls? – she flooded him with romantic faxes with salutations such as 'Good morning, Daddy Long Legs'.

These silly fun and games lasted for just a few months and didn't amount to much, other than a wild ride in the bedroom for both participants. Madonna ended the relationship when she heard that Dennis was gossiping about her to mutual friends. Later, when some of her faxes to him found their way into publication in the tabloid the *Globe*, she realized that, if anything, she had been unlucky in lust. Rodman's comments to *Playboy* that he had to end it with her when she started pressing him to impregnate her – certainly a running theme in her life at this time with the men she dated – made her even angrier at him. (Rodman recalled to *Playboy*: 'She said, "Be in a hotel room in Las Vegas on this specific day so you can get me pregnant."' He declined.)

A little more than a year later, Rodman wrote his memoir, *Bad As I Wanna Be*. In it, he was explicit about his and Madonna's foreplay and pillow talk: 'She wasn't an acrobat. But she wasn't a dead fish, either.' When the book was published, Madonna ran to the store and purchased a copy herself. According to sources, she read the chapter about her and became so agitated that she threw the book into the fire.

'A certain disgusting basketball player I made the mistake of going out with decided to publish an autobiography and devoted a whole chapter to what it was like to have sex with me,' Madonna later seethed. 'Complete with made-up dialogue that even a bad porno writer would not take credit for. It's so silly I'm sure no one will take it seriously, but I don't feel like reading the headlines and of course I feel exploited once again by someone I trusted and let into my life.'

She also explained, 'When I first knew him, I sent him a few very silly faxes with really childish drawings on them, and months after I'd stopped seeing him, they appeared on [the tabloid TV programme] *Hard Copy*, and I thought, "This is only the beginning . . ."'

Her public may be surprised to learn that Madonna was too discreet to tell the truth about her relationship with Rodman which, as it happened, bore little resemblance to the way he portrayed it in his book. According to close friends of Madonna's and Rodman's, the couple only engaged in sexual activity twice – and not 'fifty to a hundred times' as Rodman bragged in his book.

Says dancer Trina Graves who dated Rodman in Chicago, 'He told me very specifically that he and Madonna had slept together one time in Miami, and that it was a big disappointment. He blamed it on her, saying she was frigid. He said he couldn't get excited when he was with her, because she was too demanding in bed. He said that she emasculated him.

'But, after having been with Dennis myself, I can see the other side. He's much too selfish to make love to a woman in a way that would be considered memorable. Mine was a boring experience with him, bland. Nothing to speak of.' Graves recalls that the basketball star didn't even take off his silk suit for their encounter. Rather, he just dropped his pants in a way that suggested a pornographic moment rather than a love-making session. 'And, no,' she allows, 'he did not become aroused with me, either.'

A friend of Madonna's who has known her for twenty years concurs, 'Madonna made a vow a long time ago to only have sex one time with a man if he proved himself too selfish to care about her satisfaction – and that certainly defines Dennis's approach. Also, she wanted more from a man than what Dennis had to offer. Of that, she was certain.'

To this particular friend, Madonna confided that after she and Dennis became drunk one evening, they tumbled into bed together. 'The poor guy couldn't even get excited for her,' said the friend. 'She blamed it on alcohol that night. Then, the next night, she bent her rule and let him try again.

'This time, Dennis performed, but only to his satisfaction – not hers. The whole thing lasted about fifteen minutes. Then, that was it. They never had sex again.'

Madonna's friend says that, 'Madonna could have put a dent in Rodman's machismo reputation if she had decided to tell the truth about his sexual prowess,' says the source, 'but, instead, I guess she opted to have mercy on him. She told me, "I feel sorry for the creep."'

During Madonna's interview with Oprah Winfrey, Oprah noted that she had read in the press that Rodman wished to apologize to Madonna for the book (which had spent eight weeks at number 1 on the *New York Times* bestseller list and had clearly generated a lot of attention for him). Madonna said, 'Well, he'd better crawl from here to China.' In fact, Madonna and Dennis had already had a telephone conversation about the book. Somehow, Rodman managed to telephone Madonna in London to apologize 'for any misunderstandings'.

Reportedly, she said to him, 'Dennis, you and I both know what happened when we made love . . . and it was nothing to write a book about.'

Anticlimax

After all of the hard work, anxiety and anticipation, the last day of shooting *Evita*, on 27 May 1996, proved to be anticlimactic for Madonna. She would later admit that she had fantasized an emotional ending to her long ordeal. Imagining herself breaking down in front of her co-workers once having uttered her final lines, she thought she would be completely overwhelmed by the experience. While she would feel grateful that the job was over, she would also feel sad that the time had come to say goodbye to all of those wonderful people she had so grown to love and admire, and who had shown her such love and admiration in return – or at least they had in this particular fantasy. Madonna had even gone to the trouble of rehearsing a dramatic, tearful farewell speech, one that each crew member and co-star would take home as part of his or her fond memory of her, one that they would be able to recount to family and friends . . . and maybe even to future Madonna biographers. Running a trembling hand over her brow, she was all but prepared to deliver her comments in regal, Evita style at the conclusion of the last shot when Alan Parker shouted out, 'That's a wrap.' However, before she had the chance, everyone scattered and quickly went about the business of breaking down the sets. No one paid her a second thought.

Suddenly, it was all over. However, Madonna didn't feel the way she thought she would feel, as she later explained. She just felt . . . numb. She blinked as quick tears came to her eyes. Then, she looked about helplessly as if she was trying to comprehend what had just happened. Perhaps noticing her confusion, someone came over to her – she doesn't remember who – hugged her warmly and then whispered something – she doesn't remember what – in her ear.

As the crew packed up its gear, there were no speeches, no sad goodbyes. 'I was just too damn tired,' Madonna later recalled. 'And so was everyone else.'

All told, there had been 299 scenes. Forty thousand extras appeared in period dress. Almost 6,000 costumes were needed from twenty different costume houses in London, Rome, Paris, New York, Los Angeles and San Francisco. Madonna's wardrobe consisted of 85 changes, 39 hats, 45 pairs of shoes, 56 pairs of earrings and as many different hair designs – while the art department created 320 different sets including 24,000 props.

For Madonna, the filming ended just in time, for not only was her belly pressing against her tailored suits, she was on the brink of an emotional meltdown. 'I couldn't have taken one more minute of it,' she would recall.

By September 1996, Madonna had been profoundly affected by her pregnancy. On 9 September she began keeping a journal about the experience. In it, she wrote that there were days when she couldn't even function because she felt at the mercy of mood swings that made life impossible for her. She also wrote of haemorrhoids, back pains and said, 'My life has been *hell*.'

Still, she managed to have some fun with friends. 'Once she finished *Evita*, we got to spend a lot of time together,' says her good friend, Juliette Hohnen. 'It was probably the first time in years she was forced to stay in one place for a while. We giggled when we went on our trial runs from her house to the hospital in preparation for the big moment. No matter how many times we practised, we always made a wrong turn somewhere and then, like a couple of squabbling sisters, we would blame each other for bad driving or bad navigating.'

As well as a written journal, Madonna also kept a video account of her pregnancy. Friends who have seen her video history say that it is so touching it should be released to the public. Says a source, 'She talked about how hard the pregnancy was, how sick she became, how her face broke out in blemishes, how unattractive she felt, and how she knew it would all be worth it for her child. I know that when her daughter sees these videos in years to come, she will feel a special closeness to her mom that Madonna never felt with hers – which was one of Madonna's goals with this project.'

'M [many of her friends called her "M"] told me that feeling a baby growing within her made her want to make an effort to straighten out some of the things she'd done in the past that she wasn't happy about, now,' said her good friend. 'For instance, I know that during her pregnancy she at least attempted to mend her years-long rift with Michael Jackson.'

Michael hadn't spoken to Madonna since the proposed video in which Madonna wanted Michael to dress as a woman. However, in the fall of 1996, Madonna sent Michael a note to wish him luck on the beginning of a tour on which he was embarking at the time, and sent a huge floral display to Prague where he debuted his show. She tried to refrain from making critical comments about him, which was difficult for her.

'She also began calling people she hadn't talked to or seen in years,' says her friend. Said Diane Giordano: 'She told me that she wanted to be a good mother, but was afraid that would not be possible because she had become so accustomed to being a self-centred person. She became spiritual, and started looking at herself in a new and more uncompromising way. So, M's pregnancy was an emotional and very human time for her – and also for all the people in her life who were getting surprising, middle-of-the-night phone calls from Madonna asking for forgiveness. Being pregnant and bringing the baby to term was the toughest thing she'd ever had to do, tougher than anything she'd done in her career. Just as it is for a lot of women, being pregnant marked a defining time in her life.'

Lourdes

On 14 October 1996, thirty-eight-year-old Madonna gave birth to a 6lb 9oz baby girl she named Lourdes Maria Ciccone Leon at Good Samaritan Hospital in Los Angeles. Lourdes – her name inspired by the town in France associated with miracles – sported a full head of jet-black hair, just like her father's. It had been a difficult birth; sixteen hours of labour that ended in a Caesarean section. Madonna had originally hoped for a natural childbirth, with the soundtrack of a romantic 1988 Alan Rudolph film called *The Moderns* playing softly in the background. Her dream of such a tranquil birth was dashed, though, when the reality of the pain involved changed her mind. 'I just want this to be *over*,' she told the doctors. 'Screw *The Moderns*. I can't bear this!' As they wheeled her into the delivery room, a groggy Madonna turned to Carlos Leon, her newly promoted manager Caresse Norman, publicist Liz Rosenberg and several other friends and security guards and said, 'Goodbye everyone. I'm going in for my nose job, now.'

Despite the fact that she checked in under the alias Victoria Fernandez, the expected media frenzy ensued, complete with the inevitable 'Madonna and Child' articles which were quickly disseminated around the world. Outside the hospital, eleven trucks were parked, each with pop-up satellite towers, plus dozens of camera crews and hordes of photographers and reporters, all patiently waiting for any news titbits – such as the revelation that Madonna's paediatrician was Dr Paul Fleiss, father of convicted Hollywood madam Heidi Fleiss. The birth was just two months before *Evita* was set to open. The coincidental timing of these two major events in her life 'was incredibly poetic', Madonna said. 'I waited so long for this movie and it finally happened. I wanted so badly to have a child and I got pregnant while making the movie. Suddenly, God gave me two gifts that were very important to me.' She pointed out that 'everything I do is scrutinized so I shouldn't be surprised that it continued when I was pregnant. I try to have a sense of humour about it, but it does irritate me. My child is not for public consumption. It's not a career move. It's not a performance to be judged and rated. Nor is my role as a mother'.

Carlos Leon – who cut the umbilical cord with surgeon's scissors – would give Madonna sole custody of the baby. Of the notion of marriage Madonna stated emphatically, 'I don't feel the need. I'm perfectly happy with the way things are.' As for defining a father's role in raising children in general Madonna said, 'I think it's just as important as the mother's. But I won't tell you specifically that I think it's a man's job to do this and a woman's job to do that. They both have nurturing roles to play.' When pressed to answer if the ideal would be to have both a mother and father at home Madonna retorted, 'I grew up without a mother and I did all right.'

Madonna decided that she would not release an official picture of little Lourdes for mass consumption (that would come a year later in *Vanity Fair*), which only served to make a shot of the baby all the more exclusive. If a photographer managed to get a clear portrait, it was estimated it could bring in as much as $250,000. She was incensed that the price of a photograph of her baby was so exorbitant, yet she also must have understood that had she released a photograph, the price – and, maybe even the interest – would have decreased dramatically.

As Madonna recuperated from childbirth, media interest in her and her newborn did not ebb. With the *Evita* opening just a couple of months in the offing, subsequent magazine interviews that Madonna gave revolved as much around motherhood as the making of the movie. And, as the publicity machine rolled forward, the softer image that she had begun to orchestrate just prior to the filming of the movie also came into focus. Now, she was able finally to announce to the world that she was a kinder, gentler Madonna, one with new values, worthier agendas . . . and even a baby, no less.

'Madonna has repeatedly been depicted as cocky, shameless and curt,' journalist Jonathan Alter wrote after his interview with her. 'But I found none of this to be true. She was emotional about motherhood, impassioned about playing Eva Perón and surprisingly uncertain about what the future holds. In place of her legendary self-confidence, Madonna seemed unusually vulnerable.'

In a cover story for *Redbook* magazine, Madonna said, 'When I started seriously thinking about motherhood and taking care of a child, certain people that I found amusing and interesting didn't seem so terribly amusing and interesting. I did a lot of emotional housecleaning and I wound up with a much smaller handful of friends.'

For the first four weeks after Lourdes was born, Madonna didn't do anything but take care of her, hold her, and (breast) feed her. Then slowly she started getting back to work, sitting at her desk and talking on the phone, trying to run her record company. 'It was a huge adjustment,' Madonna said. 'I used to make a list and know I'd get everything done. Now a lot of things don't get done, and that's OK.'

Madonna sent for her father, Tony, and his wife, Joan, so that they could visit her in Los Angeles, and meet Lourdes. It was a joyful time. If there was any acrimony between Madonna and her father and stepmother, it certainly wasn't evident during the time they visited her after the baby was born. Other members of the Ciccone family – as well as the Leon family – also converged on Madonna's home to celebrate the new birth. Tony seemed to get along well with Carlos, and some observers noticed that he tried to convince Carlos to marry his daughter. 'Dad, stop it, please,' Madonna said, good-naturedly. She was wearing combat trousers and a white tank top, with her bra showing (which may or may not have given Tony pause). 'Carlos does what he wants to do. If he wants to marry me, he will.' Of course, whether or not Madonna became a married woman really wasn't a decision that Carlos was likely to be the one to make.

One month after the baby's birth, Madonna once again fixed her eyes on the future – and the premiere of *Evita* in December. The 5-foot-4 superstar had tipped the scales at a hefty 140 pounds before the birth of Lourdes, and she was seen furiously pedalling around Los Angeles' Griffith Park trying to slim down to 115 pounds before the movie's opening. For the next few weeks Madonna stuck to a low-fat diet and extensive exercise, and by early December she was turning heads with her slimmed-down shape.

Just before she gave birth, Madonna put her 7,800 square foot mansion – the former home of gangster Bugsy Siegel – on the market for $6.5 million. Madonna said that she felt the house, just below the legendary 'Hollywood' sign, was haunted and didn't want to live there with her baby. Her Manhattan duplex also went up for sale for $7 million. In preparation for the baby, she had bought a cosy $2.7 million house in the Los Feliz district of Los Angeles. Built in the 1920s, the Mediterranean-style home has three bedrooms in about 5,000 square feet, plus a two-bedroom cottage. The home is on two acres, and Madonna would divide her time between that residence and her $4.9 million mansion in Miami.

Evita: *The Movie and Soundtrack*

After all the publicity hoopla, *Evita* finally had its grand premiere in Los Angeles in December 1996 at the Shrine Auditorium in Los Angeles, which Madonna and Carlos Leon attended together. She wore a magenta Eva Perón-inspired dress designed by John Galliano, a feathered chapeau and veil, and sexy strapped shoes by

Manolo Blahnik. Looking confident and smart, she was flanked by bodyguards as she made her captivating entrance in a bedlam of police, limousines, klieg lights and fans, almost 2,000 of them. Truly, she was in her element as the lights played on her while the entourage of reporters and photographers yammered for her attention. Madonna's smile stretched wide. Exultant, she laughed, waved and posed as the paparazzi flashed their lights and reporters jotted down notes.

'Yes, it was such fun,' she said to one reporter.

'No, I have no plans for another movie,' she explained to another, 'but if you know a producer, tell him to call me,' she added with a laugh.

'See the movie,' she enthused to one on-camera commentator. 'It's my proudest achievement, besides my daughter.'

Once inside, she chatted with Antonio Banderas and Melanie Griffith, seeming genuinely happy even though she was facing emergency root canal surgery the following day. Then, there would be another star turn when she would fly to London with her baby for the *Evita* premiere there.

The $56 million extravaganza was a quick commercial success; generally, the movie's reviews were favourable. *Time* magazine's Richard Corliss wrote: 'It's a relief to say that Alan Parker's film, which opens on Christmas Day, is pretty damn fine, well cast and handsomely visualized. Madonna once again confounds our expectations. She does a tough score proud. Lacking the vocal vigour of Elaine Paige's West End *Evita*, Madonna plays Evita with a poignant weariness. She has more than just a bit of star quality. Love or hate Madonna–Eva, she is a magnet for all eyes. You must watch her.'

It's true; *Evita* is a spectacularly produced film. The direction and art direction are superb. The supporting cast is excellent, the sets breathtaking, the costumes captivating . . . all of which adds up to a visually beautiful movie. The film is always entertaining and, at times, moving. But what of Madonna's performance as its star?

There is no denying that she is a magnificent performer. In her pop videos and stage concerts she has a magic that, at its best, dazzles and electrifies. Perhaps, had she brought some of the flash and trash sexiness of her video persona to her role as Eva Perón (as she did in her first movie role, *Desperately Seeking Susan*), her interpretation might have been a smashing success. Her choice, though, was to downplay Eva Perón's ferocious hunger, her desire to succeed, her need to excel. Her determination to portray a more sympathetic image for the character – and for herself – ultimately strips Evita of her undercurrent of urgency. In the end, Evita's masterful manipulations become sweet suggestions; numbers that should burn with intensity instead take on a certain pallor. For example, Madonna's coy interpretation of the seduction called 'I'd Be Surprisingly Good for You', dilutes what should have been a *tour de force* and makes it sound weak and whiny.

Madonna dances expertly and looks lovely in the period costumes (although she appears too old for early scenes when – filmed in deep shadow – she plays Eva as a teenager). But always we are aware of Madonna as a performer working extremely hard at a role. We never feel that she and the role become one. She is so calculating – just as she has always been in her work – that there doesn't appear to be one truly organic moment for her as an actress in the entire movie. The viewer can almost hear her mind working: *click* – look this way, *click* – feel this way, *click* – time to cry.

During the times she is weakest, there are pleasant distractions. For instance, her performance on the much-anticipated 'Don't Cry for Me, Argentina' scene on the balcony of the Casa Rosada seems wooden and disaffected, especially considering all she did to secure that location. Yet, it is somehow boosted and lent power by sweeping camera angles, dramatic lighting changes and especially by her supporting players. Antonio Banderas' sly looks of admiration and contempt, Jonathan Pryce's proud bolstering from the sidelines, and the strong emotions on the faces of the extras playing Evita's supporters all lend power to the scene that Madonna – for all her strained neck muscles – cannot seem to muster.

Whereas there may be ambivalence from some quarters about her work as an actress in the film, as a singer Madonna could not have been more wondrous. When the two-disc soundtrack album to *Evita* made its debut, the resulting performance made jaws drop. Madonna performed with a sense of technical and emotional discipline and depth seldom heard or seen in her acts, and a commanding familiarity with the work that allowed her to get inside the Webber/Rice songs in a way that seemed even deeper and more convincing than her on-screen transformation into Evita.

As Evita Perón, Madonna is responsible for singing on most of the songs in the musical, alone or with her co-stars. When she makes her first appearance on the soundtrack – as the wistful voice of Evita, reflecting from her grave during the sad passage of 'Oh What a Circus' – she is supple and strong, and doesn't sound at all out of place. She then sounds even more self-assured during 'Eva and Mafaldi/Eva Beware of the City', a movement with complex and conflicting tempos. Bigger voices than hers have certainly sung the festive, determined 'Buenos Aires', one of the production's signature tunes, but Madonna also made it her own.

In the end, Madonna sang her way through a full musical's worth of what was unquestionably the most challenging material of her career. She didn't simply get through it, as some other singers-turned-actresses might have – but gave a performance that was, at times, captivating. Who can deny that her voice has remarkable and unmistakable presence when heard during 'You Must Love Me'?

Two singles from the soundtrack, the aforementioned 'You Must Love Me' and 'Don't Cry for Me, Argentina', reached number 18 and number 8 on the *Billboard* singles chart respectively, while the soundtrack itself went to number 2 on the trade magazine's album chart in 1996. The soundtrack sold five million copies stateside, and eleven million internationally. With this collection, she added just one more triumph to a world-class résumé already brimming with accomplishments . . . and she also silenced a good deal of snickering in the process.

If nothing else, the interest that surrounded *Evita* – the film and the soundtrack – should have given Madonna more opportunities to star in big-budget movies. The Golden Globe, given by the Foreign Press Association, acknowledged her by giving her the award for best performance by a female in a musical or comedy. Certainly, this award was a well-deserved honour symbolizing a year of extraordinary hard work, dedication and commitment on the part of Madonna. Sadly, no other offers were forthcoming, at least none that she felt were worth her time and energy. Also, she was snubbed at the Oscars, though 'You Must Love Me' did win the award for Best Song (and the award went to songwriters Webber and Rice).

'I'm patient,' she concluded in one interview. 'Roles for women are not easy to come by, especially good ones. I'd like to say that the way I handle my career is by being smart about it, but then how would I explain *Body Heat*? When the right role comes along, maybe I'll know it. Maybe I won't. I'm not a genius. I just do the best I can do.'

No Future with Carlos

After the legendary film star Elizabeth Taylor had brain surgery to remove a benign tumour in the spring of 1997, Madonna sent her a basket of fruit while she recuperated in hospital. The accompanying note read, 'You are my idol. There will never be another Elizabeth Taylor. Get well.' After Elizabeth was sent home, Madonna became a frequent visitor to her Bel Air mansion; a friendship between the two women began to blossom. When Madonna first brought little Lourdes to visit, Elizabeth was dazzled by her. She urged Madonna to marry Carlos Leon and 'give Lourdes a father. My dear, it's obvious you love the man'. Taylor was quoted as having said, 'So why don't you marry him? God knows I've married many more who've given me a lot less than Carlos has given you. He's given you a beautiful baby and will give you more. Besides, he's gorgeous.'

The two laughed about the fact that Madonna had wanted the Pope to baptize Lourdes, but he turned her down. 'Imagine, me being turned down by the Vatican,' she said, according to one of her friends. 'How dare he?' (Actually, Madonna didn't think the Pope would consent to such a baptism. After all, she wasn't even married. But what did she have to lose by enquiring?) Instead, Madonna had the baby christened at St Jude's in Miami. 'It was nice, but it ain't the Vatican,' she told Elizabeth Taylor. Madonna later indicated in an interview that she wanted Lourdes to be raised a Catholic because, 'that foundation was important to me, and important to Carlos. Say what you will about Catholicism, the things you pick up along the way do help you by giving you something to turn to when you're in trouble. Then, when you have that foundation, you can start looking at other philosophies – which is what I've done.'

The two cultural icons – Liz and Madonna – became good friends. Madonna had in common with Elizabeth Taylor her new-found spiritual pursuit; she had recently become interested in Kabbalah, a mystical, medieval branch of Judaism that emphasizes the link between self and universe. Madonna began inviting friends to study it with her, describing it as 'a mystical interpretation of the Old Testament'.

With many reasons to be exhausted by her whirlwind life and career – countless Grammys, sold-out tours, worldwide adulation – perhaps it seemed that the only thing left for Madonna to do was finally and truly to embrace who she really was, and not just who she seemed to be when attached to her career, or to a man.

In explaining her growing interest in Kabbalah, Madonna has said that she decided she 'needed to be more than a girl with gold teeth and gangster boyfriends. More than a sexual provocateur imploring girls not to go for second-best *baby*. I began to search for meaning and a real sense of purpose in life. They say that when the student is ready, the teacher appears, and I'm afraid that cliché applied to me as well.

'In the beginning I sat at the back of the classroom,' she said of her Kabbalah training. 'I was usually the only female. Everyone looked very serious. Most of the men wore suits and kippahs. No one noticed me and no one seemed to care, and that was just fine. What the teacher was saying blew my mind. Resonated with me. Inspired me. We were talking about God and heaven and hell, but I didn't feel like religious dogma was being shoved down my throat. I was learning about science and quantum physics. I was reading Aramaic. I was studying history. I was introduced to an ancient wisdom that I could apply to my life in a practical way. And for once, questions and debate were encouraged. This was my kind of place. When the world discovered I was studying Kabbalah, I was accused of joining a cult. I was accused of being brainwashed. Of giving away all my money.'

She became such a devout follower of Kabbalah that she hosted a high-powered reception in Los Angeles on 18 September 1997 to discuss the philosophy with friends and business associates. 'Kabbalah is the one place I don't feel like a celebrity,' she said. Although she had spent most of her life discussing her Catholic upbringing both in positive and negative terms, Madonna stated that nothing had ever spoken to her like Kabbalah and that only now did she feel fully equipped emotionally to take responsibility for her life. After returning to Los Angeles, Madonna surprised some of her associates by regularly attending Bible classes at the Kabbalah Learning Center in Los Angeles.

'We are all responsible for our actions, our behaviour, and our words, and we must take responsibility for everything we say and do,' Madonna would say when speaking about her spirituality. 'When you get your head wrapped around that, you can no longer think of life as a series of random events – you participate in life in a way you didn't previously. I am the architect of my destiny. I am in charge. I bring that to me, or I push that away. You can no longer blame other people for things that happened to you. There is order in the universe, even though it looks like chaos. We separate the world into categories: this is good and this is bad. But life is set up to trick us. It's a series of illusions we invest in. And ultimately those investments don't serve our understanding, because physicality is always going to let you down, because physicality doesn't last.'

Madonna's spiritual awakening would also plant the seeds for her next breakthrough – freedom from Carlos.

Although Elizabeth Taylor and other friends had urged her to marry the father of her daughter, by the early spring of 1997 Carlos Leon seemed to be rapidly disappearing from Madonna's life. Most observers believed that Madonna had ended the relationship with Carlos after she got what she wanted from him: a child. It wasn't that simple, or mean. In fact, it was Carlos who began to lose interest in continuing his relationship with Madonna and, conveniently, at just about the same time she began to distance herself from him. That they would not marry would actually be a mutual decision. After the birth of Lourdes, he told friends that he couldn't be married to a woman 'who never goes to bed before two in the morning and who then wakes up at five to see what has been published about her in some goddamn foreign country'. She has a taste for good living, he said, but no great capacity for enjoyment, 'because something is always going on in her life, some big dramatic thing, that just ruins everything that day for her. It's not fair. She works too hard to have so many bad days.'

Another problem, according to Patrice Gonzalez, had to do with the constant emphasis on Madonna's career, no matter where the couple were, or what they were doing. 'It was all about her, all the time,' says Gonzalez, 'and this was very off-putting to Carlos. He understood it – she was who she was, after all – but he didn't always like it. He was a proud man. He felt overlooked.'

Patrice and other friends of Carlos's report one instance – of, no doubt, many – when they were at a cocktail party with Carlos and

Madonna in Manhattan and able to observe as Carlos was pushed to the background.

'They arrived together,' Patrice says, 'but in a matter of moments, they were separated. The guests sort of backed off instinctively to let them pass as they walked into the room, and then they descended upon her like vultures, pushing him aside. For the next two hours, Carlos sat in the background while Madonna and her friends and associates talked endlessly about her and *Evita*.'

Looking preoccupied, Carlos walked over to the bar, where he joined a friend. As he leaned on the bar, a heart-shaped tattoo (with the date he first met Madonna) was noticeable on his left bicep. He also wore an expensive, crown-shaped ring, a gift from her on their first anniversary. Perhaps noticing his absence, Madonna sauntered over to him. 'What's wrong, Carlito?' she asked ('Carlito' is Carlos's nickname).

'To be honest, I'm sick to death of hearing about *Evita*,' Carlos answered, quickly. 'From the moment we arrived, every word has been about you and *Evita*,' he continued, trying to hold his temper in check. 'These people don't even know who the fuck I am, or what I do. And they don't care.'

No doubt, Madonna had heard this complaint before from boyfriends. She knew it was difficult for any man to walk in her shadow, especially if he wasn't also a celebrity. 'I wouldn't wish being Mr Madonna on anybody,' she once said. Still, according to Carlos's friend who was present, she looked a bit hurt. 'Everyone else here is proud of me,' she said. 'Why aren't you?'

Carlos shook his head. 'You really don't get it, do you?' he asked, giving her a hard, knowing stare. 'This isn't about you, Madonna.'

Madonna didn't respond. Instead, with furrowed brow, she examined the inside of her nearly empty glass, as if hoping to find the answer there.

'This is your life, not mine,' Carlos said sadly, while he and Madonna stood next to each other at the bar.

'I know,' Madonna said. For a moment, her expression conveyed deep despair. Then, she shook her head in annoyance and said, 'Carlos, I think you're just being a big baby. Now, come on, have fun. I'll tell you what?' she said with a grin. 'We'll talk only about you for the rest of the night. How's that?'

He didn't respond, perhaps hurt that she was making light of his frustration.

'Come on, buy me a drink,' she continued, trying to force a light moment. 'My glass is empty. A lady's glass should never be empty.'

After a silent moment which made it clear that Carlos was not in a joking – or even a drinking – mood, Madonna turned to his friend and said, 'My baby is sick of me, huh?' On tiptoes, she reached up and kissed Carlos gently on the cheek. 'Things will sort themselves out,' she said, reflecting her new spirituality and belief that all things do somehow work themselves out for the best. Carlos's friend recalls a tone of inevitability in Madonna's voice, an understanding, an acceptance. 'Trust me,' she said before taking her leave.

Carlos looked doubtful.

Rumours soon began to run riot that Madonna's relationship with Carlos Leon was over and that she had had her handlers negotiate a financial arrangement that would ensure not only his financial security but also his silence. According to the agreement, as outlined in the press, Carlos would have certain visitation rights but would have to sign documents agreeing never to seek sole custody of their child.

If her intention was to make Carlos Leon a financial offer – and, realistically, it would seem somewhat naive to believe that no such offer was made and then accepted – Madonna's proposal would have to be a generous one. He had received numerous offers to write a book about his relationship with Madonna, and one was for more than $3 million. Madonna was concerned when word got back to her of the possibility of a book by Carlos. However, she needn't have worried. Leon rejected the offer completely. Loyal to her without reservation, he promised that he would never write about her, or be interviewed about her, and that she didn't have to include such provisions in any agreement between them. 'It just goes without saying,' he told her, according to a friend of his.

Madonna suspected that she could trust Carlos to say little about her – and certainly nothing negative or revealing – and, as it happened, she could do just that. After the tangle of so many unhappy and turbulent relationships – Penn, Kennedy, Beatty, Ward, even Rodman – Madonna had finally hit upon a good guy: Carlos Leon. But it wasn't that simple. Though Carlos may have had the potential to be the ideal mate, the hard truth was that Madonna didn't feel the kind of abiding love for him that would make it work between them – and neither did he for her.

By the time of Lourdes's first birthday in October 1997, Carlos Leon was nowhere in sight. Instead, it was Ingrid Casares who accompanied Madonna and her daughter to watch the dolphins in an aquarium in Los Angeles. Meanwhile, Leon was snapped by photographers frolicking in the Malibu surf with a bikini-clad blonde. The photographs showed the pair running around in the sand, taking a dip and kissing in what appeared to be a passionate embrace. By this time, Leon even had his own 'spokesman', Eric Weinstein, who, despite the existence of the revealing photographs, declared, 'Carlos and Madonna are trying to patch things up right now.' Madonna was unhappy when she saw the photographs published in one of the tabloids – all of which she read religiously – not because Carlos was moving on with his life, but because she felt that his being able to do so made her appear to the public to be dispensable. 'You don't go from Madonna to some little blonde chippy,' she told one of her associates. 'I think Carlos should be more discreet. But what can I do? I guess he has to live his life, too.'

I chanced upon Carlos Leon in a bar in the East Village of New York in the spring of 1999 and had the opportunity to ask him a few questions. Leon said that he saw his daughter Lourdes 'as often as I possibly can. She's the light of my life.' He also stated that, 'Madonna is the best mother in the world, and I know I can trust her with our child. But Lourdes is *our* child, not just hers. I hate it when you writers act like I don't exist, like Madonna is a single mother. I do exist. We're not married, but I am involved.' When asked if there was a contractual agreement between himself and Madonna, Leon succinctly replied, 'We love each other. We trust each other. More people should try it.'

Andy Bird

In many ways, the Nineties had been tough, challenging years for Madonna. Even though she continued to enjoy great commercial success, she felt that the fame she had once so craved was now nothing more than a hungry and insatiable leech sucking her dry, keeping her from being truly happy. Much of her public had the false impression that, because she was famous, she also felt an incredible sense of self-fulfilment and of truly being loved. But people who are famous can tell you that the opposite is true – that if you are not truly fulfilled in your personal life, then many thousands of people adoring you can actually make you feel emptier. At its worst – as it had been for Madonna – fame had become a substitute for love, a disruptive influence in her life, often giving the feeling of happiness when, really, no happiness truly exists. 'I used to be so unhappy,' she said. 'Maybe that's why I was so, I don't know, maybe mean to a lot of people . . . though I don't think I'm ready to cop to that,' she added with a laugh. The birth of Lourdes helped an immeasurable amount in this regard, giving Madonna a sense of satisfaction she had never before known. 'Ever since my daughter was born, I feel the fleetingness of time,' she said. 'And I don't want to waste it on getting the perfect lip colour.'

She proved to be an excellent mother, says her close friend and confidante Rosie O'Donnell. 'She's a tough-love kind of mother,' says Rosie. 'For instance, she doesn't want her kid watching TV. Can you imagine that? Me, I use the television as a babysitter for my [four] kids. If it wasn't for the tube, I don't know what I would do to keep them occupied.' (As a child, Madonna was also forbidden to watch TV by her father, Tony, who felt there were better ways for a child to stay occupied.)

It was true that Madonna insisted that her daughter not watch television, saying that she didn't want the girl to be influenced by sexual and, also, violent images. Even though she made a career out of being an outrageous sex goddess, she believes children should be protected from such imagery.

'And no junk food for Lourdes, either,' said O'Donnell. 'So when that girl comes to my house to visit for the weekend, forget it! She leaves here a totally different child, a candy-bar-eating, MTV-watching, spoiled little kid. To tell you the truth,' said the comic, 'I think Madonna knows how tough she is on the kid and lets her spend time at my house just to give her a break. But when she goes back to Mama, she toes the line. Then, when she visits me again, I have to start the process all over again of turning her into one of "my" kids.'

In her private life, Carlos Leon had served his purpose, whether it was as a partner in a temporarily committed romance, or as just a trusted friend who was able to give her the child she so desperately desired. Now, with him all but out of the picture, she was anxious to move forward with her personal life and career.

In September 1997, Madonna embarked on what would amount to an unsteady relationship with an aspiring British actor and screenplay writer, Andy Bird, after having met him in Los Angeles through mutual friend Alek Keshishian (who directed *In Bed with Madonna*). It would be with Bird that Madonna would pick up her romantic life after Carlos Leon. While her choice in men was flawless when it came to Carlos Leon, it seemed somewhat weaker in the choice of Andy Bird.

Madonna was immediately taken with the 6-foot-2 Englishman

who wore his light brown hair at shoulder length and always dressed in black. 'It was lust at first sight,' a friend of hers revealed at the time. 'Madonna calls Andy "Geezer". He isn't exactly rolling in cash. The guy didn't look like he had two bucks to his name, but Madonna was totally smitten. When they were together, she couldn't keep her hands off of him.'

Soon after meeting Andy Bird, Madonna jetted to London for a two-month mission to search for a house there, saying that she felt that Britain was a safer place in which to raise her daughter. 'I have really fallen in love with the place,' she said. 'I've made some excellent friends in London and even thought about my daughter going to school here. I think the British are more intelligent than Americans.'

In what some of her friends called 'record time', Bird and Madonna rented a £4,500 a week house in Chelsea, while Madonna looked for a permanent home in London. Then, when she needed to return to Los Angeles on business, he moved into her Los Feliz home. He told one London-based reporter, 'I'm living over there now and trying my luck as a film director.'

Madonna's romance with chain-smoker but non-drinker Andy Bird was tumultuous from the start, generating reams of tabloid headlines over the course of about a year. At one point, she kicked him out of her California home and he ended up back in London, working as a doorman at the Met bar. Another time, she left him stranded penniless in Florida for a week before begging him to come back in a string of heart-to-heart phone calls.

Who can say why Madonna was attracted to Andy Bird? They seemed to have little in common. She was driven and ambitious, he was more laid back about his career. She was a multimillionaire, he didn't have much money. However, he was a kind man, and also fun. A gentleman with a great sense of humour, Andy made Madonna laugh. He was polite, reassuring. He wasn't cruel and argumentative, like Sean Penn. He wasn't emotionally crippled like Warren Beatty and John Kennedy Jun. Actually, he was more like

Tony Ward – loving and well-meaning while, perhaps, not terribly stable or financially secure.

To his credit, Andy treated Madonna not like a star, but like a friend, which she found irresistible. They had picnics, they talked about movies, they joked with one another. In July 1998, the two exchanged vows in a Kabbalah ceremony that supposedly united them for all time. Madonna wore a flowing white gown for the ceremony. Both she and Bird were barefoot. She told friends at the time that she hoped to have Bird's child, but that marriage might not be necessary since 'we had this very lovely ceremony'.

Madonna didn't much care about Andy's bank account – at least not at first. However, as weeks turned into months, she could not reconcile the fact that Bird was unclear about his future ambitions while, at the same time, being such a spiritual person. To her way of thinking, the purpose of spirituality was to use it to move your life ahead to the next plateau, not to fall back on it as an excuse to stagnate. Bird, however, felt that career concerns were secondary to those relating to the metaphysical. On a trip to London in the fall of 1998, at his urging he and Madonna visited the Inergy Centre in Kensal Rise, west London, which specializes in teaching yoga. Afterwards, she said, 'Yoga is very physical and strengthens me from within, not just externally. It helps me be more flexible about how I see the world and other people.'

At twenty-nine, ten years Madonna's junior, Andy did seem to have some growing up to do. He was also insecure. Perhaps a defining moment occurred in their relationship when he accused Madonna of having a fling with a young film director while she was in London making a video. Madonna was having no such affair. (At least, not yet.) Also, when it came to discretion with the media – a requirement if one is to have a relationship with a major celebrity – Andy Bird was a novice. 'She goes through boyfriends like there's no tomorrow,' Andy told a reporter. No doubt that wasn't the kind of statement Madonna liked to hear her male companions make about her. She must have known that there were problems ahead.

Madonna didn't have many people she could turn to to discuss issues having to do with Andy. Those who had known her for years were not the best to give advice, she felt, because, as she put it, 'they've all heard my stories a thousand times over, and they're sick of them . . . and of me.' Perhaps this is the reason Madonna turned to a surprising new friend in trying to sort out some of her problems with Andy Bird.

Ray of Light

By 1998, thirty-nine-year-old Madonna was all but finished with what was perhaps the most ambitious makeover in her entire fifteen-year career. For the last few years, always with great forethought, she had been going about the business of repairing the public relations damage of the downward slide that had been the result of sexually explicit projects in four different media: *In Bed with Madonna* in video, *Sex* in publishing, *Erotica* in music and *Body of Evidence* in film. Wisely, Madonna had decided to ease out of her role as a sexual revolutionary and slip into a more subdued persona as a mother and New Age thinker.

It was more than just public relations, though. She really had been affected by her experiences with *Evita* and new baby, Lourdes. 'It's just an evolution, really, since I made *Evita*,' she told *Rolling Stone*'s Gerri Hirshey. 'Because going down to South America and getting beaten up the way that I was in the newspapers every day – and sort of living vicariously through what happened to Eva Perón – then finding myself pregnant. Going from the depths of despair and then coming out the other side . . . you know, becoming a mother, I just have a whole new outlook on life. I see the world as a much more hopeful place. I just feel an infinite amount of compassion towards other people.'

Her first album issued after the birth of her daughter, *Ray of Light*, was released in March 1998. It would combine her recently adopted New Age beliefs – which she seemed to have fine-tuned with Andy Bird's help – with music that was both current and trend setting. Indeed, if ever there was a recording that proved without a doubt that Madonna still understood how to stay ahead of the game in pop music, *Ray of Light* was it.

After the movies, the soundtracks and the haunting ballads, Madonna knew that at her very core she was still a dance music artist. She also realized that trends in that genre begin in the places where people dance – which is where Madonna would find her new sound.

Techno and electronica had, for years, been the music played at so-called raves: hugely popular, illegal underground parties taking place in abandoned warehouses and deserted areas on the outskirts of town all around the world. This is where young music lovers, on alcohol and the popular rave drug Ecstasy, were zoning out on the beat of ethereal, synthesized sounds. It was a hot sound, and one Madonna knew had not reached the masses. 'It's definitely an area that's gone untapped,' Madonna observed at the time. 'And I need to be in on it.'

Just as she had once sought out the hot dance/pop producer of the moment to assist her foray into mainstream success (Nile Rodgers with *Like a Virgin*) and employed hot, urban producers to accommodate her hip-hop move (Dallas Austin with *Bedtime Stories*), Madonna smartly realized that to make an authentic album of techno-pop she'd need to go to the source of such music. Originally, she intended to collaborate with Robert Miles, Trent Reznor, Nelle Hooper, Babyface and William Orbit. In the end, probably in an attempt to give the project a strong identity, only Orbit – a writer and producer renowned in the field of techno and electronica – was retained. (Madonna historian Bruce Baron notes that there may be early demos of the *Ray of Light* songs co-produced with one or more of the original line-up. None has turned up so far, he says.)

While William Orbit brought along his crew of collaborators,

Madonna again called on the durable Patrick Leonard. Leonard would serve to musically anchor Orbit's technology and, as he put it, 'keep the resulting album sounding like it was Madonna at its core. She didn't want to lose her identity,' he explains. 'She just wanted to expand her sound.' Together, this team would create what could arguably be called Madonna's most ambitious project since she'd tackled the musically elaborate *Evita*.

With *Ray of Light*, Madonna by no means invented anything new, she simply took the essence of the techno scene – its sound and personality – and then applied it to the commercial dance music sensibility she'd come to master so well. Like pop culture heroes and icons before her, able to reshape themselves to the public's whim at a moment's notice (like the Beatles did in the Sixties when they went from the goofy and melodic 'She Loves You' to the psychedelia madness of 'Lucy in the Sky with Diamonds' in the span of just a few years), Madonna simply did what she knew she had to do to stay current: she brilliantly 'morphed' into the current trend, and did it better than most of her contemporaries, many of whose attempts at keeping pace with the musical times often appear unimaginably contrived.

The album's first single, 'Frozen', is a simple yet majestic song about spiritual growth in a person who doesn't seem to want it, made irresistible by infectious vocal melodies and musical accents that can be best characterized as Moroccan. A big success, the track reached number 2 on the *Billboard* singles chart.

The album's title track and second single, 'Ray of Light', was the essence of what Madonna sought to achieve with the project. The track begins deceptively with a quiet, melodic guitar sound before giving way to a determined beat and whirlwinding synthesized sound. Lyrically, it's a celebration of power and sense of self. Her sense of abandon is catching, and the track carries away the listener. The song was an instant hit, debuting at number 5 in the *Billboard* charts – her highest entry to date. (Previously, in December 1995, 'You'll See' debuted at number 8 and, in March 1998, 'Frozen' equalled that entry position.) 'Ray of Light', which was Madonna's fortieth chart single and thirty-second Top 10 hit, captured the heady feeling of the era – the 'new' energy of the coming Millennium.

'The Power of Goodbye', a song about the strength that comes in letting go, has a catchy Europop feel to it. Indeed, lyrically throughout, *Ray of Light* offers a certain amount of reflection on the person Madonna feels she used to be, and who she's become. For instance, 'Nothing Really Matters' has her owning up to selfish ways of the past.

'I don't really want to dissect my creative process too much,' she has said when asked by reporter Janice Dunn to explain her songwriting. 'What's the point, really? I want people to have a visceral and emotional reaction to things, rather than to have in their mind where all my stuff came from. You know, if I see a bug crawling across the floor and it inspires me to write the most incredible love poem, I don't want people to be thinking about their relationship, and then think of my bug crawling across the floor.'

Without a trace of bondage or oral sex in a single lyric, this album's songs instead spoke of ecology, the universe, the earth, 'the stars in the sky', angels and heaven and, surprising some observers, contained respectful references to God and 'the Gospel'. In one song she talks of 'waiting for the time when earth shall be as one', while in another she does her best to make a pop dance tune out of a yoga chant. However, when the album was released, the music industry at large, though usually unflinchingly supportive of an artist as commercially successful as Madonna, didn't think it would be a success. The sound of the songs wasn't radio friendly, some observers argued. Other naysayers surmised that Madonna, at least by pop music standards, was too old to do this kind of album. They were all wrong. *Ray of Light* went on to become incredibly successful for her. It also presented an older pop icon to younger audiences as an artist to whom they could relate and musically embrace.

Now nearly forty years old, Madonna had also unveiled a new physical image that included the wearing of togas and saris, and veils over long, flowing dark tresses. Gone were her come-hither looks and her underwear worn as outerwear. Now, she was photographed with reflective expressions on her face, heavenly winds whipping through her hair. Her face was retouched to give it the bronzed, flawless complexion one would perhaps only expect to see on an angel. Still, Madonna strongly objected to the perception that she was constantly reinventing herself. 'I'd rather think that I'm slowly revealing myself, my true nature,' she said. 'It feels to me like I'm just getting closer to the core of who I really am.'

With the critical raves for and commercial success of *Ray of Light*, Madonna's image transformation proved to be another triumph. Oddly, in her fifteen years of fame, she'd only received one Grammy, and that was for best video back in 1991. (It's not unusual for acclaimed artists never to receive a Grammy award. Madonna was in good company with the Beatles and Diana Ross, among other notables.) However, the stars were once again in her favour, and with a new career and image Madonna would earn three Grammys at the Los Angeles ceremony at the Shrine Auditorium in February 1999 (during which she performed 'Nothing Really Matters' in a dazzling red kimono, oriental-style make-up and straight black hair) – one for Best Pop Album, one for Best Dance Recording and one for Best Short Form Music Video. (The next year, at the 2000 Grammys, Madonna added another award to her collection when she won for Best Song Written for a Motion Picture: 'Beautiful Stranger' from the film *Austin Powers: The Spy Who Shagged Me*.)

Despite the album's success, Madonna's plans for a tour were put on hold while she concentrated on her movie career. In 1998, she was close to signing a contract to star with Goldie Hawn in the high-budget film version of the Broadway musical *Chicago* (which was released in 2002 but not with Madonna in it) and had already signed to star in a romantic comedy, *The Next Best Thing*, starring Rupert Everett, fresh from his smash success in *My Best Friend's Wedding*, a commercially successful Julia Roberts vehicle. The new script – which Everett brought to Madonna's attention – took the secondary story of *My Best Friend's Wedding* – a straight woman/gay man friendship – and brought it to the forefront. In *The Next Best Thing*, the two friends enjoy one night of intoxicated intimacy and decide to go with the resulting pregnancy and raise the child together.

Once again, though, Madonna's film career would prove to be less than lustrous. When *The Next Best Thing* was finally released (on 3 March 2000) the movie would be attacked as viciously as anything she had ever done in the past. Under the headline 'Her Best Is Bad', the *New York Post* stated, 'There hasn't been a movie as smug or cheesy as *The Next Best Thing* in quite a while.' It would go on to criticize, 'For the first half of the movie, Madonna speaks with an unexplained English accent that draws attention to the singer's apparent inability to read a line.' *USA Today* would be more succinct in its analysis: 'Madonna still can't act.' (She would have a hit record, however, with the song 'American Pie', a version of the 1971 Don McLean pop classic which Madonna recorded for *The Next Best Thing*.)

'I think half of my movies have been good and half have been shit,' she has said of her film career. 'I've got two things working against me. One is that I'm really successful in another area and it's really hard for people to let you cross into anything else. Also, because I was in a series of really bad movies, it has given people a licence to say, "Oh, she can't act. She can't do this, she can't do that." But, honestly, I can think of Academy Award-winning actors and actresses that have done more shit movies than I have.'

Exit: Andy Bird

A major schism in Madonna's relationship with Andy Bird occurred in October 1998 when he made a few choice but innocuous comments about her to the press. '[We have] a fiery relationship, but it's worth working on,' Bird told the *Daily Mail*. 'I've got a responsibility towards Lourdes . . . and towards Madonna.' Madonna telephoned him when she read the comment and became quite emotional. She felt betrayed, she said. She must have been surprised, as well, because she thought him to be much more discreet when it came to talking about their life together.

'If I can't trust the people I sleep with, who can I trust?' she asked. Bird denied that he had even talked to the reporter and apologized profusely for the fact that the news had rattled her. However, once Madonna feels that a person has betrayed her trust, it is difficult for her ever again to fully trust that person. 'She can be an open person, until she feels that you've let her down and said something about her publicly that you shouldn't have said,' observed her now former manager, Freddy DeMann. 'Once that happens, forget it. She never really trusts you again. Especially if you talked to the press . . .' (In 1997, after fourteen years as her manager, DeMann became chief executive of Madonna's Maverick label. Then, in 1998, after much publicized and unfortunate legal wranglings, DeMann left Maverick; Madonna settled with him for £25 million.)

Contrite, Andy Bird hopped on a transatlantic flight to New York and – one might wonder why he would do this – told reporters at the airport that he wanted to patch up his relationship with Madonna. 'It's worth working on and I'm certainly not going all the way to New York to have a fight with her,' he said.

Despite the truce that they called, Madonna was ambivalent about Andy Bird. In many ways, the relationship must have reminded her of the ones she had had with musicians in her early New York days. She had cared about those men, too, but felt that their potential to achieve as much in their lives as she had in hers was limited. Though she often seems to end up in relationships in which she makes more money than her boyfriends, that's not a problem for her any more. 'It is perfectly socially acceptable for a man to find a beautiful girl who hasn't accomplished the things that he's accomplished, and make a life with her,' she told American

Vogue. 'Why does the man always have to be the one who makes more money? It's pathetic and sexist and disgusting, and if people don't change the way they view this thing – the man and woman's place in society – nothing's ever going to change.' For Madonna, the issue wasn't a financial one as much as it was that she felt Andy Bird was not motivated to do with his career what she felt he should do with it. She has such great initiative and drive, and she can't help but to be judgemental about those who she feels don't match her in that regard. Also, as she once told Tony Ward, she needed more from a relationship than a man like Andy Bird could provide her. Again, whatever it was that was going to make it permanent between Madonna and a man simply wasn't there with this one.

'I can't be what you want me to be,' Andy said to her at a party in Los Angeles in front of witnesses. As usual these days, she was dressed down, in a satin shift with a long hemline and a cardigan sweater and slip-on Fendi shoes. She looked so 'normal', it was difficult for some onlookers to believe she was really *the* Madonna.

'I'm not expecting you to be what I want you to be,' Madonna shot back. 'Just find some direction . . . please!'

'I am who I am,' he said, shifting from foot to foot. His response seemed weak, even to the most casual observer.

'Well, maybe that's not good enough for me,' Madonna countered. 'I've been around the block too many times for this kind of bullshit.' As she walked away, she added, 'I want another child, but I want to give birth to it. Not date it.'

It was true that, by this time, Madonna had decided that she wanted another baby. She enjoyed motherhood. 'I have memories of sitting on my mother's lap,' she remembers, 'or lying next to her in bed and having her arms around me. I know how much I cherish those memories. I do have moments with Lola [Lourdes] when I can almost feel transposed back to those times. I don't so much see my mother mothering me as I think, *I'm* going to be the mother *I* never had.'

There had been a short time after the birth of 'Lola' when

Madonna wondered if she had made the right decision about having a child. For years, she had lived a selfish, egocentric life – she knew it, even sang about it on her *Ray of Light* CD.

Giving birth to Lourdes had 'changed everything', she explained in one interview. 'It was a tough adjustment, and she really didn't know if she could do it,' said a friend of hers. 'She said, "My God, I'm a terrible mother. I'm selfish. This baby is crying, and all I can think about is that I have to finance this video." But when she relaxed into it, she realized that, "No, this is what I *want* to do, not what I have to do."'

Indeed, with the birth of Lourdes, Madonna experienced a rebirth of her own. She had always suspected that she would probably be a capable mother, but she was truly stunned by her capacity to love her daughter. As she would tell it, she was amazed by her devotion to Lourdes. It had impacted her, informed who she was as a person, as a woman. It gave her a sense of purpose much wider in scope than just show business, and also a sense of satisfaction she had never before experienced in her life. Whether she liked it or not, there were days when her superstar plans didn't matter; Lola's needs came first. Of course, there was also something esteem-building about her ability to be a good parent. After all, it made her proud of herself, made her feel good about herself. 'Like any woman – I'm no different – I had to come to terms with the fact that I am not the most important person in my world any longer.'

Now, Madonna wanted to give Lourdes a brother or sister. Again, she found herself in a familiar predicament. She wanted a baby. Should she wait to find a suitable partner? No. She was too impatient to do that. She asked Carlos Leon if he was interested in having another child. However, he said he wasn't so inclined, explaining that, emotionally, one child was all he could claim responsibility for at this time.

As usually happens in Madonna's life, as soon as she sets her mind on a goal, the press somehow seems to be in on the scheme. Stories that Madonna wanted another baby, though not looking for a husband, began materializing earlier in 1998 when the British press reported that she had wanted Bird to be the father.

'How do they always know exactly what I'm thinking and what I'm doing?' she asked one of her advisers of the British media. 'If I miss a period, the first thing I feel I should do is read the *News of the World* to find out if I'm pregnant.'

In fact, ironically, just days after she had officially ended it with Andy Bird, Madonna learned that she was pregnant. This was bad timing for her. Those who know her best say that as much as she wanted a child, she was now completely uncertain about the suitability of Andy as a father. After all, she had to plan on a long-term relationship with whoever it was who fathered her next baby. Whereas she was on good terms with Carlos Leon, her relationship with Andy Bird was strained and difficult. 'She wasn't sure she wanted him in the picture any longer,' says one of her closest friends. 'Still, when she found that she was pregnant, she knew she would have to figure out how to get along with the baby's father, Andy Bird. An abortion was out of the question,' reports that friend. 'Not at this time in her life, at this stage of the game when she was wanting to have babies, not get rid of them. Someone suggested an abortion, and she said, "Absolutely not. Those days are over. I would never have another abortion, not after giving birth. Forget it."'

It appeared as if she would have to find a way to patch things up with Andy Bird, and even somehow make him a permanent part of her life. This would not be easy for Madonna. Once she is finished with someone, she's completely finished with that person. It's difficult for her to allow back into her life a person who has fallen out of her good graces. It's rarely – if ever – happened.

While attempting to sort out complex emotions having to do with Andy Bird as a constant in her life, the difficult decision was made for her – by Mother Nature. Madonna miscarried in her seventh week.

It isn't known if she told Bird of the pregnancy, or not. Some of the couple's friends insist that she did – and that he was two days away from a trip to America to be at her side when she miscarried and told him to cancel his trip. Others say that her ever-reliable instincts told her to wait a while before informing Bird of her condition – and that she was glad she had done just that when the information was no longer relevant.

She was unhappy about the miscarriage, naturally. She was also somewhat relieved. She also knew that she wanted another baby – and that she wanted to at least like the father, if not be madly in love with him.

Enter: Guy Ritchie

Throughout her life, it has always seemed that elements of chance and circumstance have aligned themselves in such a way that Madonna usually gets exactly what she wants when she wants it. Or, maybe it's just that once she sets her mind to a goal, there's simply no stopping her until she achieves it.

At just about the time Madonna decided she wanted another child, she became serious about English film maker Guy Ritchie, ten years her junior and the director of the popular British film *Lock, Stock and Two Smoking Barrels*. Madonna had first met Ritchie at a weekend gathering in summer 1998, hosted by Sting's wife Trudie Styler (a major investor in *Lock, Stock*, along with Peter Martin and Stephen Marks) at their fifty-two-acre country estate in Wiltshire. Ritchie later admitted that the prime reason he went to the party was to meet Madonna, 'so he must have had something on his mind,' Madonna observed, laughing. (Madonna would eventually agree to release the soundtrack to Ritchie's film on her Maverick Records, so maybe what he had in mind was just some old-fashioned show-business 'networking'.)

Madonna enjoyed a brief relationship with Guy at that time – found him to be 'cocky and charming'. However, she felt the same about Guy's producer, Matthew Vaughn, the wealthy son of *The Man from U.N.C.L.E.* star Robert Vaughn. 'And he fancied her rotten [in the worst way] for years,' Guy Ritchie has said.

While Madonna wondered about Matthew and Guy, she continued her relationship with Andy Bird. It wasn't long before word of Madonna's brief dalliance with Ritchie reached Bird, who was predictably upset. Madonna's brief affair with Guy had a certain irony to it, actually; Bird had earlier accused her of having an affair with another British film maker, a man in whom she really was not interested. He was so certain that Madonna would one day be unfaithful to him, his prophecy became a reality. At this time, Guy was in a long-term relationship with model and TV presenter Rebecca Green, the daughter of a British tycoon, Carlton TV chief Michael Green. Rebecca had helped Guy produce his first film, a short called *Hard Case*. She had also persuaded her mother and stepfather, wealthy banker Gilbert de Botton, to invest in *Lock, Stock and Two Smoking Barrels*; therefore Guy was, as one of his friends put it, 'in deep with her'.

Like Madonna, Guy Ritchie has been accused of rewriting his life story, perhaps for dramatic purposes. So, as with Madonna, one should always take what Ritchie says about his past with the proverbial pinch of salt. He is savvy enough to know that coming from the streets projects a more interesting, and even sexier, image than being raised upper class. 'I've lived in the East End for thirty years,' he was quoted as saying in 1999. 'I've been in a load of mess-ups . . . I've been poor all of my life . . .'

Guy Ritchie is, in fact, the son of upper middle-class parents. His father, John, followed his own father from army officer training academy Sandhurst into the Seaforth Highlanders, after which he became an advertising executive, responsible for the Hamlet cigar advertisements. (Guy's grandfather, Major Stewart Ritchie, was a military hero, killed in action in 1940 after the 2nd Seaforth Highlanders were ordered to remain on French soil while most British forces were evacuated at Dunkirk.)

Ritchie's mother, Amber, is a former model.

Born in 1968 in Hatfield, Hertfordshire, Guy Ritchie lived with his parents and sister, Tabitha, in Fulham, west London. When he was five, his parents divorced and, shortly thereafter, Amber married Sir Michael Leighton, the eleventh holder of a 300-year-old baronetcy who once boasted of having had '104 affairs'. Guy then went on to live a privileged life in the English countryside. He grew up at the seventeenth-century Loton Park near Shrewsbury, a manor house belonging to his stepfather.

'Guy loved it there and got on well with Sir Michael,' says John Ritchie. 'He could roam around the estate and was really keen on shooting and trout fishing. He actually wanted to be a gamekeeper or go into the army to keep up the family tradition.'

His mother Amber, Lady Leighton, divorced Sir Michael Leighton in 1980. Guy had lost touch with his stepfather Sir Michael Leighton, who later remarried. Throughout his childhood, Guy battled dyslexia and, after attending ten different schools, gave up on his education at the age of fifteen. It was then, he claims, that he had been expelled from the £4,725 a term Standbridge Earls School near Andover in Hampshire, whose teachers specialize in teaching dyslexics, for 'doing a line of sulphate'.

'Education was lost on me,' he told the *Sunday Times*. 'I may as well have been sent out in a field to milk cows for ten years. I had no interest whatsoever in what I was supposedly being taught.'

Guy's father, John, has different memories of Guy's school days. 'The headmaster rang saying he [Guy] had been a naughty boy and that if I brought him back next term he would have to expel him,' he recalls. 'But it wasn't drugs – he had been caught in a girl's room and wasn't going to his lessons.'

What followed in his life, Guy Ritchie says, was a wild period of 'hanging out with villains' and doing drugs. 'I took everything and anything, and most of the drug dealers I met along the way were in public school.'

'Guy has a certain wit, a certain humour that people don't always get,' says his father. 'He says things sometimes in joking, I think. Then the newspapers print it, and it sounds like he's pretending to be a scallywag. He hasn't really been one, though. Not that I know of, anyway.'

When he was about eighteen, Ritchie took off to Africa, and then to Greece where he dug sewers for a time before returning to England. Some press reports have indicated that Guy worked as a bricklayer when he returned to England, but his father recalls his son as having worked as a 'messenger' for Island Records, after which he worked as a barman, and then as a furniture mover – a job that ended abruptly when Guy strapped an antique table to the roof of his van and inadvertently drove through a low tunnel.

He then became a messenger for his father's advertising agency and soon after, with practically no training in the field – but by using his father's contacts – began making music videos for 'Eurotrash techno-rave bands'. He soon applied his budding directorial talents – and entrepreneurial business sense – to making short films. Eventually, at the age of twenty-nine, he found critical and commercial success as the writer/director of *Lock, Stock and Two Smoking Barrels*. With Matthew Vaughn as its producer, the movie owed much to Quentin Tarantino, particularly *Reservoir Dogs* and *Pulp Fiction*. Thanks to an audience for his films that was largely young and male, the film went on to generate £18 million in Britain alone, though it cost only £1 million to make. Moreover, after having been publicly embraced by Tom Cruise, *Lock, Stock and Two Smoking Barrels* also had a respectable – though not overwhelming – release in the United States.

It is both ironic and paradoxical that Guy Ritchie would find himself in a romantic relationship with Madonna – an entertainer widely considered to be a gay icon – since *Lock, Stock and Two Smoking Barrels* as well as Ritchie's next film, *Snatch*, both have obvious homoerotic undercurrents, as well as disturbing homophobic leanings.

For instance, in *Lock, Stock and Two Smoking Barrels*, one of Ritchie's characters explains what he believes could be the perfect scam: place an advertisement for 'Arse Ticklers Faggot Fan Club anal-intruding dildos' in gay magazines, and wait for the cheques to roll in. Then, send out letters saying that you're out of stock and enclose a cheque stamped 'Arse Ticklers Faggot Fan Club' – 'Not a single soul will cash it!'

'Do you have big brave balls,' asks footballer-turned-actor Vinnie Jones in a confrontational moment in *Snatch*, 'or mincey faggot balls?' (*Snatch* is a black comedy, gangland story, largely set in London's Hatton Garden, about diamond heists and bare-knuckle boxing. It stars Brad Pitt, who cut his normal fee by 90 per cent to take the role of the gypsy boxer and who, incidentally, is almost entirely incoherent throughout.)

Mark Simpson of the *Independent* dubbed both of Ritchie's films 'gay porn for straight males'. In an article headed 'Just What Sort of a Guy's Guy is Guy Ritchie', he wrote of *Snatch*, 'Could it be that Guy Ritchie – who lives with the woman famously described as a gay man trapped in a woman's body – is a gay man trapped in a straight man's body?'

Perhaps analysis such as Simpson's is why Guy Ritchie seemed prickly about his public image. When a reporter from male-oriented *FHM* magazine asked him about his taste in clothes, he became defensive, using words such as 'fruity', 'queeny', 'fucking fruit-tree' and 'mincey'. He also said, oddly enough, that he would be happiest 'in a gladiator outfit'. Later, in another interview, he said that he 'will not allow Madonna to dress me like a poof'.

Guy Ritchie is tall and athletic-looking, with tousled dirty-blonde hair and dark-brown eyes above sensitive, chiselled features. His charm is infectious; he draws people like a magnet.

When Guy was in Los Angeles in January 2001 for the United States opening of his film, *Snatch*, I had a chance meeting with him and was surprised by how young he seemed and acted. Though thirty-two, his demeanour was that of a friendly, outgoing college youth. There was nothing pretentious about him, as if he could be anyone's pal – all of which made his relationship with Madonna more intriguing – even confounding.

No matter how one looks at it, upon meeting her, Madonna seems anything but 'normal'. It would stretch the imagination to think that she could quickly become anyone's 'pal'. Even when she wasn't a star, she wasn't the kind of girl one would feel was accessible, easy to know. Now, because she's been a celebrity for so many years, she carries herself with definite regality and a sense of glamour that springs not so much from her looks as from her character and personality. Her presence tends to create a distance between her and any admirer. One wonders, then, how she ended up with the much more grounded and affable Guy Ritchie – and how he ended up with her.

'How many times have you interviewed Madonna?' Guy asked me.

'Hard to say,' I told him. 'A few times, going all the way back to the beginning.'

'So how would you describe her?' he asked me.

'You tell me,' I said.

'Well, I think she's probably tough,' he offered. 'I think she doesn't suffer fools, does she? And I think she's probably very lonely because, well, it's lonely at the top, isn't it?'

I had to agree.

'But I like her power,' he continued. 'She's a force, all right. That's not me, though. I'm quieter. I know who I am and don't have to shout it from the mountain tops. But,' he concluded, 'I get her. She's a woman in a tough business. It can't have been easy.'

Again, I had to agree.

While it seemed futile to analyse matters of the heart (especially when the romance was still in full bloom and could change in many ways), I felt these two probably balanced each other's personalities.

Maybe in this extraordinary mingling of contrasts, Guy added a sense of normalcy to her life and she a sense of excitement to his.

'He is friendly to me, and I remember thinking that he looked boyish and seemed like a nice guy,' Christopher Ciccone once wrote of his feelings upon first meeting Guy. 'He is conventionally dressed in a white shirt and dark-blue trousers and jacket, and I warm to him. He is personable and respectful and seems as if he might be fun to hang out with. Nonetheless, I tell myself that I doubt he'll outlast Madonna's usual two-year relationship cycle.'

From the beginning, Madonna enjoyed being with Guy Ritchie, she said, because he treated her 'like a normal person, not an icon'. When he spoke to her, he had the priceless gift of making her feel that she was the most important person in the world to him. Also, she'd never met anyone so full of compliments; he raised flattery to an art form. 'And he's not intimidated by fame,' Madonna said at the time, 'he calls me "Madge" and even makes me wash his car with him,' she said. Guy seemed to have it all: he was handsome, sexy, gainfully employed, sensible and with a sure, clear-eyed maturity about him. More importantly, he loved Madonna and she returned his affection.

In any relationship, though, there are personality traits to which both partners must adapt. One issue the two faced early in their romance was that Guy sometimes corrected Madonna in public. Rather than cause a scene, she would bite her lip. Later, she would let him have it. 'Don't ever contradict me in front of people,' she told him, according to two good friends. The four were sitting in a darkened pub, each drinking a pint of Guinness under a haze of cigarette smoke. Madonna was wearing what appeared to be a Versace turtleneck, a Gucci leather jacket and second-hand Levis. ('Never in a million years could I have imagined myself sitting in a pub, drinking,' she later said, amused at how relaxed her standards for healthy living had become.)

'But when you're wrong, you're wrong,' he said, maintaining an almost clinical composure.

'Absolutely *not*,' she insisted, dramatically. 'When I'm wrong, I'm *still* right – in public.' She took her hand mirror out of her bag and – with a rapid flourish – applied a fresh slash of what appeared to be black raspberry lipgloss. 'If ever you have a problem with something I said,' she concluded, looking at her reflection, not at him, 'do take it up with me privately, won't you?'

It was as if she had to indoctrinate Guy to the way she had been living for almost two decades. If someone asked her to do something she didn't want to do – 'which happens about thirty times an hour', she has said – she usually just fibbed and said she had other plans, rather than put the person off or make excuses. Once at a party when Madonna was being pestered by a photographer, she lied and said she couldn't allow him to take her picture that evening because she had dinner plans. Guy cut in and said, 'No, Madonna, that's tomorrow night. You're free tonight.' She shot him a glare, the intensity of which didn't escape anyone present to witness it. It's not likely that Guy Ritchie ever made that mistake again.

Possibly because of her increasingly serious romantic involvement with Guy Ritchie, and her professional involvement with Rupert Everett, one startling change in the Madonna mystique by the end of the Nineties was her habit of speaking in what seemed like an upper crust English accent that also somehow embraced Italian and was similar to the affectation Elizabeth Taylor picked up after she became involved with Richard Burton. 'True, that,' she was known to observe often. Madonna actually loved the British and was determined to make London her home base. 'I hate to use the phrase, but it's true that you can start all over again in England,' she said. 'What I really think is that even the most stupid Englishman is about ten times smarter than the most stupid American.' Soon, she traded in her $15,000 a month rented home in Notting Hill to purchase a 200-year-old, four-storey house in South Kensington for $5 million.

Madonna had grown up, and as a result she was becoming a different person than she was when she was younger and more frivolous. For instance, she was no longer a shopaholic. She used to spend thousands on clothing a week. 'I'm too puritanical for that now,' she said. 'I'm too reserved to spend my money that way. I'm careful, so careful that I actually forget I have a lot of money.'

Madonna was so careful, in fact, that people who worked for her said that she was thrifty beyond all reason. She kept flowers in her home long after they had wilted, just so that she wouldn't have to spend money on fresh ones. She insisted that her housekeeper shop using coupons, so that she could save a few dollars on groceries. She ran throughout her home turning off lights so that her electricity bill would be low. She wouldn't allow friends to make long-distance calls on her telephone. She rarely picked up the tab when dining with friends. She rarely had cash on her, and was always complaining about being 'cash poor', as she called it – even though she was one of the richest women in show business. Her spokeswoman, Liz Rosenberg, admitted that when she was performing on the road, she did her own laundry because she thought hotels charged too much. She went over hotel bills herself to make certain that she hadn't been overcharged, and if she found that she had been she then had her accountant take up the matter with hotel management.

One extravagance: shoes. She had hundreds of pairs, many of which she felt were too fragile and exquisite ever to wear in public for fear that they might be damaged in the mad crush that always seemed to surround her. She kept many of her favourites wrapped in tissue paper, stored in boxes. Now and then, she snuck away by herself, took the shoes out, admired them, stroked them, put them on . . . then took them off and put them back in storage, again.

To writer Janice Dunn in an interview (in the summer of 2000), Madonna said, 'When I go to the Versaces' homes and see the way wealthy people live, I think, "I know I can live that way," but it wouldn't come natural to me. I do appreciate that people can sort of go full-bore and get into it and live a super, glamorous, decadent life. And have gold faucets and statues everywhere. I do appreciate beautiful things, and I have nice things in my house – nice art and

I like Frette linens and all that stuff. But I just don't – I don't have to show it off. I like to show off when I'm onstage. I don't like to show off, like, "Come in and check it out. Look how rich I am." That's not my style.'

Moreover, though Madonna was worth many millions of dollars, she still feared that her fate could revert back to that of the young girl who used to eat out of trash cans in New York, back in those struggling days. 'You never get over eating from a trash can,' she says, 'no matter how much money you make. I wish people could understand me. But I guess that unless you've had my experiences, you really can't relate to them, or to me. I think I am the most misunderstood person on the planet,' she says.

'People think that my goal is to just have hit records and make movies,' she concluded. 'I don't sit here wondering if I'll still be making videos when I'm fifty. I hope that I'll have three children and that they'll be the centre of my life . . . not being on MTV.'

Guy Ritchie seemed to be the perfect mate. He loved her, he understood her need for children, and he even encouraged her to take time away from her career, to, as he put it, 'really start thinking more about what will make you truly happy in life'. Or, as Madonna had concluded of Guy, 'This one is a keeper.'

Bird vs Ritchie

It was on 19 March 1999 that Madonna's past crossed her future when Andy Bird and Guy Ritchie met for the first time in London's trendy Met Bar, which is attached to the Metropolitan Hotel in Park Lane. What happened said as much about Guy as it did Andy. The two, who just happened upon one another, began talking about Madonna – who was in Los Angeles at the time at pre-Oscar festivities, on the arm of Sugar Ray rocker, Mark McGrath.

'We were comparing notes about her when he suddenly hit me,' Andy Bird now says. 'It came out of nowhere.' Bird – two years younger than Ritchie – said the punch sent him reeling over two tables. 'I just couldn't believe it,' he observed.

Ed Baines, a London chef and a friend of Guy Ritchie's, says, 'Guy sat there listening for half an hour and got more and more wound up. He's very honourable. This guy [Bird] was going on and on. Guy got up to leave and this guy grabbed him by the arm and said, "You're not going anywhere." Guy then felt a punch on the nose wouldn't do any harm.'

The break-up with Madonna had been difficult for Andy Bird as he went about the business of unravelling their intertwined lives – shared friendships, families, living quarters, possessions. Madonna had been the one to come to the conclusion of the necessity of their break-up, not Andy. It was a huge heartache for him, says a friend of his, 'an actual physical pain because he really did have strong feelings for her'.

In late 1999, Andy Bird became romantically involved with British television presenter and interior designer Anna Ryder Richardson. Unfortunately, the relationship ended after three months. 'I think I'm a pretty confident person, but there's only so much you can take. I got pretty sick of the word Madonna by the end of our time together,' she has said. 'It was a pressure I didn't need. Ultimately, she did ruin our relationship – if only because he couldn't let go of her.'

Because he had lost something he wanted very badly, it was difficult for Andy Bird not to be bitter. Also, there was a public element involved in his break-up with Madonna, an element of humiliation since it was clear to most observers that she had been the one to make the decision, not him. Still, it probably wasn't wise for Bird to express any animosity about what had occurred to Madonna's current consort, Guy Ritchie.

Guy is a strapping man who doesn't say much in public but who, among his friends and business associates, is as much known for his tough-guy swagger as he is for *Lock, Stock and Two Smoking Barrels*. While he seemed somewhat timid when on Madonna's arm, Guy's hobbies included karate, judo and jiu jitsu and, as he put it, 'kicking a little arse'. He referred to himself as 'a smart, smug bastard'. Whereas Carlos Leon was gentle and unassuming, Guy Ritchie was a bit of a brawler, much like Sean Penn – a personality Madonna finds irresistible. Like many Englishmen, he appeared to be reserved when in public, but privately he is expressive, wild and a great deal of fun – until crossed. He has a small scar, which he wears like a badge, on his face. 'All I can say is that it came as quite a surprise to me when my opponent produced a Stanley knife,' he has said in explaining the scar. A pretty good line . . . whether or not it is true.

Though it is likely to have painted him in a chivalrous light, Guy Ritchie was discreet enough not to provide his side of the story. Unlike Bird – who discussed the fight with the media – Ritchie kept his mouth shut, which, no doubt, earned him Madonna's appreciation. About a year later, Guy commented to Steve Hobbs of GQ, 'There's something honest about violence. Some things are just better settled there and then. Of course,' he concluded, 'it helps if you are a big bastard.'

Madonna's Moment

She was becoming a better person – not only as a mother, but also as a girlfriend. By the end of 1999, Madonna's success as a mother to Lourdes had begun to influence the way she related to the man in her life, Guy Ritchie. She was more patient or, at the very least, she tried to be understanding. Of course, it was difficult for her not to be self-involved on occasion. After all, she was still a wealthy person who'd spent the better part of the last fifteen years as a pampered star. However, she was now at least attempting to be more well-rounded and giving, not only because of Lourdes, but also because she had learned a few good lessons as a result of previous failed romances. 'I finally figured out that if you want to have the right kind of man in your life, you have to be the right kind of woman,' she told *Cosmopolitan*. Madonna's relationship with Guy Ritchie was working in ways that simply hadn't really been possible with men like Sean, Warren, John, or even Carlos and Andy.

To the outside world, Guy and Madonna were an extraordinarily attractive couple – tanned and healthy, lithe and smiling, with the unassuming aura of two who have the best life has to offer. Though, try as they might to understand each other, their petty arguments and disagreements did still mirror those of any normal couple . . . albeit in abnormal situations. For instance, at the end of December 1999, Guy found himself in the middle of a typical Madonna-related drama when the couple spent New Year's Eve at Donatella Versace's Miami Beach mansion.

Madonna asked for – and received – a police escort to the Versace bash, so she wouldn't have to fight traffic getting through the millennium masses crowding the twelve-bedroom, thirteen-bathroom Ocean Drive palazzo outside of which Gianni Versace was slain in July 1997.

'Seemed a little extreme to me,' Guy later observed in front of partygoers. He looked dashing, as always, in the kind of 'couture' pinstriped suit that certain English gentlemen favour.

'Well, I absolutely detest traffic,' Madonna explained in a petulant tone. She then took off her wrap and, wordlessly, handed it to Guy. Underneath, she wore a pinch-waisted blouse and 1940s-inspired tailored skirt.

'But you weren't even driving,' Guy noted as he took the garment. 'We were in a limousine.'

'And your point is?' Madonna asked, giving him a look.

'My point is . . .' Guy began to explain. Stubbornly, he did not seem to want to abandon the subject.

'Oh, my God. Guy! Please,' Madonna exclaimed, with a smile. She then grabbed the hand of her friend Gwyneth Paltrow, and began walking with her into a crowd of people. (Gwyneth and her boyfriend, Guy Oseary – a chief executive at Madonna's Maverick label – were staying with Madonna in the guest house of her home on Coconut Grove, Miami Beach.) 'He has a lot to learn about dating a woman of means,' Madonna said of Guy, a conspiratorial grin taking the edge off her criticism. Smiling, the winsome Gwyneth, in skinny suede pants and a belted leather jacket, wagged an index finger at her friend as if to say, 'Now, now. Don't be incorrigible.'

'A double Scotch,' Guy instructed a hovering waiter. He shook his head, good-naturedly: 'No rocks.'

At the dinner for seventy-five in the mansion's courtyard, Madonna and Guy Ritchie were accompanied by Gwyneth and Guy, Ingrid Casares, Rupert Everett, Madonna's brother, Christopher, and Orlando Pita, her hairdresser. Giant plastic tarpaulins had been tied to palm trees on either side of the mansion to block the view of any fans or photographers as semi-clad men served hors d'oeuvres and champagne.

'It was a true night of decadence and debauchery,' Madonna later recalled. 'It was the best New Year's I've ever had. There were shirtless men with oiled bodies dancing on podiums and there was a mambo band playing and this really yummy food. People were pogo-ing, people were jumping up and down on the furniture. I don't know how many drinks I had. All I know is they kept sloshing out of the glass and pretty soon you have twenty half-drinks . . . I was with the perfect group of friends.'

It had been an unhappy New Year's celebration for Gwyneth, though, who couldn't stop complaining to Madonna about how much she missed her ex-boyfriend Ben Affleck. Much to Madonna's annoyance, Gwyneth spent a lot of time on her cell phone talking to Ben, who was in Boston. Madonna was overheard telling her, 'You are absolutely smothering him. Will you *please* get off the phone and just enjoy the evening.' As the willowy Gwyneth sat on the floor hugging her knees, Madonna studied her in a sad way. 'Let's go dancing,' she said, finally.

The party then moved on to Bar Room, one of the nightclubs owned by the entrepreneurial Ingrid. Within fifteen minutes, Madonna found herself surrounded by a crowd of excited people, each of whom was vying for just a single, precious second of her attention. Moving slowly and deliberately through the adoring throng, she smiled and greeted people as if the party were in her honour. Soon, she was enveloped by a group of revellers.

Meanwhile, Guy sat at the bar, alone. It never ceased to astonish him, the way he became practically invisible whenever he was with Madonna in public. 'Guy, get over here,' Madonna shouted out at him from the crowd. 'I want you to meet someone.' The weary-looking Guy turned to a man he didn't realize was a reporter for a Miami newspaper. He raised his glass to him before taking a sip. Then, he rose. 'Hopefully, next New Year's Eve,' he concluded, his voice drained and flat, 'I will be home, in bed.'

By four a.m., the New Year's party was in full, chaotic swing. As the hypnotizing strains of pumping techno music filled the room, Madonna jumped up on a table and began dancing wildly to the rhythm. 'C'mon up here,' she beckoned to Gwyneth Paltrow with a teasing smile.

After a moment's hesitation, Gwyneth leapt onto the table to join her friend. Once up there, to the delight of at least 200 partygoers, Madonna and Gwyneth locked eyes and began dancing, both seemingly in a seductive trance, their movements unabashedly voluptuous. With their hands arched over their heads, they teased and beckoned each other as they performed what looked like an impromptu version of a Greek ritualistic dance called the *tsamikos* (where each dancer clutches the corner of a white handkerchief held aloft – only there was no handkerchief between the two friends).

Though the music was already loud, it somehow seemed to grow louder.

As Madonna danced unrestrained, one can only guess at the

kinds of images that may have crossed her mind. It was the end of the millennium. Ever since Lourdes's birth, she had been feeling contemplative. While blinded by streams of colour from dazzling lights, perhaps faces from the past flashed before her – snapshots of Christopher Flynn and Camille Barbone and Dan Gilroy and Erica Bell and Jellybean Benitez and Sean Penn and Warren Beatty and John Kennedy and Carlos Leon and Andy Bird and all the rest – names and faces of friends and foes from years gone by, all charging forward in a nostalgic rush of reflectiveness, evoking feelings easily related to at that time of the year – only perhaps even more sentimental given that it was a unique period, the end of one millennium, the beginning of another.

While Gwyneth moved about the table, Madonna circled her, a predator scrutinizing her mouth-watering prey. Just as she had always sized up her career, each challenge viewed as an adversary forced to submit to her will, Madonna looked at Gwyneth with hungry eyes. Then, as if she could no longer disguise her appetite for warm young flesh, Madonna pounced. She grabbed Gwyneth and pushed her backwards so that her spine was arched. Forced to surrender to her friend's will, Gwyneth gave way. Then, as the crowd roared its approval with applause and whistles and Guy Ritchie just watched from the sidelines with a bemused – or maybe confused – expression, Madonna did what she has always done best: she defied expectations. She kissed Gwyneth full on the mouth, letting herself go, giving herself to Gwyneth Paltrow, giving herself to the moment, breathing life into it and then living it for all it was worth.

Music

By the year 2000, Madonna had been a certified, card-carrying icon for almost two decades. In the universe of pop stardom, she'd truly done it all. Equally as challenging as attaining pop stardom is maintaining it, a fact to which any million-selling artist will attest. By the late Nineties, and into 2000, the music industry at large, and in fact the entire contemporary pop music world, had been taken over by a trend for 'boy bands' and sexy, teenage female bubble-gum artists, the craze's front line of offence being at that point the million-selling Backstreet Boys, N'Sync, Britney Spears and Christina Aguilera. Still, it wasn't as if Madonna's was in the doldrums at the beginning of the new year. *Ray of Light* had sold millions of copies worldwide, the project having been hailed as bold and refreshing. However, some of Madonna's critics viewed *Light* as another calculated ruse on the part of the artist to exploit rave-inspired electronica music, which was mostly off mainstream pop's radar until Madonna got hold of it.

Madonna's detractors didn't understand that *Ray of Light* was actually where Madonna's personal tastes were at the time – she wasn't just exploiting a new sound; it was a sound she had studied and enjoyed. Being a mature pop star with a wide range of professional experiences had not diminished her appetite for adventurous new music.

One day while listening to the various demo tapes and other music that poured into the Maverick Records offices on a daily basis from both aspiring and established songwriters and producers, Madonna happened upon the tape of an album from writer/producer Mirwais Ahmadzai, who had earlier praised her musical abilities. Except for lovers of rave music, Mirwais (he rarely uses his last name) was practically a stranger to America's pop music fans. 'I heard it and was just like, "This is the sound of the future. I must meet this person," Madonna would tell *Rolling Stone*. 'So I did, and we hit it off. And that's exactly how it happened with [*Ray of Light* producer] William Orbit, too.'

In a meeting hastily assembled by Guy Oseary, Madonna and Mirwais had such a rapport that Madonna decided that the 'sound of the future' would also be the sound of her next album. Three weeks after shaking hands, she and the producer were in the studio together; most of the music was recorded in London, beginning in September 1999. By the end of January 2000, the record was almost finished.

Madonna has always considered competition between her producers to be the way to get the best out of them, but William Orbit said he didn't have a problem with Mirwais being on the scene. In any case, neither producer would hear the result of the other's toil until the album's arduous mastering process in London.

Since William Orbit was already well aware of Madonna's idiosyncrasies in the studio, it was Mirwais who had to familiarize himself with the artist's creative working style. As much technician as musician, the Frenchman would endlessly tinker with the music tracks, adding effects and taking away others, layering some sounds and remixing others. Like many artists with a clear vision of what they want in the studio, Madonna has a tendency to be impatient, and Mirwais's tedious manner would often drive her to distraction. She recalled, 'I just put my foot down and said, "It's good enough now. We're done. We're done working on it." He [Mirwais] could just sit there in front of his computer screen, changing, honing, editing, cutting, pasting – whatever. And it would never end. But life is too short for that sort of nonsense. My persona in the studio is, "I'm in a hurry." I think he was more put off by the fact that I knew what I wanted so clearly, and I wasn't interested in lots of embellishments when it came to the production.'

'She took a big risk with someone like me,' Mirwais told a reporter after the album was completed. 'When you arrive at that kind of level of celebrity, you can just work in the mainstream and just stay there. Everything she does, for her is like a challenge, and I like this kind of personality.'

When the work was done – accomplished between London, Los Angeles and New York – what would emerge was *Music*, a slick, orderless landscape of pop melodies and swirling electronic pop funk. *Music*, for all its masterful gadgetry, would be nothing if not passionate. The final selections for inclusion on the CD would include 'Impressive Instant', rife with abstract sounds and driving grooves designed to do just what the synthesized refrain suggests, put the listener in a trance, and 'Amazing', a stylized, guitar-powered, uptempo Orbit collaboration that could have been the musical cousin to 'Beautiful Stranger' (the song Madonna and Orbit had contributed to the *Austin Powers: The Spy Who Shagged Me* soundtrack). Also included would be 'I Deserve It', a moody, acoustic guitar ballad obviously dedicated to Guy Ritchie ('This Guy was made for me,' Madonna sings).

Of course, the project's flagship track would also be its first single and title song, 'Music'. The song is a shot of electronic funk-pop, a dance anthem that reaches into the future but which also slyly conjures images and feelings for the good ol' days of disco (with its affectionate call out to 'Mr DJ', a relic of disco days gone by). It's a sparse, determined arrangement that quickly gets under one's skin.

Like the song's lyrics, the accompanying playful video would have a very simple storyline that ventures no deeper than three girls out on the town, looking for fun. The concept was inspired by real days gone by of the late Seventies and early Eighties, when young Madonna Ciccone and her friends, Debi Mazar and Niki Haris used to prowl Manhattan's eclectic club and art scene in search of music and romance. Originally, actresses were cast in the roles of Madonna's video entourage. However, when the women proved to be too pretty and stiff, a frustrated Madonna, in the middle of the shoot, got on the phone and asked Mazar and Haris to join her on the set.

Just as she plugged into the electronica scene for the music, for the video Madonna would shamelessly imitate the notion of 'Ghetto Fabulous' – an over-the-top look popularized by East Coast rap and urban music stars like Sean 'Puff Daddy' Combs, Lil' Kim and Mary J. Blige and characterized by designer clothes and floor-length furs, gaudily accessorized with gold and diamonds (including in the teeth). When Puff Daddy stepped out of his Bentley dressed in this fashion, he's serious. In the 'Music' clip, however, Madonna would wear her flash and gold with a playful wink. To give the video humour, cast as the zany limousine driver was British comedian Ali G (Sasha Baron Cohen), whose brash, irreverent ways amused Madonna whenever she was in England. (Ali G hosted a television talk show in character, insulting politicians and other upstanding members of British public service.)

At the end of January 2000, Madonna had great hopes for *Music*. 'I have to stay current,' she concluded over lunch with two of her friends in Los Angeles where some of the songs were being finished. She looked stupendous in a chocolate brown Balenciaga jacket and Donna Karan trousers. Though her hair was pulled back and she wore large sunglasses, she still drew stares. While being served a tomato and mozzarella salad, she said, 'God help me, but I guess I have to share radio air time with Britney Spears and Christina Aguilera.' She shrugged her shoulders. 'What choice do I have?'

'Well, you could always retire,' one of her friends offered jokingly.

Madonna dabbed at her lips with a napkin. 'But what would the music business be without me?' she asked with a laugh.

Rocco

In February 2000, Madonna finally confirmed what the tabloids had been declaring for months, that she was determined to have another baby. 'I think Lola should have a brother or sister,' she had said in an interview. 'I think she's incredibly spoiled. She needs a bit of competition. But I would want to be in a stable relationship.' Though Madonna stopped short of saying who she thought the father should be, she probably had Guy Ritchie in mind since, by all accounts, her love affair with the British film maker seemed to be the real thing.

A month later, when Matt Lauer of the American *Today* show

asked Madonna if she was pregnant, her answer was a definitive 'no'. But, then, less than three weeks later she and Guy Ritchie released a joint statement to the media: 'We're happy to confirm rumours that we're expecting a child at the end of this year.' Actually, Madonna knew she was pregnant when asked about it by Lauer, but didn't want to announce it to the world before she told the baby's father – and she didn't want to inform Guy until he had finished his work on *Snatch*.

Having a second child seemed like a natural progression in Madonna's life. She was proud of the way Lola was being raised – of course she employed a nanny (not a team of them, just one), but she prided herself on doing most of the work herself – and she was excited about the opportunity to double her efforts as a mother.

'The last thing I'm going to do is raise my children the way I see a lot of celebrities raising their children,' Madonna stated. 'I don't want to traipse around with nannies and tutors. I think it's really important for children to stay in one place and to socialize with other children. I had that [in her childhood]. I'm not saying I don't want to go on tour or make movies anymore, but I realize I'm going to have to make a lot of compromises, and I'm comfortable with that.'

For his part, Carlos Leon offered his congratulations to Madonna via an odd medium, the television tabloid show, *Inside Edition*. 'I want to wish her all the luck in the world,' he said to the mother of his own child. He stroked his goatee reflectively. 'I am thrilled for her,' he said. 'I hope she has a very healthy and happy baby who will be a wonderful brother or sister for Lourdes.'

Her second pregnancy was, for Madonna, about as boring – and as uncomfortable – as the first, particularly during the last couple of months. Guy noted to one friend his amazement that Madonna had become so shy in the bedroom around the seventh month, always turning out the lights before undressing. Perhaps, like many expectant women, she simply did not feel attractive

On 10 August, just a couple of days after Gwyneth Paltrow

hosted a baby shower for her, Madonna began to feel unwell. That morning, she and Gwyneth had a telephone conversation (Madonna later remembered) during which they laughed about the fact that Madonna had worn the same maternity clothes during the second pregnancy that she had worn for the first – 'and I don't care what anyone thinks about it,' she said. She spoke about being photographed in a burgundy Abe Hamilton-designed sheath with a black lace overlay for a recent charity event, and not giving a second thought to the fact that she had been photographed in the same outfit a couple of years earlier. 'I guess it's safe to say that fashion is no longer my greatest concern,' she said (not in the same conversation with Gwyneth, but rather to a reporter, later).

Upon hanging up on Gwyneth Paltrow, Madonna then gave a radio interview over the telephone to Los Angeles disc jockey Rick Dees. Having finished on the telephone, she paced restlessly before going to bed, complaining of feeling nauseous. That night, Guy Ritchie attended a private screening of his film *Snatch*. At nine p.m., Madonna called him on his mobile to tell him that she was having trouble and was going to Los Angeles' Cedars-Sinai Hospital. News reports had it that Ritchie rushed home to pick up his girlfriend and then rushed her to hospital, carrying her into the emergency ward crying out, 'Save our baby! Save our baby!' Actually, Madonna was already at the hospital when he got there, 'though he likes to think he carried me inside,' she has said. (She was driven to hospital by an employee.) Months earlier, Madonna had been diagnosed with placenta previa, a condition in which the placenta covers the birth canal, causing the mother to haemorrhage and the baby's blood supply to be cut off. A Caesarean was necessary, but not as the emergency procedure also reported in the press. She had made arrangements weeks earlier to have the baby by C-section, just not two weeks before her original due date.

Madonna was placed in a room just across the hall from where Catherine Zeta-Jones had, a few days earlier, given birth to actor Michael Douglas's baby. Specialists then began monitoring her as carefully as the baby, hoping that perhaps she would be able to carry to full term. Unfortunately, like Lourdes's, the new baby's birth would not be an easy one. As she was wheeled into the delivery room, a sedated and most certainly scared Madonna was overheard telling Guy Ritchie, 'Baby, I love you. We're all going to be okay.' By this time, Madonna had lost a great deal of blood; she was actually haemorrhaging faster than the transfusions could replace the blood and was close to slipping into shock. The baby was born at one a.m. on 11 August, about three hours after she entered hospital, weighing in at a substantial 5 pounds 9 ounces. (By comparison, Lourdes, who was carried to term, checked in at exactly a pound heavier.)

Guy sat by the frightened Madonna's side, holding her hand and comforting her throughout the difficult surgery. They called the boy Rocco, a name which, it could be argued, had the requisite Italian ring but certainly also reflected Ritchie's strong cinematic interest in names associated with organized crime. Considering that there was speculation in the press that the writer-director might want to name his son Vinnie or Anthony (Ant-ny as he might pronounce it), Rocco perhaps represented a compromise.

Immediately after his birth, stories began to circulate that the baby might be brain damaged. Luckily, most of these reports were not heard by Madonna, who was sheltered from all such inaccurate speculation by the protective Guy Ritchie. In fact, because of his premature arrival, Rocco suffered a slight case of jaundice, which is normal in such births. Because his lungs were also not fully developed, he was placed in intensive care.

By 15 August, despite statements from Liz Rosenberg to the contrary, little Rocco was still in the hospital and not scheduled to leave for another few days. Rosenberg had said the child was already home with Madonna, but she was fibbing, probably in order to protect mother and child from the media storm. Guy would visit Rocco in the mornings and early afternoons, while Madonna rested at home. Then, Madonna would quietly visit her son in the hospital each day, arriving at about five-thirty p.m. and staying for four hours of feeding and cuddling. At all times, the security around the child was intense, with at least four guards assigned to his suite of rooms, plus private nurses. When Madonna visited, she arrived with a couple more guards of her own.

When the baby was finally released from hospital on 16 August 2000, five days after his birth and Madonna's forty-second birthday, his contented and relieved mother took him to her Los Feliz home. (The estate was up for sale at this time for $4.2 million; Madonna had just bought Diane Keaton's 1920s hilltop Spanish-style estate in Beverly Hills for $6.5 million and was in the process of a $1 million renovation programme.) She went into her bedroom, sat down with a breast pump and her new infant – then she noticed a paper bag on the table. She looked inside and found a box. It held a diamond ring from Guy, who had been so wonderful to her throughout the pregnancy (he even gave up drinking during those months, just so that she wouldn't be tempted). In an accompanying note, Guy told her how much she meant to him, and how proud he was of her and their son. 'This is nothing compared to the big present I will soon be giving you,' he wrote. (Madonna would insist that this was her first diamond ring. Perhaps because she gave back Warren Beatty's, she doesn't count that one. When she married Sean, she had a simple gold ring.)

Later, the good friends Madonna usually entertained at her home came by to meet the new addition to the family. Little Rocco – who resembled his father more than he does his mother – was curled up in his bassinet, sucking his thumb and nodding off, a teddy bear quilt tucked around his legs. 'Why, he's just so perfect,' gushed Gwyneth Paltrow, one of five visitors clustered in the nursery.

For her guests, Madonna had combed her shoulder-length honey blonde hair back from her face. She wore embroidered and patterned blue slacks and a simple white tank top underneath a short-sleeved T-shirt. Manolo Blahnik slingbacks with 3-inch heels added a touch of cool, uncontrived elegance. ('Better than sex,' she says of Blahnik's shoes – she missed high heels while pregnant – 'and they last longer.') Cartier earrings were another nice, unusual touch. Her skin seemed translucent. There was one word to describe her: wholesome.

'He is perfect, isn't he?' she said, gazing down at her infant son with loving eyes. At that moment, Lourdes ran into the room with a baby bottle. 'Here, Mommy,' she said, holding it up to her mother. 'For him,' she added, motioning to her brother. Madonna swooped Lola into her arms and held her, tightly. 'No yet,' she said, her voice a low and soothing whisper. 'But soon.'

'It was a feeling of such tranquillity,' said another of Madonna's guests. 'Lola then started sucking furiously on the bottle. "You're a big girl now," M said as she gently took the bottle away. "Let's go downstairs and get some juice." Then, she, Gwyneth, Lola and the rest of us tiptoed out of the room. We went into the kitchen and drank beer and ate Doritos. Doritos! I remember when she would never eat junk food, ever.'

Later, when just a few guests remained, Madonna slipped out of her clothes and wrapped herself in a soft white robe. After joining her guests in the spacious, sun-drenched living room with the Diego Rivera oil painting over the fireplace, she sank into a couch, her infant curled in her lap. 'I thought, "My, my. Here's a Madonna the public doesn't know, a relaxed, freer Madonna,"' said her guest. 'A Madonna that maybe she, herself, didn't know until recently.' (Or, as her brother Christopher said while watching Madonna as she breastfed Lourdes, 'I don't believe it. I'm looking at it, I'm watching it. And, still, I don't believe it.')

'Have you managed a routine with him yet?' one of Madonna's friends asked.

'We feed him at about ten thirty, before we go to bed,' Madonna said, sounding more like a mother than anyone who ever knew her would have believed. 'Then, he gets one feed in between two and three. Then, maybe again between six and seven. He's a good baby,' Madonna said proudly. 'He only cries when he wants something, and why shouldn't he? Guy and I agree that he should get exactly what he wants. Lord knows I always have . . .'

Happy Endings

Perhaps no one is as proud of the way Madonna has turned out as her father, Tony Ciccone. While he didn't support her dream to be a dancer and had hoped she would go to college before beginning her career, he fully understood her wanting to, as he now puts it, 'make something of herself, which she did – boy, did she ever!'

When Rocco was born sickly and prematurely, it was Tony who, by telephone from his northern Michigan vineyard, suggested that his daughter summon a priest to administer the last rites. Though Madonna is ambivalent about such sacraments, it's a testament to the respect she feels for her traditional Italian–American father that she even considered the notion of last rights for little Rocco. As it happened, such a sacrament would not be necessary. When it was determined that the baby would be fine, Tony and his wife Joan tearfully collapsed into each other's arms – and then toasted with a fine wine the new addition to the family, Tony's eighth grandchild. 'Sometimes I think I'm better as a grandfather than I probably was as a father,' he said at the time. 'But, let's face it, Madonna was a special case,' he added. 'I think anyone would sympathize with the father who had the job of raising Madonna.'

The day after Rocco's birth, Tony Ciccone continued his hard labour on the structure of the Ciccone Vineyards and Winery, a vineyard which would open to the public a month later on a hilltop between the Grand Traverse Bay resort town of Sutton Bay and the hills of the Leelanau Peninsula. Tony founded his winery in 1994 after retiring from his job as a physicist and engineer at General

Dynamics in Detroit. It is dedicated to his parents, Gaetano and Michelina, who immigrated from Pacentro, Italy, to the United States three years before he was born. The Ciccone Vineyards has been a joint project for Tony and his wife, Joan, the stepmother with whom Madonna never got along as a youngster but to whom she eventually became closer.

'It's our life together,' he proudly said of the winery, one of twenty-five in the state of Michigan, 'mine and my wife's. We have Pinot Grigio, Dolcetto, Cabernet Franc and Chardonnay planted here. I think it keeps me and Joan close, even at this old age we're in,' he added. 'We raised vegetables in Rochester [Michigan] before owning the winery,' he adds. 'My father was a vegetable farmer, too. Good, solid work. The Ciccones have always been solid workers.'

Most of his neighbours were not even aware that Madonna is Tony's daughter. 'I don't advertise it,' he said. 'It's not necessary. If they find out, they find out. I don't tell them. Some know. But they don't make a big deal out of it.'

When she became a parent herself, Madonna began to understand that Tony was doing his genuine best at the time he was raising her, and that his marrying Joan was not a betrayal of his first wife but his only alternative if he was to move on with his life – and give his children a mother.

'I love my father,' she said. 'He is a say-what-you-mean-and-mean-what-you-say kind of guy. I'm the same way. Anyone who knows me knows that I *am* my father, at least in that way. He's strict, like me. Loving, too, I hope like me. His work ethic is ingrained in me. Now that I have a family, I have so much respect for him and the way he tried to hold ours together, back when I was a bratty little kid. He didn't have the privileges I have, either. It's hard to see all of that until you have children.'

'Nonnie has said things about me in the past, probably all true,' observes Tony, reverting to the affectionate diminutive of his daughter's childhood. 'So maybe I wasn't the greatest father in the world, but life wasn't easy for any of us.' He says that he has never felt a need to address anything Madonna has ever said about him, 'Because we're Italian-Americans. In our hearts, we know that we love each other. That is all that matters. Sometimes you can't be close. But life is long and there is always another day.'

He also talked about a time, back before she had her own children, when he'd read some extremely unflattering remarks about him made by his daughter in an interview. It was the same routine from her: how emotionally abusive he'd been, how he hadn't supported her in her dreams. However, after so many years of reading about it in magazine and newspapers and hearing about it on television, Tony had enough. He decided to call her. 'This sad song you keep singing,' he told her, 'it's getting old, Nonnie. Real old. How much longer you gonna sing this sad, "woe is me" song?'

She was, he would recall, immediately defensive. 'But it's all true! You did all of those things! I'm not making it up.'

'And everyone in the whole wide world knows it,' he told her, according to his memory. 'Why don't you start painting a new picture of your life, Nonnie? Stop living in the past. Jesus Christ. Look at your life. Who cares about what happened a hundred years ago?'

Her father's words seem to resonate with Madonna. 'I sound like a cry baby, don't I, Dad?' she asked. He said that, yes, she certainly did. Considering how lucky she was, how blessed she'd been in her career, his advice to her was to stop digging up the past and just be grateful for everything she'd achieved. It really made her stop and think, or at least Tony believed so. 'You're right,' she finally said. 'It's time to turn the page. I'm sorry, Pop,' she said. 'You know I'm just being who I have always been – a little shit.' He knew it, for sure.

'Madonna and I have been closer than people know,' Tony concluded. 'There's a peacefulness about her now. Why, look at how things have changed for her,' he marvelled. 'If you were writing a book, this is how it would end. It would have a happy ending. Everyone loves a happy ending . . .'

Taking Stock

Madonna's 'Music' single, to no one's surprise, made its way to number 1 in September 2000, after six weeks on *Billboard*'s Singles chart. At the end of September, Madonna celebrated the release of her new album, also called *Music*, with a party meticulously designed to connect the new, serene-Madonna of the new millennium with the original, party-Madonna of the 1980s. To do this, the star's camp took over Catch One, a funky, ramshackle club near Los Angeles' ethnic South Central community.

On a regular night, Catch One hosted an urban cross-section of drag queens, closet gays, trendy 'Ghetto Fabulous' and a small battalion of uptown whites, who came to behold Los Angeles' black, gay culture and dance all night to techno-funk music on the huge dance floor. On Tuesday, 19 September the club hosted perhaps its strangest crowd ever – six hundred people referred to by syndicated newspaper columnist Liz Smith as Madonna's 'closest friends'. Party co-hosts Warner Bros. and the American celebrity magazine *US Weekly* paid a reported two million dollars to transform the normally gritty Catch One into a temporary haven for the Beautiful People, an A-list crowd spiced with an assortment of strippers and exotic dancers, all in the tradition of the Madonna experience of days gone by – those days almost fifteen years earlier when the young star generated all the energy whenever she walked through the club's front doors, when she beckoned her allergy-prone, older boyfriend, Warren Beatty – her 'Pussy Man' – to join her on Catch's dance floor: 'Let's have fun!'

But these weren't the old days, and Madonna – who wore her honey-blonde hair straight and parted in the middle, and boasted a black T-shirt promoting Guy Ritchie's latest movie, *Snatch* – was no longer a gum-chewing, profanity-spewing party girl. While she did mingle with the famous guests, she spent most of her time off the dance floor with a small circle of friends and associates in a so-called VIP room. She left early, after only ninety minutes. It had been her first night away from Rocco since she brought him home from hospital a month earlier, and she wanted to get back home to breastfeed him. Her career was on autopilot, anyway: 'Music' would debut at number 1 – in fifteen countries, including the United Kingdom.

The morning after the party for 'Music' was like any other at Madonna's Mediterranean-style Los Feliz home. In order to keep tabs on the day-to-day operations of her companies, including Maverick Records, Madonna's residences were equipped with fax machines and multiple phone lines. Each morning, when she was not on the road, she made a list of goals to accomplish that day, and also listed tasks for her two assistants and other associates. From eight to nine a.m., she answered and sent emails. From nine to eleven, she made business calls to attorneys, agents and to her spokeswoman and dedicated and able publicist of eighteen years, Liz Rosenberg (whom Madonna's friends referred to as 'The Validator' – the one who separated truth from rumour, or at least did her job well by protecting Madonna from negative publicity).

'My job is more casual than people might think,' says Rosenberg. 'Madonna does not wake up in the morning and plan her media campaign, nor do I. We don't think, "Who are we going to fuck over today?" There's no master plan, no army of press agents and tanks.'

If he was not similarly busy with his own career, Guy would often be found in the kitchen helping the cook prepare breakfast. (He was an excellent chef, whereas Madonna said she didn't 'have the cooking gene. I don't want to go into the kitchen and do things. I want to go into the kitchen and be served.') She kept a maddeningly detailed daily planner. 'If she wants me to look into ten things, and I'm only able to look into nine, she remembers the one thing I forgot,' says Liz Rosenberg. 'She isn't big on wasting time.' The rest of the day was devoted to rehearsals, recording sessions and interviews. Intermittently, she somehow made quality time for her two children – each of whom had their own nanny. (She also had an army of assistants helping her at home and in her Maverick office.)

By winter 2000, the media continued to speculate as to whether or not Madonna would marry Guy Ritchie, especially when she was seen wearing the diamond ring he had given her after Rocco's birth. In fact, the two had secretly decided to marry by the end of the year.

As much as he seemed to love her, some of his friends felt there could be trouble if the proud Guy Ritchie was forced to tolerate the indignities that often go along with being in a relationship with Madonna, especially given his temperament. For instance, at the party at Catch One celebrating the release of *Music*, he became involved in a confrontation with a wide-bodied security guard who refused to grant him access to a VIP section of the club.

'But I'm Guy Ritchie,' protested the writer-director. Wearing a tank-top shirt with the word 'Music' emblazoned on it, Guy's impressive biceps were on display. His hair was cut short and dyed a light shade of blonde. He wore a small diamond earring. In the background, the music was loud, pumping . . . and annoying. Ever-moving lights in every colour of the rainbow bathed the scene. An irritating, thumping cacophony, which was actually 'Impressive Instant' from Madonna's *Music* CD, could be heard in the background.

'I don't care if you're *Lionel* Richie,' said the uniformed guard over the din. He wore a headset so that he could take orders. 'Your name isn't on the list,' he declared, chewing on an ice cube. 'Not on the list, you don't get in. That's the way it goes.'

'Step aside,' warned Guy. As he tried to force his way past the guard, a camera's flash went off. He stopped, turned his head, and scowled at the photographer.

Perhaps noticing that he was distracted, the guard put one hand on Guy's massive chest and pushed.

Guy whipped his neck around to face the guard, an incredulous expression on his face. He seemed amazed – and indignant – that the guard would dare touch him. 'What, are you kidding me?' he asked in disbelief, his voice angry, his brown eyes threatening. 'Are you mad?' It was as if he had taken a page out of the 'Sean Penn Handbook of Social Behaviour'.

For a few tense moments, the two studied each other with severe expressions – their eyes inches apart – like playground adversaries about to rumble. The veins in Guy's neck were standing out. Luckily, one of Madonna's functionaries arrived on the scene. 'I felt a spasm of alarm,' she later recalled, 'when I saw that Guy's jaw was clenched.' Taking quick stock of the situation, she grabbed Guy by the arm and escorted him to the reserved area where Madonna was with friends. As Guy walked toward his girlfriend, she was laughing, gaily oblivious to what had just occurred. He whispered something in her ear and, apparently in reaction, she looked in the direction of the offending security guard and gave a disapproving frown. Just then, someone else said something to her. She tossed her blonde hair, flashed a gleaming smile and began laughing again, relaxed, chatty. Guy, standing at her side with his hands in his pockets, looked dour.

'We're better when it's just the two of us, and not all of the fans, groupies and press,' Guy told a reporter after the confrontation at Catch One. Madonna, as usual, was surrounded by her coterie of enthusiasts as Guy spoke to the newsman. 'When it's just me and the missus,' he observed, motioning toward Madonna, 'that's when it's good. This? This isn't good.'

By Guy Ritchie's definition, it was 'good' a month prior to the *Music* party when he took 'the missus' to dinner at the Palm restaurant in Hollywood. The couple were there to celebrate Rocco's release from hospital, a day earlier. The best table had immediately been theirs, of course, as it was in every place they ever ate. As Madonna sat next to – not across from – Guy, she was constantly greeted by people who knew her, thought they knew her, or wanted to know her. She took the intrusions good-naturedly, apparently happy to be out in public. Long hair with blonde streaks framed a face that seemed worry-free, content. Her skin held the translucence of youth. Her breasts were partly exposed by the cut of a daring, crimson-coloured dress – she was still Madonna, after all.

An iced bowl of caviar, plates of smoked salmon and cold chicken, and a silver basket of fruit were displayed on the table.

Though talking to the waiter, who had enquired about the health of her child, she didn't seem to mind revealing herself in an emotional, honest manner. 'My life is perfect now,' Madonna said. 'If I never do another thing again, at least I'll know I've done this.'

'Hear, hear,' Guy said, smiling broadly. He raised a glass of champagne in Madonna's direction. Giving her an admiring stare over the rim, he added, 'Here's to a new life.'

The Wedding to Guy Ritchie

Publicity, or no publicity? For Madonna, if the choice had to be made, it had always been in favour of the former, and plenty of it – as long as it was on her terms. However, that was to change when it came time to plan her two-million-dollar wedding to Guy Ritchie.

As the consort of an internationally acclaimed superstar, Guy Ritchie endured press coverage that he wasn't particularly happy about, and treatment by reporters that, in his view, sometimes bordered on the disrespectful. For her part, Madonna never stops complaining about the media's intrusion in her life. It's been her mantra for years: 'I hate the press. I hate the press.' With the passing of time, not much has changed in that regard: as much as she loves the attention, that's how much she says she hates it.

It was Guy's decision, then – and not Madonna's – that there would be no attendant publicity to their upcoming marriage ceremony. All of it – the nuptials, the reception, the parties – would be planned and conducted with an eye towards complete privacy, absolute secrecy. Madonna didn't seem to care one way or the other about the matter. If she had to deal with the press on her special day, she would do it. Certainly her staff was equipped with the means to keep it all under control. However, Guy felt strongly that their wedding shouldn't be made into a public spectacle, and so that was the way it was going to be. It's fortunate that Madonna so appreciated a man who could take charge, for that is certainly what she got in Guy Ritchie.

Two friends of the couple report witnessing a conversation between Madonna and Guy at Kensington Place restaurant in west London two-and-a-half months before the wedding, an exchange that, perhaps, betrayed some pre-ceremonial jitters on Madonna's part.

'I just don't think there should be any press at all about any of it,' Guy told his fiancée. 'I want it to be quiet, and private, don't you agree?'

'Well, look, if that's how you feel then we should just run off to Las Vegas and elope,' Madonna declared, according to the witnesses. Even though she was indoors, she wore a knee-length, snake-skin coat (dyed red), because she felt chilled. 'I guarantee you, though, it will be a circus . . . a zoo,' she continued, 'so don't kid yourself.'

'Why do you say that?' Guy wondered.

'Because everything I do is a fucking circus,' Madonna answered, snapping at him. 'Or haven't you noticed? Christ! Haven't you seen the parade that passes by whenever I walk out of the fucking house?'

'Just let me handle it,' Guy said. He paid no attention to her tone, perhaps accustomed to it by this time. 'As long as we agree: no media and no tricks. And you know what I mean, Madonna,' he concluded, pointing a parental finger at her.

Madonna sighed heavily. 'Look, I couldn't care less,' she said, visibly irritated. Perhaps she was annoyed at the suggestion that she would purposely invite press attention to their wedding. Or, maybe she was just coming down with a cold; she didn't seem particularly well. She had complained earlier of having 'the worst headache, ever since we started talking about this wedding'. Finally, she said, 'I just don't want the stress of trying to control it all. So, go for it,' she concluded. 'Knock yourself out, Guy.'

In the end, though she didn't admit it at the time, Madonna was vastly relieved to know that Guy was handling matters concerning the media. To Madonna, controlling the press's interest in her every move had always been a chore. However, to the easy-going, sports-loving Guy Ritchie, it was nothing more than a matter of gamesmanship. The way he figured it, if a photographer managed to sneak into the wedding and shoot a roll of film, Guy would lose the game. It wouldn't be the end of the world, though, because, after all, it *was* only a game. 'However, I don't like to lose,' he cautioned one confidante. 'So, I can tell you right now, there'll be no press coverage of the wedding. We'll have to find a place that's so out of the way, no one will have access to it.'

It was Guy's friend, Vinnie Jones, who suggested the 'out of the way' Skibo Castle in north Scotland for the ceremony. It's been said that Andrew Carnegie once described his Highland castle – now home of the private Carnegie Club, a residential sporting club – as 'heaven on earth'.

The fully restored twenty rooms of Skibo Castle and the twelve private lodges on the grounds provided a stately hideaway for the privileged and wealthy. The estate's beauty – perched on rolling hills overlooking Dornoch Firth – is of such magnitude and stunning clarity that it generates an emotional experience when merely looking at photographs of it, let alone actually experiencing it first-hand. The club also had a reputation for extreme discretion, especially after hosting the near-secret marriage of publicity-shy movie star Robert Carlyle. Regular guests included Jack Nicholson, Michael Douglas and Sean Connery.

When he went to Scotland to scout out this playground for the rich and famous, Guy felt that it was the ideal site for his wedding to Madonna. He wanted a spectacular affair, partly because he wanted to impress his – and her – friends and family, partly because he felt that Madonna deserved it and also because he knew that they could well afford it. At first, when shown a brochure of Skibo Castle, Madonna thought that the location was too isolated and, as she put it, 'it sounds scary, like something out of a Dracula movie'.

'Oh, you'll change your mind about that,' Guy said, knowingly. 'Trust me.'

'She did a lot of acquiescing to Guy,' said a friend of Madonna's who would speak only if guaranteed anonymity. 'She wanted a nice ceremony, obviously, but leaned towards having it in Beverly Hills. She didn't want her friends to have to fly all the way to Scotland. But she made a decision to let Guy do it his way. She told me, "Look, I and my staff manipulate everything that happens in my world. I don't want Guy to feel that he's in for that kind of life. So, let him have it his way. I'm cool with it. Honest to God," she said, "I just want to get the whole goddamn thing over with."

'With the two kids, the promotion of the new CD [*Music*], the planning of music videos and other career moves,' says her friend, 'she was always feeling completely exhausted, headachy and irritable . . . not in the mood to plan a wedding, and definitely sleep-deprived because of Rocco.'

Madonna told her friend that she would 'just as soon get married in my living room in Los Angeles wearing a nice tube top and some embroidered jeans. But,' she went on, 'if I have to put on a big show, I guess I can do it. I haven't done a tour in a long time,' she joked, 'so I have enough energy for a good show.'

She only had one concern: that Rocco's baptism – which she had promised her father would take place before the wedding – would be memorable. 'That was her only real interest,' said her friend. 'Not the wedding, but the baptism,' which she wanted to have at thirteenth-century Dornoch Cathedral, about five miles north of Skibo.

When it came to the question of security, and how much of it there would be, Guy considered Madonna's first wedding in 1985 to Sean Penn in Malibu, California. Though it is widely believed that she had actually orchestrated much of the public drama and excitement that surrounded that ceremony, Madonna never stopped complaining about it – to Guy, to friends, to the press and to anyone else who would listen. Because he hadn't been there, Guy really didn't know to what degree the madness had been manipulated by his 'missus' – though, knowing her so well, he probably suspected some involvement on her part – and how much of it was truly an unwanted intrusion. So, to be safe – and maybe to ensure that he would not have to hear her grouse about her second wedding – Ritchie hired a security force of seventy professionals from Rock Steady, a well-respected, private firm, in an effort to guarantee the security of this second ceremony.

With plans nearly finalized, Guy went on to book all fifty-one bedrooms on the 7,500-acre Skibo Castle grounds for five nights. However, there would be certain rules. Guests would not be permitted to come and go at will, and would only be allowed to leave the castle for Rocco's baptism at the nearby cathedral. They would be carefully monitored at all times, 'for your safety and ours', Guy explained to one of his more sceptical invitees. There would be no televisions or radios in any of the rooms. Mobile phones had to be turned off. In effect, contact with the outside world would be all but denied the guests for the entire duration of their stay, five days. Of course, for some of Madonna's celebrity friends who always seemed somewhat annoyed by having to live in the real world with real people, the thought of this sort of isolation was pure and perfect nirvana. For many of Guy's pals, however, it seemed a preposterous proposition. 'I do think he's been hanging round the missus too much,' said one, snickering.

Guy's guest list would be limited, anyway, since Madonna had stipulated that invitations be extended only to wives of male guests, or to girlfriends who were familiar to her. She didn't want her fiancé's single and unruly buddies bringing strippers or other women of questionable professions to the castle for a good time.

'Look, it's going to be brilliant,' Guy promised one friend who baulked at the amount of time he would have to spend at the castle accompanied by a woman with whom he was about to end a relationship, but who Madonna insisted he bring along anyway. 'It's a special place. You have to experience it. It's the good life, and it'll be good for you. And, anyway,' Guy concluded, 'what the fuck? Why not join me and the missus for some fun, eh?'

On 5 December 2000, Madonna and Guy set off from their London home for Scotland to sign certain legal papers related to the forthcoming union, and to make the final arrangements. After the private jet (carrying the couple, two bodyguards and a personal assistant) touched down at Inverness airport at 11.30 a.m., it was met on the tarmac by two Range Rovers, provided by the Carnegie Club.

As flashbulbs popped all around her from the waiting and excited media, a glowing Madonna descended from the plane wearing dark glasses, a tartan coat and embroidered jeans. Guy followed, casual in a jacket and denims. After quick smiles and a few waving gestures, the couple retreated into their Range Rover, and took off.

Before viewing the castle, Madonna had decided that she first wanted to see Dornoch Cathedral. So, fifteen minutes after landing, her small entourage began the drive to Dornoch.

The cathedral was founded in 1224 by St Gilbert de Moravia, then bishop of the diocese. It boasts a magnificent stained-glass window, unveiled in his memory by Prince Charles in 1989. While small compared to most cathedrals, it dominates the surrounding buildings in the ancient royal burgh. Transfixed, she stood in the centre of the church in the soft sunshine that poured in through colourful stained glass. All was peace and serenity in this place. Maybe too quiet, even.

She couldn't resist. What singer could? Without warning, Madonna opened her mouth to see how her voice would resonate when enhanced by the acoustics of a 776-year-old cathedral. Her personal assistant, a local resident who just happened to be praying in the cathedral, three male Spanish tourists and Guy, were the only people present to witness the impromptu performance. As Madonna sang 'Ave Maria', her voice breaking the stillness of the hallowed place and soaring to the rafters, it probably never sounded better.

'Yes,' she said with a satisfied grin. 'I think this will do just fine.' She then walked over to Guy and melted into his arms. 'Think we can make out in here?' she asked, coyly.

'Better not,' he warned her, a wide grin playing on his face.

'Oh, then, we simply *must*.' She kissed his hair, his eyes and then his lips, passionately.

After the cathedral visit, it was off to Skibo Castle. As soon as she walked onto the grounds, she was quickly transported into the past. Later, Madonna admitted to one friend that she couldn't help but note Guy's almost tender understanding of history – and of nature and its beauty – in his selection of the austere and majestic Skibo Castle, the ambience of which was wholly masculine, yet vastly sensitive. 'For him to pick this place,' she marvelled, 'well, the idea of it – that it was his choice, not mine – it really speaks to me. And it leaves me breathless.'

With Madonna and Guy back in London – the press heated up its scrutiny of their wedding plans although Madonna's press representative, Liz Rosenberg dutifully denied that any wedding was even being planned. However, once the banns had been officially posted at the register's office in Dornoch on 6 December, the news was out: the couple would definitely marry in the Dornoch area of Sutherland. It could no longer be denied. However, the location of the event would remain a mystery to all but those within Madonna's and Guy's inner circle.

On 18 December, the couple again arrived in Scotland by private jet. Though a hundred journalists gathered to document their arrival, Madonna and Guy made no statement. Madonna smiled at the crowd, though her glow seemed to dim somewhat when she heard the sounds of a bagpipe artiste known as Spud the Piper (Calum Fraser) serenading her with his odd rendition of 'Like a Virgin'. Apparently bemused by the whole scene, Guy's eyebrows lifted quizzically when he finally recognized the melody. 'I guess it proves that you can play *anything* on a bagpipe,' he said.

The guests arrived shortly after Madonna and Guy. For the most part, Madonna found herself sequestered with the women; Guy with the men. Occasionally, the couple would rendezvous to sneak off for long, romantic walks, their arms around each other. During the evenings, the entire party indulged in elaborate dinners – including haggis, a mix of lamb offal, oatmeal and spices. ('I'm sorry, but I simply can't eat that,' Gwyneth Paltrow was overheard saying to one guest. 'Why, I don't even know what it is!')

On 21 December, baby Rocco was christened in Dornoch Cathedral. A crowd of about a thousand spectators, which had gathered in front of the cathedral hours early, were kept back from the premises by a police cordon. 'Rocco is our Ray of Light to Dornoch,' read a placard proudly carried by one local resident, alluding to Madonna's Grammy-winning CD.

For his christening, little Rocco was dressed in a white, gold-embroidered $45,000 'romper' designed by Donatella Versace. During the private proceedings, the baby's godmother, Trudie Styler, read the lengthy 'Lorica' hymn while her husband, Sting, sang 'Ave Maria'. (The child's godfather is Guy Oseary, Madonna's partner in Maverick Records.) Some of Madonna's family, in town for the wedding, also attended the thirty-minute christening, including her father, Tony, and his wife, Joan, Madonna's sister, Melanie Henry, and her husband, Joe. Guy's mother, Lady (Amber) Leighton, and his father, John – along with Guy's stepmother, Shireen Ritchie, and her twenty-one-year-old son, Oliver (from a previous marriage), were all in attendance. As well as a Catholic priest, also present were about forty total strangers to the couple, the church's elders, described as parishioners with perfect attendance records.

Without them, according to strict church rules, no ceremony is permitted to take place in the cathedral. 'Well, who's to keep them from selling us out to the press?' Madonna wanted to know. 'I don't trust a single one of them.'

'The way I look at it, if you can't trust people who go to church every Sunday,' Guy said, according to what he later recalled to this writer, 'then who can you trust?'

So moved was Madonna by the baptism (performed not by the Catholic priest but by the Rev. Susan Brown), she is said to have three times burst into tears during the ceremony. Afterwards, Madonna and Guy posed outside the cathedral with their baby for just a few moments. Guy delighted the crowd by holding Rocco aloft while Madonna – her hair swept under a veiled cap and wearing a long, double-breasted and fitted Chloe coat – stood at his side, looking stunning, demure and . . . royal. Smiling broadly, she waved grandly to the score of cheering, teary-eyed fans. Meanwhile, photographers memorialized the moment on film . . . no doubt, never dreaming that this would be the only shot they'd get of anything that was to take place in the next twenty-four hours.

Later, Guy learned that authorities had arrested two men – James and Robert Jones, both former soldiers from south London – for sneaking into the church and attempting to videotape the christening. Robert, fifty-one, had actually hidden in the cathedral's organ for sixty hours – with two plastic bin-liners for body waste. He and James were discovered in the cathedral about an hour after the ceremony. 'That's one for the other side,' Guy said, gamely. 'Almost . . .

'I was actually rather amused by it,' Guy told me a few months later. 'I mean, you have to have a sense of humour about it, now don't you?' he added. 'Good show for them that they got that far, that's what I thought.'

* * *

Finally, the Big Moment had arrived. The 'main event', the wedding, on 22 December 2000, at 6:30 p.m.

As the plaintive sound of a lone bagpipe player filled the great hall of Skibo Castle, Madonna's four-year-old daughter, Lourdes, barefoot and in an ivory gown with short sleeves and a high neck, led the wedding procession. As flower girl, she delicately tossed red rose petals from a basket while descending fourteen red-carpeted stairs. Immediately, many of the women began to weep. Among the fifty-five guests seated at the foot of the stairs were Gwyneth Paltrow (who arrived alone); Donatella Versace (escorted by Rupert Everett); Sting and his wife Trudie Styler; film maker Alek Keshishian; designer Jean-Paul Gaultier; and Madonna's good friends Debi Mazar and Ingrid Casares. As well as members of Guy's family, many of his buddies and some of the casts and crews of his films – including Jason Statham and Jason Flemyng of *Lock, Stock and Two Smoking Barrels* – were in attendance.

After Lourdes's moment, music by French pianist Katia Labèque served as the background score to Guy Ritchie's entrance as he walked down a middle aisle, past the guests, and up the stairs now strewn with rose petals. Though born and raised in England, Guy had been determined to marry in full Highland dress. He wore a Hunting Mackintosh plaid kilt of navy and green, custom-made by Britain's Scotch House and boasting his ancestral Mackintosh clan tartan. Underneath the kilt, Guy wore nothing, as is the custom. ('I'm not a wuss,' he jokingly explained to a friend.) His teal blazer was tailor-made by London's Alfred Dunhill. He also boasted green and antique diamond cufflinks, a wedding gift from his bride. (Four-month-old Rocco Ritchie, wearing a matching outfit – but with a diaper on underneath – sat in his nanny's lap in the first row of the congregation.) Guy mounted the stairs and stood at the top, handsome and proud in the warm glow of hundreds of candles.

Ritchie was trailed by his two best men: Matthew Vaughn (producer of *Lock, Stock and Two Smoking Barrels*, and *Snatch*) and London nightclub owner Piers Adam who, like Guy, suffers from dyslexia (the two attended classes together to overcome the disability). They were followed to the top of the stairs by Stella McCartney, Madonna's maid of honour.

It had been expected by many of Madonna's friends – as well as the press – that Gwyneth Paltrow would be maid of honour. However, according to one intimate, Gwyneth said that she couldn't 'bear the pressure of such a performance' and begged Madonna to 'let me off the hook, please'. So, the honour was extended to Miss McCartney, designer daughter of Sir Paul McCartney. She wore a self-designed, understated, grey-and-beige silk pants outfit.

Then, at last, the bride . . .

As Madonna walked out from the wings, down the middle aisle and up to the top step of the grand staircase, she was a vision in a strapless ivory silk gown, a fitted corset bodice and a long train. An antique veil, embroidered with nineteenth-century lace and topped by an Edwardian diamond tiara, was draped over her face. It cascaded serenely to the ground. She looked slender, willowy, and dramatic. A 37-carat, 2.5 inch diamond cross hung delicately at her cleavage above a bosom that was no mystery to most of the free world. Pearl and diamond bracelets were the expensive and classic finishing touch. As she walked down the aisle, her father, Tony, in a black, formal tuxedo, stood at her side, his arm entwined in hers, his step ringing with determination. The two looked extraordinarily radiant as they walked to the top of the stairs, in perfect harmony with one another.

She had come so far that, most certainly, her middle-class youth in Bay City, Michigan must have seemed light years in the past as forty-two-year-old Madonna Louise Ciccone gazed down at her guests, her manner composed, her demeanour regal. As she stood at the top of a majestic staircase, its balustrade laced with ivy and white orchids, she was resplendent in the supernatural light of the great, old castle. She appeared as would a queen to her subjects . . . or maybe even as Eva Perón would have to her constituents, for this was a production that, at least to some observers, seemed on the same grand scale as her star turn in *Evita*.

Madonna's ensemble was the result of just weeks of planning: the gown was designed (free of charge) by Stella McCartney; the tiara – 767 diamonds, 80 carats – loaned to her by Asprey & Garrard of London; bracelets courtesy of Adler of London; the diamond cross designed for her by the House of Harry Winston in New York. It all had been co-ordinated as quickly as possible so as to get it out of the way. Madonna, her inimitable brand of efficiency well known to those who have worked for her, has never been one for dawdling. If she has agreed to give a show, she'll give one – and a good one! – but it needs to be done quickly and efficiently. No fuss. Or, as she would put it, 'Just do it!'

This isn't to say that Madonna hadn't been excited about planning her wedding. The invitations, guest lists, menus, travel plans, florists, musicians . . . she ploughed ahead with all of it, with the assistance of her capable staff. Once she became involved in the formal wedding attire, her designer's imagination and sense of style ran wild. She was soon in the swing of things, viewing the selection of each fabric with Stella McCartney and other close friends as one of her life's biggest adventures. 'How often do you choose something, the memory of which you'll have all of your life?' she decided in conversation with a friend while reviewing sketches of gowns. 'I don't want to look back on my wedding pictures in ten years and say, "What was I *thinking*?" Plus, really, look how much fun all of this is. What girl wouldn't love *this*!' She wanted perfection, no matter the cost of time, money, or energy. Those who attended the wedding would say that, as usual, she got what she wanted.

When she reached the top of the stairs, Madonna kissed her father on the cheek and then left his side to stand by Guy's. From a distance, she seemed to be crying. Touched, Guy reached for her hand, regarding his bride with obvious warmth and affection.

The Ritchies' wedding ceremony – in front of Skibo's bay window of century-old, stained glass – was just twenty minutes long

Who has more star quality? Not many . . . if any.

Above left: As sultry torch singer Breathless Mahoney in *Dick Tracy*, opposite Warren Beatty. *Above right:* Madonna and Warren Beatty made a striking couple, but there were major differences that kept them apart.

Above left: In February 1991, during a contemplative moment with Tony Ward, Madonna's rebound relationship after Warren.
Above right: On 25 March 1991, wearing $21 million in jewels, Madonna – à la Marilyn Monroe – performed 'Sooner or Later' from *Dick Tracy* during the Academy Awards presentation. The song went on to win the Oscar.

Above left: From her critically panned film *Body of Evidence* in 1992.
Above right: Gender-breaking, as always.

At the New York party to celebrate her *Sex* book in October 1992. Madonna surprised everyone by showing up looking like Heidi in a low-cut Bavarian-style dress.

In 1994, with basketball star Dennis Rodman, the man who would go on to betray her by writing about – and exaggerating – their intimacies in his memoir.

Most people didn't know Madonna had an affair with Tupac Shakur. 'I was letting people dictate who should be my friends,' he would say when explaining why they broke up. 'So, I dissed her, even though she showed me nothing but love.' Here they are at a party with Raquel Welch in March 1994.

As Evita in 1996, Madonna shone like never before.
Some felt it was the performance of a lifetime for her.

Below left: The first photo of Madonna taken with Carlos Leon. He was understanding and patient . . . and became the father of her first-born child, Lourdes.
Below right: Clearly little Lourdes looks a lot like Mom, photographed here in 1999.

Madonna, Guy and Rocco outside Dornoch cathedral after the christening, December 2000.

Madonna with her boyfriend, Jesus Lux, and her children, David and Mercy, August 2009. He became the 'Madonna go-to guy'. When she was having a tough day, he was the only one who could calm her nerves.

Above left: Madonna performs during the charity concert Hope for Haiti Now, January 2010.

Above right: Madonna and her son, Rocco, perform during the 'MDNA' North America tour opener in Philadelphia, 28 April 2012. She took him on the road with her to be close to him . . . but it had the exact opposite effect!

Right: Madonna with boyfriend Brahim Zaibat on the 'MDNA' tour. 'I know who I am,' he said. 'Madonna has a secretary. I ain't it. Maybe I'll help you find out who it is, but after that you're on your own.'

Above left: Madonna and boyfriend Timor Steffens in Los Angeles, 29 April 2014. *Above right*: 'The greatest accomplishment of my life is to be the mother I never knew,' Madonna has said. Here she is with her adopted son, David, at the 56th Grammy Awards, 26 January 2014.

Above left: Madonna with her daughter, Lourdes, at New York Fashion Week, September 2016. *Above right*: Madonna performs at the Women's March on Washington, 21 January 2017. 'Yes, I am angry,' she said, speaking of the new Donald Trump administration. 'Yes, I am outraged. Yes, I have thought an awful lot about blowing up the White House. But I know that this won't change anything.'

(as conducted by the Rev. Susan Brown, the minister who had earlier baptized Rocco). In muted voices, the couple exchanged vows which they had written, sealing their promises to one another. They then exchanged wedding bands – Madonna's a simple platinum-and-diamond ring, Guy's a gold one. Even from a distance, Madonna's face seemed flushed the moment she and Guy were pronounced husband and wife. One spectator in the third row later recalled, 'You could see, with sudden clarity, the intense love in her eyes for this man. Guy touched her cheek gently, maybe wiping away a tear, I'm not sure. It was a moment, though, like no other. There was a true bonding, on every level.'

After the obligatory wedding kiss, the newly-weds finally descended the stairs as husband and wife, their guests cheering in appreciation. Flashing a beguiling smile, Madonna seemed to glow as she and Guy stood at the bottom of the staircase and accepted the good wishes of friends and family. Those who know her well say that she had never appeared happier than she did at that moment. She seemed filled with a contentment that she, perhaps, had never before known.

After the ceremony, everyone gathered in Skibo's drawing room for champagne toasts. Dinner was then served in the castle's oak-panelled dining room. As a traditional four-piece Scottish band played, guests drank champagne and red wine and ate langoustines, salmon, mussels, Aberdeen Angus beef, roast potatoes and red cabbage. For dessert, a caramelized profiterole cake was served. At 11 p.m., the party moved on to a disco that had been set up in the basement of the castle. By this time, Madonna had changed into an ivory-white pantsuit. The new bride was also adorned by millions of dollars' worth of jewels: diamonds that were on loan from Harry Winston. Guests then danced into the early morning hours to recorded music by Madonna and Sting, as well as artists who had contributed to the soundtrack of Guy's movie, *Snatch*.

Thanks to such careful planning by Guy Ritchie and certain members of Madonna's experienced staff, the event had been successfully shrouded in unprecedented secrecy, and had been a total media blackout.

Slowly, over the course of three days after the ceremony, sketchy – and often contradictory – details of what had occurred behind the castle's gates began to emerge. Surprisingly, no wedding picture of the couple was issued to the press, though noted photographer Jean Baptiste Mondino had documented the entire experience. 'If we're playing the game, we go all the way with it,' Guy told one of Madonna's press representatives. 'So, no photos.'

In the end, the only real breach came from Guy's father, John, who had told a reporter – prior to his arrival at the castle – that Guy would be wearing a kilt of the family's Hunting Mackintosh tartan. Once he arrived in Scotland, the elder Ritchie was given a severe dressing down from one of Madonna's representatives. When he later heard about the rebuke, Guy became incensed – perhaps the only time he was angry during the five days at Skibo. 'He's my father,' Guy hissed at Madonna's handler upon confronting her. 'How dare you speak to him in that way?' An argument ensued, a blow up that quickly ended when Guy walked away with a fierce expression, muttering something about 'the fucking assholes that work for the missus'. Though instantly forgiven by his son and his fiancée for the innocent transgression, the senior Ritchie was still shaken by the internal fracas. At the cathedral just prior to the baptism, a reporter from Associated Press asked him what was going to transpire at the ceremony, John Ritchie responded, 'I wouldn't dare ask.'

After the wedding, Madonna's father, Tony, and his wife, Joan, left Scotland for the United States. Everyone who knew Madonna felt that her father's presence in Scotland had been a strong indicator that his relationship with Madonna was now on firm ground. Whatever unpleasantness had occurred between them had been assigned to the past where, hopefully, it would remain.

One close friend reports overhearing a conversation between father and daughter in the grounds of Skibo Castle. Tony, awed by his surroundings, spent much of the time with Guy's father, John, soaking up the environment, feasting his eyes on the scenery. On the morning of the wedding, he and Madonna enjoyed one of many heart-warming moments in the grounds. Wearing what appeared to be a cashmere, pale-pink turtle-neck sweater with straight-leg jeans, Madonna sat under a sycamore tree, holding baby Rocco in her arms, close to her bosom. A cheerful nanny played 'tag' with Lourdes, three feet or so away. Friends milled about, watching Madonna with the new baby and gazing out at the spectacular vista spread before them. This peaceful scene played out gently in the early morning hour's sunlight, abundant with beauty, harmony and a sense of timelessness that made it all seem so far removed from the outside world.

As Tony approached his daughter, she smiled at him. 'Well, we've sure come a long way, Dad,' Madonna said.

'I'll say,' Tony agreed, 'I never thought we'd be here in this place together,' he added, waving a hand at their lush surroundings.

'No, Dad,' Madonna responded. 'I mean you and me. We've come a long way.'

According to the witness, Tony's eyes began to fill with tears. He shook his head, a slow smile spreading across his face. 'My God. Just look at you,' he told his daughter. Madonna lifted Rocco in the air, and made a funny face at him. 'A mother . . . soon a wife. Look how good you turned out, Nonnie,' Tony concluded, his face filled with genuine pride.

'Da-ad!' Madonna exclaimed, drawing the word into two syllables. She seemed embarrassed, probably because she knew that people were listening.

'No, I mean it,' he insisted.

'Well, stop it,' Madonna said, her face softening. 'You're gonna make me cry.'

'And we couldn't have that, now, could we?' asked another voice. It was Guy, approaching from behind Madonna. He was wearing comfortable corduroys, a heavy, wool sweater and a big smile.

Madonna's head spun around. 'Oh, I get it. You guys are gonna gang up on me, now,' she concluded, good-naturedly. She handed the baby to Guy. 'Take this kid,' she told him as she stood up. 'I'm getting out of here.'

'Where to?' Guy asked.

'Somewhere I can have a good cry,' she answered.

Guy carefully placed the infant into the arms of the nearby nanny, and then followed Madonna. Joining her, he put his arm around her waist. They walked off wordlessly, looking safe with each other, seeming to belong together, maybe lost in their own thoughts, no words necessary between them.

'Drowned World'

For the entire time she had known Guy Ritchie, Madonna had not been in what her business associates refer to as 'full Madonna mode' – meaning that she wasn't planning a full-scale concert, and then travelling and performing while living the grand life of a pop superstar. True, she'd recorded, made videos and appeared on a couple of awards shows. However, Madonna and Guy were fortunate that, as a couple, they had been able to enjoy the space and time needed for an ever-deepening, steadily maturing relationship. As it would happen, they would need the strength of the bond they forged during her 'down time' to keep the marriage strong through the first tour since 1993.

The announcement of Madonna's 'Drowned World' tour was met with great enthusiasm from her public: tickets for the forty-eight dates in seventeen cities worldwide sold out within hours. Madonna's take would be nearly £2 million per show – and she would have to work for every pound. She realized that the pressures of a major international tour – the planning, the details, the show, the huge entourage, the travelling, all problems with which she had lived for years – were enormous challenges.

Over the years, Madonna had made tremendous sacrifices to achieve her unparalleled success, her great wealth and her undeniable power in the world of show business. However, it had always been her, and her alone, against the world – at least that's how it had sometimes felt to her. Now, added to the landscape would be her two children: Lourdes four, and Rocco, less than a year old. Guy also planned to be with her for most of the dates. Gone, then, would be the days when she and her dancers would be able to lounge around on king-size beds, talking about penis sizes and plastic surgery.

'We routed the whole tour so it would be manageable for the family,' noted Caresse Henry, Madonna's close friend and manager, 'and in Europe we wanted to stay in the same city for a week at a time so the kids wouldn't have to change planes so much. Madonna builds *everything* around her family.'

When the show's song line-up was finalized, many in Madonna's camp were concerned that the final presentation would disappoint, mostly because she had decided not to include her most famous hits, such as 'Like a Prayer', 'Vogue', 'Papa Don't Preach' and a legion of others. In fact, most of the twenty-two songs in the act were drawn from her two most recent CDs, *Ray of Light* and *Music*. Madonna's strategy was at odds with most veteran artists at the time, such as the Rolling Stones and U2, who toured with many of their old hits in order to keep the high-paying customers satisfied. Tickets for Madonna's show cost up to $250. It was unusual for Madonna, who has always managed to strike a careful balance between what she wanted to deliver artistically and what she knew her fans wanted from her, to make the decision to completely disregard her public's probable needs for this tour – already sold out by the time word leaked that she would not be performing her most popular songs. However, as she put it to interviewer E. Jean Carroll, 'I don't see the point of doing a show unless you're really going to make some great theatre. I'm pretty bored with most live shows I see. I don't want to go and watch someone just stand on stage and play music. I want my senses overwhelmed.'

'Oh my God, we're gonna suck,' background singer Niki Haris remembers having thought. 'They're gonna boo us off the stage.' She recalls Madonna saying, 'Please just trust me. I've been very successful. I know what I'm doing.'

Of course, this is the same woman who wore a Britney Spears T-shirt to bed every night for a week during the time she performed on *The Late Show with David Letterman* in New York in the winter of 2000. She had decided that Britney was her 'talisman for the week', she privately explained, and that wearing shirts with Spears' face emblazoned across them would bring her good fortune. 'And it did,' she said. (Just when one thinks of Madonna as perfectly calculated and logical in the way she lives her life, out falls that Britney Spears anecdote and her entire image is once again transformed.)

Haris and Donna DeLory – both of whom had worked with Madonna for more than a dozen years – did manage to convince their employer to climax the show with her first major hit from 1983, 'Holiday'.

Madonna's concept for the 'Drowned World' tour was loosely inspired by British author J.G. Ballard's portentous 1962 novel *The Drowned World*, the second of four disaster novels set in the future – each with a theme of air, fire, water and earth. In these books, the protagonist journeys through wondrous and dangerous landscapes until finally discovering the 'truth'. It was in Madonna's 1998 *Ray of Light* CD that she first drew an analogy between Ballard's work and her own ideas, to do with ambition and eventual success, but at a cost. In that work and, two years later, in *Music*, Madonna concluded her own 'truth' to be inner peace, restitution and family values.

Like Ballard's books, Madonna's 'Drowned World' show had four distinct sections, each a mini-opera with its own set pieces and costumes, drawing on elements of punk, geisha, cowgirl and a weird flamenco/ghetto fabulous fusion, and also involving martial arts, country and western, rock and roll, Japanese *butoh* dance and even the circus. Would any of it make sense? In Madonna's hands . . . somehow, yes. Having admired Ricky Martin's 1999–2000 'Livin' La Vida Loca' world tour, the first thing she did was recruit its director and choreographer Jamie King to assist her with her ideas. She also hired much of Martin's production crew, including production designer Bruce Rodgers, and video director Carol Dodds. Madonna's costumes (later valued at about $200,000) would be designed by Gaultier, Versace, Dolce & Gabbana and DSquared, right down to her black vinyl bra.

Once Madonna knew how she wanted the show to be outlined – the line-up of music and the four set pieces during which the songs would be performed – she turned the ideas over to Bruce Rodgers. Throughout the subsequent planning and rehearsal process, Rodgers says that Madonna was just as she's always been about her stage presentation: meticulous. If someone couldn't implement something she wanted done, he or she was fired. To Madonna, it was a simple matter of achieving her goals. She had a vision, she wanted to see it through, and if a person wasn't with her – perhaps trying to convince her that an idea wouldn't work for a logistical or fiscal reason – he was against her, and thus dismissed. After all, she didn't get where she was in life by acquiescing or thinking in a limited manner.

'One of the hardest parts in the beginning was getting everybody who was involved in making the production to stop saying, "That's impossible,"' says Bruce Rodgers. 'Madonna constantly supported the design, saying, "Go for it." Also, I'm used to trying to get the most out of the least amount of money. But because of the time frame, costs were running up and it made me – and everyone else – panic. Yet Madonna knew where every nickel was going . . .'

Madonna's steady calm throughout the planning process was no surprise to her friends. She had been practising Ashtanga yoga for the past five years, and was certain that meditative moments spent alone would get her through any difficult times during the organization and final execution of her show. She wanted it all to appear effortless, not sweaty. To that end, she scheduled eight weeks of production rehearsal time.

For this production, Madonna even wanted to appear to defy gravity while engaged in an elaborate martial-arts battle inspired by the film *Crouching Tiger, Hidden Dragon*. To that end, she took 'flying' lessons, learning to leap and float about adeptly in an uncomfortable harness, on cables breathtakingly high above the 4,900-square-foot stage. Nothing was too big a challenge, for her as well as for anyone else. If she wanted nearly nude dancers to dangle from the rafters by their ankles in Act One, then that's exactly what she expected to see in Act One. Or, as tour director and choreographer Jamie King put it, 'She wanted something new, she wanted change, and she wanted to do something she hadn't done before. If someone's not cutting it, or they're not inspiring her in a new way, there's no reason for them to be there.'

For the accommodating Guy Ritchie, now witnessing his wife's entire process for the first time, it was disconcerting to see so many heads on the chopping block. Ten people were fired in one week. 'I wouldn't want to work for her, I can tell you that,' he said. Wisely, though, he seldom ventured an opinion, preferring to just watch 'the missus' in action.

The first performance of the 'Drowned World' tour took place on 9 June 2001 at Barcelona's Palau Sant Jordi stadium, in front of about 20,000 people. Finally seeing the act in all its dazzling glory was awe-inspiring for everyone who had watched as Madonna and her team put it together – including Guy, who said, 'How she does it, I don't know. And I'm married to her.'

The raucous punk opening segment included songs such as 'Drowned World/Substitute for Love', 'Ray of Light', and 'Impressive Instant'. As an unsmiling Madonna performed, ten dancers in boots, Mohicans and gas masks stalked her menacingly, alternately humping and then tormenting her. Defiance being a rock attitude, and one embraced by Madonna, she didn't hesitate in wanting her public to know that she hadn't mellowed over the years (even though she has). 'Fuck you, motherfuckers!' Madonna shouted at her adoring crowd between 'Candy Perfume Girl' and 'Beautiful Stranger'.

At the beginning of the second segment – the Japanese *butoh* sequence – Madonna rose centre stage in a stunning kimono with a flabbergasting fifty-two-foot sleeve span. This section featured 'Frozen', 'Mer Girl', and 'Nobody's Perfect'. Later, during 'Sky Fits Heaven', she engaged in her show-stopping martial-arts battle.

The third act, rooted in her cowgirl routine, included 'I Deserve It', 'Don't Tell Me', and 'Gone', along with two of the older hits of the evening, 'Secret' and 'Human Nature'. During this section, Madonna jumped on a mechanical bull and transformed this cowgirl experience into an act almost – but, thankfully, not quite – as sexual as her 'Like a Virgin' masturbatory routine from the 'Blond Ambition' tour.

The final act, more thematically vague than the others, was Spanish/flamenco/ghetto fabulous in concept, including 'Lo Que Siente La Mujer' ('What It Feels Like for a Girl'), an acoustic, flamenco-style version of 'La Isla Bonita' (one of several songs on which she would play guitar) and 'Holiday'. When it all ended with a raucous and finely executed finale of 'Music', most observers had to agree that the show had been breathtaking – if odd. It had clocked in at only one hour and thirty-seven minutes.

'Through it all, Madonna made a display of arrogance, tossing off profanities, striking tough postures and glaring more often than she smiled,' noted John Pareles in his *New York Times* review. 'She represents self-love backed by plenty of gym time and a whole troupe of devoted flunkies – enough to delight an audience she only seems to disdain. "Music makes the people come together," she sang in the finale . . . together that is, if Madonna is in charge.'

There were no encores. Instead, British comedian Ali G popped up on giant video screens to announce, 'She ain't comin' back, so go on, piss off. We got the Backstreet Boys in this venue tomorrow and let's face it, none of us want to be around for that.'

Opening night had been an unqualified success. Though emotionally and physically drained after the first performance, Madonna was pleased with her work. After it was all over, her tears flowed unchecked backstage, she was so filled with gratification. The sense of nervous hysteria that had hung in the air in her dressing room prior to show time now gave way to pure peace, satisfaction. Sadly, this state of euphoria did not last long.

About an hour after her performance, a misguided person in Madonna's camp showed her a story that had been published in the German magazine *Stern*. In it, Guy complained about Madonna. He was quoted as saying, 'It's still too early to know how my wife will influence my life, but I do already know it's sometimes hard work living with her.'

Madonna might not have cared about this kind of press at another time – after all, she probably would have reasoned, Guy might have been misquoted. Anyway, she knew she could be 'difficult to live with'. That was not news to her. However, on this stressful night, the comment set her off. She asked Guy to join her in her dressing room. There, the two were heard exchanging loud words about the interview. She said, 'How do you think that makes me look?' to which he was overheard saying, 'Since when do we care about *that*?' Guy left the dressing room after about five minutes, annoyed. She ran after him, perhaps not wanting her bad mood to ruin the triumph of this important night for her, for them. Later they seemed fine together, looking at each other with great admiration while greeting guests at an after-concert party. However, Madonna's small outburst was a harbinger of things to come.

Guy would have to get used to the fact that irritability would characterize Madonna's mood for most of this tour. She had already worked to the point of exhaustion, and she still had months ahead of her. 'I saw her in Paris and it was so hot, I thought she was going to collapse,' recalls Marty Callner (who directed the Grammy-nominated 1993 HBO special *Madonna Live Down Under: The Girlie Show* and who would go on to produce *Madonna Live: The Drowned World Tour* for the same network). 'She just kept trudging through it, up there dancing in heavy costumes under hot lights. You say to yourself, "Where does that come from?"'

While Madonna is usually at her creative best during times of extreme pressure, she's also at her moodiest. Anyone who has ever lived with an artiste would agree that, often, there's an offstage price to pay for onstage brilliance. Guy Ritchie was not to be spared his wife's frequent eruptions of anger and frustration. Indeed, for the next couple of months, Madonna would be at her most demanding and imperious.

Drama Mama

After France, the 'Drowned World' tour made its way to London, where Madonna would play Earl's Court in July 2001. While in Britain, Madonna and Guy would find themselves tightly locked in arguments for three consecutive days.

The first fracas occurred while the couple were with friends at the San Lorenzo restaurant. On this summer night, Guy was formally attired in pinstripes and wingtip shoes. Madonna appreciated it when he dressed up to go out at night, saying that her husband's comportment demanded old-world tailoring. For her part, though, she preferred to be more casual, especially when she had to spend so much time dressing up for stage work. This evening she wore curve-hugging black leather from head to toe. She also wore fingerless lace gloves, an elegant touch. Her mood, though, was as dark as her attire.

'It's completely bonkers,' Guy exclaimed, while in a lengthy discussion with friends about the 'Drowned World' tour. As Guy spoke, Madonna was silent, picking at her food.

'Two jumbo jets full of stuff [1,500 storage trunks], another jet for the crew, and a fourth [Madonna's luxury twelve-seat Falcon 900 series] for me, the children and the nannies. And toys for the kids,' Guy went on, according to the recollection of one witness. 'Do you know how many stuffed animals are being carted around the world?' he asked. 'Why, it's unbelievable.'

Guy explained that he and 'the missus' were 'up at the crack of dawn', every day. 'We're on the planes, we're in hotels, we're in venues, sound checks, rehearsals. I mean, her kimono is, what, fifty feet wide?' he asked. 'Try packing that thing.' Ritchie, who seemed to know every detail of what was going on with the tour, noted that it took seven people to get Madonna in and out of the kimono. He also mentioned that she had four versions of each costume on hand for the entire tour, each hand-cleaned, steamed, pressed and ready to wear.

'It's chaos all day with rehearsals and sound checks,' he added. 'Then, she's on stage and has to be bright and energetic when she's not feeling that way at all,' he continued, talking about Madonna as if she wasn't present. After the show, he went on, there were the inevitable crowds of people backstage wanting their picture taken with Madonna. He said he would prefer that she left the venue quickly to go back to the hotel, and to bed. 'But she wants to pose with this person and that person,' he observed. 'And, meanwhile, the kids are back at the hotel, crying for their mum.'

Madonna took a deep breath and closed her eyes, perhaps waiting for some kind of yoga-induced inner peace. 'The lighting in here sucks, doesn't it?' she snapped, looking around. Later, someone in her camp would explain her disposition to a witness by saying that she'd had a bad reaction to the chemical Botox, which she'd supposedly had injected into her armpits to prevent her from sweating into her stage costumes. Madonna's contract 'rider' called for two bottles of Absolut vodka – not for drinking but, rather, to remove unsightly sweat stains from her costumes . . . perhaps in case Botox failed her.

Guy ignored his wife. 'Anyway, the whole thing is quite the spectacle,' he concluded.

'My God, Guy. Please,' Madonna suddenly exclaimed. 'I've been doing this for fifteen years.'

Of course, Madonna was known to be dismissive of Guy, and in public. It's part of her personality to sometimes be short with people. If one knows her well, one realizes that her detached, impatient persona is mostly facade and is, therefore, not offended by it. (Or, as her brother Martin put it, 'She's a real softie and most people don't get that about her. She's afraid that side of her will get out, and then everyone will know she's not as fierce as she wants people to think she is.')

'Look, I'm just saying—' Guy began.

'Exactly,' Madonna said, cutting him off. 'Excuse me,' she told her friends as she got to her feet. 'We'll talk later,' she told Guy. She threw him a sharp look and walked out of the restaurant.

'Well, there she goes, popping off again,' Guy said. 'See you later,' he called with a wave of his hand.

'For the next fifteen minutes Guy seethed,' said the witness. 'Finally he said, "Well, look, I guess I'd better go find my bird." He got up. "She's so difficult," he said, as he took his jacket from the back of his chair and put it on. "But she's under a lot of pressure," he concluded, gamely. "So what can you do?"'

Ten minutes later, he returned with Madonna, who had apparently cooled off. 'I'm really not a bitch,' she told her friends, apologetically. 'I'm just a very good actress.' Then, she added, with typical humour, 'Contrary to what some have said.'

While in London, the Ritchies had checked into the Berkeley Hotel because their new £5.7 million, four-storey Georgian terraced home near Oxford Street was being re-modelled. However, due to the Berkeley's faulty air-conditioning system, they were forced to move to nearby Claridges. Because the weather in London was particularly hot and humid, Madonna and her children couldn't rest without cool air. She didn't care that the press made her out to be a diva by changing hotels in a hasty middle-of-the-night switch . . . as long as she could get the good night's sleep she needed to function while on tour.

The next night, the same group of friends who had been with the Ritchies at the San Lorenzo restaurant joined Madonna and Guy at the bar at Claridges. By the time they got there, the Ritchies were already involved in a heated discussion about Rocco. While she and Lola were close, Guy observed, she hadn't spent enough bonding time with Rocco. When their friends arrived, Guy was in the middle of saying '. . . nursemaids are doing all of the messy work with the nappies, and all, and you pretty much stay out of it, don't you?'

'Excuse me,' Madonna said, brusquely, 'but that's what they get paid for.'

It's true that, after she became immersed in rehearsals for her show, Madonna seldom changed Rocco's nappies. When her schedule became full, she decided to prioritize her time and find other quality moments to spend with the baby, rather than times when he needed changing. 'If other mothers could do so, they probably would, as well,' she had said.

Guy went on to say that there really wasn't much else to do with a new baby, other than 'change his nappies' and 'coo at him', and, he added, 'you don't seem to do much of that, either.'

One of the witnesses tried to defend Madonna by saying, 'No one can gauge the love a mother has for her child.' At that, Madonna erupted. 'I don't need anyone to defend me,' she said. 'The whole subject is ridiculous. I'm not even going to respond, it's that insulting.'

She put down her drink, and picked up her handbag. 'When are you going to stop picking on me?' she asked Guy. Unexpectedly, tears welled in her eyes. She seemed to swallow hard, as if trying to push them back. She couldn't. Soon one rolled down her cheek. Clearly, Guy had hit on a sore spot, maybe one that touched upon delicate emotions having to do with Madonna's childhood, the loss of her mother. Only Madonna would know for sure what it was, but something in his criticism had hit her hard, there was no doubt about that. It was written all over her face. 'Excuse me,' she said as she took her leave.

The others talked awkwardly among themselves as Guy sat in silent contemplation.

Ten minutes later, Madonna returned. Guy asked how the matter could be settled. According to the witness, Madonna suggested that an apology was in order.

'You're a great mum,' Guy conceded. 'I was being ridiculous and I do apologize.' He held her hand and kissed her fingertips.

'Well, that's good for starters,' Madonna said with a sly smile at her friends. 'Later we'll see just how apologetic he can really be.'

Round three between the Ritchies occurred the next night, again at San Lorenzo's. Madonna was wearing a black long-sleeved catsuit and matching choker, her shoulder-length blonde hair was parted in the middle. Her face seemed tight, as if smiling would have depleted every ounce of energy.

There were no witnesses to their disagreement; the two had dined alone. When they left the restaurant and headed back to Claridges, they were again in a heated discussion. Madonna was crying. Guy exited the limousine first, she followed. A friend greeted Guy as he entered the hotel. Without saying a word to him, Guy bolted into the lobby, leaving a shaken Madonna to fend for herself with the waiting paparazzi. Their photos published the next day caught her looking distraught.

The rest of the tour saw professional triumphs and personal challenges, each day bringing equal measures of excitement and despair – and more fights and reconciliations with Guy, as well. There were also memorable moments that had nothing to do with the show or Guy, but, rather, moments of personal experience for Madonna. While in Germany on 24 June, Ingrid Casares, Gwyneth Paltrow and Stella McCartney (all three of whom travelled with the tour to certain cities) accompanied Madonna on a visit to the former Nazi concentration camp Sachsenhausen in Oranienburg. One of the first of the Nazi concentration camps, Sachsenhausen housed more than 200,000 inmates. Jews, Czech dissidents and others oppressed by the Nazis were imprisoned arbitrarily here, and many were killed, from 1936 until it was liberated by Soviet troops in 1945. It was also a training centre for the elite Nazi police, the SS, as well as for concentration camp guards.

A photograph that later circulated around the world showed Madonna, in a black leather jacket and matching jeans, pointing to the infamous slogan 'Arbeit Macht Frei' ('Work Sets You Free') in iron letters at the camp's entrance. Another photo showed Madonna and Gwyneth walking by Barracks 38 where Jews were imprisoned in especially cruel conditions. Both women were moved by the thought of the tens of thousands of deaths that had occurred on these grounds. 'It's more than I can bear,' Madonna later said. 'Just being there affected me so deeply.'

Some of those who worked on the 'Drowned World' tour later expressed the view that the visit to Sachsenhausen took a toll on Madonna at a time when she didn't have a lot to give. For days afterward she was distracted and seemed particularly sad. The European dates were tough enough, but by the time she got to the American leg of the tour – the third week of July in Philadelphia – she was exhausted. In recent weeks she had become so ill-tempered, some members of her touring troupe had begun calling her 'Andrea' behind her back – as in 'Andrea Yates', the troubled Texan woman known in America for having drowned her children.

In Las Vegas, in early September, where she played the MGM Grand Theater, Madonna and Guy stayed at the Mansion (the MGM's expensive VIP suite). Madonna hates Las Vegas. With the exception of gambling – 'and I don't throw away my money, I save it,' she says – there's nothing to do there for recreation. Because she knows that the city is teeming with tourists from all over the world who would love a mere glimpse of her, she was loath to leave her suite.

The first day in Las Vegas had been a gruelling one of rehearsals and sound checks. Wearing baggy blue jeans (with a chain wallet) slung low on her hips, a thick black belt and a sleeveless T-shirt with the words 'You Suck' emblazoned across her chest, Madonna looked more like a sculpted triathlete than a female pop star, especially with biceps still bulging from the rehearsal workout. But, appearances aside, she really wasn't well. With her throat raw from constant coughing, she was exhausted and listless. Though her body felt broken down, she wouldn't allow herself to deviate from her usual work schedule. She'd cancelled a couple of shows earlier because of laryngitis, and had felt terrible about doing so to her fans. No, she would carry on – somehow. Some inner determination would push her forward, just as it always had in the past. 'How I will ever get through the performance tonight,' she said, fretting about a tightness in her chest, 'I don't know. Someone had better start praying,' she added.

In the early evening, a butler, assigned by the hotel to tend to the Ritchies, brought Madonna and Guy a complimentary lobster meal along with a bottle of champagne. Once he had served the lobster, the butler popped open the bottle. He poured Guy a sample glass. Guy tasted it and nodded approvingly.

The server then poured a glass for Madonna. Slumped in a chair across the table from her husband, her legs spread mannishly open, she leaned over and touched her glass to Guy's. She took a sip. Then, with a great flourish, she spat the champagne from her mouth. 'Why, this tastes like piss!' she exclaimed.

Guy had a stunned look in his eyes, according to the butler's later recollection. 'What the missus means to say,' he explained, 'is that this champagne may be a bit on the bitter side.'

'What the missus means to say,' Madonna corrected her husband, 'is that *this tastes like piss*! And not only that,' she said, 'this lobster isn't fresh, either. Taste it, Guy,' she said.

He took a taste. 'I don't know,' he said in his most non-committal tone. 'It tastes fresh to me.' Guy wagged his finger at Madonna, and then made a slicing motion across his neck with his hand, as if to say 'cut it out'.

Meanwhile, the butler picked up a nearby telephone and called the kitchen to say that 'Mrs Madonna' ('and don't call me that!') was unhappy because the lobster wasn't fresh.

He hung up, turned to 'Mrs Madonna' and told her that, according to his best information, the lobster was, indeed, fresh.

'They don't call me Drama Mama for nothing,' Madonna said later, when recounting the story of the butler to members of her touring troupe. 'I'm simply awful, and I know it. Okay? *I know it.* So,' she concluded with a wicked grin, 'deal with it.'

What seemed to make Guy Ritchie an ideal partner for Madonna was that he understood her and her world, and wouldn't make matters worse by challenging her unless completely necessary. No doubt he would have preferred that she refrain from diva-like behaviour with functionaries – but that might be asking too much, he probably realized. After all, who was a bigger diva than his own wife? Say those who knew the couple best, Guy realized that Madonna had always had a fear of connecting deeply with another person, and that it had to do with old abandonment issues. He quickly learned to pick and choose his arguments, marshal his senses even when they were reeling, and cool his rage.

Also, it wasn't as if Guy had nothing to do with his time. If all he did with his day was follow his wife about and observe her theatricals, it's not likely that she would allow him to be a part of her life. While accompanying Madonna on her tour, Guy was making plans for two major films. One, to be called *Love, Sex, Drugs and Money*, would star his wife, filming mostly on the island of Malta; the other, *The Siege of Malta*, was intended to be an epic movie based on the siege of Malta in 1565 and was projected to cost nearly $40 million to produce.

As always, Madonna was full of surprises. When Carlos Leon was arrested in New York for smoking pot in Manhattan's Washington Square Park, most of the people in her entourage felt she was going to telephone him and explode about how he'd embarrassed her. After being arrested, he had spent one hot August night in jail and then, a legal aid attorney at his side, pleaded guilty to a misdemeanour the next morning. 'Poor geezer,' Guy said when he heard the news. 'But how can anyone smoke pot in broad daylight in the middle of a park? That makes no sense to me.'

Madonna telephoned Carlos and spoke to him for an hour, telling him that she thought the charge was ridiculous and that he shouldn't worry about it. 'You'd think the police could find better ways to spend their time, especially in New York,' Madonna reportedly said to him. It was an unpredictable reaction – she is vehemently opposed to drug use – but one that probably shouldn't have surprised anyone. Carlos has always shown the utmost loyalty to Madonna. Nothing matters to her more than the loyalty of those in her life, and her loyalty to them.

A real test of Madonna's allegiance to her husband came at the end of the 'Drowned World' tour. In early September, statuesque twenty-seven-year-old television presenter, Tania Strecker, again implied that she and Guy (whom she had known since the age of thirteen, and whom she described as 'the love of my life') had been dating just months before he married Madonna. Whether or not Tania and Guy had been romantically involved after he met Madonna had been a running theme of news reports about Strecker in the past. 'I'm not saying when the last time was because that's a bit of a sore one – not for me but for her,' Strecker had said in a previous interview.

Of course, Madonna knew of the younger woman – sixteen years her junior – and had even told friends that she suspected Guy was still attracted to her. However, when Guy denied that he'd had anything to do with her once he and Madonna had outlined their relationship as committed (about three months after they first started dating), she believed him.

Now, more than a year later, the British press had again alleged that their relationship lasted longer than people had thought. Madonna and Guy were in Oakland, one of the last stops on the tour, when the news broke. According to a source close to them, they had a brief discussion about it. He denied it was true, and that was the end of it.

Madonna later said that she wouldn't demean what she has with Guy by bringing up the subject of these 'revelations'. She told a friend, 'He finally mentioned it to me, told me that it was all bullshit. That's where it ends for me. Look, he's the most trustworthy man I have ever known,' Madonna concluded. 'Would I have married him, otherwise?'

Instead of pressing Guy about these claims, Madonna decided to be sweet to him. She arranged for her personal chef to make him his favourite English breakfast of fried eggs and sausages with croissants and jam. (Both he and Madonna were usually on a macrobiotic diet but they did slip from time to time.)

11 September . . . and Beyond

The eleventh of September 2001 was the ghastly day terrorists used United Airlines aircraft as weapons against the US, downing four US passenger jets, damaging the Pentagon, destroying the World Trade Center in New York and murdering nearly three thousand innocent people in the process. These cataclysmic events did for Madonna what they did for most Americans, indeed for most people around the world: they reaffirmed what matters most in life. It truly wasn't the 'Drowned World' tour – despite the boundless energy she had devoted to it – or any of the sensational headlines constantly swirling about her that really mattered, Madonna now realized. Rather, it was Guy, her children, her friends, the life she had created for herself . . . all of that was what she was most grateful for in the wake of 11 September.

After the attacks, Madonna could barely continue with the tour, she was filled with such profound anger, such dumbfounded grief. Guy shared his wife's sense of incredulity, shock and disbelief. They watched the television coverage together for many hours. How, they wondered, could they possibly continue with the show – a production once so important in their lives that now seemed so trivial? Soon sorrow gave way to rage, though Madonna said that she felt strongly that she should resist hatred. Still, it felt as if nothing would ever be the same. Evil had run amok in America. The country – the world – had been savaged by the most insane acts of violence. How could Madonna now go on and sing 'Music makes the people come together'?

Making matters more complex for Madonna, Lourdes and Rocco had become increasingly cranky and difficult. These days, they were not the well-behaved children their mother had been so proud of prior to exposing them to her drowned world. Lourdes had taken to scribbling graffiti with her crayons on wardrobes and equipment cases, as well as luggage and even walls. Frustrated with the new scheduling of her life, she had become selfish and unreasonable. During one fit, she threw her $300 Christian Dior sunglasses across the room and announced, 'I want my daddy, and I want him *now*.' Meanwhile, Rocco couldn't seem to stop crying unless Mum was in the room with him, holding him in her arms, nuzzling his neck, wiping tears from his sad, young face. Both tots were accustomed to a regimented and sensible schedule, now completely ruined during their first worldwide tour with a pop icon who happened to be their mother. Madonna said that her heart ached every time she thought of the upheaval she had caused in their young lives. 'Never again,' Madonna told her publicist Liz Rosenberg, probably wondering if she could really mean those words. 'Never again.'

Fortunately, Madonna had only the last few California dates to play. She cancelled the performance scheduled for Tuesday,

11 September at the Staples Center in Los Angeles. Two days later, ticket-holders were told to arrive at least one hour before each sold-out performance to allow enough time for them to make it through heightened security procedures. That night, and during the shows that followed, Madonna offered a moment of silence for those killed and injured in the terrorist attacks. She also pledged the proceeds from her remaining shows to help victims' families. Wearing an American flag skirt instead of tartan, and using the stage as a platform to voice her views, she expressed pacifist comments that were perhaps not as understood or appreciated during this tragic time as she may have wished. 'I think that each and every one of us should look inside our own hearts and examine our own personal acts of terrorism, hatred, intolerance, negativity, the list goes on and on,' she told her audience at the Staples Center. 'We're all responsible. It's not just [Osama] bin Laden, it's all of us, we've all contributed to hatred in the world today.'

Implying that her audience was somehow responsible for the horror that had taken place in the United States was more than some present could comprehend – there were scattered boos and hisses. Speaking from a metaphysical viewpoint, however, Madonna holds fast to the belief that we are all responsible for our actions, that our thoughts create our environment, and that those thoughts are creative in both a positive and a negative way. Every choice produces a consequence. Hers is a philosophical and spiritual way of thinking that may be difficult for some to comprehend without a full explanation, especially in times of great terror when people tend to feel the most powerless. While her words seemed to assign blame, that was not her intention. In Madonna's view, there is a big difference between blame and global consciousness. It's a fine line, however, and one that escaped many of her fans and critics, especially at this time. The fact that she wasn't really connecting with her audience only made her feel more depressed, and more anxious to end the tour. She was glad when it was over.

Perhaps making matters even more stressful for Madonna at this time was a medical concern. On 19 September, she decided to have a health problem checked at Cedars-Sinai hospital in Los Angeles. Some thought that her months of riding the mechanical bull had caused her to have a hernia. However, she rarely – if ever – even broke a sweat on that contraption.

After her examination, it became clear that Madonna had really just pulled an abdominal muscle. However, while at Cedars, a bomb threat was called in to the hospital. The wing in which she was being examined had to be quickly evacuated. Though still in pain, she had to flee to the parking garage, from where she was whisked away in her car. She later confided that, as her driver raced away from the hospital, she thought she was going to have a nervous breakdown, or at least some sort of physical collapse. She was truly at her breaking point after so many months of stress and anxiety. Now *this?* It was more than she could take, underscoring her deep sense of despair and fear. 'I want my kids out of here,' she said, privately. 'I wish I could take all of my loved ones with me, but I can't.'

By the time the tour ended, plans had already been finalized for Guy and Madonna to work together on the Mediterranean island of Malta where, in early October, they were scheduled to begin shooting *Love, Sex, Drugs and Money*. The new movie was to be a remake of Lina Wertmüller's 1974 Italian film *Swept Away*, which had starred Giancarlo Giannini and Mariangela Melato. Guy was set to direct the romantic comedy; Madonna would play a wealthy woman who has an affair with a communist sailor she meets on a yachting vacation (played by Giannini's son, Adriano Giannini). Guy had earlier directed Madonna in her video of *What It Feels Like for a Girl*. He'd also given her an unaccredited role in his darkly comical BMW commercial, *Star*. His wife was so intimidating a presence on the set, he had to admit, 'the only way to direct her is to grab her by the balls.'

* * *

After her final 'Drowned World' tour show, she was wondering if it had been worth it to put herself and her family through such an ordeal. For now, she was happy to assign the tour to the past, never to visit that particular place again.

Somehow, at the end of a long but productive day of filming on the Italian seaboard, she managed to look elegant in a simple blue athletic outfit, her light hair tumbling loosely around her face. After just a few weeks away from the grind of the road, she felt renewed. It showed. Her skin glowed again. She seemed full of health and vitality and – in the wake of the terrorists' horrors – she had vowed at least to try not to obsess over things that don't really matter in the bigger scheme of things, to be mindful of every moment. 'Easier said than done for me, I know,' she told one confidante. 'But I'm going to try.'

As Madonna strummed a guitar, Guy sat across from her, massaging her bare feet. With the brilliant sun setting in the stillness of the afternoon, they seemed suspended in time and space, the deep-blue of sea and sky stretching away from them endlessly. A soft and balmy breeze gracefully buffeted their sleek sailboat forward through calm and dreamy water. They drifted quietly with their thoughts.

Something in the distance approached rapidly, a speck on the horizon, the only blemish in an azure blue sky. There was no mistaking the source of that chopping noise as it came closer, those gusts of wind, the awful cacophony now laying ruin to any tranquillity. In moments, the helicopter was directly above its target.

When Madonna looked up, she saw a man leaning precariously out of the aircraft's window, a camera held in front of his face. Tossing her hair, she smiled and gave him a flirtatious look. Then, extending her arm, she thrust her hand into the sky, middle finger extended. 'This is for you,' she shouted above the din. 'See this? All for you, you jerk.'

Guy bolted to his feet and leapt for his wife.

As Guy tried to force Madonna's arm down, probably hoping to prevent the global circulation of an unflattering picture, the two of them tumbled onto the floor of the boat in a heap. They then began wrestling, flipping each other, struggling with one another, laughing the whole time. Eventually, one of them gained dominance over the other and ended up on top.

Of course, it was her.

Swept Away

So, what can we make of *Swept Away*? Probably, the less said about it, the better. It was difficult to know what Guy Ritchie had in mind with his direction of the film or why he would even want to see his wife in such a terrible, degrading role. It was even more perplexing as to why Madonna would want to do it. In the film, she plays 'Amber Leighton', a rich, spoiled, and arrogant woman – unlikeable from the first frame onward – who takes a private cruise from Greece to Italy with her husband. After a storm, Amber ends up on a desert island with the ship's first mate, 'Giuseppe'. A communist sailor with a chip on his shoulder, he begins to annoy Amber from the moment she lays eyes on him. Movie viewers can't help but share her contempt. In fact, as played by Adriano Giannini, Giuseppe is such a miserable, misogynistic character it's almost unbearable to watch. From the start, Amber treats him like a second-class citizen, making it clear that she looks down upon him and his station in life. However, Giuseppe soon has the chance to return the favour after they are shipwrecked. Once alone with her, he berates and humiliates her mercilessly, reversing their roles and showing her what it's like to be on the other end of such abuse. Midway into this misadventure, Amber is worn down, a shell of her former caustic and egocentric self. She then does what the viewer hopes she won't do (but fears is possible simply because movies this bad usually have bad plot twists): she falls in love with him. From then on, it just gets worse.

Seldom had any cinematic venture received such scathing reviews when *Swept Away* was finally released in October 2002. Actually, the notices were a lot more entertaining than the movie! 'If there is one thing worse than a Guy Ritchie movie, it's a Guy Ritchie movie with Madonna in it,' wrote Rex Reed for the *New York Observer*. 'No yacht was harmed during shooting. It's the movie that's the shipwreck,' added Peter Travers of *Rolling Stone*. 'Butt-numbingly b-o-r-i-n-g,' chimed in Megan Turner for the *New York Post*. 'New ways of badness need to be invented to describe exactly how bad it is,' wrote John Anderson for *Newsday*. 'It's hard to imagine another director ever making his wife look so bad in a major movie,' added Paul Clinton at CNN.

'I think twenty-one papers in America ran on how appalling it was,' recalled Guy. 'We had the absolute faeces kicked out of us.' Madonna publicist Liz Rosenberg agreed, calling it 'a public hanging'.

Because of the bad reviews, *Swept Away* ran for just three weeks in the United States and then didn't even open in the UK, going straight to video and DVD there instead. 'It's not being released in England because it's shit,' Guy blustered, when asked why *Swept Away* was not given an opportunity to find a UK audience. 'I can't answer more eloquently than that.' The movie cost $10 million to make but generated just a half million dollars at the box office, a devastating turn of events for both star and director.

Perhaps it was just a matter of human nature, but the Ritchies couldn't help but blame each other. In fact, because it was the failure of something in which they'd both invested so much, *Swept Away* caused tension between them. Simply put, Madonna felt that Guy had let her down, partly because she'd been photographed in such an unflattering way. Though her body looked amazingly athletic for a woman of her age, she *did* appear to be haggard, no doubt the result of poor lighting and make-up – indeed, all in Guy's purview as director.

'Why did you make me look that way?' she complained to him.

'I'm not sure that how you *looked* was the issue,' Guy countered, according to someone privy to the discussion.

Guy's suggestion seemed to be that Madonna's acting was what had ruined his movie and, as one might imagine, that notion didn't go over very well with her. The fact that Madonna wasn't very good in the role shouldn't have come as a big surprise, anyway. Playing someone's doormat? She has often been convincing in her films, but even *she's* not a good enough actress to pull *that* one off.

In time, Guy would become more philosophical about the movie's failure. For him, it became old news quickly; he soon moved on and decided he would just have better luck next time. However, Madonna couldn't help but hang on to the hurt and disappointment a while longer. After all, she's always wanted to be taken seriously as an actress. She'd certainly made great strides in that regard with *Evita* back in 1996. However, as a result of *Swept Away*, she'd now taken a giant step backward. Even though she'd made sixteen films by the time *Swept Away* was released, Madonna still couldn't help but feel a sense of injustice about the response to her movie career. On several occasions, she had been heard to have observed, 'I just don't know why people can't be, I don't know . . . *nicer*.'

'The thing is this: the woman cannot act,' observed Mary McNamara of the *Los Angeles Times*. It was almost as if McNamara was addressing Madonna's concerns when she further wrote, 'And unlike some of her initially wooden peers who went on to achieve excellent performances – Farrah Fawcett comes to mind, as does Cher – she seems incapable of learning on the job. So the question is not, Why is everyone being so mean? It's, Why does Madonna keep doing this?'

One friend of Madonna's recalls a conversation the two had about *Swept Away* in the expansive kitchen of Madonna's countryside home in England. 'I tried so hard,' Madonna said, according to her friend's memory. 'I still don't understand the cruelty. You don't like it? Fine. But, why be so vicious about it? I'm still not over it.'

Madonna's chum was unsure how to respond, so she didn't.

She definitely seemed defeated, recalled her friend. Her face was tinged with sadness.

'Oh, Mo, you know you'll recover,' observed her chum. 'You always do. You'll make many more movies.' (Some of her friends call her 'Mo'.)

'That's true, isn't it?' Madonna agreed with a rueful smile. 'After all, what would the movie industry be without me?' In fact, all of these many years later, Madonna still has not followed *Swept Away* with a starring role in a major motion picture. It's as if that one, well-intentioned movie pretty much ruined her in Hollywood.

American Life

By the beginning of 2003, forty-three-year-old Madonna was living a calmer, more introspective and – gasp! – even *wholesome* lifestyle with her thirty-four-year-old husband, Guy, and their children, Lourdes, six, and Rocco, three. Guy had been a good influence on her and of that there was little doubt. A grounded and usually reasonable man, it took a lot to get him riled. In some ways, his calming presence in her life had settled Madonna, easing her temper and insecurities. Or, maybe she was just open, at the time he came along, to the idea of being a more mature person. Whichever was the case, the marriage had definitely worked for her. For his part, though, Guy downplayed any sway he might have on his other half. 'Look, my wife has a mind of her own,' he said with a chuckle. 'I like to think I have some way of influencing her, but that could be an illusion.'

It could be argued, though, that Guy's influence on Madonna's career had not been such a good one, as evidenced by *Swept Away*. Things were about to get even worse on the show-business front with the release in the spring of 2003 of Madonna's ninth studio album, *American Life*. This was, perhaps, her most daring album in some time, with most of the song's lyrics geared toward decrying mythical aspects of the so-called 'American Dream', such as society's obsession with fame and fortune. Produced by Madonna and Mirwais Ahmadzai, the album went on to receive decidedly mixed reviews, which were mostly a response to the cold and robotic sound of the music. There was nothing warm about the production, that's for sure. It sounded impersonal, jarring and disjointed. There were a few gems to be found – 'Nothing Fails', 'Nobody Knows Me' and the surprisingly strong 'Die Another Day' from the James Bond movie of the same name come to mind – but as a whole, it wasn't a convincing, cohesive package.

The music video for the first single, 'American Life', caused a bit of a controversy in the United States when it was released on 24 March because it contained scenes that suggested the violence of the ongoing war in Iraq. However, a week later, Madonna changed her mind about the video's content, no doubt as a consequence of adverse publicity that was strongly suggesting she was being less than patriotic in releasing it. Instead, she recalled it and then issued an edited version which, basically, showed her singing in front of an international selection of flags. Though its lyrics don't make much sense if one analyses them closely, there's still something oddly haunting about Madonna's voice on the chorus of this song as she sings about living 'the American Dream'. Still, the rap in its mid-section having to do with nannies and lattes remains one of the silliest things she's ever recorded, forcing the listener to once again marvel at the inconsistency of her songwriting ability.

One of the performances promoting *American Life* did cause a bit of a flap on 28 August 2003 when Madonna sang 'Hollywood' with Britney Spears, Christina Aguilera and Missy Elliot at the MTV

Video Music Awards. During the routine, she kissed Spears and Aguilera squarely on the lips, which resulted in a memorable picture for the press and predictable headlines around the world. However, if anyone was to benefit from the publicity, it was to be Britney. (Interestingly, no one seemed to care that Madonna had also kissed the less sensational Aguilera. It was almost as if that particular lip-lock had never even taken place!) Not coincidentally, young Spears was about to embark on a comeback tour with a new CD at the time, and so this controversy put her right back into the public consciousness. Madonna had even provided guest vocals on Spears' song 'Me Against the Music', which went on to become a hit. Though obviously advantageous for Britney, the duet amounted to yet another questionable career move for Madonna. It's clear by listening to it that she had been added to it as an afterthought. After all, it's called '*Me* Against the Music', in the singular, meaning Britney . . . and just Britney. The way the production was put together suggested that Madonna had virtually nothing to do with it and had recorded her vocals after the song was essentially finished. However, Madonna did take Britney under her wing at this time, even convincing her to give Kabbalah a try. She said that she couldn't help but see some of herself in the younger entertainer, especially in the way Spears was constantly scrutinized by the media. In truth, there are so many obvious differences between the two women and the way each approaches her life and career, it's not even worth enumerating them all. Suffice it to say, each has had her own path. Anything Madonna saw in Britney that reminded her of her own experience was, doubtless, superficial. Maybe she eventually discerned as much because her alliance with Britney was definitely short-lived.*

---

* Actually, Jennifer Lopez was supposed to be on stage with Britney and Madonna at the MTV Awards. She cancelled, citing a conflict in her schedule, thereby leaving the door open for Christina Aguilera. Jennifer also had some concerns about 'the big kiss'. She told this writer, 'I think Ben would be a little unhappy if he saw me on TV kissing another woman, especially after what we

Historically, *American Life* is viewed as having failed to perform well in the United States sales charts because it peaked at just 37 on the Top 100. But, in fact, it did debut at number 1, which, obviously, isn't so bad at all. In the United Kingdom, it rose to number 2. However, it seemed as if once Madonna's diehard fans made their purchases, it began to sink. In all, *American Life* sold about five million copies in the USA, the poorest-selling album of her career. There were a few more single releases from it in the States, all failing to reach the charts there, but enjoying Top 10 success in various European countries. Though it did sell more millions abroad, it was clear that *American Life* was to be largely a commercial disappointment. It seemed surprising to many observers that a performer with Madonna's credentials as a pop icon could release an album that would not go on to massive success. It certainly proved, if nothing else, that the record-buying audience was as fickle as ever and that an artist was only as hot as her latest product.

In September, Madonna came out with her book, *The English Roses*, a glossy, illustration-driven children's book having to do with the evils of envy and jealousy, 'And,' as Madonna put it in one interview, 'how these emotions cause so much unnecessary suffering in our lives.' This was to be the first in a series of morality-themed books authored by the entertainer, the stories of which have all been loosely based on Kabbalah teachings. It was interesting to some observers that when Madonna went about the business of promoting these books in stores, she would sometimes show up in lovely 'mumsy' attire – floral-printed dresses and reading glasses – as if she was playing a role.

Though her two children probably enjoyed *The English Roses*, the book certainly wasn't going to do much for Madonna's career as a

---

both went through with the whole stripper thing.' She was referring to a recent controversy having to do with her fiancé-at-the-time, Ben Affleck, and an exotic dancer in Canada with whom he allegedly had an encounter – which, by the way, he vehemently denied. 'Look, Jennifer's okay,' Madonna said at this time. 'Her high-profile romance with Ben? I've been there, done that. With Sean [Penn].'

pop star. Some critics felt it would make matters worse for her because it appeared as if she was trying to find *something* to do . . . and she had settled on this easy project. In fact, she was obviously just biding her time, staying busy until something better in the music business struck her fancy. 'The music business has been a certain way for many years, and it's changing rapidly,' explained her manager, Caresse Henry. 'Everyone is trying to figure out, how do we restructure thirty-five years of doing business? The traditional music video and promo is just not enough.'

Then, during the Christmas season of 2003, Madonna released *Remixed & Revisited*, a remix EP (extended-play CD) that included rock versions of some songs from *American Life*, as well as a song called 'Your Honesty' (which was a leftover from 1994's *Bedtime Stories*). Another disappointment, this collection failed to even chart in the *Billboard* Top 100.

It should be noted that Madonna's lack of commercial success at this time really meant little in the bigger picture of her career, and virtually nothing at all in terms of her life. After all, she was, by this time, worth more than $350 million. She owned a New York apartment overlooking Central Park. Also, along with Guy, she owned three multimillion-dollar properties: two estates, one in Beverly Hills and another in Wiltshire, England, and a five-storey Georgian townhouse in London's West End. Plus, she'd been paid millions to write the series of children's books. She was doing just fine. Still, it would have been nice to have another hit . . . though it wouldn't be long before she'd have just that.

The 'Reinvention' Tour

At the conclusion of her last concert tour in 2001, the 'Drowned World' tour, Madonna had said that she wouldn't go back on the road for some time. Of course, that decision didn't last long. She's a woman who lives for the stage, loves performing . . . loves being *Madonna*. Indeed, by 2003 she was planning a new show. This spectacular concert presentation would be called the 'Reinvention' tour and hit the road in May 2004. As always, her work ethic and commitment to her craft would amaze fans and critics alike. Her imagination and creativity seemed to know no bounds. This writer saw the show twice in California. It doesn't overstate it to say that the concert – which featured most of her hits from 'Material Girl' through 'American Life', and including 'Vogue', 'Like a Prayer' and 'Papa Don't Preach' – was the best and most satisfying concert in Madonna's record-breaking twenty-five-year career.

By the end of its four-month run, the 'Reinvention' tour would encompass fifty-five concerts in the United States, Canada and Europe, grossing about $120 million. However, the gruelling show with its many costume changes and choreographed routines sometimes proved difficult for its star. Though she got through the dates, she was totally exhausted by them. Ten years earlier, she could do pretty much anything with ease. But by 2004, it was tougher. After some shows, she couldn't even hold a cup of tea steady without jittery hands! While that may have been the adrenaline, there must have been times when her forty-five-year-old body felt totally broken down, but there was no way to deviate from the schedule.

Those who had the chance to observe Madonna in her day-to-day activities during the tour couldn't help but notice the toll it was taking on her. Indeed, the pressure of mounting a major, international extravaganza remained an enormous challenge – the advance planning, the attention to every detail, the show itself, the organization of such a huge entourage and the myriad of other logistical concerns with which she has dealt for years. During times of crisis, she sometimes had to fight the urge to revert to the bitch-goddess of days gone by, the temperamental star who would lash out at anyone in her presence if she was in a bad mood. However, by 2004, in an effort to be more evolved, she would usually try to swallow her anger. As it happened, though, such control could sometimes be more difficult for those around Madonna than it might've been if she had just let out her frustration. One tour employee recalled an incident in Anaheim on 2 June:

'She and one of the musicians accidentally collided into each other on stage during a routine. She was very upset about it. When she got off stage, she went straight towards her dressing room. "I don't want to discuss it," she said. "I am not going to fly off the handle. I'm just going to be . . . cool." She then went into her dressing room and slammed the door. Guy followed her. Five minutes later, he came out looking a little red in the face. "Best to leave her alone," he said. "She's got a lot on her mind. Not feeling well. Stomach flu." The next day [again in Anaheim] was stressful. She didn't want to be bothered, was snapping at everyone . . . very unhappy. Someone who works on her team came over to me and said, "Please stay out of her way, she needs some down time." My feeling was that if she had just ranted and raved like the old Madonna, it might have made things better for her and everyone else.'

Three days later, by the time the tour got to San José, California, Madonna was in better spirits. At a meeting with the entire company, she said, 'I'm still a little pissed off about Anaheim. Maybe some people around here aren't doing their jobs. If so, you know who you are. Straighten up, or get out, that's all I have to say.' Then, as if to ease any tension, she pointed to young Lourdes, who was sitting nearby, and said, 'And that includes you, Lola.' The kid, who was playing with some kind of red string on her wrist, pointed back at her mother and said, 'And that *also* includes *you*.' (The red Kabbalah string Lourdes wore is supposed to ward off negative influences.) It was a funny moment; things seemed better.

On 2 August – the final North American date of the 'Reinvention' tour in Miami, Florida – Madonna received annoying news. She had just finished rehearsing 'American Life' with the dancers when an assistant approached her with an advance copy of a newspaper article everyone had been whispering about all day. 'Give it to me,' Madonna said, anxiously. She snatched the newspaper from the assistant and scanned it quickly. Unexpectedly, tears welled in her eyes. She swallowed hard, as if trying to push them back, and then recovered, quickly. 'What crap,' she said, handing it back to the assistant. 'You'd think the American press could make up better stories than this, wouldn't you? You'd think they'd have more imagination. Has Guy seen this?' she asked. When told that he hadn't, Madonna said, 'Well, show him. The sooner the better. This is all we need right now . . .'

According to the story, Guy wanted a divorce because he believed she'd been cheating on him during the tour. It was totally ridiculous. She usually ignored such prattle from the press. However, this report bothered her. After scanning it, she turned to her troupe of dancers. 'Okay, one more time,' she commanded. 'And this time, let's at least *try* to get it right, shall we?'

'But . . .' someone protested.

She threw that dancer a sharp look. 'Just do it,' she commanded.

A Marriage Not Always Perfect . . . But Perfect Enough

The notion of Madonna cheating on Guy at any time in their marriage, let alone while she was in the middle of a concert tour, was far-fetched. Anyone who knows her knows that she has too much integrity to play around behind her husband's back. She'd had her wild times and she certainly enjoyed them, but by the time she married and had children those days were well behind her. Moreover, there were times during the 'Reinvention' tour when she could barely walk after a concert, let alone find the energy for a romantic fling. Besides, Guy was always around. He had decided to go on the road with Madonna and the children. His presence was invaluable in that he helped give the children a sense of normality while on tour. He became a sort of 'house husband' – except the family was usually nowhere near their home. As one of his friends put it, 'I think, on some level, it bothered him that he couldn't do much about his own career while on the road supporting hers. "Look, I've got my own midlife crisis going on here," I heard him tell her at one of the tour's opening-night parties. "What are you talking about?" she joked. "Don't be ridiculous! Why, you're not even forty yet. Just wait. You'll see what a *real* midlife crisis is."'

'Normally their fights end with him being the one to say "I'm sorry",' said her former manager Caresse Henry of this period in their marriage, 'but she's trying to change that.'

'I think she's trying to be a good wife,' her father, Tony Ciccone, told me at this time. 'When I see her with Guy, I can't get it in my head that she's the same Madonna I raised. It's hard to take it all in. I'm proud that she's been able to keep the marriage going this long.'

He said that he talked to her about 'once a month' and that she seemed very determined to make sure her marriage worked. 'She has seen a lot of divorces in the family,' he said, 'and she doesn't want one. She worries about the children and what it would do to them. She's a lot more traditional than people know. It's how I raised her. She can be strict, too. She got that from me,' he said with a chuckle.

Tony recalled his first interaction with Guy, which was in Michigan when Madonna brought him to meet her father. 'She's tough, that one is,' Tony told Guy of his daughter.

Guy chuckled. 'Tell me about it,' he said.

'Just don't let her get away with running things,' Tony advised. 'She has a habit of wanting to be in control.'

'Has she always been that way?' Guy asked.

'From as far back as I can remember,' Tony said, according to his memory of the conversation. 'She's headstrong. It's not bad usually. I mean, if you like that kind of woman.'

Despite all of the rave reviews on the road, the most important one was still her husband's. 'It's not always perfect between them,' said a good friend of Madonna's. 'But, as she told me, "It's perfect enough".'

After her final North American concert date on the tour in Miami, Madonna hosted a private dinner party for thirty-five of her friends at South Beach's Delano Hotel to mark the end of the USA leg of the tour. Wearing a pink top and blue jeans, her body was as svelte and trim as ever. However, she did look somewhat drained. 'This damn tour has been the toughest thing I have ever had to do,' she told one of the guests. 'And hard on my family, too. My poor husband. He's a saint, I swear to God.'

'Good for you that you've been able to get this far with the show,' the guest responded. 'With the States finished, you only have Europe to go.'

Madonna forced a smile. 'Yeah, well I'll be dead by the time we get to Lisbon [the last stop on the tour, 14 September],' she said. 'But it's worth it,' she added. 'It's hard, but so satisfying . . .' Her voice trailed off. Then, with a thoughtful expression, she added, 'This is not my last tour, though. I'll do it again in a few years. And again a few years after that. I love it too much, even with all the bullshit.'

For his part, Guy seemed absolutely giddy at the after-party – maybe it was the Guinness he was drinking, or maybe he was just happy that he and the 'missus' were about to return to England. Truly, they considered England – in particular their Ashcombe House estate outside London, once owned by British society photographer Cecil Beaton – their home, *not* anywhere in the United States. 'I love to rise to the challenge the UK provides,' she enthused to one reporter. 'You've got the media there [in the United Kingdom] that loves to hate me, and you have the fans there who expect perfection,' Madonna once observed. 'When you're good in England, you know it. And when you suck, you know that, too. It's real. Not like America, where you never know where you stand. In England, they have respect for their icons. In America, everyone is disposable.' (As it would turn out, the eight scheduled British concerts – two in Manchester and six in London – would each go off without a hitch.)

Guy put his arm around the missus as the two left the party, well after two a.m. 'Let's get the hell out of America, shall we?' he said.

His words brought a quick, pleased smile to her face. 'Yes, let's do,' Madonna agreed. 'Let's go home.'

The 'Confessions' Tour

Guy Ritchie thought – *hoped*, actually – that there would be a nice, long break for Madonna after the 'Reinvention' tour because it had been fraught with so many logistical problems and was such a headache for everyone involved (though it was also hugely profitable). However, Madonna had never stopped hinting that she would eagerly embrace the opportunity to go back on the road. Indeed, by mid-2005, she was already planning another big show. Did she really need to tour again and, thus, risk more tumult to her family life? For her, the answer was, unequivocally, *yes*. It obviously wasn't about the money. She just loved performing – always had – and simply did not feel completely fulfilled as an artist unless she was on stage communicating with her audience.

Like most of the previous tours, the new one would be many months in the planning and strategically timed with the release of a new recording for Madonna. In fact, she had just finished a new CD, her tenth and called *Confessions on a Dance Floor*. It was, as the title suggested, a dance package, taking her back to her original roots. It promised to be great fun and maybe even a welcome departure from her more introspective concept albums of late. Because three of the new songs – 'Hung Up', 'Sorry' and 'Get Together' – had been scheduled for eventual release, lavish videos had to be produced for each. It was, as always, a busy time. However, there was a surprising interruption in her plans when Madonna suffered injuries in a horse-riding accident.

Madonna had not been riding horses long and certainly wasn't an experienced equestrienne when she was thrown from one on 16 August 2005. After taking a nasty tumble, she broke her clavicle, scapula, five ribs and the bones in one hand. The injuries were actually much more painful than she let on to the media. However, she was lucky. Obviously, she could have been paralysed – or even killed.

As well as the obvious physical consequences, the accident also took a bit of an emotional toll on Madonna. Indeed, she'd been experiencing quite a few aches and pains in recent years and had become accustomed to not feeling 100 per cent well. However, from the horseback riding accident onwards, she really wouldn't feel quite the same at all. It was as if her age – forty-seven at the time – had finally begun to catch up with her. Some of her joints and muscles would ache more than ever and she would just have to get used to it. It wasn't easy, though. Like most active people as they age, Madonna became frustrated any time she woke up with a stiff back and achy knees. However, to say that such weaknesses slowed her down much would be overstating it. In fact, her next stage show – which she was planning at the time of the accident – would be more physically taxing than any other she'd ever mounted. She would even face any lingering fear of horseback riding she might have had by staging an unbelievably rigorous – and seemingly even dangerous – bronco-riding sequence within the act. When finished, this set piece was produced in a way that suggested that she was defying the notion of anything ever really getting to her or causing her to be anything less than the Madonna she's used to being – including the recent horseback-riding accident.

Work on the new concert monopolized the rest of 2005. In October, Madonna released a short film – *I'm Going to Tell You a Secret* – which was primarily a behind-the-scenes look at the planning of the new tour. However, it was a lot different from her 1996 *In Bed with Madonna* documentary, in that this 'new' Madonna was, obviously, a more mature, sensible woman. Also, the programme allowed a closer look at her family and, during it, Lourdes, in particular, came over as a revelation, as she spoke fluent French and revealed herself to be sophisticated beyond her years.

Meanwhile, in 2005, a gangster film Guy directed called *Revolver* was released (with Ray Liotta and Vincent Pastore) to mixed reviews and not much box-office excitement. It did little for his career.

In the winter of 2005, Madonna and Guy brought Lourdes and Rocco back to Michigan to meet some of her relatives. 'I guess the thing that surprised me most is how well-adjusted she was,' said one of those relatives. 'I had the impression that she was a happy child.

'An interesting thing happened while we were all in the back yard, having a relaxing moment. Madonna spotted a photographer peeking around a corner with a long lens. "Him, over there," I heard her say to Guy. He bolted out of his chair and ran over to where the paparazzo had been seen. By the time he got there, the guy was gone. Guy didn't return, though. When we asked about it, Madonna said, "Guy is very protective of our privacy. He'll stand guard out there until the photographer shows up again, and then he'll let him have it." Maybe an hour later, Guy came back to the gathering. I asked him what happened and he said that, yes, the photographer did show up and, yes, they did have words. "I'm not Sean Penn," he said, laughing. "So, no, I did not beat him up. I just told him to bugger off, and promised that when we got back to Europe I would set something up for his photo agency to get some shots of the missus and Lourdes. It doesn't have to be a big war," he told me. "Sometimes things can just be settled peacefully." I asked him how

Madonna would handle it. He laughed and said "The guy would have a black eye about now if I let her handle it."'

In November 2005 the *Confessions* CD was released to great critical and fan response. Then, in February 2006, Madonna made official her tour plans with an announcement on *The Ellen DeGeneres Show* – a USA chat programme. She revealed that the dates would begin in the summer.

'Uh-oh. Here we go again,' said Guy, who was home in London. He was having drinks at a pub with close friends. 'Just what we need,' he said with a resigned smile. 'Another tour.'

Guy hadn't gone to America with his wife for her TV appearance because he had business commitments in England. 'And that's the truth,' he insisted, according to one observer. 'Plus, I wanted to stay home with the kids, anyway.' (Lourdes was nine and Rocco five.) 'The missus knows I am with her in spirit, all the time,' he concluded.

Of course, the fact that Guy didn't make it to America only served to heat up yet more ongoing rumours of marital discord. Some stories even had it that he was upset that Madonna had been spending too much time with twenty-eight-year-old Stuart Price, who worked with her on *Confessions on a Dance Floor*. Even *she* was taken aback by the rumours about Price – and it takes a lot to surprise her when it comes to stories about herself in the media.

In fact, Madonna had been spending time with Price because the two were busy collaborating on how to translate the *Confessions* CD into a successful road show. Stuart is actually a dedicated professional who has only spoken well of his experiences with Madonna both with the *Confessions* album and the subsequent tour. 'The real eye-opener was about how focused she was on avoiding the kind of over-the-top, excessive, entourage-in-the-studio environment that I had expected,' he recalled in an interview. 'It was the total opposite, really. She helped to create an environment where we were like two kids working together in a studio. She was really . . . I don't want to say "smart", but she was really *honest* about music. She's really instinctive in understanding that dance music comes from a very minimal way of working. It doesn't come from throwing lots of money on a lavish production.

'We spent five or six weeks in my apartment; the studio used to be upstairs in the loft. I would work on a track overnight, then she would come in and we'd start messing around. She would do vocal melodies and I would come up with a few ideas, and then she'd go, "Okay, I'm gonna go home and think about it." Then she'd come back the next day and have the hook for "Hung Up" or the chorus for "Sorry". Then I would carry on working on more tracks to keep us going. It was more of a really fluid and almost childlike environment than anything that seemed too serious.

'They always say that an album sounds like the time that you had making it,' he concluded. 'I know that with that album, it was a super-productive time, but it was also really fun and natural. And I think that comes across in the way it sounds.'

When asked to comment on such stories as the Stuart Price rumour on the DeGeneres programme, Madonna laughed off the gossip, saying: 'Really? We [she and Guy] split up? Oh, okay. Well, he's still calling me every five minutes,' she added, her tone purposely sarcastic. She insisted that her visit to the States without Guy was not a sign of any problem in their relationship, adding, 'He works and I work and we can't always co-ordinate our schedules together.' However, she added that the longest they had been apart was 'two weeks about five years ago. And now it's never more than a week.' She also denied the stories that the two had grown apart because she was more devoted to Kabbalah than Guy. 'I would say he studies but probably not as enthusiastically as I do. He does in his own way – he's more into the intellectual side of it than I am.' She further insisted that raising their children was more important than religion. 'I didn't meet him and say, "Oh, you have to believe in the same things I believe in." Anyway, when I met him he was an atheist and I was a Christian.' However, she said that, like her,

Guy now had a strong faith in God, adding: 'Maybe he always did, but Brits are sort of allergic to the idea.'

Backstage at *The Ellen DeGeneres Show* a fan actually approached Madonna to ask again about the rumours. Though she was racing to get somewhere, Madonna made a point to stop and talk with the admirer. Clearly, she wanted every opportunity to set the record straight. 'I'm sort of amazed that people would think I could do that, have an affair, I mean,' she said while signing a glossy photograph. 'It's as if everything I have ever said about being fair and decent and honourable – all of my spiritual beliefs – means nothing. How could anyone believe that I'm the kind of person who would do this to my husband and my family? *That*, to me, is what's really shocking.'

'Well, I never believed it, anyway,' said the fan.

'You'd better not,' Madonna said, embracing the devotee. 'If my fans don't know me, who does?'

Lucky

8 February 2006. Wearing a lavender leotard with a glittery corset, her blonde hair falling to her shoulders in soft waves, Madonna looked at least twenty years younger than forty-seven. Perhaps a giveaway to her true age, however, was that she was so out of breath, perspiring heavily. She had just walked off stage after her performance for the Grammy Awards at the Staples Center of Los Angeles, California. 'Oh my God, I'm too *old* for this shit!' she exclaimed, maybe only half-joking. 'Look at me,' she concluded. 'I'm half dead, and I'm *soaked*!'

Suddenly, as if on cue, she was engulfed by frantic-looking people. Someone handed her a towel. Someone else, a bottle of water. Another person ran to her with a piece of cardboard and began fanning her furiously. 'And who the hell are *you?*' she asked him. 'You don't even work for me!' He just kept fanning away, all the while babbling about how great she had just been on stage. She couldn't help but laugh.

It was true: her performance of her recent international hit, 'Hung Up', had been stunning. Culled from *Confessions on a Dance Floor*, it's a terrific song, sampling the ABBA classic 'Gimme, Gimme, Gimme' and combining it with one of Madonna's most infectious melodies.

Three months later, in May 2006, the 'Confessions' tour would begin in Los Angeles, California. It was scheduled to end in Tokyo in September of that same year (though it would end earlier). The show's choreography was more intricate than ever – if that was even possible – demanding from her everything Madonna had to give to it. The music was taxing her voice, pushing her to hit notes on some of the songs in the same way she did almost two decades earlier. There were seven costume changes. Still, Madonna persevered every night, usually even topping the previous evening's performance.

Frank Bruno of Los Angeles has been a Madonna fan since the age of fifteen, in 1983. Given his unabashed admiration for her, he may seem a less than objective witness of her 'Confessions' show. However, his review of the concert does reflect a general consensus not only of fans, but also critics. As he put it: 'One of the reasons I've always loved Madonna is because she's consistently thumbed her nose at convention. She's done pretty much what she's wanted to do every step along the way. But after the *Sex* and *Erotica* period it was as if she felt she had to bite her tongue and conform to societal standards. And when she had her children and married, I was afraid we'd lost her for good. Though subsequent concerts – the 'Drowned World' and 'Reinvention' tours – were amazing, those performances did lack a certain spirit. Was she concerned that her children might be watching? Was her behaviour appropriate for a wife? I'm not sure what was going on in her head, but those shows lacked the edge and grittiness of what had shot her to stardom. But then, along came the "Confessions" tour.

'As if a magical finger had been snapped, the show began with the goddess descending from the heavens above in a giant disco ball. Everything I had loved about the Queen of Pop seemed to suddenly resurface. She looked more beautiful than ever. Her dancing was the most active since the "Blond Ambition" tour, tearing up songs like "Music Inferno" and "La Isla Bonita". She was brash while grabbing her crotch and suggestively riding a boom box. Her voice was impeccable on "Substitute for Love". She was controversial while suspended from a cross in "Live to Tell". Most importantly, it felt as if she was finally having fun again, letting her hair down. On "Let It Will Be", the audience was treated to seeing Madonna cut loose on stage like she never had before in any concert.

'This show, more than any other, was the culmination of Madonna's entire career wrapped up into one tightly woven spectacle, aiming to please her core fans as well as excite a younger new audience. Truly, it brought her full circle. From her roots as a street urchin to musical icon, she delivered to her audience *exactly* what they wanted: pure entertainment – and all as she approached her twenty-fifth year in the business.'

Amazingly, all thirty-four shows in the States and Canada would be sell-outs. The tour was a success, but, one had to wonder, at what price? After Madonna finished her opening night performance at Madison Square in New York on 28 June 2006, she and Guy hosted a small gathering for the show's cast. At one point, a photographer asked them to pose for a picture. Madonna – taking control, as always – grabbed Guy by the waist and pulled him in for the shot. He glared at her. She returned the look. Finally, they posed – but both with frozen smiles. 'He can't wait for this tour to be over,' Madonna explained to the cameraman. 'I can't blame him. It's tough on him and the kids. I keep saying I'll never do it again, but after every tour ends I'm somehow ready to go back and do another.'

'Yes, well, that's true, isn't?' Guy said.

'You love it, and you know it,' Madonna remarked, trying to keep things light.

'No, dear. It's *you* who love it,' Guy said, his voice flat and devoid of expression. 'Not I.'

Later, the two of them were seen huddling in a corner, each with a stern expression.

Afterwards, this reporter asked Guy if there was any sort of troubling issue between him and his wife. 'If there was a problem, do you really think I would stand here and tell you about it,' he asked with a tolerant smile. 'No,' he said. 'I would lie to you, wouldn't I? And then, later, you would figure it out that I had lied, and you and I would be at odds, wouldn't we? So, rather than have all of that be the record, let me just say this to you now: "No comment."' Then, with a smile to ease the moment, he walked away.

Years later, in 2016, Madonna would tell Howard Stern that one of the reasons she continues to work is 'because I'm an artist and I'm tortured. I'm a masochist and I like to create.' Guy would have to agree; however, in his defence, it can't be easy living with such a character. Adding to the couple's stress level, no doubt, was the fact that he hadn't been able to latch onto a project that would reinvent him in the eyes of critics and fans after the critically assailed *Swept Away*. His most recent film, *Revolver*, had done nothing to enhance his reputation. 'He has to work. It's important to his image of himself,' says his friend Lawrence Solomon, 'and work was hard to come by. So, yes, it's safe to say that the last year or so has been a struggle.'

'Look, they've been married a long time,' Madonna's father, Tony, explained to me at this time. 'They're not in the honeymoon phase, they're in the *real life phase*. If you don't see them kissing and hugging all the time, it doesn't mean they aren't getting along. It means they're married.'

It was decided early on that Guy would not accompany Madonna on all of the stops on the 'Confessions' tour but, instead, be present for select dates. He would spend the rest of the time on his own, working on new film ideas. 'This was a decision the Ritchies came to on their own,' adds a source. 'I would say that they realized that it's important for Guy to have a career, as well as Madonna. And he can't do that following her all over the globe.'

As it happened, the time away from one another was time well spent for Madonna. Being away from Guy for weeks at a time definitely seemed to remind her of what she had in him and in her marriage. She was unhappy without him at her side, say those in her circle, and on the phone with him as much as possible. In June, she reached what might be considered a somewhat ironic turning-point when she went to see Carlos Leon, Lourdes' father, play a small role in *The Threepenny Opera* while she was in New York.

After the show, she went backstage to say hello. According to one friend who witnessed their backstage meeting, Carlos spent most of the time raving about how lucky Madonna was to be so happily married.

'You have it made,' Carlos told her.

'What do you mean?' she asked.

'Look, you have a great guy, he's devoted to you, he's an amazing father to Lourdes and Rocco. You don't know how lucky you are, Madonna. Say,' he asked, looking around, 'where is he, anyway?'

Madonna seemed a little embarrassed, according to one account. 'Well, you know, he has a life, too, Carlos,' she said. 'He can't be at my side every single second. Yes, I know I'm lucky. I do.' She looked sad, though. Carlos knew her well. 'Come over here, girl, let me talk to you,' he said. He then pulled her aside and had what appeared to be a heart-to-heart conversation with her. He probably felt he knew how to appeal to her to not take a chance on jeopardizing what he viewed as a special relationship not only in her life, but in his daughter's.

After that conversation with Carlos, Madonna decided to cut the tour short and end it in September, cancelling the Australia dates. Who knows for certain if Carlos influenced this decision; there were probably other factors, but he may have helped things along. For the record, Madonna said the decision was made so that she could get the kids back to school. 'Of course, Guy could have done that for her and she could go on with the show as planned,' said one source at the time, 'but she's starting to see, I believe, that she needs to be home with her husband and kids for a while.'

In fact, by the time she returned to England, Madonna was seriously considering something she'd been thinking about for some time: adoption. Her decision was in alignment with another important choice she'd made at this time. At the end of the summer in 2006, she announced a major effort to assist orphans in Malawi, Africa, pledging to raise at least $3 million for charity programmes there. 'Now that I have children and now that I have what I consider to be a better perspective on life,' she explained, 'I have felt responsible for the children of the world.' She said that she was also planning a $1 million documentary about the orphans' plight in Africa, as well as helping to implement medical and financial aid programmes through a new venture called the Raising Malawi Foundation.

Adopting David

It was 4 October 2006 when Madonna and Guy Ritchie arrived in Africa to visit her Raising Malawi project and establish facilities to care for and educate more than 4,000 orphans in the impoverished small African republic of Malawi. In five days, construction would commence on a new children's home for AIDS orphans in the village of Mphandula, thirty miles outside the Malawian capital. However, there was another intention behind the Ritchies' visit. For months they had been sorting through reams of paperwork necessary to adopt a baby from Malawi. In fact, this visit to Malawi was not their first. They'd previously managed to sneak in and out of the country twice without press scrutiny while going through the adoption process. They'd met the baby – an infant named David Banda – a couple of months earlier at the Home of Hope Orphan Care Centre in Mchinji, a village near the Zambian border. However, contrary to cynical press reports, a gaggle of infants had not been paraded in front of Madonna for any sort of callous 'selection process'. 'Because I'm financing a documentary about orphans in Malawi, I was allowed to view footage and photographs of a lot of the children,' she later clarified. 'An eight-year-old girl who is living with HIV was holding this child [David]. I became transfixed by him, but I didn't know I was going to adopt him. I was just drawn to him . . .

'I decided that I had an embarrassment of riches and that there were too many children in the world without parents or families to love them,' Madonna would also explain many years later, in 2013. 'I applied to an international adoption agency and went through all the bureaucracy, testing and waiting that everyone else goes through when they adopt.

'As fate would have it, in the middle of this process a woman reached out to me from a small country in Africa called Malawi and told me about the millions of children orphaned by AIDS. Before you could say "Zikomo Kwambiri", I was in the airport in Lilongwe heading to an orphanage in Mchinji, where I met my son David. And that was the beginning of another daring chapter of my life.'

Actually, it would seem that Madonna had adoption on her mind all the way back to the 1990s. I remember once interviewing her in the fall of 1992 when the subject rose. It was on the occasion of the publication of her notorious *Sex* book. In that book, she had a great line – she actually had quite a few – which was really about female empowerment, but could still be deemed offensive: 'My pussy has nine lives.' One had to wonder if it was something she would ever wish to repeat to any children she may one day have. Of course, I had to ask the question. 'Well, *my* kids aren't going to care about any joke I ever made about my pussy, which by the way is pretty funny and very true, or about any artsy pictures I ever took,' she told me. 'In fact,' she added, 'the children I adopt are going to have a healthy and well-regulated home life.'

I was taken aback. 'Adoption?' I asked.

'Yes, adoption,' she said. 'I absolutely will adopt one day, and that's all I want to say about it, for now.'

Flashing ahead fourteen years, Madonna was now in the process of officially adopting David Banda, whose biological mother had died after childbirth. His father – a poor thirty-two-year-old farm worker named Yohane – eagerly approved of the adoption plans when he was approached by officials. As it happened, David had spent most of his life at the Home of Hope Orphan Care Centre with about 500 other babies. Though he was taken care of, he was unwell. Madonna brought a paediatrician with her to examine all of the children at the orphanage and learned that David had tested negative for tuberculosis, malaria, HIV and other common illnesses striking African orphans. Yet still, he had some other problems. 'When I met him, he was extremely ill,' she would recall. 'He had severe pneumonia, and he could hardly breathe. I was in a state of panic, because I didn't want to leave him in the orphanage because I knew they didn't have medication to take care of him. We got permission to take him to a clinic to have a bronchial dilator put on him.'

Even given the baby's dire condition, the Ritchies did not lightly come to the decision to adopt. Matthew Hamilton, a friend of Guy's in Los Angeles, says, 'There was some concern as to how Lourdes and Rocco would take to the idea. Madonna and Guy spent a lot of time discussing it with them, making sure they were okay with it. Lourdes told Guy, "I think we have to do it, it's our *responsibility* to do it." Honest to God, the girl seems like a forty-year-old woman living in a nine-year-old's body . . .'

Despite Madonna's global celebrity, she found that it would be far from easy for her to adopt a child. She wasn't going to be given any kind of preferential treatment, that much was clear. In fact, there were to be quite a few upsetting missteps along the way. At times, the uncertainty would be almost more than Madonna could bear – especially when news of her plans leaked out prematurely on 5 October, the day the Ritchies arrived in Malawi. On that day, an official in Malawi stated publicly that Madonna had *already* adopted. Of course, he was wrong. In fact, to the contrary, the Ritchies had actually just learned that they might not be able to circumvent Malawian legislation that, if interpreted a certain way, prohibited inter-country adoptions. Madonna thought her attorneys had been able to cut through such red tape because it wasn't an actual law as much as it was just an interpretation of an old restriction. However, that had not been the case. Making matters even more sensitive, by this time she had already bonded with David after having spent time with him at the orphanage. The thought that it might not work out for her was heart-wrenching.

Madonna also feared that certain important government officials might think the premature announcement was her idea too, and maybe even some kind of publicity ploy designed to strong-arm them in the matter. Liz Rosenberg quickly issued a curt statement saying, simply, that the story was not true. Indeed, who knew if the adoption would even happen now? 'I'm heartbroken,' Madonna said. 'I truly wanted to do this, and I still think I will – though, now, I'm not sure how.'

Somehow, Madonna's attorneys were eventually able to come to terms with the Malawi government and work out the adoption process in a way that made everyone happy. So, on 12 October, Judge Andrew Nyirenda authorized an 'interim adoption' of David. Penston Kilimbe, director of child welfare services in the Ministry of Gender, Child Welfare and Community Services, said of the Ritchies, 'They have followed the normal processes. This has been going on for some time. Now, this is the completion point.' Actually, two things had occurred: first of all, the Ritchies were given permission to take the baby out of the country for eighteen months while the rest of the paperwork was being finalized. Secondly, a new law was established to make such a thing even possible.

Of course, to some observers, it looked as if Madonna had somehow used her money and power to influence the government to get what she wanted. Her critics were mistaken, though. 'I assure you it doesn't matter who you are or how much money you have, nothing goes fast in Africa,' she would say. 'There are no adoption laws in Malawi. And I was warned by my social worker that because there were no known laws in Malawi, they were more or less going to have to make them up as we went along. She said, "Pick Ethiopia. Go to Kenya. Don't go to Malawi because you're just going to get a hard time."'

While at the courthouse on the twelfth, Madonna and Guy also had the opportunity to finally meet David's natural father, Yohane Banda. 'They are a lovely couple,' he would later say of them. 'She asked me many questions. She and her husband seem happy with David. I am happy for him.' Banda added that his son would make regular visits to Malawi. 'He will know his roots,' says Banda.

Damage Control

Madonna is a woman who has long been accustomed to problem-solving in her life and career. She's been doing it for years, leaping seemingly unscathed from one controversy to another, all the while building the image of a strong, self-reliant and enlightened woman. Of course, it's not all an act. She actually has been all of those things at different times in her life, but it's only because she, as a celebrity, has availed herself of so many PR opportunities that the masses actually know about it. However, it was not as easy for her to be as understood by the public after she and Guy were finally home in London with David. Any joyful time she might have had with the family was interrupted by ongoing public criticism of the adoption. For instance, the conveners of the Scottish Parliament's cross-party group on Malawi accused her of exploiting the poor children of Malawi for publicity. Spokeswoman co-convener Karen Gillon put it this way: 'This smacks of celebrity-itis and I think it's more about Madonna's needs than the child's. Family is important in Malawi and I think this child belongs with his relatives. Perhaps the money she spends on this child would have been better invested in the whole community.' Moreover, in an open letter to Madonna, the private Malawian child advocacy group, Eye of the Child, questioned whether foreign adoptions were in the best interests of children. Simply put, there was a lot of negative press. Madonna felt she had no choice but to embark on a sort of media blitz to explain her position.

On the morning of 24 October 2006, Madonna walked into a London hotel suite to prepare for a satellite interview with talkshow host Oprah Winfrey. She carried with her the stress of recent times. 'Bring back my youth, will you?' she asked a make-up artist before going on camera. 'After what's been going on,' she said with a sigh, 'I feel twenty years older than I did last month.' Her blonde hair hung loosely at her shoulders, her dark roots seeming more pronounced as if hairstyling had been the last thing on her mind.

Once she was on the air, though (the show was taped and broadcast the next day), Madonna appeared completely composed and in control. 'I didn't realize that the adoption was causing any controversy until I came back [to London],' she said. 'There were a million film crews in the airport and press camped outside my door. I don't read newspapers or watch television, but all of my friends have let me know what everybody's talking about and what's going on in the news. So, it didn't really hit me until I got back to England. It's pretty shocking.'

Madonna often says that she does not pay attention to the media. However, that seems a little hard to believe. She's too smart about world events to be as closed-minded about 'newspapers and television' as her comments suggest. Unless she gets her information by osmosis, she must depend on the media in some way. In fact, people close to her say that she does keep abreast of what's going on, especially when it relates to her and her family. If one looks at her career, she has obviously never been opposed to using the media to explain herself. Of course, the very reason she even appeared on the Oprah Winfrey television programme was to explain her side of the adoption story, rehabilitate her image and show pictures of David with the family in order to demonstrate how well he had already adjusted to the Ritchie home.

It was only when she spoke of David's biological father, Yohane, that Madonna's confidence seemed to crack. 'He looked into my eyes and he said to me that he was very grateful that I was going to give his son a life, and that if he had kept his son with him in the village he would have buried him,' she said, her voice cracking. 'I didn't feel that I needed any more confirmation that I was doing the right thing and that I needed his blessing.' She seemed hurt, maybe even a little worried, and perhaps with good reason.

Yohane Banda – a potato and onion crop farmer – lives in Lipunga, a village of just 300 people in the foothills of far western Malawi. He has buried two other children, one as a result of malaria. As earlier stated, his wife died giving birth to David. He first contributed to the headlines about Madonna's adoption on 12 October by publicly declaring that he was happy about giving up his son. 'I know he will be very happy in America,' he said at that time. A week later, he criticized human rights organizations that had been attempting to stop the adoption. 'Where were these people when David was struggling in the orphanage?' he asked. It definitely seemed that he was on Madonna's side. However, in a startling twist, he reversed his position on 22 October. It was then that he claimed he'd totally misunderstood the adoption process and had been under the impression that Madonna was merely taking the baby to educate and raise . . . and that she was then going to return him! 'It would have been better for him to continue staying at the orphanage,' he declared, 'because I see no reason why my child should be given away forever when I can feed him.'

In truth, as Madonna explained on *Oprah*, every detail of the adoption had been explained to Yohane Banda. She personally told him of her intentions, and in the presence of the judge. Banda was then asked several times in court if he understood what was going on, and he had said he did. 'So what is going on?' Madonna asked privately when told of Banda's claims in the press. 'Someone needs to find out what's happening here!' Naturally, she was quite upset. 'She wasn't really angry at Yohane,' said one of her intimates. 'How could she be? Look at his tragic circumstances. He's uneducated. He's poor. She understands the way the media works.'

Indeed, Madonna soon came to the conclusion that because Yohane doesn't speak English (he speaks the local language of Chichewa) he was easily manipulated by a reporter looking for a new angle to a story that had already received too much international coverage. As she told Oprah, 'This is a simple man who comes from a village, who has nothing, and suddenly he is besieged by the media of the world and they have spun things out of control and brought nothing but chaos to his life. I believe that the press is manipulating this information out of him. I believe he's been terrorized by the media. They have asked him things repeatedly and have put words in his mouth. They have spun a story that is completely false.'

Who knows if Madonna's suspicions are true? After she gave the interview to Oprah, *Time* sent a reporter to Banda's native home for comment. He held his own with the *Time* journalist and did what he could to set the record straight . . . or at least he changed his story, again. He told *Time* that he would not contest the adoption nor would any of his relatives because doing so would be 'killing David's future'. Moreover, he said that he was 'grateful to [Madonna] for helping my child'. He'd been spending more time with reporters, he added, than he had been 'tending to my onions and tomatoes'. Then, in yet *another* interview with another publication, he suggested that it wasn't just the media that had become an intrusion in his life. Apparently, representatives from the Human Rights Consultative Committee would also not stop pestering him. He said that he had actually been hiding from them, they'd pestered him so much. Then, referring to his earlier statement about not understanding the adoption process, he concluded, 'My comments were taken out of context and I hope Madonna is not angry. I am afraid she may get angry and frustrated and decide to dump my son.' Of course, since Banda's many statements to the press had to be translated from Chichewa, who knows what he really said – or the context in which he said it?

As a result of the controversy, there was some talk in Madonna's organization of possibly having her return to Malawi to personally request that Banda stop giving interviews as this would be in David's best interests. However, she must have realized that if she did so and he spoke to the media anyway, the first thing out of his mouth would likely be that she'd gone all the way to Africa to shut him up. And how would *that* play out in the court of public opinion? Truly, she was in a tough spot where this man was concerned, especially since she and Guy were still in an evaluation phase of Malawi's ever-evolving adoption process. They had not been officially approved – thus the 'interim adoption' – and so anything that occurred during the eighteen-month trial period that reflected poorly on them could prove damaging to their case. Though it seemed inconceivable after all they'd been through, the baby could still be taken away from them. Therefore, the problem posed by David's natural father was more than just one of public relations. 'It's unthinkable, but it is something they are dealing with,' said a relative of Madonna's in Michigan during this time. 'They could lose David! But they've already integrated him into the family. They love him. Rocco and Lourdes, as well. Last week, they had a gathering of friends at their home [in London] to introduce David. But a dark cloud hung over the proceedings . . .'

The Big Five-Zero

By the fall of 2007, Madonna had almost finished the recording of a new album. Her fans were excited about the possibilities of still more hits for her when word leaked out that she'd been working with Justin Timberlake and popular hip-hop producers Timbaland and Pharrell on a few of the new album's tracks. When pressed for information about the recordings, Timberlake told this writer, 'I don't want to give you details, because she'll either kill me or she'll have *me* kill *you*. And I think we have enough celebrities going to jail!'*

Also in the autumn of 2007, Madonna was in the planning stages of another tour, set to be launched in 2008. Predictably, the Ritchie household balance was bound to be thrown into chaos by the decision to tour. However, they had all been down that road so many times before that, by this time, it was old news. 'Obviously she can be demanding and a little difficult when she's planning these things, and that's an ongoing problem,' said a source at the time.

Perhaps another problem faced by the Ritchies by the autumn of 2007 was that Guy's career still had not taken flight, whereas everything Madonna touched, as usual, seemed to turn to gold. For instance, the previous year's 'Confessions on a Dance Floor' tour set the record for the highest-grossing tour *of all time* by a female artist – more than $260 million in ticket sales. However, the last

* In the spring of 2007, Madonna released a song called 'Hey You', recorded specifically for the Live Earth charity concert at Wembley and available to the public as a free download on the Internet. An underwhelming folk-like production, it's not really considered even by fans to be a legitimate release by her, but more of a novelty record. Madonna's 7 July performance of it before 70,000 people at Wembley (and many millions of international TV watchers) also wasn't memorable, though the rest of her set – 'Ray of Light', 'La Isla Bonita' and 'Hung Up' – couldn't have been more dazzling.

time Guy had had any kind of success had been his film *Snatch* in 2000. When *Forbes*' annual list of the 'Celebrity 100' was released in 2007, Madonna came in at number 3, after having earned a whopping $72 million in the previous year, mostly her take from the 'Confessions' tour. It was difficult to imagine how much Guy might have made in the same period, but it was obviously much less. And now, as if she didn't have enough on her plate, Madonna had even begun venturing into *his* territory by directing her own short film – a movie called *Filth and Wisdom*. Might this have proved an irritation for Guy? Did she have to conquer *every* challenge, even those that were customarily his? But, in her defence, Guy knew who he was marrying when he married Madonna: a multitasker of the highest level. Eventually, her many ambitions were bound to cut into his own.

Not surprisingly, Madonna also acquitted herself well at Guy's profession. Eugene Hutz, frontman for the New York gypsy/punk band Gogol Bordello (who contributed to a raucous rendition of 'La Isla Bonita' with Madonna at the Live Earth concert), appeared in the 'short' and praised Madonna's directorial skills. 'I think she was fantastic,' he recalled of the production. 'She's such a dynamic force. You can always measure a director by how specific he or she is, and she was very specific. She had very energetic visions but at the same time there was a lot of room for me to do my own thing. It was super fun and perfectly respectable, and it ended up being quite a collaborative project.' Hutz said that he contributed dialogue for the script of the forty-five-minute piece – requiring him to dress in drag – which also stars Richard E. Grant (*Gosford Park, Spice World*) and Stephen Graham (*Snatch, Gangs of New York*). Gogol Bordello also performed in the film, with the soundtrack scheduled to feature three of its songs. *Filth and Wisdom* was expected to debut at the 2008 Sundance Film Festival.

With Madonna getting early high marks for her skills as a director, there was – as always – much media commentary in the autumn of 2007 about the effect of her ambition on her relationship with Guy. Obviously, Madonna – who turned forty-nine in August of 2007 – and Guy – thirty-eight – had always had an explosive relationship and it remained that way. The first time I met Guy in 2001, I wondered how he would ever survive as Madonna's mate. As he sat at the bar of the Polo Lounge in the Beverly Hills Hotel, he struck me as being easygoing and charming. He even looked young and naive, at least to my eyes. I remember thinking, 'Well, he can certainly forget about ever winning an argument with Madonna. Nice guys always finish last with that one.'

I was wrong. From the beginning, he presented a real challenge to Madonna. It was one of the reasons, in fact, that she was first attracted to him. She wanted an intellectual equal, and she found one in Guy.

In the autumn of 2007, Guy was at work on a new action film called *RocknRolla*, due for release in late 2008. Madonna visited the set several times, much to the enjoyment of his stars, including Gerard Butler, who described her as being 'very cool'. Guy was still surprised to see the stunned reaction to his wife's presence. 'One tends to forget,' he said, 'that there's somewhat of a drum roll whenever Mrs Ritchie walks into a room.'

It had become clear that Malawian child welfare officials were still at a loss as to how to process the adoption of little David. Much to Madonna's and Guy's dismay, they had even missed an appointment to monitor David's progress in the Richie home, which had been scheduled for April 2007. Though unthinkable, it remained a possibility that the Ritchies could actually lose David and that he could actually be sent back to Malawi! Of course, Madonna never gives up on anything without a good fight, especially something in which she's truly invested. She would fight for David, just as she has over the years for everything else that's truly mattered to her.

As she approached fifty, Madonna had to be proud of herself. Doubtless, when she was a kid growing up in Michigan she could never have imagined the kind of life she'd create as an adult. Or could she? After all, she always did seem to know exactly what she wanted and how to go about getting it, didn't she? It was clear that she had no intention of slowing down, either. At a time when the shelf life of most pop stars expired by at *least* the age of forty, there always seemed to be a new commercial proposition for Madonna. In fact, one would be hard-pressed to name any other contemporary performer who remained relevant in middle age, who still inspired as well as entertained – and who worked as hard as Madonna did – and does – in the recording studio and on the concert stage.

In her private life, though, Madonna was actually like many people her age. She had her daily aches and pains – despite her stunning athleticism on stage – and couldn't help but sometimes fret: about her marriage, her children and sometimes, though not very often, even her career. She said that she didn't sleep as well as she once did because she's got so much on her mind. However, it's not all that bad. 'I'm living a good life,' she concluded in 2007. 'How dare I complain about anything? I'm blessed beyond my wildest imagination.' Moreover, as she approached her milestone birthday, she said that 'along with age comes the freedom to be authentic' – as if she ever had any trouble doing that in the past. 'Just watch out,' she concluded with characteristic humour. 'When I hit the big five-zero, if you think I was a bitch before, well . . . just you wait!

Cracks

Maybe it was inevitable that Madonna's marriage to Guy Ritchie wouldn't last. However, its failure most certainly wasn't for lack of trying on both their parts. Some in their lives felt that, by early 2008, they were such different people than they'd been when they wed that there was simply no way they could stay together. This isn't exactly true. In many ways they hadn't changed at all – and maybe *that* was the problem. Madonna was still as invested in her career as ever, determined to do her best work at all times, interested in every small detail, and often at the expense of her private life with Guy and the children. Meanwhile, Guy was just as adamant that he was tired of the pace his wife had been keeping since their marriage began, and he wanted nothing more than for her to take a break, not only for his sake but for the sake of their children.

Madonna had always known how seriously her split focus could affect her marriage. For the last seven years, it had been a difficult tight-rope walk for her as she pursued her passion while, at the same time, tried to give her all not only to Guy, but also to Lourdes, now 11; Rocco, 7, and, of course, David 2. 'I was with them one night in London when they were having a very heated argument about the raising of their children and how to square it with Madonna's career concerns. Guy became so flustered, he accidentally poured his coffee into the creamer, instead of the other way around,' recalled one of their friends. 'That's how upset he was!'

For how many more years could they continue to engage in the same disagreements? Add to it Guy's exasperation about his own career and desire to continue to do his own best work, and it was a recipe for marital disaster. 'If you were to really look back on his relationship with Madonna, it's been one scene of emasculation after another,' said a friend of Guy's back in 2008. 'For instance, he is constantly thought of in the media as "Mr. Madonna", which upsets him no end. He knows he's been viewed as a purse holder for a long time.'

It was also true that the press was crueller than ever to Guy during coverage of the adoption of David Banda. The process, at least as described by the media, certainly didn't sound like an equal decision for the Ritchies. In fact, Madonna was the one who'd found the baby in Malawi, she was the one who felt an immediate connection to him, and she was the one who then convinced Guy they should adopt him. Guy didn't fight it, of course. However, it also wasn't his idea, and the media knew it. Suddenly, they had three children and it looked as if he had nothing to say about it.

Before he met Madonna, Guy was an open, accessible person. What had become frustrating to him in recent years was his inability to be specific about the problems in his life, even to his closest friends and relatives. Because he felt he was living under a shroud of secrecy, he had little to talk about. After all, one can only talk about sports and politics for so long before the conversation turns to a personal life. However, he was afraid to say anything to anyone about his problems, about Madonna, about any of it. To live like that, afraid that whatever he said could end up in one of the tabloids and cause a huge row with the missus became, as one source put it, 'not the kind of life Guy wanted to live.'

Madonna had her own problems. In early March 2008, she and a few friends had lunch at a small café in New York. As she picked at her salad, it was clear from her demeanour that the last couple of months had not been easy for her, either. She looked pale, her face drawn with anxiety. 'You know me,' she told the two friends with whom she was dining, 'and you know that I don't like failure. People are thinking my marriage is over? Well, I can tell you that it's not. There's always been stress between me and Guy. That's nothing new.'

It was true, of course. They'd always had their issues. However, they'd also always been able to work through them. Not lately, though.

On Tuesday night, 18 March 2008, Madonna and Guy made their first public appearance in quite some time when they dined at the upscale Italian restaurant, Harry's, in Mayfair. Seldom had a famous married couple seemed more uncomfortable to be with one another. Madonna, her blonde hair parted in the middle and then pulled into a short ponytail, seemed sad and lost in her own thoughts. Guy looked prickly and annoyed by the attention they received from paparazzi. 'How are things going?' one of the lens men asked. Guy didn't respond, and he usually did at least try to chat with photographers. For her part, Madonna forced a weak smile. Then, as they were getting into their car, she let something slip that was perhaps telling. 'It's been like this all week,' she was heard telling Guy. 'I just hope tomorrow is a better day.'

If, with their night on the town, the Ritchies were hoping to send a message that all was well between them in order to refute persistent rumours, it didn't work. In fact, it might have been better if they had just stayed home because their awkward appearance only served to convince people that there really was trouble on the home front.

One reason for the scrutiny of the Ritchies' marriage at this time was because Guy had become noticeably absent from major public events in his wife's life. For instance, he hadn't been present when Madonna was inducted into the Rock and Roll Hall of Fame in New York earlier on 10 March.

The Hall of Fame's twenty-third annual induction ceremony was held at the Waldorf-Astoria in New York City and telecast live on VH1 Classic. Madonna – in her first year of eligibility – was named alongside John Mellencamp, Leonard Cohen, the Ventures and the Dave Clark Five. She was introduced by Justin Timberlake, who had just collaborated with her on the song '4 Minutes' from her upcoming album, *Hard Candy*.

Justin recalled that while they were working on the song, he came into the studio not feeling well. Madonna suggested a B-12 shot. He thought she was going to call a doctor. Instead, she pulled from her designer purse a Ziploc bag of B-12 syringes. 'Drop 'em,' she said, before she gave Justin a shot. Then, she added, 'Nice top shelf,' referring to his bum. 'It was one of the greatest days of my life,' he joked. 'That is what Madonna will always be to us. The shot in the ass when we really need it.' During her acceptance speech Madonna, who agreed with Justin that she is a 'control freak' corrected him. 'I said, "pull your pants down",' she asserted. She then gave a thoughtful (if also a tad long) oration during which she acknowledged not only many of her chief supporters, such as her dance teacher from thirty-five years earlier, Christopher Flynn, but critics of her life, too: 'The ones that said I was talentless, that I was chubby, that I couldn't sing, that I was a one-hit-wonder. They pushed me to be better, and I am grateful for their resistance.'

For Guy to have missed such an important moment in Madonna's life definitely suggested a growing discord between them. Then, to make matters even troubling, Madonna had acknowledged just about everyone in her life – including people she hadn't seen or talked to in decades – yet, she didn't even mention her husband.

Prior to the Rock and Roll Hall of Fame induction, Guy had also missed Madonna's Oscar party in Beverly Hills in February. And before that, he was a no-show at the celebrity-studded gala she hosted in New York at the United Nations for her Malawi charity. He didn't make the premiere of the opening of her movie *Filth & Wisdom*, either.

Besides Guy's noticeable absence at important events, statements made by his own father at this time also served to advance the story that the Ritchies were headed for divorce. 'Madonna and Guy are not spending any time together,' John Ritchie said in late February 2008. 'Madonna is busy in America with the children, and Guy wants to stay in the UK. They won't be spending Easter together, either.'

Madonna was used to controlling most things, but she couldn't control everything that came out of the mouths of friends and relatives, could she? The best she could do was hope that the public believed Liz Rosenberg when she issued statements – as she did in early 2008, when she announced that the Ritchies were 'joyfully back together'.

There was a new rub in the Richie's relationship, though, one that had become a major source of irritation for Madonna: Guy had started suggesting to her she 'act her age'. He wasn't fond of some of the concepts she'd been coming up with of late in terms of her sexy image and felt she was just 'too old' for certain style choices.

Also, when she would talk to him about particular song lyrics with which she was toying, he was not at all supportive. He told her that the suggestive ideas for which she'd long been famous had become old and tired. To her ears, though, it sounded as if he was saying the same about her.

In other words, Guy wanted his wife to age 'gracefully'. Did he not have a clue as to who he'd married? His ideas about where she should be headed in her career as she turned fifty were nothing at all like what she had in mind. In her view, Guy had become provincial and out of touch. She still felt young, a pop star at heart. 'I think when you get married you have to be willing to make a lot of compromises and that's fair enough,' Madonna reflected, when later talking about her marriage. 'I think that's the way it goes in relationships. However, you know, I did find myself sometimes in a state of conflict. There were many times when I wanted to express myself as an artist in ways that I don't think my ex-husband felt comfortable with. There were times when I felt incarcerated. I wasn't really allowed to be myself. It doesn't mean that marriage is a bad thing. But if you're an artist you've got to find someone who accepts who you are and [who] is comfortable with that.'

Guy would disagree. 'Who's in charge at your home?' an interviewer once asked him.

'I've got to tell you,' he answered, 'we're just like any other married couple.'

'So she's in charge?'

'Yes.'

Guy's wit and sense of humour aside, despite any problems they were having, the Ritchies also had to be careful to not allow rumours to get out of hand. David's adoption would not be formalized until the end of April 2008. Until then, they had no choice but to play nice. They certainly wouldn't do anything to jeopardize the adoption by making it appear that their home in which David was about to be temporarily placed wasn't a happy one.

Hard Candy

In April 2008, Madonna released her eleventh studio album, *Hard Candy*, a collection of carefully constructed songs taking her more into R&B and urban territory than any of her previous releases. This outstanding album – which included collaborations with Justin Timberlake, Nate 'Danja' Hills, Pharrell Williams and Timbaland – would debut at number 1 on *Billboard*'s Top 100 as well as at the top of the charts in countries around the world. Its lead single, '4 Minutes' (with Timberlake) would peak at number 3 on the *Billboard* charts; Madonna's thirty-seventh Top 10 hit. This would also be Madonna's final studio album with Warner Bros. prior to a deal she'd just signed with Interscope (though it would be almost four years before the issuance of that first Interscope album, *MDNA*, the lag time being filled with two more Warner albums, *Celebration* (a 2009 greatest hits package) and *Sticky & Sweet Tour* (a 2010 live recording of the concert of the same name).

'She's a little baby tiger cub on the inside but outside she's as tough as anything,' Pharrell said of her. 'Once you are fighting with her you can't let your guard down, she'd beat your ass to a pulp. She could definitely beat me up. But you know, making Madonna cry has just cemented our relationship. We're tight now. Seriously tight. She's probably the best person I've ever collaborated with.'

'She was cool,' added Danja of working with Madonna. 'She had a dark sense of humour that I can't explain. She might just say something crazy that you might feel is out of line. But it's not. It's just her sense of humour. She was in the studio chilling with us, being open and the whole nine.'

Madonna originally had an entirely different concept in mind for the cover art. 'I did a photo shoot with Steven Klein for my last album cover, and I painted my face black, except for red lips and white eyes,' she explained. 'It was a play on words. Have you ever heard of the Black Madonna? It has layers of meaning, and for a minute, I thought it would be a fun title for my record. Then I thought, '25 per cent of the world might get this, probably less. It's not worth it.' It happens all the time because my references are usually off the Richter scale. That's why I have people like Guy [Oseary, her manager] in my life who look at me and go, 'No, you are *not* doing that.' She ended up going with a sort of S&M image, no less controversial but definitely less sacred in meaning.

A lot of *Hard Candy* was thematically biographical, such as the lilting 'Miles Away', about which Madonna told the *Daily Telegraph*, '[It's] a song most people who work can relate to. If part of your work is travelling, and the person you are with also works and travels, you find yourself separated a lot and it can be very frustrating. I'm American and he [Guy Ritchie] is British, and I have to come to America all the time. Especially at the beginning of our relationship, that long-distance thing was very frustrating. I also think it's easier for people to say things from a distance; it's safer. In "Miles Away" I'm tapping into the global consciousness of people who have intimacy problems.'

Ben Thompson, in his review for the *Guardian*, reflected what a lot of critics thought about *Hard Candy*, which was that Madonna was perhaps too reliant on her producers and, in the process, lost some of her own vision and voice. Still, he felt the collection had a lot to recommend it. 'Whenever *Hard Candy* threatens to get boring, something always happens to recapture your interest,' he wrote, 'but the three songs in which Madonna actually seems to forge a genuine connection with her music help leave the rest of the album in the shade.'

In the end, *Hard Candy* was considered by her fan base to be a triumph and one of Madonna's best, most accessible albums. There actually isn't a bad song in the bunch. 'I never know what is going to happen in the studio,' Madonna said at the time, 'whether the people I put together for an album are even going to get along. With this album, I had a lot of strong-minded men in the studio, which can be challenging. They had ideas as to how they thought I should sound, how I should sing. There were a few times along the way when I had to remind them that nobody tells me how to sing,' she added with a chuckle. 'Plus, these guys, they wanted to be up all night working and, sorry, but I have kids at home and I have things to do. So, I had to keep them on a short leash. But at the end of the day, I think it's a very good album, a lot of autobiographical songs, some really good production values.'

Divorce

At the end of June 2008, two friends of Madonna's visited her at her New York apartment and, during a chat over tea, raised the thorny subject of her marriage. 'How are things going with Guy?' one of the women asked. 'Fine,' Madonna answered, tersely. 'But there have been so many news reports . . .' the friend continued. Madonna's faced darkened. 'If you think I have any idea what's being reported in the media,' she said, 'you're wrong.' Then, she added, 'And if you think I'm going to now discuss this matter with you, you're *very* wrong.' Apparently not yet dissuaded, the friend continued to push. 'Well, what they're saying is . . .' Madonna raised both hands, palms out. 'Stop right there,' she warned. 'This subject is definitely off limits. I'm very serious.' With that, the conversation uneasily shifted to the more acceptable topic of *Hard Candy* and the upcoming 'Sticky & Sweet' tour.

Also foremost on Madonna's mind at this time, though, according to one of those at the luncheon, was a book about to be published that was authored by her brother, Christopher Ciccone, called *Life with my Sister Madonna*. For a woman who has controlled her public image for as long as she could remember, having a sibling release a book about his relationship to her, wholly unauthorized of course, wasn't easy to accept. 'I'm really pissed off about it,' Madonna said. 'Christopher should know better.' She said that someone gave her a copy of the book and 'I couldn't help it, I just sort of hurled it across the room at a wall, that's how enraged I was about it. Then, I thought, okay, I'm not really mad about this book, I'm mad about other stuff, and this damn book just happens to be the thing in my hand that I can throw.'

Liz Rosenberg said of Madonna's reaction to the book and its author, 'I would have to assume she has come to terms with the fact that they do not have a close and loving relationship. And with the book coming out,' she added in what sounded like a veiled threat, or maybe promise, 'I assume that will remove the chances of that ever happening.'

Further alienation from a sister with whom he already had a chequered history was, of course, the chance Christopher took when he decided to write about Madonna. Obviously, he knew she wasn't going to like it. However, it's his story as much as it's hers and he certainly had every right to tell it. It was a good and compelling read, too; it debuted at number 2 on the *New York Times* bestseller list, which said as much about Madonna's continuing fame as it did about the book. Christopher would pay a steep price for the tome, though; many of his show-business friends would drop him, feeling he had been disloyal. 'You're friends until you aren't,' he would say. 'I saw a great deal of people in my life vanish. It's shocking and difficult to find, wow, the room is that empty! After publication I had to recreate my world. There were maybe five people who still were in my life at that point, apart from family.'

Knowing her, it's difficult to imagine that Madonna didn't retrieve that copy of Christopher's book she flung against a wall, secrete it away in her Gucci bag and then dip into it from time to time. How could she resist?

Alex

Prior to her marriage, it had always been the case that whenever Madonna was seen with a man, there would be an onslaught of rumours suggesting a romantic relationship with him. This was still true of her in the summer of 2008 when she became linked to the handsome baseball player Alex Rodriguez even though, of course, she was still married to Guy. Though she and Alex were said to be having an affair, it turns out that it simply wasn't true. As it happened, the two had the same manager, Guy Oseary, she took her children to a Yankees game . . . had a few dinners with Alex . . . but that was it.

Alex was going through a painful divorce after five years of marriage, giving him and Madonna some common ground for commiseration. Apparently, Alex also became a little infatuated with Madonna. *The New York Daily News* would report in June that his wife, Cynthia, found a note from him to Madonna in which he professed his affection for her, and said that he felt she was his soul mate. The paper reported that Cynthia believed Madonna was trying to convert the ball player to Kabbalah. 'I feel like Madonna is using mind control over him,' she was quoted as having said, 'I don't recognize the man he's become. He was a sweet, beautiful, loving husband and father. Today he's very cold and calculating.'

While it may be difficult for people to believe that Madonna would be able to resist being intimate with a handsome, thirty-two-year-old athlete, in fact she wasn't – and the reason had to do with Lourdes, eleven at the time, and Rocco, eight. She cared deeply about what they thought of her, and would never have an affair while she was still married. Also, as a woman who'd been in the public eye for as long as she has been – and someone who has been the subject of not only present scrutiny but historical – she's always been one to look at the bigger picture of the story of her life. 'She would not want her children to ever look back and think the worst of her, it's as simple as that,' said one of her confidantes. 'As liberated as she is, she can also be puritanical. She wants to be a positive role model, especially for Lourdes. How could she ever hope to do that if, one day years from now, Lourdes would be able to say, "But *you* were having sex with someone else while you were still married, so why can't I?" This is how Madonna thinks. She's always looking at how things will play out in the future.'

'The correct analysis is . . . a *relationship*,' Cynthia Rodriguez's attorney, Earl Lilly, said of Madonna's time with Alex Rodriguez. 'Some people categorize an affair as something as sexual infidelity. We're not claiming that. It's an affair of the heart. Madonna's name is not mentioned in the [divorce] papers,' reminded Lilly. 'We don't want the public to think this is an aggressive action against Madonna.'

If anything, Alex Rodriguez began to personify exactly what Madonna *didn't* want in her life at this time – more complications. She actually wondered if maybe the stories about the two of them having a sexual affair were coming from his camp. Were these rumours being circulated in order to boost his public image, or in some way generate publicity for him? He was a nice enough person, but she really didn't know him. It was difficult for her to not be suspicious. She has been famous for so many years, she pretty much always assumes that people are out to use her for their own gain. Assuming the worst in that regard is just a consequence of her fame, a war within herself she has waged for many decades. She hates to be so cynical but, in fact, she *has* been used for purposes of publicity so many times in the past, it's not as if she doesn't have valid reason to wonder.

* * *

Settlement with Guy

Though Alex Rodriguez wasn't a factor in their decision, by the summer of 2008 Madonna and Guy finally agreed that their marriage was over. Now it was just a matter of working out some sort of settlement. For Madonna, the fact that she was so busy with her career at this time – as usual – was both a blessing and a curse, the former because it allowed her to be distracted from the heartache of her broken union but the latter, of course, because her hectic life was exactly what had jeopardized her marriage in the first place. At this time, she was preparing to mount her 'Sticky & Sweet' tour, which would run for more than a year, all the way through to 2 September 2009 in Tel Aviv.

For a woman not used to failure in her life, the end of her marriage was a big one. Her tough exterior aside, the personal heartbreak of what had happened with Guy hurt her deeply. She was anxious about the future, fearing she might end up alone, a fifty-year-old woman raising three children in a big, American metropolis. She tried to remain positive, though. 'You can't really reach a level of enlightenment without going through a period of darkness or a period of doubt,' she said at the time. 'We all get sort of angels that come into our lives and they sometimes come in very strange packages. Sometimes they look like the devil and they end up pushing you in the direction you need to go in.'

Madonna and Guy agreed to announce the divorce on 15 October while she was in Boston with the tour. That afternoon at sound check, the pop star sat at the edge of the stage taking in the surroundings of the huge TD Banknorth Garden venue that in a few hours' time would be filled with thousands of devoted fans. 'Another city, another show,' she said, looking downcast. 'And, no matter the drama, I'm just expected to keep going on and on and on, aren't I?' She was clearly depressed; obviously, this was not a good time for her but, as per usual, she knew she would have to rise to the occasion and do whatever necessary to put on a spectacular show. That night, Madonna couldn't help but give voice to her frustration. Before singing 'Miles Away', she explained, 'This song is for the emotionally retarded. You might know a few people who fall into that category. God knows I do.' To some critics it sounded like a swipe at Guy. Actually, though, that was pretty much the way she had been describing the theme of the song since the time she recorded it.

Surprisingly enough, Madonna didn't have a prenuptial agreement in place with Guy. How was that even possible? She's so smart about such things, always thinking about the future and how to protect her business, that her friends and associates were astonished. In fact, Madonna went into the marriage with Guy never imagining that it would ever end. She's such a great visualizer when it comes to her life and always so certain that whatever she puts forth in thought will materialize in form, she didn't want to project even the slightest suggestion that the marriage could fail. '[I know that] consciousness is everything and that all things begin with a thought,' she once said. 'That we are responsible for our own fate, we reap what we sow, we get what we give, we pull in what we put out. I know these things for sure.'

In her mind, the composing and executing of a pre-nuptial agreement with a man she planned to marry was an admittance that maybe the union would fail. She would not go into the marriage with that belief. One might think her to be more pragmatic. However, at the time she married Guy, she was so swept away by him and by their relationship she wanted to think only positive thoughts.

The fact that no pre-nuptial agreement existed complicated Madonna's divorce ten-fold. In the end, Guy would receive an astonishing 92 million dollars in the settlement – *92 million dollars!* 'It's one of the largest payouts ever in a divorce settlement,' Liz Rosenberg would have to admit, and for her to be so specific about a private matter suggested that Madonna really *did* want the word out there about it. She was said to be worth about $500 million at the time – maybe more – so it's not as if shelling out almost $100 million to Guy did a lot of damage to her bottom line but, still, it was a huge price to pay in a divorce and she felt the emotional sting of it. 'If I think about it for even five seconds, it's more than I can take,' she said at the time. 'Did he deserve a hundred million for putting up with me?' she asked. 'Hell. If I thought he was going to get *that* much, I would have been a *much* bigger bitch to him. *Much bigger!*' (Guy would deny that he received as much from Madonna, but it's not likely that he would have confirmed it, is it?)

Some felt it ironic that the very career about which Guy Ritchie always had such reservations was the very reason he was able to bank such a huge award. In Madonna's mind, though, there was plenty more to do and a lot more money to make. She decided she wasn't going to begrudge Guy his little hundred million. She was just glad to have somehow survived a very tough year.

Jesus

By the beginning of 2009, fifty-year-old Madonna was a woman in transition. Some felt she was flailing, trying to find her new footing as a single woman and mother while, at the same time, continuing with her ever-demanding career. In retrospect, she would probably be the first to admit it was true, and that it was hard. Some decisions she made during this time were difficult for outsiders to fathom. Case in point: her new relationship with a model barely in his twenties named Jesus Luz, whom she'd met at a photo shoot at the end of the previous year.

Jesus Luz was born on 15 January 1987 in Rio de Janeiro, the son of a public official and a hairstylist. He was named by his father after, of course, Jesus Christ. His parents separated when he was five; he then remained closer to his mother. 'I grew up with many ups and downs,' he said. 'I also saw the beauty of people who were living an intellectual life and also people who were humble and had nothing.' As a teenager, Luz became interested in modelling and signed his first contract at the age of seventeen. Not only was he extremely handsome, he was intelligent and ambitious with a contagious personality. He struggled for about five years in his new profession. Then, his agent, Sergio Mattos, managed to book him for a sexy photo shoot with Madonna in *W* magazine; who can ever forget the photo of Luz, his toned back to the camera with its elegant tattoo of his name, and Madonna seated before him, admiring him with lustful eyes and looking as if she was about to pounce. Then, of course, there were those naked shots of Luz; he definitely made an impression.

After Madonna took him under her wing, that was the end of the obscure life for Jesus as he had known it. 'At the moment he met Madonna, I never see him after that,' his agent, Sergio Mattos recalled. 'I sent him to the job and after that he changed phone numbers and I never see him again.'

Soon after the photo shoot, Jesus signed a lucrative deal with Ford Models. Some have said over the years that by the time he met Madonna, he was already on his way to a successful career. That seems doubtful. What we do know is that being at her side for the next two years certainly didn't hurt; he would walk the runway in Milan for Dolce & Gabbana in June; appear in the winter collection of Pepe Jeans; be featured in the spring-summer collection of Ona Saez, and even become the subject of an in-depth feature in the *New York Times* in November, all within a year of meeting the pop star. As a guest DJ in clubs, by the end of 2009 he was asking for $30,000 an appearance! (He wasn't always getting it, but he was asking for it, anyway.)

When Madonna brought him into her life at the end of 2008, Jesus was about to turn twenty-two. Of course, some in Madonna's circle began to speculate that the pop star was in the midst of a serious mid-life crisis and that Jesus was a consequence of inner turmoil. To an extent, maybe that was true. 'She tried to act like turning fifty was not a big deal for her,' said her relative, 'but it was. I know for sure that it was.'

Judging by her appearance as she approached the big five-zero, one would certainly never know Madonna took any issue with the milestone. This writer bumped into her as she was leaving a Los Angeles recording studio at the beginning of 2009. She looked marvellous in black, velvet pants outfit with matching pumps. 'Hey! How are you? So lovely to see you!' she said as she rushed by me and flashed a big smile of recognition. Then, turning back to look at me, she said, 'I am in *such* a hurry. But you know me. I never stop, do I?'

Her body was slim and toned, the result of regular yoga workouts not to mention that strict macrobiotic diet of hers. Her skin was clear and her face was lean and angular, its rawboned sharpness softened by just a touch of make-up. She seemed to have no lines (and still insisted in the press that she'd had no plastic surgery, though it was fairly obvious to people aware of such things that she had regular Botox injections). Her blondish hair was pulled into a simple pony-tail. Her ebullient spirit more than matched her youthful appearance.

Madonna's very essence has always emanated youth. She radiates it. She lives it. The reality that she was getting older was sometimes hard for her to accept. Maybe it's a cliché but having Jesus in her life did make her feel young and attractive; the fact that she could still interest a man in his early twenties filled her with self-confidence. Madonna wasn't ashamed of it, either. She actually felt comfortable enough to joke about the relationship. When asked how young was too young in a mate, she quipped, 'As long as they're old enough to dress themselves, they're good enough.' Then, she added, 'Younger people are more adventurous. Have you met many guys my age?' she asked. 'They're usually grumpy and fat and balding!'

When Madonna made her first official public appearance with Jesus at the Metropolitan Museum Costume Institute Ball in spring 2009, he looked like the mature adult in his dapper tux and she the youngster in an unconventional Eighties-inspired ensemble. Here's what *Marie Clare* said about the appearance: 'The Queen of Pop brought out her '80s side, taking the evening's dress theme – "The Model as Muse: Embodying Fashion" and running with it.

'Dressed in a navy blue ruched, Louis Vuitton mini dress, thigh-high black boots and the black fingerless gloves of old, Madge completed her ensemble with a teal-colored hair piece tied around a top knot. The style chameleon's get-up didn't put off beau of the moment though, as twenty-two-year-old toy-boy, Jesus Luz, showed up at fashion's most stylish annual bash, looking super suave in a slick black dinner jacket and waited attentively as the flashbulbs went into overdrive for his date.'

Another reporter for *Marie Claire* – Amy O'Dell – took a more humorous approach to the evening, writing that Madonna arrived, 'looking like a cleaning lady moonlighting as a stripper who washed her Xanax down with one too many margaritas before she changed outfits. And it was a genius, if not very attractive, fashion moment for her and Marc Jacobs, who designed the Louis Vuitton ensemble. Because on a night dedicated to the world's most beautiful women, no one – especially a non-model – could win by trying to look the most beautiful. So looking a bit drunk before you actually got drunk wasn't a bad way to steal attention from Kate Moss and her paltry headpiece.'

Though Madonna generated a lot of heat for herself, few men that night at the Met were as sexy and good-looking as Jesus Luz with his tousled curls, penetrating blue-green eyes and toned, muscular body. However, as expected, in their private life he wasn't a very dominating person. He did what he was told; he never challenged Madonna. He was great in bed, though. Madonna later confided that the sex with him had been better than it ever had been with Guy and, in fact, she insisted it was 'the best I have ever had – and that's saying a lot.' (It should be noted here that it was rumoured that Madonna and Guy hadn't been intimate in at least two years prior to their divorce – some say three – and so, by the time Jesus came along, Madonna was understandably eager to be reacquainted with real passion.)

There were moments when Jesus intrigued Madonna on other levels, too. He was so full of hope for the future, brimming with optimism about his life, he reminded her of herself at that age. Nothing ever seemed to get him down. He woke up every day raring to bite into it and make it his very own. He had big plans, spoke endlessly about his dream of being a successful model, a singer, a DJ. 'It never even occurs to him that at any moment his whole life could just go to shit and for no good reason,' Madonna told one confidante. 'I remember being like that,' she said, before adding with a smirk, 'before this business turned me into the jaded shrew I am today.' In that respect, Jesus was a breath of fresh air for Madonna. He was also a follower of the Kabbalah, having been introduced to it by a former girlfriend, so he had that in common with Madonna, as well.

Importantly, Jesus was also unequivocally supportive of Madonna; they spent hours talking about . . . *her*. Her new album, her new tour, her plans for new movies, her many goals and aspirations for the future. She had become so accustomed to Guy feeling angry and resentful about everything having to do with her ambition, that being with Jesus was fun and somehow invigorating. He was impressed with pretty much everything Madonna said or did; the way he lapped up every word, every idea, every thought made her feel that her beliefs were still valid and worthwhile. He was sincere about it too, he wasn't just kissing up to her. He admired her so much! Maybe it sounds superficial and even silly that a woman of Madonna's great stature would need such validation, but Jesus became her biggest cheerleader at a time when she'd all but forgotten what it was like to have this kind of unequivocal support from the man in her life.

'Nobody works harder than she does,' Jesus told me in 2009 of Madonna. 'Can you imagine what it is like just talking to her about her career, about what she has seen and experienced? Every day, it's like an honour for me, as I think it would be for any person. She is not selfish, either. She wants to share her knowledge, she wants people to not have to go through what she went through to get where she is, all the shit she has had to go through, all of the crap people threw at her when she was first starting out. She's told me all of it, wanting me to, you know, *learn* from it. *Grow* from it. That kind of generosity is rare, I think, in people who have become that famous. She just wants to give. I think she's a good mother, too. People have a lot of ideas about her, but most of them aren't true. I see a different side to her.'

When I asked what their life was like outside of the public eye, he smartly replied, 'If I told you that, it would no longer be outside the public eye, would it?' He said that he and Madonna had discussed in-depth how much of their private lives he should share with the public and the decision they'd come to – not surprisingly – is that the least said about it, the better. He had a couple of scares with the media early in their relationship, he recalled, with reporters claiming to know details that may or may not have been true. He was concerned that Madonna might think he had spoken out of turn. However, she told him not to worry about it. She promised that she would not believe anything she ever read had come directly from him – and, not only that, she said, she practically never sees anything that is ever published about her, anyway! 'She doesn't allow entertainment magazine or newspapers in the house,' he observed. 'She doesn't want to know what people are thinking or what they're saying.' (This was, of course, at the beginning of the overwhelming proliferation of social media; today, Madonna may not have show-business-related publications in her home, but because of the Internet she is all too well aware of what is being said about her these days – and often wishes she was still in the dark about it.)

Even with everything that may have recommended him, Madonna was still not romantically serious about Jesus. She suspected he was just a passing fancy, which is why she didn't mind the career mileage he was gaining from becoming involved with her. He was a nice kid, she figured, so why not cash in while he can? It wasn't as if he was a major celebrity, like Alex Rodriguez, perhaps using her to generate headlines for himself. He was her 'rebound relationship' after Guy and – his age and maturity aside – another reason she couldn't fully commit to him was because, deep down, she still so desperately missed Guy. She would tell intimates that she couldn't shake the nagging feeling that maybe she'd made a mistake in divorcing him. Of course they'd had their problems. However, once he was gone from her and replaced by a young man barely out of his teens, Madonna realized that she'd underestimated what it was like to be with someone with whom she was on truly equal ground, psychologically and emotionally.

One friend of Jesus', a model named Anne Wilder, recalls being with him and Madonna at the Hiro Ballroom in Chelsea, New York. As she described it, it was a crazy scene – people dancing, drinking and having a good time as expected in a crowded, popular place like Hiro. Madonna was in Jesus' lap, her head rested against his chest as the two whispered to one another. When he got up to go to the men's room, he left Madonna alone in the booth. She seemed awkward sitting by herself, not really fitting in, maybe even afraid of being approached by fans and feeling vulnerable. Anne sat next to her. 'Jesus is so sexy, isn't he?' she shouted at Madonna, trying to be heard over the noise. 'Yeah, he sure is,' Madonna shouted back. Then, after a pause, Madonna said, 'Is he a friend of yours?' Anne nodded. 'Have you fucked him?' Madonna asked. A little taken aback, Anne answered, no. Madonna then sidled up to her and whispered in her ear, 'Well, you should watch out for him because I think he's falling for me.'

'I was confused,' Anne Wilder recalls, 'thinking I hadn't heard her right. Finally, she leaned in again and said, "He's a good boy but he's in way over his head with me. You're young and beautiful and just his type, I would think. Make sure he still has your number. He's going to need it in a few months." I was a little surprised, and I guess I showed it because then she said in an oddly affected British accent, "Oh my dear, how *tragic* can it be to say you've had Madonna's left-overs? Don't act so appalled! Millions of women *wish* they could be so lucky. Or," she added, "who knows? Maybe a three-way?"'

At that moment, Jesus returned. 'Come on stud, let's dance,' Madonna said as she took him by the hand out to the dance floor. On her way, Madonna turned, looked over her shoulder, naughtily licked her lips and winked at Anne.

She'll never change.

Mercy James

'I come from a big family – there were lots of kids – and that's what I want for myself, a big family like the one I was raised in.' Those were Madonna's words to me many years ago during the press junket for her movie, *Evita*. It was in November 1996, a few months after she gave birth to Lourdes. Back then, most people were astonished that she'd have even one child. 'But my history is one of family,' she told me. 'However that looks, in whatever shape it takes, it doesn't matter to me. Family is important. It gives you structure. I have had problems in my own family and God knows me and my father have not always gotten along. But the older I get, the more necessary I know it is to have that foundation in your life. I don't want to be alone. I don't want to be some old superstar by herself in an ivory tower wondering what happened to my life.'

By the time she was ready to turn fifty-one in August 2009,

Madonna was well on her way to achieving her goal of a large family, especially as she sought to adopt three-year-old Chifundo, 'Mercy' James, from the same Malawian village as David.

Back in April, the Malawian government had ruled that the adoption would not go forward unless Madonna first lived in Malawi for more than a year. Though crushed by that decision, she would not take no for an answer – not when the girl's entire life was at stake. 'It's bigger than just me, than just what I want,' she said. 'This child is at a crossroads of either a wonderful life or one that will be very, very difficult. I cannot let this go.' However, she was not about to move to Malawi for a year – 'let's be reasonable', is how she put it.

The fact that Madonna was now a divorcee also worked against her. She would recall, 'When I adopted Mercy James, I put my armour on. I tried to be more prepared [than she'd been when she went through the process with David]. I braced myself. This time I was accused by a female Malawian judge that because I was divorced, I was an unfit mother. I got the shit kicked out of me, but it didn't hurt as much. And looking back, I do not regret one moment of the fight.'

Eventually, the government reversed its decision after Madonna appealed it all the way to Malawi's Supreme Court. The court would ultimately rule in her favour, granting Madonna the right to adopt Mercy James.

This latest adoption would be an important piece in the new puzzle of Madonna's single life as she finalized the move of her home base of operations to Manhattan where she'd purchased a town house *Rolling Stone* described as 'massive'. In a sense, it was as if she had gone full circle. After all, New York was where she had got her start. Going back was symbolic in many ways, another new beginning for her – post Guy. There was a great deal of re-organization going on in her life; it was an exciting time for her.

Guy had first met Mercy a couple of years earlier in Malawi, with Madonna. Therefore, he was just as invested in seeing the child safely adopted. Now that she was ensconced in Madonna's home, it was bittersweet for him in that he had once envisioned himself as her father. 'Life goes on and things change,' he said, trying to keep a stiff upper lip. He remained available to Madonna during her transition and took the boys, Rocco and David, to his country home in Wiltshire for a few days when Mercy arrived so that Madonna and Lourdes could bond with her.

As 2009 wore on, Madonna continued to display the intellect, brains, energy and drive of her youth, while also remaining focused and clear-eyed – not always easy considering the chaos of her world. She continued to be influenced by Kabbalah and tried to incorporate its teachings into her life and, indeed, into her personality. 'I don't think I was cruel, mean or heartless in the past, but back then I could gossip or speak badly about people, or say things without thinking what the consequences would be,' she told Austin Scaggs for *Rolling Stone* in 2009. '[Kabbalah] has changed my way of looking at life, so naturally it will change the way I think about life: not thinking like a victim, taking responsibility for my actions and my words.'

In terms of her career, Madonna was preparing a new greatest hits collection at this time, *Celebration*, for release in September 2009. It would include thirty-four hits along with two new songs – the title song, written and produced by Madonna, Paul Oakenfold and Ian Greene, as well as 'Revolver', by Madonna, Brandon Kitchen, Carlos Battey, Justin Franks, Dwayne Carter and Steven Battey. (Another song, 'It's So Cool', would later be available digitally.) She also applied herself heart and soul to the 'Sticky & Sweet' tour, which continued throughout the year as the top-grossing tour, generating $280 million with 58 concerts in 17 countries. Meanwhile, Forbes named her the number 3 celebrity on their '2009 Celebrity 100', behind Angelina Jolie and Oprah Winfrey.

Six months into the relationship with Jesus Luz, Madonna began to become a little concerned about things. Her children had become attached to him, which worried her because she had to admit to herself that she was beginning to lose interest. 'He helps the children with their school work, they watch movies together, talk on the phone quite often when he's not around,' confirmed one source at the time. 'He and Lourdes share the same taste in music – and not Madonna's music, either. They both love Lady Gaga. He and Rocco have special jokes and a language all their own. Jesus also loves to get down on the floor and play with David, wrestling around, tumbling and laughing. I do think the kids would be sad if Madonna broke up with him.'

While she enjoyed Jesus' company and he was fun to have around, Madonna had always known that his feelings for her were stronger than hers for him. She didn't want to hurt him, but how long could this relationship continue? The longer he was around and the more her children grew to love him, the harder it would be, she knew, to let him go.

By the end of the year, Madonna and Jesus had been globe-trotting for over twelve months on her tour. He'd been a tremendous help to her, lending the sort of emotional support she'd become used to from Guy on the road but without all of the annoying whining about it all. The two ended the year in Brazil where she was hoping to drum up support from businessmen to aid a children's charity. While there, Madonna met Jesus' father – a hospital worker named Luis Heitor Pino da Luz – and his mother, Cristiane Regina da Silvan. Previously, Cristiane had made some statements to the press along the lines of her believing that Madonna had somehow 'brainwashed' her son. Therefore, it was incredibly awkward between them, especially given that Cristiane was almost fifteen years younger than Madonna. Everyone was polite but the meeting with Jesus' folks did cause Madonna to want to stop and assess exactly where the two were headed. Maybe it was good that she was so distracted by her career, though – good for Jesus Luz, who, it would seem, was on borrowed time.

'The Go-To Guy'

Madonna began 2010 by performing at the Hope for Haiti Now: A Global Benefit for Earthquake Relief on 22 January. *The Sweet & Sticky* live album was released in April, debuting at number 10 on the *Billboard* 200 – not bad for an album of stage performances without any new material, but still a bit of a disappointment. In March, she collaborated with Dolce & Gabbana on a new line of sunglasses, named MDG – the initials of the company and its collaborator. 'She is very exacting and a professional who seeks perfection in everything she does, and this was no exception,' the company said in a statement. 'The oversized and wraparound designs are sexy and very feminine, like our clothes. Madonna's creative contribution and unique point of view were key, even in designing the MDG logo.'

In July, Madonna began principal photography on her next directorial effort, *W.E.*, which she wrote with Alex Keshinishian (who she first worked with on 1991's *In Bed with Madonna*). *W.E.* was a romantic comedy with a bit of a convoluted plot that had something to do with a woman named 'Wally Winthrop' who'd become obsessed with King Edward's abdication of the British throne for Wallis Simpson. In her research into their lives, Wally learns startling facts relating to Edward's and Wallis' love for one another.

Towards the end of the year, Madonna knew she had to do something about Jesus. If it were up to him, they would probably have married. He was crazy about her. Madonna knew this was never going to happen, however. He had been a pleasant diversion after Guy, but now that she'd had time to at least partially recover from the trauma of her divorce and begin to put the shattered pieces of her life back together, she knew Luz would have to be a casualty. They'd run out of common ground. One funny story: Madonna was annoyed by something a reporter had written about the age difference between them. Disgruntled, she said, 'My God, it's not like I'm Joan Collins!' To which Jesus responded, 'Um . . . who's Joan Collins?'

When the two began bickering over nothing, Madonna knew it was time to end it. 'I have this bad habit,' she would confide in one friend, 'of being judgmental and critical when I'm losing interest in a guy. That's sort of my thing, being a real bitch. I'm self-aware enough to know it. I'm just not self-aware enough to stop it.'

One friend of Jesus' recalls being in London with the couple toward the end of the year and watching as Madonna berated him for being late for dinner, almost as if he was her disobedient son. She was very hard on him in front of stunned friends, embarrassing him until he finally blew up at her and told her to 'knock it off and stop being such a bitch!' It was as if she were picking a fight with him, maybe hoping he would end it with her right then and there, and in front of witnesses in case he changed his mind!

Jesus would never break it off with Madonna, though. It had got to the point where he'd begun to believe he was invaluable in her life, and with good reason. Quite often, there were people in Madonna's organization that used him to access her. They knew he had her ear and hoped he could influence her or have some sway when they would have trouble with her. In other words, he became the 'Madonna go-to guy'. When she was having a tough day, Jesus was the only one who could calm her nerves. He was the one who could make her laugh at herself or at the sheer absurdity of whatever was going on in the moment of her crazy life. He took a certain amount of pride in this purpose, too; it became a major facet of his identity. After all, she was a pop icon doing important work, in his view, making tough calls every day, seeing to it that her artistic vision was being fully realized.

Madonna's days were hectic from morning to night, a myriad of problems always in the offing, situations that demanded everything she had in her to handle. If Jesus could be of assistance to her, he definitely wanted to do it. After all, he knew her like no one else, or at least it felt that way to him. For instance, he knew that if she was being bitchy to people it was because she was sleep-deprived. If she was distracted, it was because she was worried about her kids. He understood her good days and her bad, and having such specific, intimate knowledge of her made him feel almost a part of her very soul.

For Madonna, it had to have been as if she had the best, most capable and trustworthy assistant in the world. She began to expect Jesus to be there for her, to listen to her complaints and to help solve her problems. One day, though, she looked up and realized that the poor guy had made the uneasy transformation from boyfriend to functionary. It was a hop, skip and a jump from there to the point where she began to view Jesus as weak, as not having a life of his own. Then, when *that* happened, she was *really* done with him.

Jesus took the break up badly. An intensely sensitive person, he told people he was as worried about Madonna as he was hurt by her decision to end it with him. Because he knew she had depended on him, he was concerned about how she would fare without him. He also wondered what he had done so wrong in being available to her 24/7. In fact, as it happened, that was *exactly* what he had done wrong.

Of course, Jesus Luz had benefited from his relationship with Madonna, his modelling career at a zenith by the time they broke up at the end of 2010, and his work as a club DJ also generating a lot of money for him. 'So, he couldn't complain,' said Anne Wilder. 'He was sad, though. She had just opened a bunch of fitness centres around the world [Hard Candy Fitness, the first of which opened in Mexico City in November 2010] and he was hoping to have an involvement in that since he was with her at its genesis. When it was over, he told me he had to look in the mirror and try to remember who he had been before she was in his life, he was so used to being Madonna's guy he didn't even know who he was, anymore.'

As many men over the years have testified, being with Madonna does tend to swallow up a person. She's a very big presence. It's easy for a partner of hers to wake up one day and feel an absence of personal identity, especially since every day is about her life and her career. Luz's friends say it was difficult for him to find himself, again. Maybe making matters tougher, Madonna was fairly cold with the break up, not wanting to drag it out. One day she was with Jesus, the next she was gone.

Once they were over, word in the street began to spread that it had actually been Jesus Luz who had ended it with Madonna, not the other way around. Indeed, it would seem that Jesus really *had* learned a thing or two from the master. When Madonna heard the rumour, she couldn't help but laugh. 'Good for him if he started it,' she said. She had no animosity toward him at all, knowing in her heart that the relationship had simply run its course. In her eyes, he was a good kid. Hopefully, he would go on to a productive, rewarding life without her. 'I would have done the exact same thing in starting that rumour,' she concluded, 'if in fact he did start it. Good boy.'

Brahim

Madonna had a number of valid reasons for cutting Jesus Luz loose, but the great difference between their ages was not amongst them. When it came to the opposite sex, she had a distinct 'type' and no matter how much she aged it would never change: she liked 'em young, and she liked 'em hot. She wasn't going to apologize for it, either. Of course, she knew that her iconoclastic stature made it so that she was able to interest sexy, young guys . . . and so what? What she brought to the table was money, travel, celebrity and a fantastic lifestyle. If some young man wanted to jump aboard for the ride, so be it. She wasn't going to discourage it. In fact, she wasn't looking for a real partner, an equal, anyway. She'd had that in Guy;

it had stopped working for her and, now, she no longer wanted it. What she did want was the ease of being with someone who would make little to no demands of her. She wanted fun at the end of a stressful day, good sex, a few laughs. She wasn't looking for a husband as much as she was looking for a companion. Self-aware, she understood what she was after, even if others around her seemed a little baffled by it. By the end of the year, the latest lad on the menu was Brahim Zaibat (also known as Brahim Rachiki), a talented French dancer who'd once worked as a choreographer for Michael Jackson. The two had met earlier, in September 2009, at the launch of the Material Girl Collection at Macy's in Manhattan. Brahim was born on 6 September 1986, making him twenty-three when he met Madonna, twenty-nine years her junior.

As it happened, a friend of Brahim's had been a dancer on Madonna's tour and also her personal trainer; he'd asked Brahim to perform at the Material Girl launch. Afterward, he was introduced to Madonna. 'It wasn't like meeting a monster,' Brahim recalled. 'She's just a woman like all the others. She's an extraordinary artist and world famous, but of course a woman above all. I was delighted to meet her but not stressed out.'

With Jesus officially banished from her world, it didn't take long before Madonna was with Brahim. Brahim, said to be a devout Muslim, cited Madonna's early desire to be a dancer as an interest the two had in common. (He'd become popular years earlier in Japan with the dance group, The Pockemon Crew, which he formed in 2003.) Though Madonna didn't speak French, and his English wasn't fluent, the two had a sexual chemistry neither could deny. The new relationship was confirmed by – of all people – Brahim's mom, Patricia Vidal, who said, 'My mouth fell open when I realized that my son was Madonna's new boyfriend. It's something I'm still trying to come to terms with. Madonna was already a big star when I was a schoolgirl, let alone when Brahim was growing up. The whole situation is very strange indeed – surreal even.'

Suffice to say, Madonna wasn't exactly thrilled with Patricia

Vidal's commentary about her private life; her representatives immediately denied any romance, especially given that Madonna was eight years older than Brahim's mom. Again, yet another mother speaking out of turn! Madonna probably had to wonder why the nosy parents of her young boyfriends couldn't just keep their mouths shut.

Like Jesus before him, Brahim could only benefit from being with Madonna, though he insisted that this was not his primary intention. He quickly learned that with all eyes on him, people he hadn't seen in years suddenly wanted to befriend him; he had to change his mobile phone number several times.

Zaibat's intimates say that the new relationship with Madonna was, as Lance Dixon – one of his friends in New York – put it, 'totally problem free. He got along great with her kids. Because he was a pop culture junkie, he and Madonna have plenty to talk about. Madonna had said he is very mature for his age. He told me that she wished he was more well-rounded when it came to current news and to politics. It's in those areas that I think he felt a little intimidated by her.'

W.E. would open towards the end of the year 2011 to mixed – but unfortunately, mostly negative – reviews. It was too bad; as always Madonna had put everything she had into it, just as she did with every endeavour. In the end, though, *W.E.* – three whole years in the making – was weighed down by a mediocre script and weak performances.

Though Madonna's lovely ballad, 'Masterpiece', which she wrote for the film's soundtrack, would win a Golden Globe Award for Best Original Song, she was deeply disheartened by the critical response to *W.E.* For months after it opened, Madonna fought sadness over the response to it, vowing to never make another movie again while, paradoxically and true to form, at the same time trying to come up with new and better ideas for films. Brahim was surprised. He said he never imagined that an icon such as Madonna could have such a thin skin. Though he tried to make her feel better about things, there was no way a person of his limited life experience was ever going to influence Madonna in this regard. Therefore, she shut him out; she told him she needed time on her own to process things. Wisely, he gave it to her.

It was to Brahim's advantage that he didn't push Madonna. 'He was beginning to understand the lay of the land when it came to being with her, and a big part of remaining in her life was in knowing that terrain,' said Lance Dixon. 'She needs to process stuff in her own way,' he told me. He said that a problem she'd had with Jesus was that he became too involved, too invested in trying to help her through tough spots, such as her divorce, trying to be of assistance to her. Brahim was smarter. 'I think that the best thing I can do is stay out of her way,' is what he told me. 'She can get dark, moody. My gut tells me she'll be back when she's ready. If not, I'm good. I still have a life. She's not my life.'

Of course, Brahim was right in his assessment. Though Madonna froze him out for a couple of weeks, she came back to him when she was ready. 'I felt, though, that he would have been fine if she told him to take a hike,' said Lance Dixon. 'I also felt that this sort of independence that he had, this inner resolve to not become just an attachment of her, was what would maybe keep the two of them together. "She hates needy people," he told me. "She hates weakness in people, too, because she hates it in herself whenever it rears its head, which is like pretty much never. Show her that you are needy or that you are weak, and it's all over for you." So, throughout the *W.E.* experience, Brahim kept his distance, let her figure things out on her own.'

'I think she won't rest until she gets an Oscar for writing and directing a movie,' said someone who worked closely with her on *W.E.* 'She would call me very upset about a review – and she somehow saw them all, I don't know how – and wonder if maybe these critics knew what they were talking about, second-guessing herself, thinking maybe she just didn't have a clue about movies. 'This is their business,' she would tell me, 'they must know *something*. Can

I just disregard it all?' But then, in the next breath, she would be convinced that they were all full of shit and that she knew *exactly* what she was doing, that *W.E.* was a magnificent film, and that she was determined to do another one, and this time prove them all wrong.'

The source's recollection is not surprising. Madonna is not going to be discouraged, at least not permanently. She hasn't got this far in her career by taking to heart everything every critic has ever said about her. However, she still has the basic insecurity most artists have of feeling inadequate, of not being 'good enough,' and it's most evident in her conflicted response to critical reaction to her films.

When it comes to her pop music career, of course Madonna has the tough skin Brahim had expected of her. She has obviously proven herself in that arena, and there's not much a critic from *Billboard* can say about her that will matter to her. However, if the *Hollywood Reporter* or *Variety* is critical about one of her movies, *that* hurts. It's a pain that also motivates her, though, and propels her forward; it's not likely she will ever truly abandon her dream to, as she once put it, 'makes great movies, even if it kills me'.

MDNA

Brahim Zaibat would go on to perform as one of Madonna's many dancers in her stunning half-time performance for Super Bowl XLVI on 5 February 2012. The show was conceived by the production staff of *Cirque Du Soleil* as well as Madonna's longtime choreographer, Jamie King, as a kick-off to the upcoming release of Madonna's album, *MDNA*. It would also feature performers CeeLo Greene, LMFAO, Nicki Minaj and M.I.A. Madonna had to have been heartened by the fact that it would become the most-watched half-time show in Super Bowl history with 114 million viewers – more than the viewership for the game, itself. She performed, 'Vogue', 'Music', her new single, 'Give Me All Your Luvin'', and 'Like a Prayer'.

It was difficult to fathom why she released a mediocre song like 'Give Me All Your Luvin'' considering its 'L-U-V Madonna/Y-O-U You Wanna' cheerleading chant. With lyrics like, 'Don't play the stupid game/Cause I'm a different kind of girl/Every record sounds the same/You've got to step into my world', it was hard to escape the notion that, as far as Madonna was concerned, so long as words basically rhyme they are perfectly acceptable as song lyrics. It's long been a bit of a problem in her songwriting. On one hand, Madonna's fan base felt she was having a good time – and certainly her performance of the song during the Super Bowl half-time show with all of the pom-poms and cheerleading choreography against marching drums was fun. On the other, some of her greatest admirers couldn't help but be a bit conflicted. Sceptics felt she should have been more evolved as an artist by 2012 than 'Give Me All Your Luvin''. Let's face it: she was fifty-one, nobody's high-school cheerleader. (The late comic, Joan Rivers, had a funny line: 'Madonna as a cheerleader? What school does she go to? Our Lady of Osteoporosis?')

Journalist Neil McCormick from the *Daily Telegraph* really let Madonna have it, and a lot of what he wrote in his essay just can't be argued: 'Madonna's current sound is effectively the same banging electro you can hear blasting out of a teenager's bedroom or fizzing on headphones in the playground, the sound of Rihanna and Lady Gaga. It is as if Madonna is competing with her own offspring. At her worst, her lyrics are lumpen appropriations of teenspeak, obsessed with sex and dancing, declaring with a tiresome addiction to cliché that 'girls they just wanna have some fun' and attempting to woo a lover by promising 'you can have the password to my phone.' I mean, please. Most people I know of Madonna's age don't even know the password to their own phone, and have to ask their kids how to open it . . . There is neither wit nor wisdom to Madonna's songwriting, no sense of emotional depth or musical progress, just a relentless chasing after trends that sees her moving in musical circles in which she is no longer entirely comfortable.'

In Madonna's defence, 'Give Me All Your Luvin'' served a purpose. Coming after the heaviness of *W.E.*, and especially the bleakness of its release and poor reception, she described a definite sense of relief and fun with, once again, songwriting. 'It's amazing to be back in music,' she said. 'I like the intimacy of a recording studio and songwriting. I'm using a different part of my brain when I work on music versus when I'm directing a film. There are a billion more people on a film and I don't have that visceral outlet of being able to sing, scream . . . jump around. It's very different. I love doing both but it was nice to have the simplicity of songwriting after three years of writing a script and directing and editing and talking about my film, to sit down and play my guitar and sing a song. I almost cried.'

Considering that 'Give Me All Your Luvin'' was the highly anticipated first release in her exciting new three-album deal with Interscope and the lead single from her long-awaited *MDNA* album, many people were hoping for more. Or better. Still, it would become her thirty-eighth Top 10 hit on *Billboard*'s Hot 100. She still had her fan base, and it was a loyal one, as also evidenced by the impressive sales of *MDNA*. It debuted at number 1, with her biggest opening week sales since 2000's *Music*. It was her fifth consecutive studio album to debut in the top spot.

Though 'Give Me all Your Luvin'' was a weak first single for *MDNA* and gave some the impression that the album would be all fluffy nonsense, it really wasn't the case. It's actually one of Madonna's better albums, very candid in nature and exposing of her private life. Maybe Joel Levy said it best for *Rolling Stone* when he wrote, 'Yup, *MDNA* is our lady's divorce album. Seven out of sixteen songs address her split directly, and that's low-balling if you think the chick with "fake tits and a nasty mood" in "Some Girls" could be the lingerie model who became Guy Ritchie's new baby mama. [He was referring to Guy's new relationship, Jacqui Ainsley.] Revealing herself has always been part of her art, and this is hardly her first album that's dark, messy and conflicted. But *MDNA* stands as Madonna's most explicit work.'

Madonna had a small dinner party in New York to celebrate the release of *MDNA* and the beginning of her world tour to promote it – just a few friends at her home, something intentionally intimate in contrast to the bombast of everything else going on around her at this time. The tour would kick off in Tel Aviv on 31 May 2012 and continue through to the end of the year, finishing on 22 December in Argentina. Her children, of course, were there, as well as trusted friends, and Brahim Zaibat was on her arm. Obviously, no one present would ever go on the record about the evening at the end of May. However according to one of the guests, Madonna seemed revitalized and ready to get back on the road.

'I remember that when I was married to Guy and it was time to tour, I used to dread it,' she told one of her friends that night. She said that 'all of the bitching and moaning about it', had almost made her feel it wasn't worth all of the trouble. Putting together an act and then going on the road with it was such an ordeal on so many levels, the last thing she needed, she said, was Guy in the background bemoaning the time they would have to spend apart, and what it was doing to their family. Now that she was free of all of that opposition, she said, the planning and execution of a complex show like the 'MDNA' tour was once again a joyous experience.

Madonna didn't know it at the time of her dinner party, but the 'MDNA' tour would go on to gross more than $300 million. It would be the tenth highest-grossing tour of all time, and the second highest among female artists – the first being her own 'Sticky & Sweet' tour! 'If ten people show up, I'll be fine,' she would say, though not one person who heard her say this believed her. Brahim would be going on the 'MDNA' tour with Madonna, as one of her dancers. 'If we're still together by the end of the year, it will be a freakin' miracle,' she said, maybe only half joking. He didn't seem worried, though. 'Nah. It'll be a good time,' he said, self-confidently. 'I ain't worried. I got this.'

'There was enough instability in her life just by virtue of her career,' said someone who knew her well at this point, 'that if the man in her life was solid, it went a long way to keeping her sane. Brahim had a calming effect on her. You could see it when they were together. Somehow, she was able to resist the urge to tell him what to do, to mother him. People didn't understand it. You looked at them and you thought, "No way. He's just way too young. And she's just way too . . . *Madonna*." But, hey, it worked.'

Madonna Does Not Get Dumped

By the beginning of 2013, Madonna was exhausted from the 'MDNA' tour and anxious for some time off. The relationship with Brahim Zaibat ended up being compromised during the later part of the tour, and for reasons not entirely surprising. It had been a difficult experience, as is always the case with global Madonna tours, with no end to the various technical snafus and other problems. There was obviously a huge company of choreographers, directors, production designers, costumers and musicians on the road with her but, as always, final decisions in most areas fell to Madonna. As usual, she tended to micro-manage, often second-guessing choices made by those she'd hired. She couldn't help it. When she was on stage and all eyes were on her, everything going on around her had to be working at optimum efficiency otherwise she would lose focus and her performance would then suffer. She'd been around long enough to know how it all worked, what she needed in order to perform, and if it wasn't in order, would it be any surprise that it would rattle her?

Also, it's worth noting that the older Madonna got, the harder the rigorous choreography was on her. She didn't hold back on the 'MDNA' tour; she never makes allowances for age. She was determined to give it her all, and that included the level of dance that had always been a chief hallmark of her performances, no matter the wear and tear on her body. She hadn't been the same, though, not since that nasty horseback riding accident of eight years earlier during which she broke a number of bones. Since that time, she had recurring and sometimes chronic pain, especially when under the demands of a strict dance regimen when touring. 'Every time I do a show, I die a little bit,' she once said, 'but no shit is worth doing unless you're willing to die for it.'

Brahim – who celebrated his twenty-sixth birthday while the tour was in New York City and performing at Yankee Stadium – could barely comprehend the stress his fifty-four-year-old girlfriend was under from one day to the next. She was also loath to complain about it to him, not wanting to appear old in his eyes, or in anyone else's for that matter. Of course, it could probably be argued that what Madonna really needed at this time was a companion of or at least *around* her age who could empathize with not only her physical issues but emotional as well. After all, by the time the tour was over, she was depleted in almost every way; she had nothing left to give anyone but her children, and the last thing she needed was another child – which was how, unfortunately enough, she had suddenly begun to view Brahim.

Brahim Zaibat was an interesting study in paradoxes. While he wanted to be present for Madonna, he refused to become her whipping boy, or even her assistant. Unlike Jesus Luz before him, he didn't become the 'go-to' guy for anyone wanting to have entrée to Madonna. He wouldn't put himself in that position. If a person on the production had any sort of pressing issue and approached Brahim with it, he figured out who on the team had that particular responsibility and helped arrange a meeting, but he made it clear early on that he wasn't going to appeal to Madonna on anyone's behalf. 'I know who I am,' he would say. 'Madonna has a secretary.

I ain't it. Maybe I'll help you find out who it is, but after that you're on your own.' Instead, Brahim focused on his dancing – dedicating himself completely to his performance on stage with Madonna every night – and, not surprisingly given his youth, he also focused on having fun.

For Madonna, being on the road is not fun. Put it this way, she's no longer that young girl with the blonde ponytail who used to hang out with her dancers from the 'Blond Ambition' tour. She does her show; she goes to bed. She wakes up; she travels to the next city. Then . . . she does her show; she goes to bed. She's a dedicated workhorse and, after so many decades of touring around the world, she long ago realized that the road is no place for a good time.

While Brahim found Madonna's work ethic admirable and even inspiring, it wasn't easy for him to conform to it; he liked hanging out with the other dancers and, also, seeing sites Madonna had been to a dozen times or more in the past. He would eventually find his way to their hotel suite. By the end of the tour, they were sleeping in separate rooms; she was in no mood to have sex. One evening, though, Madonna rose in the middle of the night and began storming through the hallways of the hotel in which they were staying, banging on people's doors, and demanding to know, '*Is Brahim in there? Where the fuck is he? Is he in there? Goddamnit, where is he?*' She was unravelling, very upset, and no one seemed to know why. By morning, whatever it was that had been troubling her had blown over, and the company was off to the next stop. There was no time for high-stakes drama, not while on the road, anyway. However, by the time the 'MDNA' tour wound down in Argentina on 22 December 2012, the gulf between Madonna and Brahim had grown to the point where he was thinking about leaving her.

He was thinking about leaving *her*? No. Not so fast. Madonna does not get dumped. Madonna does the dumping. While she may have once written that 'rejection is the greatest aphrodisiac' (in her song 'Forbidden Love' from *Bedtime Stories*), she definitely prefers to be the one doing the rejecting. Therefore, the couple limped along throughout the year 2013, not seeing eye-to-eye on pretty much anything, before the relationship then ended badly. Depending on whose version of the story one believes, either he left her around the end of 2013, or she left him. Either way, it was over, and not in a sweet, sad way as had been the case with Jesus Luz. This one was explosive and acrimonious, though the details are not really known. All that is known is that it's best not to mention Brahim to Madonna – not unless you want something thrown at you.

Three years later, at a concert in the Philippines during her 'Rebel Heart' tour, Madonna would tell the crowd, 'Once I had a Filipino trainer, this beautiful girl, but she fucked my boyfriend, so I fired her. In this case, it was not a happy ending,' she continued. 'I know I sound like I'm cynical and I don't believe in romance and that I think everybody is backstabbing.' There was immediate speculation that the boyfriend was Brahim but he and the trainer denied the allegation, admitting they had slept together but that this was before he was with Madonna. Whatever the truth about Brahim, the particulars of the scandal hardly mattered. The fact that Madonna made a point of addressing it in her act and seemed quite bitter about it made it clear to any observer that, as far as she was concerned, even the passing of three years had not eased her discomfort where a younger man was concerned . . .

Still, true to the paradox of her nature, as angry as she was at whatever happened, she was still sorry to see Brahim go. After all, he'd been her longest-running relationship after her break-up with Guy. He'd proved himself to be his own man, and she liked that about him. However, *he proved himself to be his own man* – and she hated that about him, too! She still wasn't in the market for an equal. Those who know her best say that by the end of 2013, she was still trying to sort out her feelings about Guy, still unable to reconcile what had happened between them. It also couldn't but vex her that he had gone on to a happy, fulfilling relationship with the afore-mentioned model, Jacqui Ainsley – thirteen years his junior.

Despite the hit his film-making career took as a result of it, Guy, according to all accounts, is not conflicted about the particulars of his marriage to Madonna. 'I enjoyed my first marriage,' he would later tell *Details* in December 2017. 'It's definitely not something I regret. The experience was ultimately very positive. I love the kids that came out of it, and I could see no other route to take. But you move on, don't you? I stepped into a soap opera, and I lived in it for quite a long period of my life. I'll probably be more eloquent on it ten years from now.

'When you end up with a lot of the things you set out to chase and find that you've stumbled into all sorts of hollow victories, then you become deeply philosophical,' he added. 'I'm quite happy that that experience was accelerated for me. I'm glad I made money, in other words,' he concluded, oddly – hopefully, he didn't mean it the way it sounded. 'And I'm glad I got married,' he concluded.

Guy moved on. Madonna, though, not so much; barely a month after Brahim, she found herself with yet *another* young man, twenty-six-year-old choreographer and dancer Timor Steffens, from the Netherlands. This one lasted only eight months, though. On 11 August – Rocco's birthday – something apparently happened between the two of them in the South of France which, at least according to what was widely reported, caused Madonna to demand that he pack his bags and leave. The poor chap hardly had a chance to register as a figure in Madonna's world, so we don't know if he was anything like the always-available Jesus or the stubbornly independent Brahim; he was out of Madonna's life before being able to prove himself one way or the other.

Ciccone Family Values

In May 2014, Madonna went back to her home state of Michigan to see family and friends. This also gave her an opportunity to have her children reunite with relatives they hadn't seen in some time; by this time Lourdes was seventeen; Rocco, thirteen; and David and Mercy were both eight. Madonna's father, Tony, and her stepmother, Joan, still owned the thriving Ciccone Vineyard, fourteen acres in Suttons Bay, Michigan.

Madonna was proud of the fact that she'd been able to keep her children on an even keel as they got older. She was determined that they not fall into the same life traps of some of her siblings – their aunts and uncles – many of whom have had extremely difficult relationships with Madonna in the past. In many ways, the Ciccone family was fairly fractured in 2014, some of its members in alignment with their most famous sibling and others not able to see eye-to-eye with her at all. In the past, Madonna has blamed the instability of her natural siblings on the death of their mother. 'I have a very large family who are all emotional cripples in one way or another. Emotionally, we're all pretty needy because of my mother.' In truth, though, it would seem that her incredible fame has also had a lot to do with the complexities of her relationship not only with her natural siblings, but her step siblings as well.

At this time, Madonna was at least somewhat friendly with her brother, Marty, fifty-seven, a former disc jockey who'd also worked as a voice-over artist in Los Angeles. In the early Nineties, during Madonna's 'Blond Ambition' tour, Marty was the one who famously had a setback in his recovery just a day after being released from a rehabilitation centre (paid for by his sister). Perhaps somewhat unfairly, *In Bed with Madonna* showed him apparently incoherent and irresponsible, and either too inebriated or too disoriented to attend his sister's concert and visit with her afterwards. The way the scenes were framed, it was as if Madonna was let down by his behaviour – making her the victim, as opposed to maybe a more sympathetic notion that the troubled, heavily scrutinized Martin was actually a casualty of her celebrity. In 1994, he told a US newspaper: 'Madonna won't lift a finger to help me. This is not the sister I grew up with, who mothered me, who was so full of compassion.

I guess fame really changes people.' Of Marty, Madonna countered: 'He's very tortured. I've had to get him out of the habit of calling me whenever he needed something from me. I have to feel that Martin loves me for just me and not my money.' By 2014, the siblings seemed on somewhat steadier ground, but it would never be easy between them. However, they were at least *trying* to have a better relationship.

Madonna's sister, Paula, now fifty-five – who'd worked for the Ciccone vineyard in its marketing division – also had a sometimes stormy relationship with the pop star. Fans remember that she attended Madonna's wedding to Guy, though Madonna famously made her pay for her own ticket! (In fact, though, it was reported that Madonna had made *all* family members who wished to attend – including her father and stepmother and Christopher – pay their own ways to Scotland.)

Of course, Madonna fell out with fifty-four-year-old Christopher six years earlier when he wrote *Life with My Sister Madonna*. The contentious siblings had begun occasionally emailing one another, though they hadn't actually seen each other since the publication of the book.

Madonna's sister, Melanie, fifty-two, a former publicist now married with children, remained the closest to Madonna of her siblings; she was present when Madonna gave birth to Lourdes. Her half-sister, Jennifer, forty-seven, was now an art teacher in Michigan; they had never been close. Madonna was somewhat closer to half-brother, Mario, forty-six, who once worked for Maverick. Mario, also an addict, has had his own share of problems, though. 'My big sister can't tame me,' he once said. 'I am what I am and she has no right to lecture me.' By 2014, the siblings were rarely in touch.

The problem Madonna has faced with her family members is that, as is the case with many famous and wealthy people, she's never been able to find a balance between giving them money to help them out of tough times and drawing a line in terms of how much. None of her siblings are well off. The consensus amongst some of them is that Madonna could do a lot better by them, maybe give them each a few million dollars that would completely transform their lives. After all, such gifting would mean almost nothing to her bank account. However, Madonna feels that she has worked hard for her money and has helped them all out at one time or another – which is true. She has never been a woman who just hands over millions, even to family members. From their perspective, though, it's never been easy being related to someone like Madonna. 'Little things seep into your persona,' says Christopher, 'whether it's that you judge yourself against this massive thing, or the way other people look at you because of that massive thing – their expectations that you must be great, that you must be rich, that you must be famous, and why aren't you?'

The fact that Madonna donated money to the city of Detroit in the spring of 2014 and made headlines doing so did ruffle the feathers of certain family members. Believing in the old adage that charity should begin at home, they felt she could help them out a bit more if she really wanted to do so. However, Madonna was more focused on how run-down the city appeared; this had been the case for years, since Detroit was still reeling from bankruptcy and was in very bad shape. There were more unemployed than ever, and the homeless rate had quadrupled in recent years. Madonna wanted to help. To that end, she decided to donate money to three personally chosen organizations.

The Downtown Youth Boxing Gym, which offered sports activities to underprivileged kids from Detroit's Eastside would benefit from Madonna's largesse in that she would finance the construction of a new building for the facility. She would also support the Detroit Achievement Academy, which provided art and music supplies to inner-city classrooms. Also, she would give funds for the Empowerment Plan, which employed homeless women in the manufacturing of coats and sleeping bags for the underprivileged.

'I was deeply inspired by the efforts of so many people who I met who have dedicated themselves to helping the kids and adults in

Detroit elevate themselves from the cycle of poverty,' Madonna said in a statement in May 2014. 'I have seen the results their commitment and hard work have already accomplished.

'From meeting the kids at Downtown Youth Boxing Gym, who have a 100 per cent high-school graduation rate, to seeing how eager the students at the Detroit Achievement Academy are to learn about the arts, to understanding the value of giving homeless women the opportunity to become self-sufficient through the Empowerment Plan, it was obvious to me that I had to get involved and be part of the solution to help Detroit recover. A piece of my heart will always be in Detroit and I'm humbled to be able to give back to my community.'

Anthony

While Madonna was happy to be able to do something for the city of Detroit, she was a lot less eager to assist one family member whose life had gone completely off the rails. At this time, her oldest brother, Anthony, was suffering from debilitating alcoholism and had been homeless for almost four years. He was fifty-six, and bitter. The problem the Ciccones faced for years with Anthony is that he'd been unwilling to address his drinking problem. It had all but destroyed him, alienating him from family members like his father Tony – now in his mid-eighties – who had tried everything to help him. 'My father would be very happy if I died of hypothermia and then he would not have to worry about it anymore,' Anthony had said. 'He's old-school. He grew up in the depression. He doesn't want to be bothered. He doesn't like me. He doesn't want me to be me; he wants me to be somebody else. He thinks the way I live is intentional.'

Anthony started giving press interviews about his tragic life and suggesting that Madonna was somehow to blame for it or, at the very least, not very concerned about it. 'Madonna doesn't give a shit if I'm dead or alive,' he told the *Mail Online*. 'She lives in her own world. I never loved her in the first place. She never loved me. We never loved each other.' In fact, Madonna had paid for Anthony to enter rehab programmes four times in the past; each time, he left early and refused further treatment. Madonna does not believe in enabling bad behaviour. She's always been pragmatic about the way life works – or, at least how it does in her view. 'We are responsible for our own lives,' she said when speaking of her brother. 'I don't blame other people for my mistakes. I just don't do it. There are people who do that, and I'm fine with it – for them. However, I will not allow them to drag me in. I just won't.'

Madonna had actually been at the end of her tether with Anthony for many years. Of course, publicly, she was painted in a poor light in relation to his tale of woe. For instance, when the *Mail Online* interviewed Anthony, it noted that Madonna had 'a billion dollars' and that despite this great wealth, she didn't care if her brother was dead or alive. 'In his rucksack he carries a photo of Madonna printed off the Internet,' said the article, 'where he also keeps a bottle of cheap wine in a brown paper bag, his gloves and his rolling tobacco – which he smokes constantly. Luckily for Anthony the local churches take turns allowing the homeless night-time shelter during the winter and cooking them hot meals – otherwise he admits he would already have frozen to death.'

Madonna was furious when she saw the story in the *Mail Online*. 'It really riled her up,' said one relative. 'She crumpled it up and threw it into the trash can.' It wasn't so much that she was angry at Anthony as much as she was dismayed by his decision to tell his story to a reporter. 'Does this help him in any way?' she asked in a phone call to one of her relatives in Michigan. 'Is he trying to shame me into giving him money? What is the point of a story in a London newspaper? How does *that* help him?'

'Obviously, he is trying to embarrass you,' said the relative.

'And the newspaper is after the exact same thing,' Madonna said. 'All of it designed to make me feel bad.'

'Does it work?' the relative asked. 'Does this make you feel bad?'

She was more concerned, she said, about her brother. However, she was also not going to do anything to help him, not at this time, anyway. She said she'd given it all she had to give, and wouldn't do anything else until Anthony agreed to go into rehab. At that point, she said, she 'might' then agree to pay for it. 'I'll see how I feel,' she concluded. 'But I am not inclined to help him. The only reason I might do it is for Pop. He shouldn't be made to suffer because of Anthony's mistakes.'

In 2012, a radio station in Detroit orchestrated a stunt that saw Anthony and some down-and-out friends who appeared in similarly bad shape posing in front of the venue in Indianapolis where Madonna was performing her Super Bowl half-time show. While she sang, he and the others drank beer outside. They could hear the echoes of her voice as it wafted into the parking lot. Since they didn't have tickets, of course they couldn't get into the venue. When Madonna saw the photos of her brother in the paper a few days later, she was angry – not only at him but at the radio station who sponsored the weird photo opportunity.

Now, two years later during her visit home, Madonna's heart broke when she learned that Tony had been driving around Detroit looking for his son to give him some food. 'He's too old for this kind of stress,' a concerned Madonna told one relative at the winery during her visit. 'We can't allow this to continue.'

'Tony does what he wants to do,' said that relative. 'He's heartsick about Anthony. No one can get through to him. That's his son, after all.'

Madonna was as angry as she was upset. She got into a car with that relative, determined to find Anthony and, once and for all, try to talk some sense into him. She and the family member drove all over the outskirts of Traverse Bay, Michigan, looking for Anthony, stopping at homeless shelters and at bus stops and liquor stores, asking other indigent people if they knew him or knew of his whereabouts. When recognized by one homeless person, Madonna said, 'People say I look like her but, actually, I think I'm better looking.' She smiled, reached into her purse and pulled out a hundred dollar bill. 'Take this,' she said, handing the money to the poor woman. 'Save it. Buy food. Not liquor, though. Do you promise? I need you to promise me!' The woman nodded her head then took the gift. 'I know I shouldn't tell her how to spend the money,' Madonna later said. 'I feel like a real bitch, making her promise. Like she doesn't have enough problems? But I just can't watch people destroy themselves.'

In the end, Madonna wasn't able to find Anthony, and maybe it's just as well because she was in no mood to be understanding of his plight. She had intended to tell him that if he couldn't straighten himself out, that was his choice. However, he should stop torturing their poor father.

I tracked Anthony down at a soup kitchen outside of Traverse Bay. He looked quite sick, a full beard hiding his gaunt face. He talked a lot about the past and, in particular, the loss of his mother and the long-ago re-marriage of his father to Joan Gustafson. 'We all hated her,' Anthony said, pointing out that she was only twelve years older than him. He said it was as if his older sister had become his mother. It seemed as if he was living in the past, keeping a record of old grievances against his father and stepmother, blaming them both for his present dire situation, and also blaming Madonna by insisting she could 'at least try to act like she gives a shit about anyone other than herself.'

He said that Tony once promised him that the vineyard would be 'all mine'. However, somehow, his half brother, Mario, had ended up running the place. He now felt that Tony preferred Mario over him, and seemed to not recognize that, in fact, his own alcoholism had come between him and his dad. 'My father just is who he is,' he said.

Three years later, at the end of 2017, Anthony would return to the Ciccone fold when, after a final stint in rehab, he was welcomed back into the family. However, from all accounts, Madonna would still not have much to do with him.

Piracy

On 28 November 2014, almost a full four months ahead of the release date of Madonna's next album, *Rebel Heart*, two songs – the title track and 'Wash All Over Me' – were leaked on the Internet. While they were immediately taken down, Madonna was understandably upset. The way she saw it, it was nothing but sheer piracy (and there are few, if any, artists of her calibre who would argue the point). 'Nothing is done until the day it is released,' she said in a meeting at Interscope, according to someone present who would only speak candidly if guaranteed anonymity. '*How did this happen?*' she demanded to know. No one knew the answer. In this cyber age, there's really no way to protect songs from being leaked, she was told. She wasn't about to accept that answer, though. For now, she was just happy that the songs had been removed. It vexed her, however, that there were people in the world who had them in their possession.

Then, on 17 December, a true catastrophe occurred – or, at least that's how it felt to Madonna: *thirteen more songs* were leaked. 'Thank you for not listening!' Madonna wrote to her fans, amid reports of the breach. 'Thank you for your loyalty! Thank you for waiting.' Then, in a follow-up post on Instagram, she accused the hackers of trying 'to destroy [her] artistic process'. 'This is artistic rape!! These are early leaked demos, half of which won't even make it on my album,' she insisted. 'The other half have changed and evolved.' The leaked material even included artwork suggesting that the album was to be called *Iconic*. 'My music has been stolen and leaked!' Madonna complained in a 4 December Instagram post. 'I have been violated as a human and an artist! #fuckedupshit'.

It's easy to conclude that Madonna was overreacting, that there are worse things in this life than having one's songs leaked on the Internet. If one understands an artist like Madonna, however, it becomes clear that the assault feels very real to her. Like most artists of her stature, she is immersed in her music for many years before its release, constantly honing the material, always working to make certain it's her very best effort. Even when it's finally released, she usually isn't completely satisfied with it. In fact, it's safe to say that the only reason any album is ever released is simply because she has run out of time, and the label is now demanding it. Otherwise, she'd probably still be working on her first album! Therefore, to have songs disseminated into the public domain before completion, when they are still just rough demos or preliminary mixes, does feel to her like a personal attack.

Now that so many of the songs were out there for scrutiny, and in variations that weren't even finished, Madonna felt she had no choice but to officially release the final mixes of the songs, and to do so earlier than intended. 'I wanted to plan everything in advance,' she said. 'Release the single, shoot a video, start talking about my record. And you know, prepare for the release of the entire album and have everything set up just so . . . But we sort of were left with no choice', she concluded.

On 20 December, five songs were made available for download on iTunes (six in the United States). The leaks continued, though, with fourteen new demos being revealed between 23 December and 27 December!

Many artists in this same situation might have just secured their laptops and 'cloud' access and hoped for better luck next time. Madonna, though, wanted the perpetrator found and punished. Somehow, Interscope was able to track the leak to Israel. It was then suggested to Madonna that she hire Lahav 433, a crime-fighting division of the Israel Police, specializing in national crimes. After a month-long investigation that incorporated the FBI, the culprit was found and arrested, on 21 January 2015. It turned out to be the same man who had earlier leaked a demo of Madonna's lead single from *MDNA*, 'Give Me All Your Luvin'.' The first time, with that song, he was let go with a stern warning. This time, though, he was sentenced to fourteen months in prison. Hopefully, he learned his lesson. 'I know he's a fan,' Madonna said of the perpetrator to one of her associates. 'How do you punish a fan? How does that feel good? But what else can be done?'

Rebel Heart

It's difficult to gauge whether or not the illegal downloading of Madonna's songs impacted the release and then sales of *Rebel Heart*. In a marketplace that finds some albums dropped suddenly with no advance notice – as Beyoncé has done in the past – shock and awe goes a long way toward generating public recognition and, hopefully, acclaim for the music. Besides that, Madonna has a specific formula for releasing her music, as she has said, which has to do with a tried-and-true, careful strategy of videos coinciding with single releases and a slow build-up of expectations to the Big Day – the day of official release. She also likes press interviews and other forms of marketing to coincide. Lately, she's also a proponent of social media and the power it has to reach her fan base. Did having those plans laid to waste by an obsessed fan in Israel hurt the release of *Rebel Heart*? Maybe. After all, it was her first album not to debut at number 1 on the *Billboard* chart since 1998. However, Arthur Fogel, who heads up Live Nation's Entertainment Global Touring Division, which has sponsored Madonna's tours of late and was gearing up for the 'Rebel Heart' tour, felt that maybe no damage had occurred. 'It's kind of strange how it all came out,' he said, 'but it certainly hasn't been a negative in terms of getting people engaged with the new music. Anything that helps put it out there is good, even if it happens in a weird way.'

Madonna would have to disagree with Fogel, though. There is a right way to release music, and a wrong way – and, as far as she is concerned, *Rebel Heart* was done the wrong way.

'What started out as an invigorating, life-enhancing, joyous experience evolved into something quite crazy,' Madonna told Jon Pareles of the *New York Times*. 'A strange artistic process, but a sign of the times. We're all digital, we're all vulnerable and everything's instant – so instant. Instant success and instant failure. Instant discovery, instant destruction, instant construction. It's as splendid and wonderful as it is devastating. Honestly, to me it's the death of being an artist in many ways.'

As it happens, *Rebel Heart* really is one of Madonna's most satisfying albums. Unlike many of her best records, on which she tended to work primarily with one producer – such as William Orbit on *Ray of Light* – with *Rebel Heart* Madonna implemented her more recent strategy of working with a variety of producers, such as the late Avicii (known for his work with Chris Brown) and Toby Gad (who's worked with Beyoncé). That said, she still had the final say on every aspect of each song. 'I never leave the room,' she said. 'Sometimes I think that makes them mad. Like, "Don't you have to go to the bathroom? Don't you have somewhere to go? Don't you want to go make some calls?"'

Of this, her thirteenth studio album, the *New York Times*' Ben Ratliff wrote: '. . . it uses sex as an arena of pleasure and challenge, just as she was doing in her mid-30s; it reminds you that her ballad voice was one of the ubiquitous pleasures in American pop twenty-five years ago. It goes into EDM, trap and reggae, pulling on the songwriting and production contributions of Avicii, Diplo and Kanye West."

Much of the album harks back to Madonna's glorious past – even if just in terms of the way her voice is recorded, so upfront in the mix, not obscured by orchestral elements. Especially if one is a longtime fan, listening to this album serves to remind that she remains a force to be reckoned with, an artist who has stood the test of time – and also, the superficiality of 'Give Me All Your Luvin'' from *MDNA* really does *not* define who she is as an artist.

'I don't like to dwell in the past, but it seemed like the right time to do so,' she said at the time. 'After three decades one has to look back. Because there's a lot of times I just stop and think, "Wow." I'm thinking about all the people that I've known, that I've worked with, that I've been friends with, that I've collaborated with, from Basquiat to Michael Jackson to Tupac Shakur. I survived and they didn't. And it's bittersweet for me to think about that. It just seemed like a time where I wanted to stop and look back. It's kind of like survivor guilt. How did I make it and they didn't?'

Rebel Heart is a personal statement, the songs reflective of where Madonna has been in her career – such as 'Joan of Arc' which points to the widespread criticism she's received over the years. It also suggests where she may be headed – the stripped-down 'Ghost Town' is a singer/songwriter masterpiece, showcasing her voice and songwriting ability, along with a scintillating production.

In January 2017, Madonna addressed the question of retirement to *Harper's Bazaar*, and took a shot at Guy in the process: '[My ex-husband] used to say to me, "But *why* do you have to do this again? *Why* do you have to make another record? *Why* do you have to go on tour? *Why* do you have to make another movie?" And I'm like, "*Why do I have to explain myself?*" I feel like that's a very sexist thing to say. Does anyone ask Steve Spielberg why he's still making movies? Hasn't he had enough success? Hasn't he made enough money? Hasn't he made a name for himself? Did someone go to Pablo Picasso and say, "Okay, you're eighty years old. Haven't you painted enough paintings?" No. I'm so tired of that question. I just don't understand it. I'll stop everything that I do when I don't want to do it anymore. I'll stop when I run out of ideas. I'll stop when you fucking kill me. How about that?' Of course, there was probably a more artful, elegant way of expressing herself, but she'll never change, will she? She knows who she is, and so does her public.

The response from critics to *Rebel Heart* was overwhelmingly positive. In terms of radio play, though, appreciation for the album's songs was lukewarm. No one is hot forever on radio, however, and that's just a fact. Once an artist hits 40, he or she usually suffers on radio.

'Living for Love', the album's first release, didn't even make the *Billboard* Top 100. Also, while the UK's BBC Radio was reluctant to give it a shot, despite that wrong-minded decision it entered the UK singles chart at number 26. It became her seventy-first Top 40 single in the UK, a record number. However, even though it reached the Top 20 in some other countries, it really can't be considered a successful release.

The next single 'Ghost Town', also didn't make the *Billboard* Top 100, which was astonishing considering its stellar reviews. In the UK, it charted at number 117. While in the top twenty in several other countries, again, this also cannot be considered a success for Madonna. It did make number 1 on *Billboard*'s dance charts, though – giving her the distinction of having the most number 1s ever – forty-five in all – by an act on a singular *Billboard* chart.

'Bitch I'm Madonna' also went to number 1 on the dance charts, but stalled at 84 on *Billboard*'s Top 100 and didn't even chart in the UK.

'Hold Tight' did worse, not charting in the USA or the UK.

The fact that Madonna couldn't seem to score with a radio hit was frustrating to her; she had just as much to offer as she ever had and, in fact, maybe more just by virtue of her life experience. However, ageing in the record industry wasn't easy, especially when people kept bringing it to her attention. 'I'm sick of people saying

I'm too old for this or that, to shake my ass, or whatever. I'd like to see your ass when you're my age,' she has said. In fact, when was the last time the Rolling Stones were played on the radio? Or Billy Joel? Or Paul McCartney? Or Diana Ross? Indeed, as Pete Seeger once wrote, 'To everything there is a season . . .'

While radio programmers were reluctant to play her music, it certainly didn't stop her fans from swarming to Madonna's concerts. From 9 September 2015 to 20 March 2016, she was on the road – again! – with the 'Rebel Heart' tour. It looked like she was having a terrific time, completely in her element, still vital, still fresh. 'Throughout nearly the entire two-hour event, Madonna could barely stop grinning,' wrote Jim Farber of the *New York Daily News* of the opening night in Montreal's Bell Center.

'. . . It helped that she was supported by her best-choreographed, and most rewardingly theatrical, show since her peak "Blond Ambition" show twenty-five years ago. Together, it made for an infectious night that brought the Canadian crowd to a series of spontaneous, and escalating, standing ovations. It didn't hurt that she sang "La Vie En Rose", both in French and in surprisingly bold voice. The bright tone of the show made for a striking contrast to the star's last tour, "MDNA", a dark and violent affair that often ended up puzzling to boot. "Rebel Heart" had no such pretense. In fact, it may be Madonna's lightest road show to date.'

While clearly having a good time on stage, behind the scenes Madonna was very lonely with no romantic interest on the road with her. Or maybe that's not exactly true; she was seen with a couple of young men during the tour, but no one who appeared to be impacting her life in any significant way. She had her son, Rocco, with her, though, as she did on the 'MDNA' tour (when he would sometimes come on stage and dance with her), this time as a production functionary, though he was not listed as an employee on the tour's official staff.

It started out fine with mother and son, but within a few stops things began to go downhill. Soon, they were arguing. Maybe it was understandable. After all, Rocco was now fifteen and going through what most youngsters do when it comes to puberty and teenage rebellion. Madonna's joking about him on social media probably didn't help, either, such as when she posted a video of him performing a back flip on Instagram with the caption: 'Rocco's preferred profile #nosausage'.

As a parent, Madonna was – is – quite strict. Some find it ironic that she has taken after her father, Tony, in this regard. Most of what she got away with as a youngster she would never allow for any of her children. She has always had stringent rules. For instance, her kids have had to follow her macrobiotic diet, which they've all inevitably hated. No sweets, no chocolate – a rule which even Tony has tried to break with his grandchildren. No TV, except under special circumstances. No cell phones until they turned fifteen. If they left clothing on the floor in their rooms, those clothes were taken from them. Madonna once explained of Lourdes, 'She has to earn all of her clothes back by being tidy, picking up things in her room, making her bed in the morning. She wears the same outfit every day to school until she learns her lesson.' Back in a 2005 interview with *Harpers & Queen*, she said, 'I'm the disciplinarian, Guy's the spoiler,' she said. 'When Daddy gets home they're going to get chocolate. I'm more practical.'

It's worth noting that the nature of the trouble Madonna had with Rocco on the road was so minimal, it's practically not even worth examination. For instance, he wanted to stay out late at night; he wanted to smoke; he wanted his mother to butt out of his business; he wanted his independence – nothing unusual. She was also annoyed with him for not doing his homework while on the tour and took away his cell phone – all classic, well-meaning, determined, mother–rebellious son business. At one point, he even blocked her on his Instagram!

What *is* worth examination is how much Rocco took after Guy in one major and, for Madonna, extremely troubling respect. For most of his life, Rocco had heard one constant refrain from his father about Madonna and her job: too much work and not enough home life. Suddenly, as Rocco became a teenager, he started repeating that exact same refrain. Simply put, he didn't want to share his mother with the world. Of course, Madonna is who she is, she still had a fire in her belly for her career and she wasn't going to change. Moreover, she felt that it was precisely *because* of her job that her children were able to enjoy such an entitled, privileged lifestyle and that they should just be grateful for it, and toe the line.

Lourdes didn't take much issue with her mother's work; she had her own aspirations in fashion and was even working with Madonna on different projects relating to that interest. Rocco, though, wasn't sure what he wanted to do with his life. He just knew he was tired of having it turned upside down every time Mom decided it was time to go back out on the road and entertain her fans. Madonna couldn't believe she was now hearing the exact same critique of her lifestyle she'd heard for years from her recalcitrant husband, but now coming from the mouth of her son! 'I thought I was done with this,' she complained. 'And here I am! It's Guy all over again!' Therefore, she did what she had once done with Guy: she brought Rocco out on the road with her, thinking that perhaps it would be fun and exciting for him. It was – for about a month on the 'MDNA' tour. After that, Rocco was over it. So by the time they got to the 'Rebel Heart' tour, being on tour was anything but enjoyable for either him or for Mom. Maybe it was only natural, then, that Rocco tended to gravitate toward Guy, who was not only much more permissive, but also, in some ways, more understanding. 'Everyone told me that to be good at school was important, but for me it wasn't,' Guy would observe when talking about his parental responsibilities. 'So, I am anti-school. And I'm anti people putting so much pressure on kids and robbing their childhood by giving them so much homework. I think if kids want to arse around, then they should.'

Fighting Over Rocco

In December 2015, Rocco Ritchie left the 'Rebel Heart' tour when it made its way to England. He adamantly refused to carry on to Scotland with his mother and ultimately go back to New York with her for the holiday. Instead, he said he wanted to stay with Guy and his wife, Jacqui Ainsley, with whom he had a very good relationship. Madonna was furious, not only with Rocco but with Guy for encouraging their son in his decision.

It couldn't help but still bother Madonna, who was fifty-seven by this time, that Guy, forty-seven, had found true happiness after her with the beautiful model, Jacqui. He had moved on successfully and, in the process, had got what he'd always wanted – a secure and stable home life. As far as he was concerned, Madonna got what she'd always wanted, too – the continuation of a record-breaking career that just kept getting bigger and better, at least as far as her concert tours went, anyway. Hadn't that always been her goal? Of course, Madonna would see things quite differently. She would say that *never* did she want to sacrifice her home life for her career.

Understandably, it would eat away at Madonna every time she spoke to Guy – which was often because of co-parenting – and she'd find him nothing but content, just loving his life and living it up. After all, had she been happy since the divorce? Really, truly happy? With Jesus? With Brahim? With Timor? On the road, trying to prove herself, pushing herself to top one tour after the other? Yes, of course she'd had her happy moments, but she knew that her life left a lot to be desired – and, maybe worse yet, she knew that Guy knew it, too. The spectre of the failure of her marriage to him seemed to haunt every relationship she'd had since, influencing many of her decisions relating to those men in her life.

When Rocco decided to stay in London with his father, Madonna made quick moves to force him to return to New York for the 2015 holidays, and then for reenrolment for the next term at his school, the Lycée Français de New York. Of course, she was concerned about her son and wanted what she believed was best for him. She was heartsick that he didn't want to be with her, as would be any mom who loved her boy and had to face the harsh reality that he'd rather be with Dad. However, if anyone thinks that her mixed emotions for Guy had nothing to do with the war she would wage against him for possession of Rocco, that would be a person who doesn't understand Madonna very well.

First of all, Madonna is used to having her way and doesn't like being defied. It practically never happens in her life. When was the last time a person said 'no' to her and got away with it? It's not hyperbolic to say it probably hadn't happened in many years. For Guy to tell her she couldn't have Rocco when she wanted him was more than Madonna was willing to accept. As far as she was concerned, Rocco was just a kid; he didn't have a say in what happened. Guy could have and, as far as Madonna was concerned, *should* have insisted that the boy return to the States. However, Guy was only acquiescing to their son's wishes. Was he to force the teen to return to his mother when clearly it was not what he wanted? The short answer from Madonna was: '*Hell* yeah.' Therefore, she went before a judge in New York on 23 December and pleaded her case for custody of Rocco.

Manhattan Supreme Court Justice Deborah Kaplan ruled for Madonna; courts usually side with the mothers in these sorts of custody cases. During the hearing, she ordered Rocco to return to New York immediately. However, Guy's attorney, Eric Buckley, told the judge, 'He [Rocco] has expressed very clearly that he does *not* want to return to New York.' Madonna – in a long black skirt with a fur-trimmed coat and large celebrity sunglasses – became instantly annoyed and began to speak up, no surprise there. Fearing whatever it was she was about to say, her attorney, Eleanor Alter, asked her to please be quiet.

'Has he [Guy] prevented the child from returning to the US?' the judge asked.

Buckley responded, 'Effectively, yes.'

The judge then ruled that Rocco would have a court-appointed attorney in New York to whom he could personally plead his case as to whether or not he wanted to live with his mother. However, the teen would have to first return to New York in order for it to all be sorted out. The judge also told Madonna that she and Guy should try to work this problem out between them, rather than drag the family into what she feared could become a very nasty, public dispute. 'Meanwhile, I'm granting you all the relief you have requested,' the judge declared. Madonna was appreciative; she smiled and nodded. 'I'm directing the child to be returned to New York,' said the judge. 'If he wants to stay with his father, he must [first] return to his mother.'

In the end, much to Madonna's dismay, Rocco simply defied the court's order. He did *not* return to New York. Instead, he posted a message on Instagram to a friend: 'I'm staying here, bro.' She simply couldn't believe that Guy was allowing such insubordinate behaviour. Of course, by this time, Guy had also lawyered up so he wasn't doing anything he didn't think he could get away with; he certainly would not put his son in legal jeopardy.

What was Madonna to now do? Have the kid arrested? She had no choice but to just let him have his way, especially since time was running out and she was due to return to the 'Rebel Heart' tour on 6 January, in Mexico. From that point onward, she was scheduled to be on the road until the tour ended on 20 March in Sydney, Australia. Now, unfortunately enough, it made sense for Rocco to stay with Guy in London since he definitely didn't want to be on the road with his mother. However, *something* would have to be worked out before the end of the tour because Madonna was not going to allow him to live with his father indefinitely.

Madonna was also dismayed when she did a little soul-searching about her interaction with Rocco earlier on the tour. She now felt that maybe she hadn't given him enough of her time. She'd hoped that the tour would be a sort of bonding experience for them, that it would make them closer. However, true to her nature, she became fixated on micro-managing every aspect of it to the detriment of any time she might have spent with Rocco. In her defence, though, trying to carve out quality parental time in the middle of an exhausting world tour would not have been easy under any circumstances. Now, though, she was very sorry about it and, basically, she just wanted one more chance to make things right.

Given what was going on in her private life, Madonna was miserable – and she still had more than thirty shows to go in the States, Puerto Rico, Thailand, Taipai, Japan, China, the Philippines and New Zealand. 'This was the worst of all experiences,' said someone who was on the tour with her. 'She was worried sick about her son and her relationship with him. She didn't know if she was ever going to see him again; she truly didn't. She was so bereft, it was everything she could do to get on stage and give her audiences what they had paid a whole lot of money to see – which was prime, grade-A Madonna. There were shows when she would just walk off the stage in tears. She was calling her boy, he wasn't willing to speak to her. She was fighting with Guy. It was a mess, the whole thing. "I can't go on," she said one night. "But how can I cancel? These people *deserve* the best of me, but I'm just a fraction of me these days." It's to her credit that she did it, though. Those shows on the "Rebel Heart" tour were probably amongst her very best. We were all amazed. I mean, when she digs down, she finds herself and she gets results. She never lets anyone down, least of all her fans. It just never happens.'

It's always been difficult for Madonna to suppress her feelings; she gives her all with every performance and, in doing so, often feels the need to express herself and, sometimes, her most private emotions. Of course, this impulse often flies in the face of any plea she may later issue to the public or to the press for 'privacy', but the conflict as to how much she should keep to herself and how much she should share with her public has long been one of her biggest inner struggles. Of course, she leans towards sharing – over-sharing, actually. She knows no other way, not after being in the public eye for almost thiry-five years.

In Mexico City on 6 January, 2016, Madonna told the audience, 'I, too, go through challenging times in my life, and right now is one of them.' About two weeks later, in Nashville on 18 January, a fan in the audience shouted out that he wanted to marry her. She reportedly shouted back, 'I'm looking for a husband. Not a cunt. I already married a cunt.'

About a month later, in February, Madonna went to London to try to talk Rocco in returning to the States with her. He refused. Shortly thereafter, pictures of him appeared in the *Sun* in which he seemed to be smoking a joint. '[Madonna] has been shocked by evidence that her son is in danger of being drawn into a seedy and dangerous world of soft drugs and teenage hoodie gangs,' read the report. Really? Because of one joint? Even Madonna, as protective as she was and as unwilling as she was to allow her teenage son to indulge in marijuana, would not be so over-reactive.

In Australia in March, as the 'Rebel Heart' tour came to a merciful end, Madonna – dressed in costume as a clown – dedicated 'Intervention' (from *American Life*) to Rocco saying, 'There's no end to the mistakes I've made. Anyway, everybody knows the saga of me and my son, Rocco. It's not a fun story to tell or think about. I probably could have enjoyed myself a little bit more on this tour if he hadn't disappeared so suddenly and also if I knew when I would see him again.' As she sang the emotional song, touching images of her eldest son were projected behind her on the jumbo screens.

Though she was distracted and unremittingly sad throughout the tour, the reviews were incredibly positive just the same. The response was gratifying to her, of course, but did nothing to help settle her mind over private affairs at home. That same month, March, a judge in England again urged the Ritchies to work things out between them, and to try to do so without further litigation. 'I renew, one final time, my plea for both parents to seek and to find an amicable resolution to the dispute between them,' Mr Justice MacDonald said. 'Most importantly, as I observed during the course of the hearing, summer does not last forever. The boy very quickly becomes the man. It would be a very great tragedy for Rocco if any more of the previous and fast receding days of his childhood were to be taken up by this dispute.'

At this same time, Madonna began seeing Aboubaker Soumahoro, a twenty-five-year-old model and former employee of Harrod's department store. 'They were at a party together back in November when they got chatting, and hit it off straight away,' reported one friend of Madonna's. 'Over the next few weeks, they got together a couple more times and she invited him over to her place, where they sat up all night talking.'

'It's just what happens,' Madonna would blithely explain of her ongoing fascination with much younger men. 'Most men my age are married with children. They're not datable. I'm a very adventurous person and I also have a crazy life. I'm a single mother. I have four children. I mean, you have to be pretty open-minded and adventurous to want to step into my world. People who are older, and more set in their ways, are probably not as adventurous as someone younger.'

Unlike Jesus or Brahim, though, Aboubaker (also a model) seemed not to want to inject himself into Madonna's life in any way but superficially. This was the way she wanted it, particularly in light of what was going on with Guy and Rocco. Things were complicated enough, especially since, in March, Rocco's court-appointed attorney, Ellen Sigal, testified that the dispute was causing the youngster great stress. 'It's been very difficult for him,' she said. 'We hope to put an end to this as soon as possible without exposing him to more litigation, press innuendo, any of that kind of thing.'

'No one is disrupting his household other than the inability of the parents to reach a resolution,' Judge Deborah Kaplan declared. 'If they cannot resolve this matter then eventually the court will.'

Unfortunately, the conflict would continue to drag on throughout the spring and into the summer months. Madonna and Guy would have many heated telephone conversations during this time, airing their differences (sometimes explosively) and, in the process, re-examining their lives together and their failed marriage. If anything, the battle over their son forced Madonna to come to terms with Guy, once and for all; she had no other choice. She had to face the fact that he had moved on and that he was very happy in his new life.

'She also had to face the fact that all she had was her kids,' said one of her intimates, 'and that losing one of them to Guy hurt a lot. It was devastating in so many ways. The rejection stung. She had to sort through it, come to terms with it. "I see my part in this," she told me, "and I have to claim it. I can't continue to blame Guy for everything that went wrong between us." I think she was finally seeing her way through the muck that had been her messy divorce, including the outrageous settlement, Guy's happy re-marriage . . . all of it. I had the sense that she was ready to finally put it all to rest and just move on with her life.'

Rapprochement

Emotional support for Madonna during this extremely dark time in her life came from a rather surprising source: Carlos Leon, Lourdes' father. Madonna had always had a good relationship with Carlos, who was now forty-nine. She had never really been in love with him, which may be why the two of them were able to continue as such good friends long after Lourdes was born back in 1996. For the last three years, Carlos had been married to Zac Posen designer, Betina Holte; Lourdes attended the wedding in Gillelje, Denmark. The two had one child, a son named Meeka, born in February 2015.

Like Guy, Carlos was also a permissive parent whenever he had Lourdes under his roof. 'I'm a lenient dad,' he told *People* when speaking of his daughter who had recently landed a modelling campaign with Stella McCartney. 'I'm very empathetic, and I'm good at listening to my daughter. I'm probably a bad dad when it comes to disciplining her.'

Carlos strongly urged Madonna to work things out with Guy, to come to terms with him and put to bed any animosity or conflicted feelings she may have had for him. 'He rightfully believed the fight was as much about Guy as it was Rocco,' said one source. 'He, of all people, knows Madonna so well. He knows how stubborn she can be, especially when she can not have her way. He urged her to examine her relationship with Guy and accept the fact that it was over. "It's not a defeat, the end of your marriage," he told her. "It's not a mistake in your life. It's not a failure on your part. It just is what it is. So, stop punishing yourself and stop punishing Guy." She needed to hear those words, *really* hear them. He urged her to put her ego aside. "You don't always have to win," he told her. "Sometimes, it's not worth the fight."

"*You don't always have to win*"? This was a little hard for Madonna to accept, of course, but in the end she knew that Carlos was right. She knew it in her heart.'

Because she trusts Carlos so much, Madonna did what he suggested; she called Guy and said she wanted to work things out. Whatever needed to happen for all of them to move forward in peace, she said, she would make happen. Once she opened herself up to the possibility of losing the fight, and once she decided to also put aside her strong emotions about the demise of her marriage to Guy, her life seemed to fall into order quickly. The result was that, once again, Rocco wanted to spend time with her. 'Funny how that works,' she concluded, wryly.

On 29 April 2016, mother and son finally reconciled in London. Usually not one to shy away from advertising every little moment – private or otherwise – Madonna shared a heartfelt photo of the two on Instagram, she with her arms around Rocco's neck and her head on his shoulder. She has explained, 'I like Instagram because it's like keeping a diary and every day I get to share different aspects of my personality, my life, and what inspires me, what infuriates me, or what causes I want to fight for. It allows me to be mysterious, ironic, provocative or proud. I get to use it as a platform to bring attention to people or issues that I think are important. It allows me to be the curator of my life.'

Madonna and Rocco then did that which mothers and sons in the real world rarely do after finally seeing eye-to-eye on important personal conflicts: they posed for a fashion shoot. The pictures, taken by the famous photographer Mert Alas, who is a personal friend of Madonna's, later ended up in *Love* magazine. *Love*'s editor-in-chief, Katie Grand, explained that Madonna and Rocco agreed to the photo shoot when Alas pitched the idea to them. 'The morning after Madonna's reconciliation with Rocco, nine stunning images of Madonna arrived,' Grand reveals. 'They had been taken at 2 a.m. at Mert's house in Hampstead, where he and Madonna often hang out and have casual dinners.'

In June 2016, Rocco returned to New York to spend quality time with Madonna. They had a relaxing time together; she took him and Lourdes to the off-Broadway show *Sleep No More* at the McKittrick Hotel on Tuesday night, 14 June. The three exited the theatre wearing creepy, Venetian beak masks, which had become a hallmark of the presentation, allowing audience members who happened to be celebrities to enjoy the show anonymously.

For Rocco's sixteenth birthday on 11 August, Madonna posted three photos of him to celebrate the big day, one with the caption: 'Happy Birthday to my First Born Son! A true Warrior with a beautiful Heart. Let the Sun shine!' she wrote. 'Once my baby always my baby. Happy Sweet 16!'

Finally, on Wednesday 14 September, Madonna and Guy reached a reasonable settlement that would see Rocco continue to live with Guy in Belsize Park where the teenager had already enrolled in school. He would spend most weekends with his father and Jacqui and their children at their country manor in Wiltshire. He would also make regular visits to the States to be with his mom. Afterwards, Madonna posted on Instagram one of the photos taken by Mert Alas, a picture of herself with a crown scribbled on her head and the word 'Bitch' scrawled across the image. The caption read: 'Because sometimes soccer Moms need to be a . . .' In another photo, the word 'Bitch' was replaced by 'Queen', and she added, 'And be treated like a . . .'

On 16 September, Madonna posted a photo of all her children – Lourdes, now nineteen and a college student at her mom's alma mater, University of Michigan and fashionista in her own right; Rocco, sixteen and David and Mercy, both ten, with the caption: 'We are family! No matter where we are in the (world),' along with globe and heart emojis.

Since that time, Madonna has managed to keep the peace not only with her children, but also with Guy. 'Family is everything,' she has said. 'It's not what I expected it to be, but nothing's perfect.' At the time of writing, Rocco – who his mother says wants to be a painter – still lives primarily with Guy in London. It's an arrangement Madonna has fully accepted. She doesn't want to fight any longer or, as she put it to one confidante in 2018, 'I have learned, finally, that not everything has to be a battle to be won.'

Is her conflict with Guy completely over? Of course not. She still has her moments, according to people who know her best. She was not instantly and completely changed by what happened during the custody battle over Rocco. However, it had gone a long way towards settling old scores between her and her ex-husband. Madonna now seems better equipped to move forward with her life and – who knows? – maybe even do so with a man deemed perhaps a little more 'age appropriate' – though that phrase absolutely infuriates her. She has admitted privately, however, that it might be nice to be with someone 'who might actually remember the TV show *Friends* [from the 1990s].' She was joking. Or was she?

Woman of the Year

In December 2016, Madonna was honoured as *Billboard* magazine's 'Woman of the Year'. This was such a prestigious honour and distinction, especially because previous notables feted by the publication in recent years included such contemporary artists as Beyoncé and Lady Gaga. If anything, it demonstrated that Madonna was still relevant and, for her, such recognition of her life and times meant the world.

In what some critics considered an odd miscalculation, Madonna used her platform at the ceremony to discuss – and some felt complain – about the slings and arrows she's suffered as a recording artist blessed with longevity in the music business. In her speech, she noted the 'blatant misogyny, sexism, constant bullying and relentless abuse' with which she has had to do battle for her entire life in show business. Camille Paglia – who has both supported and indicted Madonna over the years – was disappointed and wrote for the *Hollywood Reporter*: 'It was a startling appropriation of stereotypical feminist rhetoric by a superstar whose major achievement in cultural history was to overthrow the puritanical old guard of second-wave feminism and to liberate the long-silenced pro-sex, pro-beauty wing of feminism, which [thanks to her] swept to victory in the 1990s. Madonna's opening line [was] . . . "I stand before you as a doormat – oh, I mean a female entertainer". Merciful Minerva! Can there be any woman on Earth less like a doormat than Madonna Louise Ciccone? Madonna sped on with shaky assertions ['There are no rules if you're a boy.'] And bafflingly portrayed the huge commercial success of her 1992 book, *Sex*, as a chapter of the Spanish Inquisition, in which she was persecuted as "a whore and a witch".'

It's a little surprising that Madonna's critics, like Paglia, so missed the point of her speech. She wasn't whining. 'Life's too short to be bitter,' she once said. '*I'm* too short to be bitter.' On the contrary, she was telling the truth of her life based on her own experience, and who better to explain how she survived in a cutthroat record industry dominated by men than the biggest-selling female artist of all time?

In her speech, Madonna spoke about her early days in New York. 'I started off in a difficult time. People were dying of AIDS everywhere. It wasn't safe to be gay, it wasn't cool to be associated with the gay community. It was 1979 and New York was a very scary place. In the first year I was held at gunpoint, raped on a rooftop with a knife digging into my throat. And I had my apartment broken into and robbed so many times I just stopped locking the door. In the years that followed, I lost almost every friend I had to AIDS or drugs or gunshot.'

She also spoke about her greatest role models and inspirations at that time – Maya Angelou, James Baldwin and Nina Simone. While she was at it, she also took a shot at Camille Paglia, 'the famous feminist writer, said I set women back by objectifying myself sexually. So I thought, "Oh, if you're a feminist, you don't have sexuality, you deny it." So I said, "Fuck it. I'm a different kind of feminist. *I'm a bad feminist*."'

In the end, though, Madonna's speech was really a victory lap. 'People say I'm controversial,' she noted. 'But I think the most controversial thing I have ever done is to stick around.' She closed by saying, 'To the doubters and naysayers and everyone who gave me hell and said I could not, that I would not or I *must* not – your resistance made me stronger, made me push harder, made me the fighter that I am today. It made me the woman that I am today.'

The applause was thunderous. The fact that some people, including a few major and widely respected feminist voices of our time like Paglia, found fault with the speech by feeling Madonna was painting herself as a victim, says maybe more about our culture than it does Madonna. Especially in our present point-and-click society, where little lasts longer than a Facebook post, a tweet or a photo on Instagram, we tend not to look back and consider where we've been – we're too busy worrying about where we're headed. For Madonna to take just a moment to reflect and come to terms with her storied past in such a public way says a lot about the woman she is today. She's grateful. Not bitter.

She still speaks her mind, too. In January 2017, at the Washington DC Women's March that followed the controversial inauguration of America's President Donald Trump and disavowed many of his separatist policies, she dropped the f-bomb three times and also told the huge crowd, 'Yes, I am angry. Yes, I am outraged. Yes, I have thought an awful lot about blowing up the White House. But I know that this won't change anything.'

Some people were stunned, but probably only those who forgot that Madonna is never going to stay silent when infuriated, especially if she feels she can make a difference. One of her best lines remains: 'Listen, everyone is entitled to my opinion.' She's also said, 'I think that life is a paradox and you have to embrace that in your work and your belief systems . . . you can't be a literalist, and that's the trouble that people always find themselves in. That's why people always hit a wall with any of my stuff, because you can't take it literally.'

A couple of days later, she clarified her comments about the White House – on Instagram, of course. 'I do not promote violence and it's important people hear and understand my speech in its entirety rather than one phrase taken wildly out of context. My speech began with "I want to start a revolution of love". I then go on to take this opportunity to encourage women and all marginalized people to not fall into despair but rather to come together and use it as a starting point for unity and to create positive change in the world. I spoke in metaphor and I shared two ways of looking at things – one was to be hopeful, and one was to feel anger and outrage, which I have personally felt. However, I know that acting out of anger doesn't solve anything. And the only way to change things for the better is to do it with love.'

In February 2017, Madonna added to her family when she adopted two more children from Malawi – four-year-old orphan twins Estere and Stella, both of the Home of Hope from which she had adopted David. 'Six kids, no husband, single mom . . . I never thought that would be me,' she said, 'but pretty much everything that's ever happened to me in this life is something I never imagined.' Maybe that's true in her personal life. However, the woman who famously told American TV host Dick Clark during her first major television appearance in 1984 that she wanted to 'rule the world' can't now act as if her show-business success was much of a surprise. In fact, as we have seen, she always knew exactly what she wanted out of her career and just how to get it. It's true, though, that her personal life has been more unpredictable, and she thinks that perhaps that's been for the best. 'You can't appreciate the success without a few flops along the way,' she has said, 'and I'm talking about unhappy marriages, that sort of thing. You can't fail with the kids, though. It's trial and error every day, but you have to get it right.' Her philosophy about parenting? 'I'm in charge. I'm the boss,' she says with a laugh – but she's not joking! 'I'm not a popular parent,' she says – but also one who allows her children to make their own mistakes just as she made hers when she was young. In a social media post in May 2017 to commemorate Mother's Day that year, Madonna captioned a photo of her and her mom: 'The Greatest Accomplishment of my life is to be the mother I never knew! Happy Mother's Day to my Mama whom I hope is watching over me and. [*sic*] to all who have nurtured and suffered and experienced the Joy and sacrifice of Motherhood!'

Not surprisingly, Madonna is nothing if not exceedingly proud of her brood; her friends report that, like most doting moms, she's anxious to scroll through photographs stored on her mobile phone for any person who shows the slightest interest. She says that the youngest four of her children (who call her 'Mambo') 'don't have a clue', as to her pre-eminence in the entertainment world, nor do they care about it. Once, Rocco tried to explain their mom's pop music history to the young ones by playing them a bit of her 1983 hit, 'Holiday'. It went right over their heads. 'They were like, huh?' Madonna recalled, laughing. Today, Madonna and her children divide their time between homes in New York, London and Portugal (where she purchased a home after eleven-year-old David joined the Benfica football team youth academy).

Madonna remains committed to her charity, Raising Malawi, and in 2017 opened the Mercy James Center for Pediatric Surgery and Intensive Care, the country's first children's hospital, in Blantyre, Malawi. 'You can't imagine the red tape and other nonsense they put her through, not only in opening that hospital but in everything she has ever done in Malawi,' said one person who knows Madonna well. 'Everything has been a struggle, but Madonna has never given up. She's someone who has really shown up for those kids, who really cares about them. It's easy to just look at it as a headline in another cover story about her, but the actual doing of it all is incredibly challenging. I'm not sure how she does it. She's also enrolled her oldest kids in the crusade, having them chip in and contribute in any way they can. They've all been to Malawi many times; it's a family venture now, not just Madonna's.'

She's done it all, seen it all and faced every challenge with an unquenchable thirst that still somehow surprises some people in her close-knit circle, and, yes, she's survived in an industry that is sexist, no matter how much some people – mostly men – try to downplay it. Somehow, she also remains relevant. Even with the sometimes spotty record sales of recent years and a true deficiency in radio play, she still sells more internationally than most artists and her concert tours remain among the top grossing of all time. How she continues to manage it all, it would seem, is relatively simple: she wakes up every morning and, whether happy or sad, triumphant or pissed off, plants both feet on the ground and just keeps going. She never allows herself to feel defeated, and if so, not for more than a passing, very human moment. 'One set of circumstances does not complete you,' she has said. 'Maybe nothing ever does. So, you work on your life and you work on your "work" and you try to live every single day like it's your last. And you try to be better, to yourself and to others. I don't always succeed. But I try and it's my goal.'

Is she obsessed with ageing? Obviously. Should she perhaps settle down with an age-appropriate mate, someone who can present as much a challenge to her as she to him, someone she can think of as an equal? It probably couldn't hurt. However, trying to tell Madonna how to age is always going to be useless. She has lived her life on her own terms, and, as she turns sixty, that determination to be independent and true to herself remains a true and organic part of her character, defiant as ever.

Or, as she put it for one of her signature songs on *Rebel Heart*: 'Bitch, I'm Madonna!'

And who could argue with that?

Source Notes and Other Information

I first began developing this book in January 1990 as the intended follow-up to my first bestseller, *Call Her Miss Ross: The Unauthorized Biography of Diana Ross*. Though my career turned in other directions, I and my team of researchers never ceased developing a full-scale biography of Madonna.

It is impossible to write accurately about anyone's life without many reliable witnesses to provide a range of different viewpoints. A biography of this kind stands or falls on the cooperation and frankness of those involved in the story. Over the years, a great number of people went out of their way to assist me in this endeavour: hundreds of friends, relations, journalists, socialites, lawyers, celebrities, show-business executives and former executives, associates and friends as well as foes, classmates, teachers, neighbours, friends, newspersons and archivists were contacted in preparation for this book over a twenty-year period. Obviously, considering the span of Madonna's life and career, I and my researchers had the opportunity to interview a wide range of sources. We purposely decided to focus on those who had not previously told their stories. These people were interviewed for this work over the last two decades, either by myself or my trusted researchers – Cathy Griffin in the United States, Thomas DeWitt in the United Kingdom and Teri Donato in Italy. Many of these sources are people I haven't seen or talked to for years, but my appreciation for their cooperation and assistance will not fade with time.

Whenever practical, I have provided sources within the body of the text. Some people were not quoted directly in the text but provided observations that helped me more fully understand Madonna and her life and career.

In writing about a person as powerful and as influential as Madonna is in the entertainment world, a biographer is bound to find that many sources with valuable information prefer to not be named in the text. This is understandable. Throughout my career, I have understood that for someone to jeopardize a long-standing, important relationship for the sake of a book is a purely personal choice. I so appreciate the assistance of many people close to Madonna over the years who gave of their time and energy for this project, and will respect their wishes for anonymity. Those who could be named are named in these notes.

I had the opportunity to interview Madonna on several occasions during the early years of her career, in 1983, 1984, 1985 and 1987 and all the way into the 1990s and 2000s. I have also attended several press conferences given by Madonna over the years. In this work, I utilized many of Madonna's memories from those encounters.

Interviews Conducted Relating to Madonna's Relationships (some dates in parenthesis)

With John 'Jellybean' Benitez: thanks to Jellybean Benitez (1984, 1984, 1990), Erica Bell (1991) and Melinda Cooper (1994). Also: *Teen Machine*, June 1991, 'Spillin' The Beans With Jellybean' by Marie Morreale.

With Steve Newman: thanks to Steve Newman (1995) and April Dougherty (1999, 2000).

With Prince: thanks to T.L. 'Boom-Boom' Ross (1998) and Jerome Quigley (2000).

With Tommy Quinn: thanks to Tommy Quinn for five interviews (1998–2000).

With Sean Penn: back in 1988, I spent six months researching a book entitled *Sean Penn: Lone Wolf*. That biography remains unpublished. However, I used much of the material from it in this work about Madonna. I also referred to my own interviews with Sean Penn in 1987, 1988, 1990 and 1991. Thanks also to Meg Lowery (2000), Lori Mulrenin (2000), Isaac Benson (2000), Todd Barash (1999), David

Wolinsky (1989) and Martin Ciccone (1992), Al Albergate (1999), Deputy District Attorney Lauren Weiss (1988), and Lt. Bill McSweeney (1989). I reviewed the police documents from the LAPD relating to Sean Penn's arrest in December 1988.

With Sandra Bernhard: thanks to Sandra Bernhard for the interviews I conducted with her in 1996, 2001, 2005 and 2010. I also referred to: *Penthouse*, November 1988, 'Sandra Bernhard: The Queen of Comedy' by Richard Dominick.

With John Kennedy Jun.: as the author of *Jackie, Ethel, Joan: Women of Camelot*, *After Camelot* and *Jackie, Janet & Lee*, I have cultivated many contacts within the Kennedy circle. For this text, I utilized a number of them to learn about John's relationship with Madonna. Some asked for anonymity. However, two who did not are Steven Styles and Thomas Luft, both of whom I interviewed on ten different occasions regarding Madonna and John (1990–2000). I also interviewed two former members of the Secret Service, both personal friends of John's who requested anonymity. My thanks also to Richard Wiese (1999), Senator George Smathers (1994) and Chris Meyer (1995, 2000) for their interviews. I also referred to: *New York Post*, 4 October 1991, 'The Real Story Behind Madonna's Fling With JFK, Jr.' by Marsha Kranes.

With Warren Beatty: thanks to Diane Giordano (1990, 1994) and Bill Hollerman (1990). Also thanks to Cathy Griffin for certain details and valuable information regarding Madonna and Warren. I also referred to: *National Enquirer*, 20 June 1989, 'Madonna To Wed Warren Beatty' by Tony Brenna, Diane Albright and Jerome George; *Entertainment Weekly*, 20 December 1991, 'Warren's World' by James Kaplan; *Interview*, September 1991, 'Sean Penn' by Julian Schnabel.

With Tony Ward: thanks to Tony Ward for the interview I conducted in 1992; Jayme Harris (1993); and Sandra Bernhard (1996). Thanks also to Keith Saltar (2000) and Tina Stanton (2000). I also referred to: *National Enquirer*, 26 February 1991, 'What Madonna Doesn't Know About Her Live-In Boyfriend' by John South, David Duffy and Alan Braham Smith.

With Ingrid Casares: thanks to Chita Mavros (1999, 2000). I also referred to: *New York Post*, 7 February 2000, 'Casares Speaks' by Jared

Paul Stern; *New York Post*, 11 April 2000, 'Now It's Madonna [And Pal] With Child' by Linda Massarella.

With Carlos Leon: thanks to Carlos's parents, Maria Leon and Armando Leon (1996, 1999). Thanks also to Michael Gacki (1996), Patrice Gonzalez (1998, 1999, 2000).

With Dennis Rodman: thanks to Dennis Rodman (1996) and Trina Graves (2000). The faxed correspondence between Madonna and Dennis had been published in the *Globe* in 1995, and also broadcast on the television show 'Hard Copy'. I also consulted: *Bad as I Wanna Be* by Dennis Rodman (Delacorte Press, 1996).

With Andy Bird: thanks to Andy's mother, Kathleen Bird (1998), Joseph Lafferty (2000), Elvin Bishop (2000); I also referenced: *People*, 5 April 1999, 'Two Guys, A Girl And A Punch In The Nose' (no byline); Reuters, 22 March 1999, 'Fighting Over Madonna) (wire service); UPI, 23 March 1999, 'Bird And Ritchie Clash Over Madonna' (wire service); *Now*, 4 December 1997, 'Madonna's English "Geezer"' by Jon Clark.

With Gwyneth Paltrow: thanks to Jeannie Misterling (1999, 2000). I also relied on research for these stories about Miss Paltrow which I authored: *Women's Day*, 6 December 1999, 'Why Gwyneth Can Never Please . . .' by J. Randy Taraborrelli; *Women's Day*, 13 December 1999, 'Gwyneth's Search For Love' by J. Randy Taraborrelli; *Daily Mail*, 16 February 2000, 'Gwyneth Paltrow' by J. Randy Taraborrelli.

With Guy Ritchie: thanks to the many friends and family members of Guy Ritchie's who, because of his marriage to Madonna, asked for anonymity. And thanks also to Guy for all of the moments we spent together in which he shared information, on and off the record.

With her father, Tony ('Happy Endings'): thanks to Silvio Ciccone for the many telephone conversations I had with him and his wife, Joan, over the years.

Evita

My thanks to all of those interviewed in Buenos Aires, including Simoné Sarella (1998), Isidrio Alvarez (2000) and Cecilia Nuñuz

(2000) for pointing me and my researcher Jorgé Rodriguez-White in the right direction and giving us so many details – and so much colour – relating to Madonna's meeting with President Carlos Menem. Thanks to the aides of Menem's who spoke off the record about that meeting. Also, the patrons of the La Cigale Bar (who asked not to be identified) in the Bajo area for leads and tips given to Mr Rodriguez-White. As he explains it, the Costanera Norte and Las Cañitas in Palermo are where the city's young and wealthy go to drink and eat . . . and when Madonna was in town for *Evita*, she was the subject of great fascination there. We thank all of the people who gave Jorgé so much information, and so many names and numbers. I also referred to 'The Madonna Diaries' in *Vanity Fair* (November 1996) for background. Thanks also to Martina Logan (2000), Joan Layder (2000) and Louis Keith (2000).

Among the volumes I consulted: *The Making of Evita* by Alan Parker (HarperCollins, 1996).

Madonna's Childhood and Early Years

Over the last twenty-something years, I have spent a great deal of time in Michigan where a number of people opened their homes – and their scrapbooks – to me as they remembered the young Madonna Louise Veronica Ciccone. I am indebted to so many people who lived in Michigan when the Ciccones did – many of whom live elsewhere today – and, also, to the sons and daughters of people who were friendly with the Ciccone family whose memories of them and of Madonna remain intact. I was impressed by their affection for the Ciccones and appreciate their trust.

Thanks, also, to those who submitted to interviews, including: Christopher Ciccone (January 1993), Martin Ciccone (January 1993); Carol Belager; Karen Craven; Clara Bonell; Beverly Gibson; Tanis Rozelle; Russell Long; the late Christopher Flynn (1987, 1989); Carol Lintz; Nancy Ryan Mitchell; Whitley Setrakian (1991, with me, and also with late literary agent, Bart Andrews, for the purpose of a possible memoir, which remains unpublished); Gay Delang; Tony Castro, Gina

Magnetti; Pearl Lang (1989); Susan Seidelman (1991); Moira McPharlin Messana and Walter Pugni. Thanks also to Silvio 'Tony' and Joan Ciccone.

I culled quotes from many published interviews, as well as previously unpublished radio broadcasts and television interviews, with Madonna.

I also studied the tapes of many television programmes that aired for these years, including 'Robin Leach's Madonna – Exposed (March 1993)', on which I appeared as a guest discussing Madonna, as well as 'Madonna – The Real Story – An Unauthorized Video Documentary'.

The Eighties and Nineties

I want first to thank Camille Barbone, who I believe is the unsung heroine of Madonna's life and early career. It is my hope that, with this volume, she is fully recognized for her contribution to the legend. She's a wonderful woman. I know that she has expressed interest in writing her own memoirs, *Making Madonna*. It's my hope that this project of hers is one day published.

I want to also thank Tommy Quinn who has never before spoken of Madonna, and chose to trust me with his precious memories of her. His stories have so enriched this work.

Many notes, memos and correspondence relating to Madonna's early career can be found at the Lincoln Center Library of the Performing Arts. I utilized a great many of them throughout my research and I thank the staff of the Lincoln Center Library for all of its assistance throughout the years of research on this project.

Among those who submitted to interviews: Camille Barbone (1991, 1993); Erica Bell (1990); Martin Burgoyne (1988); Stephen Bray (1990); Gregory Camillucci; Anthony Panzera (1991); Martin Schreiber (1991); Norris Burroughs (1989); Dan Gilroy (1990); Stephen Jon Lewicki (1993); John 'Jellybean' Benitez (1990); Bill Lomuscio; Mark Kamins (1988); Seymour Stein; Steven Sterning (1994); Rosanna Arquette (1996); Nile Rodgers (1995); Manny Parish (1991); Mark Kamins (1985, for 21st Century Publications); Bobby Shaw (1991);

Carlos Leon (1989); Patrick Hernandez (1985); Michael Rosenblatt (1990); Reggie Lucas (1995); Ed Gutham (2000); Veronica Edwards-Long (2000) and Beatrice Furnell-Jarecki (2000).

Thank you Barbara Manchester, David Morehouse and Stephen Witneki for allowing me to go through dozens of their photo scrapbooks about Madonna's life and career, and for making themselves available to answer my endless questions about Madonna's New York experiences.

Thanks to Betty Freeman and Thomas Styler, two generous people who were friends of Madonna's in New York. They spent hours with me, individually and together in the year 2000, and helped me recreate moments in Madonna's life, based on what she had told them. They also shared with me much correspondence from Madonna, which cleared up inaccuracies that had been published in other books. I am so grateful for their help and trust.

David Kelly allowed me access to his complete collection of Madonna memorabilia. This material was invaluable to me in that it provided many leads along the way. I am so grateful to him for his assistance. I am also grateful to Deidra Knight for her diligence in keeping such excellent notes relating to Madonna's early music.

Most important to my research was the *Advocate*'s two-part interview with Madonna, 7 May 1991 and 21 May 1991, 'The Saint, The Slut, The Sensation . . . Madonna' and 'The Gospel According To St Madonna' both by Don Shewey.

Among the volumes I consulted: *Madonna In Her Own Words* by Mick St Michael (Omnibus Press, 1990); *Madonna: The Rolling Stone Files* (Rolling Stone Press, 1997), by the editors of *Rolling Stone*; *The Madonna Companion: Two Decades of Commentary* by Allan Metz and Carol Benson (Schirmer Books, 1999).

The Nineties and 2000

For this and other sections of this book, I referred to my research in: *Daily Mail*, 27 March 1999, 'In Bed With Madonna' by J. Randy Taraborrelli; *Daily Mail*, 30 March 1999, 'The Truth About Madonna' by J. Randy Taraborrelli; *Daily Mail*, 29 March 1999, 'Madonna . . . Prince . . . Michael Jackson' by J. Randy Taraborrelli.

My thanks to Theresa Lomax for all of the hours of interviews (1999, 2000) relating to Madonna and Warner Bros. Records.

I referred to and am grateful for my interviews with Deidra Evans-Jackson, Doris Jenkins, Mark White, Joe Mantegna (1990), Ron Silver (1993), André Crouch (1995), Jean-Paul Gaultier, Diane Demitri, Sallim 'Slam' Gauwloos (1990), Gabriel Trupin (1990), Kevin Stea (1990) and Oliver Crumes (1990), Peter Cetara (1990); Raynoma Gordy Singleton (1991); Neal Hitchens (1998); Judith Regan (2000), Rob Van Winkle (1995), Rocky Santiago (1995), Paul Shaffer (1997), James Lucas (2000); Vinnie Zuffante (1991) and Camille Paglia (2000).

Other miscellaneous material consulted for this section:

Throughout this section, I relied on Larry King's television interview with Madonna on 18 January 1988 for certain quotes and other background information.

The Arts & Entertainment Biography series was invaluable to my research. My thanks to the staff of A&E who assisted me in my research, providing me with tapes, transcripts and other materials having to do with Madonna's life.

Thanks also to Eileen Faith, Nancy Wood-Furnell and Laura Cruz for their insight.

I am also indebted to the staff of the Department of Special Collections of the University of Southern California which provided me with much material relating to Madonna's career.

Among the volumes I consulted: *Madonna* by Rikky Rooksby (Omnibus Press, 1998); *Madonna Superstar* (Schirmer's Visual Library) (Schirmer/Mosel GmbH, 1988); *Madonna* by David James (Publications International Ltd, 1991).

Special thanks to Matthew Rettenmund for his comprehensive work, *The Madonna Encyclopedia* (St Martin's Press, 1995). Wow.

Thank you to Debbie Monroe Thompson for her time, boundless energy and astute observations, and for ten hours' worth of interviews in the year 2000. Also to Betty Trundle, Debra Stradella, Marjorie Hyde, and others who provided me with audio tapes of rehearsals and concerts, and all of those out-takes from the *Sex* book. Thanks also to Steven Bishop who had so much backstage footage of the 'Blond Ambition' tour; it took me weeks to view it all.

Thanks to David McClintock and Terrence Donahue for all of their notes, personal papers and other documents relating to Madonna's most recent recording career.

Thanks also to the following people for enlightening me on Madonna's current life: Buddy Adler, Diane Phipps, Mary Jenkins, Monica Hallstead, Beatrice King, Allan Melnick, Nelson Richards, Jessica Morgan, Paula DeLeon, Thomas Calabrino, Ethel Anniston, Bob Anthony, Patrice Mallard, Ida Banks, Josephine Barbone, Marjorie Nassatier, Joseph Langford, John Parker, Steve Capiello, Carl Rick, James McClintock, Harold Chapman, Paul Clemens, Doris Corrado, Andrew Wyatt, Joseph Godfrey, William Godfrey, Shirley Jones, Thomas Lawford, Marilyn Lowry, Marion Bush, Elliot Schreiber, James Silvani, Steve Tamburro, Johnathan Treddy, Betty Wilkinson and Douglas Prestine.

Specific Notes Relating to 2008 to 2018

Interviews conducted:

Madonna, September 1992, November 1996; February 2009 (conversation, not interview); Madonna and Guy Ritchie, 28 June 2006, backstage at Madison Square Garden (conversation, not interview); Silvio 'Tony' Ciccone, August 2004 and April 2014; Conversation with Guy Ritchie, Polo Lounge, January 2001; Sergio Mattos, 5 February 2009; Conversation with Madonna, Los Angeles; Jesus Luz, 5 March 2009; Brahim Zaibat, 15 October 2010; Lance Dixon, 29 October 2010, 15 December 2016; Anthony Ciccone, 12 November 2015; Anne Wilder, 12 October 2016; Armon Stewart, 4 November 2016; Devon 'Pooch' Arnold, 3 January 2017.

Radio interview:

Madonna interview, The Howard Stern Show, 11 March 2015.

Volume consulted:

Life with My Sister Madonna by Christopher Ciccone.

Articles consulted:

'Madonna' by Jonathan Moran, *Daily Telegraph*, 20 April 2008; 'Madonna – Hard Candy' by Ben Thompson, *Guardian*, 19 April 2008; 'Alex Rodriguez . . .' by Linda Hervieuxm, *Daily News*, 5 July 2008; 'Cynthia Rodriguez's Mom Tells News She Pities A-Rod' by Lisa Lucas, *Daily News*, 6 July 2008; 'A-Rod Pal: "Cynthia Spent $100G in Paris"' by George Rush and Corky Siemaszko, *Daily News*, 8 July 2008; 'Carlos Leon Raising Lourdes' by Rennie Dyball, *People*, 4 August 2008; 'Guy Ritchie Reveals Why Love in Madonna Marriage Died' by Graham Brough, *Mirror*, 16 October 2008; 'Thoughts on Madonna's Ingenious Met-Gala Outfit' by Amy Odell, *Marie Clare*, 5 May 2009; 'Madonna Looks Back – The Rolling Stone Interview' by Austin Scaggs, *Rolling Stone*, 2009; 'Madonna Splits from her Muslim Toyboy . . .' by Ben Todd, *Daily Mail*, 9 May 2011; 'Awkward? Madonna to meet mother of toyboy Brahim . . .' by Holly Thomas, *Daily Mail*, 19 August 2011; 'I don't regret marriage to Madonna' (no author) *Daily Telegraph*, November 2011; 'Guy Ritchie Interview', *Details*, December 2011; 'Christopher Ciccone: No One Sees Madonna's Children . . .' by Nick Curtis, *Evening Standard*, 14 September 2012; 'Madonna's New Album, *MDNA* . . .' by Neil McCormick, *Daily Telegraph*, 7 March 2012; 'Madonna: *MDNA*' by Joel Levy, *Rolling Stone*, 26 March 2012; 'As Madonna joins the billionaire club, her tragic homeless brother says: "She doesn't care if I'm dead or alive"' by Hugo Daniel, *Mail Online*, 29 March 2013; 'Madonna's Back' by Madonna, *Harper's Bazaar*, 4 October 2013; 'Madonna: "I Was Raped at Knifepoint"', *Daily Telegraph*, 5 October 2013; 'Madonna Splits from Boyfriend Brahim Zaibat . . .' by Stephanie Webber, *Us*, 11 December 2013; 'Stewart Price and the Truth about Madonna's Confessions', *Thump*, 15 September 2014; 'Madonna' by David Blaine, *Interview*, 1 December 2014; 'Madonna on "Rebel Heart", Her Fall and More' by Jon Pareles, *New York Times*, 5 March 2015; 'Madonna, Rebel Heart . . .' by Neil McCormick, *Daily Telegraph*, 9 March 2015; 'Madonna seemed to be happy at last during upbeat "Rebel Heart" tour opener' by Jim Farber, *New York Daily News*, 10 September 2015; 'Madonna is Still Madonna on "Rebel Heart"' by Ben Ratliff, *New York Times*, 6 March 2015; 'Madonna's former trainer slept with her ex Brahim Zaibat' by Mara Siegler, *New York Post*, 29

February 2016; 'Madonna's Rebel Heart Tour a tour de force of power and eroticism' by Will Huxley, *ABC News*, 15 March 2016; 'Madonna Covers a Special Edition of Love' by Eddie Roche, *Fashion Weekly Daily*, 15 August 2016; 'Madonna, Guy Ritchie Settle 8-Month-Long Custody . . .' by Jeff Nelson, *People*, 7 September 2016; 'Madonna & Guy Ritchie Settle Son Rocco's Custody Case', Associated Press, 7 September 2016; 'Inside Madonna and Guy Ritchie's Custody Battle' by Jeff Nelson, *People*, 23 September 2016; 'Carlos Leon: "I'm a Lenient Father to Lourdes"' by Paul Chi, *People*, 23 September 2016; 'Madge Son Drug Bust' by Tom Wells, *Sun*, 22 November 2016; 'Reasons to be Thankful' by Rebecca Pocklington, *Sun*, 24 November 2016; 'How to Age Disgracefully in Hollywood' by Camille Paglia, *The Hollywood Reporter*, 6 January 2017; 'Madonna Defends her Anti-Trump Speech at Women's March', Associated Press, 22 January 2017.

Finally, thanks to Madonna Louise Veronica Ciccone for inspiring so many people with her life and career. Whatever one thinks of her, one fact remains: her success is the result not only of extraordinary talent but also many years of hard work, dedication and persistence.

'If I'm going to make it,' she told me in 1983, 'it's not going to be because anyone ever handed me anything, already I can see that. I'll probably have to fight my way to the top.'

I asked her, 'In the end, what do you want to achieve?'

She answered quickly. 'Not much. Just the best of everything there is to have.'

And so it is.

Personal Acknowledgements

This book would not have been possible without the assistance of many people and institutions. First acknowledgment must go to my venerable editor, Ingrid Connell, for her encouragement and professionalism. We've done many books together at Macmillan, and I look forward with great anticipation to our next project.

My deepest appreciation also goes to Dorie Simmonds of the Dorie Simmonds Agency. Dorie is always there for me during the development and actual writing of any work. She is truly a positive force in my life, a trusted and valued friend. How she manages to elicit the best from me under some of the circumstances in which we find ourselves, I'll never know. I appreciate her dedication, assistance and encouragement.

Thanks also to my USA agent, Mitch Douglas, who always does such a fine job of representing me in so many ways. We've had a great run, and it just keeps getting better with the passing of the years.

Warmest thanks to Cathy Griffin for her professional assistance over the years, as well as her friendship. Cathy, a journalist and reporter in her own right, worked as an investigator and researcher on *Madonna* at the beginning of its development in 1990 and in 1991, in 2008 and, again, in 2018, locating scores of sources and conducting in-depth interviews with them.

Special thanks to all of those who assisted me in tangible and intangible ways, including: Andy Hirsch, George Solomon, Jillian DeVaney, Andy Skurow, Steve Ivory, Andy Steinlen, Hazel Kragulac, Richard Tyler Jordan, John Passantino, Linda DiStefano, David Spiro, Jeff Hare, Brian Newman, Corey Sheppard, Sam Munoz, Brandon Anjeleno, David Gunther, Michael Coleman, Rob Kesselring, James McQuillan, Samantha McQuillan, Eric Edmonds, Terik King, Samar

Habib, Skip Bolden, Charles Thomson, Robin Roth, Jon Cassar, Susan Kaya, Stephen Kronish, Keri Selig and Jonathan Hahn.

Thanks to Dale Manesis for all of his help with Madonna-related memorabilia, to which I would never have had access without his assistance.

Thanks to Camille Sartiano-Glowitz for all of the travel accommodations relating to *Madonna*. You've been so helpful and are very much appreciated.

Thanks also to my incredibly supportive Italian-American family: Roslyn and Bill Barnett and Jessica and Zachary, Rocco and Rosemaria Taraborrelli and Rocco and Vincent, and Arnold Taraborrelli. Special thanks to my late father, Rocco, who has always been my inspiration and who has encouraged me in ways too numerous to mention. This book is dedicated to him because of the challenge it presented his son. I most certainly would have abandoned it years ago if not for his influence. Also, this book was written in memory of my mom, Rose Marie Taraborrelli, who taught all three of her kids how to just be better people.

And finally, to those loyal readers of my work who have followed my career over the years, who have sent me letters of support and encouragement about my previous works (and who have also doled out harsh criticism when necessary), I humbly thank you for adding *Madonna: An Intimate Biography of an Icon at Sixty* to your collection of books.

J. RANDY TARABORRELLI
May 2018

Index